This new edition of *The 1* ....per dive into these concepts that have become even more critical as we struggle to sustain a workforce to provide care in serious illness. This book is essential reading for any clinician providing compassionate care and to all of those who prepare and support them. It is a gift of wisdom and inspiration to sustain the work of caring.

—Betty Ferrell PhD, FAAN, FPCN, Professor and Director of Nursing Research, City of Hope Medical Center

Rooted in science and infused with soul, this latest edition of *The Helper's Journey* is a gift to a new generation of caring professionals. It is steeped in the wisdom of experience of those who feel called to caring and intentionally walk close to the fire of human suffering.

—Ira Byock, MD, author of *Dying Well and The Best Care Possible*, active emeritus professor of Medicine, Geisel School of Medicine at Dartmouth

In this very well written book, Larson helps readers to explore their motivations for caregiving and to find a balance between under- and over-involvement when working with patients and others. This book is a mandatory read for all helpers and caregivers.

—J. William Worden, PhD, ABPP, Harvard Medical School, Massachusetts General Hospital

You will likely identify with the histories of those helpers featured in this book, tear up at many of the examples of how and with whom they work, and learn much about the ways that you can care for yourself while giving so much to others.

—Barry A. Farber, PhD, Professor, Clinical Psychology Program, Teachers College, Columbia University

Dr. Larson beautifully incorporates recent research and theories as he demystifies the art of helping and addresses the critical and often ignored concept of helpers' secrets.

—Patti Anewalt, PhD, LPC, FT, Director of Pathways Center for Grief & Loss, Hospice & Community Care

Deep insight like this is more essential every day as societies worldwide are aging, and the burden of caregiving is growing exponentially. This empowering and inspiring guide is essential reading for the hospice and palliative care workers who care for this growing population of our most vulnerable patients and families.

—Stephen Connor, PhD, Executive Director, Worldwide Hospice Palliative Care Alliance, Author of *Hospice & Palliative Care: The Essential Guide*

Dale Larson writes clearly about loss, empathy, compassion, personal distress, burnout, compassion fatigue, moral distress, and how to keep going when the going gets tough. Drawing on the latest research and his personal wisdom, he shows us how caring is good for us and integral to our health and wellbeing as human beings, but only if we practice self-compassion and are not drawing from empty wells. *The Helper's Journey* is a masterpiece for our time and the coming decades in the field.

—Mary L.S. Vachon, RN, RP, PhD, Registered Psychotherapist in Private Practice, Adjunct Professor, Department of Psychiatry and Dalla Lana School of Public Health, University of Toronto and Clinical Consultant, Wellspring

Dale G. Larson

The Helper's Journey

Empathy, Compassion, and the Challenge of Caring

Second Edition

RESEARCH PRESS
PUBLISHERS

2612 North Mattis Avenue, Champaign, Illinois 61822
800.519.2707 / researchpress.com

Composition by Jeff Helgesen
Artwork by Marc Ramos
Cover design by Cuttris & Hambleton
Printed by Seaway Printing

ISBN 978-0-87822-726-6
Library of Congress Catalog Number 2019933780

To Deborah

To Hann'a
Celebrating your
helping Journey!
Warmly, Dale   11/21/22

Contents

Preface

The Helper's Journey: Empathy, Compassion, and the Challenge of Caring is a guide to help you navigate the challenges of working with people facing grief, loss, trauma, life-threatening illness, and other highly distressing life events. My personal experience of these challenges as a clinician and consultant, and as a social scientist who studies them, motivated me to write this book. In it, I address some of the key questions being asked by today's clinicians and researchers:

- Why do so many professional and volunteer helpers struggle with burnout, compassion fatigue, and moral distress?

- How can we strengthen our resilience against stress, and remain caring and emotionally involved as helpers?

- What are the essential helping and self-care skills needed to be effective and healthy clinicians, and how can we learn them?

- What attributes characterize effective and high-functioning interprofessional health care teams, and what skills and strategies are needed to create and maintain them?

- What are the forces that nourish empathy, compassion, and helping, and how can we maximize these in ourselves, in our caring teams and organizations, our society, and our global community?

- Finally, how can our service to others be a journey of discovery and personal and professional growth?

These questions and the answers to them can be embraced under the umbrella of what I call the *challenge of caring*: How can we be emotionally involved in this work, and maintain our empathy, compassion, and commitment as we support others who suffer in a world where loss and often trauma are inescapable? I addressed these and related questions in the first edition of *The Helper's Journey.* Since then, these questions have become increasingly relevant in our lives, and the answers to them can provide a compass to guide our personal and collective helping journeys.

My continuing search for these answers has been informed by the rich and extensive research and clinical work that has appeared in the literature since the first edition. Myriad studies of mindfulness, self-compassion, compassion fatigue, resilience, and moral distress now inform our thoughts about stress, coping, and the helping relationship. Burgeoning brain research and the new field of interpersonal neurobiology, which tracks these phenomena at the cellular level, have served to support and complement these studies. Our everyday clinical and research conversations now include terms such as disenfranchised grief, end-of-life conversations, posttraumatic growth, and self-concealment, to name just a few. These and other advances make it possible to significantly deepen and extend the themes and practical skills presented in the first edition.

This proliferation of ideas and research reflects a widely recognized need to attend to the human dimension in health care and psychotherapy, especially in the current era when the emphasis on technological advancement can often displace the human values of compassion and understanding. As technology catapults us into the digital age, we need to ensure that the clinical promise of telehealth modalities, virtual reality applications, and digital therapeutics strengthen, not diminish, the human dimension in health care and psychotherapy. We have the insights and practices to ensure this dimension remains precious and intact; we need only to nurture our personal and collective will to make sure empathy and compassion always come first.

I believe many of the needed critical perspectives and practices can be found in the clinical and scientific work shaping the evolution of person-centered care. This concept of care is now a ubiquitous organizing theme for conferences, academic journals, blogs, and books, and represents a concerted effort to refocus on how we provide health care and psychotherapy. Work within this paradigm is deepening our understanding of empathy, compassion, resilience, altruism, health, and healing.

The Helper's Journey is intended for multiple audiences, including nurses, physicians, social workers, marriage and family therapists, psychologists, clergy, volunteers, and others who work at the frontline of helping. Because my research and clinical experiences have focused on psychotherapy, oncology, and hospice and palliative care, most of my examples are drawn from those fields. If you work in those areas of care, many of the vignettes and issues will be familiar to you. However, I hope that professional and volunteer helpers and students in an even broader variety of settings will find the ideas and skills presented here useful as well.

This is a practical book, one that seeks to empower the reader with new skills and working knowledge. We become more effective helpers, more capable of coping with stress as we acquire knowledge and specific psychological skills and resources. I don't believe we can just pick up these ideas and skills along the way, as the popular (mis)conception dictates. To enhance your learning in these areas, *The Helper's Journey* includes several exercises and activities. I strongly encourage you to practice and personalize the ideas and techniques presented here.

A central goal of this book is to offer you an opportunity to learn about the lives of fellow helpers who, though they remain anonymous, can become your valued teachers. You will read verbatim disclosures from others describing their self-doubts, deepest fears, and frustrations, as well as their joys, rewards, and greatest moments. Some of these disclosures will startle you; some will inspire you. Many will offer you the relief of knowing you are not alone in your thoughts and feelings.

Part One of the book focuses on the innermost personal experiences of helpers. It explores personal mission in the work, our innate altruism, and the *empathy-compassion-helping connection*. Emotional involvement doesn't often come without some impact on the helper. We will examine difficult issues such as burnout and stress while discovering ways to build stress resilience. We will also shed needed light on the power of secret keeping and disclosure in helping and healing. Part Two looks at the interpersonal dimensions of clinical work, focusing on the helping relationships and communication skills that empower our expressions of caring. Part Three examines helping teams and our nation and global community as caring systems, exploring both the healing potentials and barriers they present to caring.

Each of the helping situations discussed here—whether counseling a bereaved family member, having an end-of-life conversation with a dying patient, or resolving a conflict with a coworker—holds a lesson for us. I hope I have justly portrayed the significance of these moments. They all have far-reaching implications for our efforts to create a more compassionate society and world.

I extend my best wishes to you on your helping journey. My deepest hope is that, in the pages that follow, you will find renewed strength, inspiration, and ideas that will not only enhance your life but will have positive ripple effects on the lives of those under your care—effects that can reverberate far into the future.

> **A note on style and terminology:** I have used the terms patient and client interchangeably throughout the book to refer to the recipient of help, with greater use of patient when discussing helping in medical contexts.

Acknowledgments

This book reflects my life and work over several decades. During that time, many extraordinary individuals have shared their ideas and lives with me. To all—thank you!

Certain people have played special roles in my professional work leading to this second edition. I will list the names of some key people and organizations. They know how they helped and how much they mean to me: Sally Adelus, Wes Alles, Patti Anewalt, Barbara Bouton, Ira Byock, Robert Chastain, Connie Connor, Stephen Connor, Joel Crohn, Kenneth Doka, Barry Farber, Christopher Hall, Edward Holland, William Hoyt, Marcia Lattanzi-Licht, James Monahan, Barbara Sourkes, Daniel Tobin, Amy Tucci, Mary Vachon, and J. William Worden; my colleagues at Santa Clara University, where I have had a stimulating and supportive home for my intellectual and personal growth; the Hospice Foundation of America, the National Hospice and Palliative Care Organization, the International Work Group on Death, Dying and Bereavement, the Australian Centre for Grief and Bereavement, the American Psychological Association, the Association for Death Education and Counseling, Santa Clara University, and the terrific team at Research Press. Thank you to all these friends, colleagues, and organizations for inspiring and valuing me and my work.

Others have taught me about life, courage, and helping. My students have helped me test out new ideas. My clients and participants in my research have taught me about stress, loss, and life's trials, and how we respond to them. At conferences and in seminars and retreats throughout the world, and at the *Compassion in Action* conferences we held at Santa Clara University over the years, many thousands of people have shared their experiences as helpers with me, teaching me most of what I know about the challenge of caring and how to meet it.

My family has been my greatest source of support. My wife Deborah Kennedy, author and artist, somehow birthed a healing book of her own—*Nature Speaks: Art and Poetry for the Earth*—while supporting me through the long hours needed to write mine. Our son Evan is an inspiring and positive force in the world. My family is a caring team, and that has made all the difference.

PART ONE

Exploring the Inner World of Helping

1

This is the true joy in life, the being used for a purpose recognized by yourself as a mighty one; the being thoroughly worn out before you are thrown on the scrap heap; the being a force of Nature instead of a feverish selfish little clod of ailments and grievances complaining that the world will not devote itself to making you happy.... Life is no brief candle to me. It is a sort of splendid torch which I have got hold of for the moment, and I want to make it burn as brightly as possible before handing it on to future generations.[1; 2]

George Bernard Shaw

The Helper in Us All

Most professional and volunteer helpers can relate to George Bernard Shaw's words. They feel a sense of purpose in their work. For them, helping provides a way to express deep values and personal goals, and an opportunity to make a positive difference in the world. Caring is their "splendid torch," their charge.

Reflect for a moment on your motivations as a helper. Search inside, asking: "What drove me to engage in this work? What reasons led me to choose this path initially?" Think back to the time in your life when you made the decision to pursue your current involvement as a helper, whether in counseling, nursing, medicine, social work, the clergy, or volunteer work. What were your goals, hopes, and expectations? What led you to make that choice back then? What did you originally want to achieve in this new role? What mattered most to you?

Perhaps you hoped to prevent unnecessary pain and suffering, to save lives, or to learn about life and death. Your broader goal might have been to make a difference, to give back, or to make the world a better place.

Reflection on the life events that shaped your helping motivations, and your decision to be a caregiver, can reveal a great deal. A personal encounter with grief or life-threatening illness might have deepened your empathy for the needs of others in similar circumstances. Or perhaps a skilled and sensitive caregiver—a counselor, physician, nurse, minister, or social worker—guided you through a personal life crisis, inspiring you to pass along this care to others.

Events early in our lives are sometimes the roots of our passion for caring. For example, an oncology nurse recalled an aunt saying to her, "You'd be a great nurse," when she was 6 years old. This nurse identified that moment as the beginning of her nursing career. As a young girl, Florence Nightingale, the iconic 19th century British nurse, escaped from the routines of everyday life through daydreaming of a life of heroic action helping others. She spent the remainder of her life realizing her vision.[3]

The motivations and life events that drew you to engage in this work define who you are, both as a person, and as a caregiver. My own helping motivations probably began during my early childhood. They were rooted in my grief for my older brother, Dickie. I was 5 years old, and he was my 11-year-old big brother—a Little League All-Star, a paperboy, and in my eyes, a champion at just about everything—when he died from a concussion. This loss, I believe, significantly shaped my empathy, compassion, and career.

What life events shaped you and your caring motivations? Which brought significant personal meaning to your work and defined your vision of your goals as a helper?

This personal vision might express itself in many different forms such as comforting a frightened child, giving chemotherapy, writing a successful grant proposal, directing a palliative care program, leading a bereavement support group, or helping a seriously ill mother talk to her son about her illness. Any of these diverse, caring acts can express your unique mission as a helper.

Mission Moments

Your purpose in your work can become vividly clear to you at specific moments in helping. At these times, you find the results of your actions profoundly rewarding. They seem an expression of your core being. Think back to those helping encounters that touched you most, the times when you thought "This is it," or "This is why I'm doing this." These self-revelations don't happen every day, but when they do, they can renew your commitment to your core mission.

I first discovered the deep significance of these clarifying and inspiring moments while conducting a retreat for the staff and volunteers of a hospice organization in the Midwest. Rain poured down as the last remnants of a dying hurricane swept over our retreat site. Inside the meeting hall, we shared difficult and embarrassing thoughts and feelings about ourselves and our work. These are things we don't usually share with colleagues—things we sometimes actively conceal. The similarities of our painful disclosures surprised us. Some relief came with the knowledge that we were not alone in our problems, yet we also had a feeling of incompleteness. Something was missing. Responding to this sentiment in the group, I asked each participant to think of the most rewarding encounter or event he or she ever had as a helper. We wrote our descriptions on note cards, distributed the cards to ensure anonymity, and slowly read the vignettes aloud, one at a time:

✦ After entering the hospital room of a middle-aged man dying of kidney cancer, I spoke with him about many things. Having known him for some time, we talked about his family, and his hopes for the future. Finally, I asked him what one thing I could do for him. He replied, "Help me get home to my own big bed." We made the arrangements and he left me, saying, "I love you, kid." That's where he died—in his own big bed.

✦ When a patient said to me, "I'm so glad you're my nurse today because I wanted you to be the one to be with me on the day I die." She died at the end of my shift that day.

✦ A young wife and mother, terminally ill and hooked up to IV pain medications, died 2 days before Christmas. Her husband was grief-stricken but coping well. Before he allowed his children to come in and say goodbye to their mother, I helped him dress her in a beautiful robe, comb out her few strands of hair, and place flowers near her bed. He looked at me and said, "Thanks for making my kids able to see their mommy as they remembered her."

✦ A mother of a child with leukemia once said, "We come to this clinic every week, and know you care for many, many children. But when you come to see us, I feel like we are the only people you have seen that day."

✦ When I worked with terminally ill prisoners, I was helping a young man work through his anger and other feelings, listening to him while he vented. As I left his room, he hugged me. With a new look of peace and a beautiful smile, he said "You mean the world to me."

✧ As I sat with a family whose father had just taken his own life, they said they could not have gotten through it without me. I had made a difference.

✧ A moment that feels fresh to me—being present, listening, and feeling with one of my staff, a social worker, who was going through a significant personal grief/loss/health crisis. As we sat together, sharing tea and a poppy seed muffin, she said, "I'm really not so different from the people we take care of." Then she hugged me, and we cried.

✧ I visited a man in his 20's, dying of brain cancer. He shared his deep feelings and his faith with me in a powerful way. I was able to share words of encouragement with him, my own feelings, and we prayed together. He tearfully, but with a smile on his face, said to me that he knew I'd been sent to him by the Lord. At that moment, I knew I was in the right place at the right time doing what I was supposed to be doing.

✧ A young mother with two young children was dying. The family would not allow her to hold her children because they thought this was a terrible thing and would scare the kids. So when they weren't around, I asked the kids if they wanted to get in bed with her, and they said yes—so I put them in her bed, and she held them.

During these poignant encounters, these helpers said they felt "peaceful," had a sense of "connectedness," and believed they had "made a difference." Their purpose in the work was being fulfilled. Through sharing their most meaningful experiences, the group members had answered the implicit question, "But why do I do this difficult work?" Now in that clearer lens, the struggles disclosed in our earlier conversation took on a different meaning.

Sharing these uplifting stories, these *mission moments*, brought tears to our eyes more readily than discussing our difficult feelings.

The intense emotion in the room made it difficult to continue reading the cards. It was as if, in these individual acts of helping, the fabric of human existence unfolded before us, and at its center, we found love, compassion, caring, and meaning.

Helping is tough work: it is unavoidably stressful, conflicted, and exhausting at times. Yet when you make a difference, and you see the real impact of your caring, any doubts about the value of your efforts disappear.

A whole lifetime of caring can be affirmed in just a few words. On his deathbed, James Vizzard, a Jesuit priest and dedicated helper, described one such instance to me. He had fought for the welfare of migrant farmworkers for more than 25 years. Several years earlier, Jim was thrilled to learn that he and John Steinbeck were attending the same social gathering in New York. At the party, he shyly approached Steinbeck and disclosed how *The Grapes of Wrath* had inspired his lifetime of caring work. Steinbeck overwhelmed Vizzard with his response: "Then it was worth writing, Jim," and went on to say he had followed and respected Vizzard's work for many years. This simple yet profound exchange validated the caring contributions of both men.

The Caring Helper

Think of the people you work with. What are your colleagues like? Do they evoke words like dedicated, committed, caring, and concerned? I am sure other less endearing words come to mind as well, but the general picture probably reflects these highly positive qualities. This is because the nature of your work acts as a powerful screening device. It's a filter selecting more altruistic individuals who want to work with people in these challenging situations.[4]

The altruistic person is inclined to act in prosocial as opposed to self-centered ways. He or she cooperates, donates to charities, shares with friends, gives directions to strangers, or helps someone with a disability to cross a street. These are acts of kindness that can reflect deep moral values.[5]

You might not self-identify as an altruist if you compare your actions with those of, say, nondirected kidney donors and other ultra-altruists. However, the flame of caring is most likely burning a bit brighter in you than in someone randomly selected from the rest of society.

In addition to having a more altruistic personality, and with it, strong prosocial motivation, you probably also possess greater empathic capacity. To assess this dimension in yourself, reflect on how much you agree with the following items used to measure empathy.[6; 7; 8; 9]

- When I read an interesting story or novel, I imagine how I would feel if the events in the story were happening to me.

- I often have tender, concerned feelings for people less fortunate than myself.

- After being with a friend who is sad about something, I usually feel sad.

- I sometimes try to understand my friends better by imagining how things look from their perspective.

- Empathy is an important therapeutic factor in medical treatment.

- It makes me sad to see a lonely stranger in a group.

You probably tend to agree with most of these statements. You bring heightened empathic capacity—along with your purpose in the work and your altruistic tendencies—to every helping encounter. Research on empathy, compassion, altruism, and helping shows how these essential elements combine to promote and guide caregiving. Helping is a natural outcome of these psychological forces—a product of what I call the *empathy-compassion-helping connection*, or what Batson refers to as *empathy-induced altruism*.[10]

Indeed, our helping often has an almost automatic quality. Imagine you are taking a nature walk, and as you come to a clearing, you see a young woman lying on her back, groaning and holding her leg. You see her mountain bike on the ground behind her, its frame bent. No one else is in sight. What do you do? Most people would certainly do something to help this person.

Put yourself in the place of the clinician in the following situation:

A patient of mine was devastated. She had awakened and clumps of her hair were all over her pillow. I immediately got a large selection of wigs and went to her. After we talked, we tried on the wigs and laughed about being a blonde or a red-head. She felt better, so did I.

Why do we help in these situations? For most of us, the question we ask is not why we should help, or whether we will help, but how we can help. We listen, give pain medication, have difficult end-of-life conversations, or grab the wigs.

Of course, much of our helping is simply what is expected of us in our professional roles. We might sometimes perform these roles reluctantly, or even grudgingly. However, think of all the "normal helping" you do in an average day. What motivates you to do so? A salary might sustain you, and a sense of responsibility keep you focused on tasks. Yet, a deeper motivation for most of your helping comes from within. As a helper, your helping goals are connected to the flame of caring burning brightly within you.

These observations of helping probably seem reasonable to you. You might be thinking, "Yes, that sounds like me, at least on my good days." What is not so obvious are the powerful and pervasive invisible forces arousing, shaping, and supporting our helping. The most fundamental, and perhaps most overlooked of these forces, is our innate altruism.

Innate Altruism: The Pilot Flame of Caring

Are love, caring, and compassion at the core of human existence? Few would say there is enough caring in the world. Cruelty, not kindness, often seems to have the upper hand; conflict, not cooperation, seems to rule the day among people and nations. The media reinforce this view, with nonstop reporting on the negative aspects of society. The belief that good news is no news often appears to be their guiding principle.

We can become deeply discouraged by daily exposure to the many staggering social and health care problems we face, such as poverty and homelessness, gun violence, physical and sexual abuse, racism and discrimination of all kinds, and disparities in health care. Exposure to these and other social maladies can readily coalesce into a negative image of our fellow humans.

This cynical view of human nature—a social Darwinism—can be profoundly demoralizing. It's encouraging to work with committed and caring people. It's reassuring to know you are helping people in distress. But it can too often feel like an uphill, losing battle. This is especially true when you begin to doubt your caring or grow disappointed in your colleagues or organization. As our cynicism increases, the image of a caring world where all people—healthy and sick, rich and poor—are treated with dignity and compassion moves farther and farther from our collective consciousness and social reality.

Indeed, history and our everyday reality tell us that there is a more malevolent side of human nature. This less noble side of human nature has now become a focus of personality research as psychologists study the interrelated traits of narcissism, psychopathy, and Machiavellianism—what they have dubbed the *Dark Triad* traits. Individuals high in these traits demonstrate greater callousness to the suffering of others, manipulative interpersonal styles, and a lack of empathy. Dark Triad traits are more common among men than women. Health care professionals, it is good to see, have lower mean scores than the general population.[11; 12] However, the existence of Dark Triad traits is not a condemnation of human nature. A closer look at the world reveals a more encouraging perspective, and we begin to see altruistic behavior as a ubiquitous and frequent human activity.

This altruism takes many forms. According to the United States Department of Labor, about 25% of Americans are now volunteering through or for an organization at least once in a given year.[13] Today, millions of Americans participate in online or in-person self-help or mutual-aid groups, voluntarily assisting one another to cope with shared problems.[14] Add the informal support occurring among friends and relatives, and the estimate of voluntary helping occurring in the United States rises to a staggering figure.

Paradoxically, it is often disasters that most dramatically display this brighter side of our natures. This might, on its face, seem unlikely. That's because horrifying events, such as mass shootings, seem to carry the potential to permanently sour our opinion of humanity as a whole. Senseless tragedy often tempts us to take a step away from our fellow humans. Natural disasters, like hurricanes, wildfires, and earthquakes might also seem likely to dampen altruistic motivations, thus elevating self-interest over concern for others. However, when we closely examine each of these terrible events, we always find many, often countless, acts of kindness and heroism during and after the violent act or disaster.

The helper in us all also sometimes appears unexpectedly in everyday life. A friend of mine was once ice skating at a public rink when a large group of blind teenagers arrived. The group included only one sighted companion. My friend and the other sighted skaters at the rink realized that the blind skaters would have to skate one at a time with their companion. Slowly, without discussion, a line of people formed, waiting to guide the blind skaters around the rink. These volunteers remained for the entire evening as this group of strangers joined in their common humanity.

This positive view suggests that we are prewired as a species to be cooperative, helpful, and altruistic—to be our brother's keeper. It proclaims that there is a hero in us all: that compassion and caring are part of the fabric of human existence, and human nature is essentially good and constructive. This alternative, more hopeful view of humankind proposes that if we create the right environment, helping will naturally unfold, and both the helper and the recipient of care will grow and develop through their participation in it.

What other evidence tells us that helping and caregiving are the default condition of humankind? Although a harsh and unloving childhood can interfere with the full expression of these human tendencies, nurturing and growth-promoting parenting can enhance them. Evidence from evolutionary psychology and neuroscience decidedly points to the conclusion that humans possess innate altruism, and that cooperation and the tendency to help suffering others are part of our biological inheritance.[15; 16] The human capacity for altruism begins expressing itself early in life, as Zahn-Waxler and Radke-Yarrow note:

> Many children, it appears, are able to perform a caregiver function well by the age of 1½–2 years. Not only do they comfort another person by patting, hugging, or presenting an object, but they also have more sophisticated and complex

methods of attempting to help. They express verbal sympathy, they give suggestions about how to handle problems, they
are sometimes judgmental in their helping, they appear to try
to cheer others up, and they sometimes try alternative helping responses when a given technique is not effective... The
behaviors appear to be intended to reduce suffering in others and to reflect concern for the victim in distress. Many of
the acts would undoubtedly be judged as altruistic if an older
child or adult were performing the very same behaviors.[17]

A tendency to help suffering others is not unique to *Homo sapiens*.
Jean-Pierre Hallet recounts this instance of elephant altruism in
Congo Kitabu:

The trunkless tembo [elephant] stood by idly while his companions tore into the trees, then he opened his mouth and
every member of the herd moved toward him with trunkfuls
of twigs and leaves. Two of them jostled each other, anxious to
feed him first, but the rest waited their turns patiently. In all,
they brought so much food that he hardly had time to chew it;
he gulped furiously until, finally, he closed his mouth tight and
shook his mutilated head from side to side. Only then did the
other tembo move away and at last start to feed themselves.[18]

Other mammals also display altruistic behaviors. Primates share
food, cooperate, and respond to their fellows' distress.[19] In one fascinating study, experimenters taught rhesus monkeys to obtain a food
morsel by pulling one chain when a red light flashed and another
when a blue light flashed. The monkeys could do this with ease. Then
the experimenters created a new situation: One chain administered
an electric shock to a monkey in the next cage. Ten of the 15 monkeys
in the experiment shifted to the non-shock chain, and two refused
to pull either chain. When the shock victim was a cagemate, this
altruistic behavior was much more pronounced. The monkeys that
had been shocked in the past were most likely to engage in selfless
behavior.[20] Rats behave in much the same way, sacrificing rewards to
decrease the shocking of their peers. Like the monkeys, those familiar with shock are most likely to cease shocking others.[21]

In another intriguing study, white albino rats were more likely to release another rat of the same strain than to release a rat of a different strain (in this case, black-hooded rats).[22] However, when the albino rats were housed for only 2 weeks with black-hooded rats, they then began to help stranger rats from that different strain. Thus, social experience expanded the rats' prosocial motivation, a finding with implications for empathy and altruism in our own species and our society.

These experiments and other naturalistic observations of animals reveal an almost universal tendency to become provoked in the presence of a distressed member of one's own species and to act in ways to reduce the other's suffering. Animals that demonstrated a closer connection showed this tendency even more strongly, and even stronger still, if the altruistic partner can "empathize" with such distress.

Like the rats and monkeys, we humans have greater empathy for the suffering of others when we have shared their difficulties, and less empathy when we have not. As Shakespeare's Romeo observed, "He jests at scars that never felt a wound."

Compassion energizes a desire to help, but it does not necessarily lead to a decision to help.[23] When our compassion is aroused, and the goal of relieving the suffering of another is activated, other competing goals or considerations can quickly arise. What is the personal cost of helping? How much effort, time, money, or personal vulnerability will be required in helping the other? Although compassion motivates us to help, competing values and goals can block its expression as helping behavior. We will see that burnout and other emotional struggles we have as helpers can also dim the flame of caring, making helping more effortful and sometimes less likely.

Empathy: The Bridge To Compassion and Altruistic Action

Whatever the origins of altruism, it is our empathy that eventually transforms it into caring, compassionate action. To understand the role of empathy in helping, Harvey Hornstein argues we must journey back to the African savannahs about 3.5 million years ago, when our 60-pound ancestors struggled for survival.[24] Their continued existence hinged on whether they could develop coordinated and cooperative activities. Physically, they were no match for other predators. Only their superior intelligence could save them. At about that time, Hornstein notes, their brains fortunately underwent a significant spurt of growth. This enabled them to think and feel their way into the minds of their fellow hominids, making cooperation and other forms of prosocial and helpful behavior possible. Without this ability to empathize, to feel emotionally and sympathetically aroused in the presence of another's suffering, our species would in all likelihood not have survived, falling prey to physically superior species. Of course, the survival of our species also required an intense empathic bond between mothers and their infants. Consequently, our phylogenetic inheritance promotes prosocial and benevolent behaviors.

Contemporary neuroscience supports this view. In *The Altruistic Brain*, neuroscientist Donald Pfaff marshals extensive evidence showing our brains are "wired to propel us toward empathic behavior and feelings leading to altruistic behaviors."[16] We now believe that mirror neurons or mirror cells play an important role in the empathic process as corresponding neural activity. The right angular gyrus and the parietal cortex brain regions linked to empathy are the same cortical and subcortical structures of the brain that are activated when we have pain, and also when we view another person in pain.[25; 26; 27] Also, the peptide hormone oxytocin, often referred to as the *moral molecule,* plays an important role in cooperative behavior and empathy-induced altruism and in the relation between prosocial behavior and health.[28; 29; 30]

We may be wired to help when encountering suffering in others, but a prerequisite is to detect that distress. In a set of experimental studies, Abigail Marsh found that individual differences in the ability to detect distress strongly influenced helping outcomes. People who more accurately identified fear (a form of distress) in a set of 24 photos of adults' facial expressions were more likely to behave altruistically, pledging greater donations of money and time to assist a victim in need.[31] This fear recognition capacity better predicted prosocial behavior than gender, mood, or scores on an empathy scale. Psychopaths, the authors argue, are the reverse of altruists. They are insensitive to distress cues, and so lack the other-oriented emotions of empathy and guilt.

Myriad studies demonstrate empathy is indeed the built-in mechanism for mediating natural helping behaviors.[32; 33] As we empathically engage with someone's suffering, a tension or motivation to relieve it develops in us, leading us to help the person. We empathize, suffer together, feel compassion, and then act altruistically. Other variables come into play, and thoughts are involved. Yet our emotional responses are most important. We can mentally take the role of the suffering person, but without the corresponding empathic feeling response, helping isn't likely.[34]

Empathy changes as we grow and develop. A newborn baby cries reactively, but an adult can take the role of the distressed other and imagine how it would feel to be in those same circumstances. Thinking and feeling our way into a state of empathy with the other person arouses and guides the instinctive need to help others in distress.

We begin to develop our role-taking ability in the second year of life, as we come to recognize that others have inner states independent of our own.[32] By late childhood, we can empathize beyond our immediate circumstances and become empathically aroused by someone else's general life circumstances or prospects for the future.

Bonds of We-Ness, Barriers of They-Ness

Our compassion develops as we extend our caring and understanding to others. Our empathy and helping usually begin with a recognition of a social bond with people needing assistance. Our hearts are open to them and we include them in our psychological worlds; these *bonds of we-ness* encourage our empathy, compassion, and helping.[24] This feeling of we-ness is a precursor to our empathy. Remember even rats and monkeys are more likely to act altruistically toward their former cagemates, the members of their "we-group." However, the empathy-compassion-helping connection can be blocked before it begins. We often fail to empathize with and help others with whom we do not feel this social bond. The expanded neocortex enables us to take the role of the other, and to develop bonds of we-ness, but it also enables us to create *barriers of they-ness* that inhibit helping and cooperation.

Barriers of they-ness are a central psychological feature of many social ills in our society, such as the actions of hate groups, racism, the dehumanization of our enemies, and the failure to care for suffering members of our society. These barriers are even reflected neurologically. In an electroencephalography study, white participants were shown clips of hands being pierced by syringes, some belonging to an ethnic ingroup (White) and others to an ethnic outgroup (Black). Responses were significantly stronger for the ingroup than the outgroup.[35]

In 1968, a team of psychologists studied everyday altruism in the streets of New York.[24] They "lost" 40 wallets each day and later counted the number of wallets returned by Good Samaritans who chanced upon them. An average of 18 wallets were returned each day—45%, a respectable rate of altruism. The study was in full swing on the day Sirhan Sirhan assassinated Robert Kennedy, and not a single wallet was returned on that day. The psychologists speculated the brutal killing of Kennedy weakened the social bonds making us concerned for another's welfare, especially an anonymous stranger. The boundaries of "they" had expanded, separating the people who found the wallets on that day from the anonymous other who lost it, and empathy for this anonymous other did not develop. Maybe people thought something like, "Why should I return this wallet? This person might have shot someone or done something else horrible. What's the use? People are pretty screwed up."

Other studies also show that remote events in the news may influence whether we help someone in distress. Good news enhances our general concern for others and promotes cooperative and helping responses. Bad news, news that sours us on humanity—headlines of child kidnapping, greed, rape, killing—has the reverse effect, increasing apathy, competitive behavior, in-group favoritism, and even guilty verdicts in trials.[24; 36] Perceived differences between us and those we aid can also interfere with our helping efforts and caring connections. Differences in faith, race, ethnicity, personality, lifestyle, sexual orientation, and political views can all create barriers of they-ness.

Opening one's heart, and being compassionate to others who are different, requires mindful awareness of nonempathic inner reactions and constant efforts to express the best in oneself. Sometimes the barriers take more extreme forms and can seem insuperable. One nurse described the enormous inner conflict she felt when saving the life of a murderer:

✧ A patient came in for emergency surgery. This patient had gone for a killing spree. He had killed four men in 1 hour. Police had to shoot him to stop him, but it wasn't fatal. When he was in surgery, I had mixed feelings. Let him die by not moving quickly, or save him to prove my efficiency.

Conflicted feelings of anger and guilt can occur when these barriers of they-ness thwart our empathy and caring:

✧ I'm angry I now have to care for an old man who is sleeping with his young daughter and has a prison record for abuse. It's hard for me to keep the spiritual side of this man in focus and hard for me to relate to him lovingly and nonjudgmentally.

✧ I hated the husband of a patient because he wanted her to die and did not want to care for her or be with her. I couldn't be totally effective because of my antipathy. He was selfish, and I didn't help him through the crisis as I should have.

✧ It is easy to love and help those who are kind and considerate and want your help. But how about those who hate you and the whole world? How do you get close to them and give them encouragement, keep upbeat and caring toward them, when they have never cared about anyone or anybody?

Have you ever been pinched, cursed, spat upon, or kicked by the people you care for or felt the brunt of a grieving family member's displaced anger? Many helping professionals certainly have. How can you extend your caring to an anonymous stranger who is mistreating you? It seems like a tough assignment. A saint could do this, but we mere mortals have trouble with it. This dynamic leads to even more trouble if we are not compassionate with ourselves when we have what are understandable negative reactions to mistreatment.

Situations like these highlight how our social connectedness—or lack of it—can influence helping. When in great discomfort, we can oscillate between feelings of amity and enmity, between a sense of we-ness and of they-ness. One of my psychotherapy clients taught me about this dynamic. An irate, emotionally-disturbed customer had brutally attacked and nearly killed him. As he physically and emotionally recovered from multiple stab wounds, he continued to run his business, serving many customers of the same nationality as his attacker. He once told me, "When I am a victim, I don't want to help them; but as a human being, I want to."

The ability to establish bonds of we-ness may reflect a more general orientation of the helper. In their study of rescuers of Jews in Nazi Europe, Samuel and Pearl Oliner concluded that rescuers had a greater capacity than non-rescuers for *extensive* relationships, described as a "stronger sense of attachments to others and their feeling of responsibility for the welfare of others, including those outside their immediate familial or communal circles."[37] Non-rescuers had a more *constricted* orientation characterized by detachment and exclusiveness. When the ability to take the other's perspective and feel compassion is severely limited, bonds of we-ness shrink to include only a small group.

Spiritual teachers throughout history have, of course, championed the reverse: the importance of loving all people, of having an expanded sense of we-ness. Developmental thinkers also emphasize moving away from attention focused exclusively on the self, and toward a focus on others as we mature. Abraham Maslow described a hierarchy of needs progressing from physiological needs to higher needs, such as those for love and belonging. The self-actualized people he studied had a commitment to something beyond themselves.[38] In his Pulitzer Prize-winning work, *The Denial of Death*, Ernest Becker concludes: the "only real problem in life" is discovering our unique talent and finding a way to express it and devote it to something beyond oneself.[39] Finally, Lawrence Kohlberg and other psychologists have shown moral development advances from self-interest to a concern with universal principles.[40] For these and other theorists, a caring extension of self toward others is the capstone of human development.

Time to Help?

In an influential study, professors John Darley and Daniel Batson studied how time pressure can affect helping. They asked Princeton theology students to walk across campus to give a talk on the parable of the Good Samaritan as part of an experiment on religious education.[41] In the original Biblical parable, perhaps the classic helping story of all time, a man going from Jerusalem to Jericho was attacked by robbers who left him half dead on the roadside. A priest and a Levite, two leading religious functionaries of the day, passed him without stopping. Next, a Samaritan came upon the man and helped him, binding his wounds and taking him to an inn to give him further care. Because the priest and the Levite were headed to an important religious event, they did not want to be distracted. The Samaritan, however, saw someone in need, was moved by compassion, and helped.

In the experiment, the theology students encountered a slumped "victim" in an alley on their way across campus. The students had been divided into two groups: some were told to hurry, others to walk in a leisurely fashion. Who helped? As it turned out, 63% of the students who were not hurrying offered help, as opposed to only 10% of those who were hurrying. The students who didn't help did report having noticed the man, and recognized he was in distress. The experimenter reviewed with them what happened: "You were on your way to give a talk on the parable of the Good Samaritan, you saw someone in trouble, and you didn't stop to help?" The students admitted the irony, but countered they had helped the experimenter: They had faced a conflict between helping the experimenter (by hurrying across campus) and helping the man in distress, and the experimenter won out. Darley and Batson concluded that situational variables, such as how hurried we are, can significantly determine whether or not we help someone in need.

When we don't have enough time, for whatever reason—excessive paperwork, unexpected crises, too many patients—natural helping can miscarry, and we may not respond to the needs of others.

For example, decreasing the contact time between physicians and patients can limit important end-of-life discussions. A study of how physicians communicate about advance directives showed that conversations about them averaged 5.6 minutes, and physicians spoke for two thirds of this time.[42] Although the physicians introduced advance directives, their patients' values and attitudes toward uncertainty and their questions and concerns were infrequently dealt with, rendering the discussions of limited usefulness in their decision-making. Time pressures like these, now constantly increasing throughout the health care and psychotherapy fields, pose significant challenges to both the quality of care and to the well-being of the providers who must contend with them.

The Feel Good—Do Good Effect

Although our individual personalities dispose us to certain ways of responding, our moods also strongly influence our disposition and openness toward the people we help. We are most likely to help and give of ourselves when we feel good. *Feel good-do good* is the rule. Sunny weather, thinking happy thoughts, feeling competent—all stimulate helping.[43; 44]

Simple everyday events—unexpected positives—can have a significant impact on kindness. Some of us still remember the now extinct phone booth. We may recall finding a dime in the coin return slot. An early social psychology experiment on the effect of finding that dime on helping behavior reported that 88% of subjects who found a coin stopped and helped someone (a confederate of the experimenter) who dropped her papers outside the phone booth, whereas only 4 percent of the people who didn't find the coin helped her.[45] Similarly, students who unexpectedly receive free cookies while sitting in a library are more likely to help someone outside the library.[46]

A series of studies show even briefly inducing the positive emotion of awe can promote prosociality and helping behavior. In one study, participants were asked to spend one minute looking up at the towering eucalyptus trees on the campus at the University of California, Berkeley.[47] Participants in the control condition looked instead at an adjacent, tall building. The experimenter approached subjects in each group and spilled a box of pens in front of them, seemingly by accident. The subjects in the awe condition picked up more pens, and also scored higher on other measures of prosociality. Piff and colleagues believe awe fosters prosocial tendencies, and does so "by broadening the individual's perspective to include entities vaster and more powerful than oneself and diminishing the salience of the individual self." This new viewpoint then energizes collective concern.

Uplifting events of all kinds seem to ignite a feeling of goodwill, a concern for the well-being of others, and helping. Think of those days when you find a flower on your desk, receive a thank-you note from a patient or family member, get a positive evaluation at work, or receive unexpected aid from a colleague when you're behind in your work. On days like these, helping is probably a bit easier—yesterday's hassles became today's challenges, there seem to be fewer "problem patients," and you feel less enervated when the day ends. A clinician shared one such uplifting event. It was a note from a family reading, "You made a difference to all of us. What could have been a terrible time for our family turned into something special. We have never been so close. Thank you."

Positive emotion can clearly fuel the fires of altruism, but how does it lead to increased helping? Why do you help when you feel good? The answer may lie in the expanded sense of self you feel at these times. Unexpected good fortune and positive events expand caring and we-ness. You feel "like a million dollars," and you are unusually responsive to diverse people and situations. These extended bonds of we-ness facilitate the first, necessary step in helping: recognizing the needs and suffering of others. These bonds allow you to take the perspective of the other person; you don't overlook his or her suffering. This is the opposite of self-preoccupation, which can block any awareness of the cues leading to empathy.

Another reason for these altruistic effects is that feeling good alters your internal calculations of how much you can afford to give to others. Precisely because you feel good, you may seek to share your good fortune without being concerned about the returns from your giving. Your emotional largesse stems from the perception that there is an imbalance of resources in your favor, and you give to help those less fortunate.[48] Also, once your helping is activated, altruism is intrinsically reinforcing; it can make you feel better, especially when the costs of helping are low and the benefits high. Because altruism functions as a self-reward, we can feel good, do good, and then feel even better.

This model of helping underscores the importance of what you bring to the helping encounter. Your empathy and compassion connect you with the people you help, and keep the flame of caring burning within you. When you are high on humanity and feeling good, spontaneity suffuses your caregiving.

This does not mean these positive feelings are necessary for helping to occur. As a professional or volunteer caregiver, you are obligated to continue to help others even when you feel cynical or angry, when you dislike the people you care for. Still, when these positive psychological forces are present, and the empathy-compassion-helping connection is activated, your caregiving will be less stressful and more creative, effective, and rewarding.

Do Good—Feel Good: How Helping Benefits the Helper

When all the ingredients for natural helping are present, helping can unfold in an optimal fashion. The benefits for the recipients of this care are obvious—ideally their pain is controlled, their suffering is reduced, their relationship is repaired, and their coping ability and growth are enhanced. The possible benefits to the helper are less apparent and have been, until recently, largely overlooked. A growing body of research and theory supports the idea that, in most circumstances, helping is a natural expression of the healthy human heart. Our caring connections with others, in turn, sustain our health.

For example, we find that close, supportive ties to others are extraordinarily good for our psychological and physical health.[49] The associations of social integration and social support with positive health and lowered mortality are among the most consistent findings in the social sciences.[49; 50; 51; 52]

We also know that not opening one's heart to others has significant negative health consequences. When these connections are lost, a host of medical and psychological symptoms are more likely to develop. For example, loneliness (the perception of social isolation) is a major risk factor for morbidity and mortality.[53] Responding to this clinical reality, pioneering cardiologists Meyer Friedman and Ray Rosenman advised Type A individuals to bring more people into their lives through increased caring and communication.[54] When we participate in a network of caring and reciprocal relationships, and secure a feeling of belonging and a reason for living that transcends our individual lives, we tend to live longer and more fully.

Social connections are good for us, but what about helping relationships, where one-way giving is the norm, and reciprocal or mutually advantageous benefits are not built in? Data on volunteer helpers certainly support the *do good-feel good* theory. Volunteer researcher Allan Luks surveyed 1,500 members of a large women's volunteer group and asked how helping feels.[55] More than half the respondents reported feeling a *helper's high* when helping others. Large percentages indicated feelings of strength, calmness, greater self-worth, and fewer aches and pains during and after helping. Similarly, more hours of volunteer work are associated with greater happiness, life satisfaction, self-esteem, feelings of mastery, physical health, and reduced depression.[56]

The relative contributions to one's health of helping others and of active social relating must still be disentangled. Michael Poulin and colleagues conducted a survey addressing this question. In their sample of 846 respondents from married couples, help given to valued others predicted reduced mortality. Extensive analyses led the authors to conclude that "help given to others is a better predictor of health and well-being than are indicators of social engagement or received social support."[57]

A singularly one-way helping situation, or at least one commonly seen this way, is caregiving for a family member with a chronic illness or disability. Widely-reported research and popular public beliefs emphasize negative psychological and physiological consequences resulting from caregiving, including higher mortality rates for strained spouse cargivers.[58; 59]

In an important paper in *The Gerontologist*, however, Roth, Fredman and Haley bring together findings from extensive population-based studies presenting a markedly different perspective. They report strong evidence for reduced mortality and extended longevity for caregivers compared with non-caregiving controls. A majority of caregivers reported benefits from caregiving and saw it as positive. They reported little or no caregiving-related strain.[60] The authors also emphasize that there are many extraordinarily stressful and burdensome caregiving situations, for example, when internal (e.g., coping skills) and external (e.g., finances, help from other family) resources are insufficient, or in progressively deteriorating situations, such as care for a spouse with Alzheimer's. These situations, however, are not seen as representative of most family caregivers.

A key point of Roth, Fredman, and Haley is that caregivers can simultaneously have "both emotional distress and psychological satisfaction and growth." They propose significant national policies and practices to reduce stress in caregiving, while at the same time, endorsing this positive view of its role in human society. The authors reflect on the larger implications of this new perspective:

> To be connected through caring relationships with other human beings, especially within one's own family, is a common human experience desired by virtually everyone. Providing care for an older family member or friend with a chronic illness or disability is an increasingly common and important type of caring relationship. We assert the "caregiving-is-stressful" assumption is an overly narrow, simplified, and limited view on these types of human relationships. Multiple perspectives, from research on altruism, volunteerism, and evolutionary perspectives on prosocial behavior, are currently emerging to provide a broader and more balanced view on the range of caregiving experiences and health outcomes.[60]

Ask yourself the following questions: What about helping is healthy for you? Is it the good feelings you get when you help someone? Or is it the compassionate stance, the social connectedness, or the significance you feel doing this work? When are these benefits missing or more negative consequences present? The philosopher and humanitarian Albert Schweitzer reflected on the benefits of helping and caring: "It is only giving that stimulates. Impart as much as you can of your spiritual being to those who are on the road with you, and accept as something precious what comes back to you from them."[61] And a great deal does come back, often as intensely accelerated emotional, intellectual, and spiritual growth.

Through his study of self-help groups, Frank Riessman pointed to these gains and formulated the "helper therapy principle" to describe the benefits helpers receive from taking the helper role.[62] Our helping is rooted in more than compassion for suffering. We are also inspired and energized as we witness the healing and growth of our clients— their insights, creativity, courage, and resilience. These uplifting thoughts and feelings sustain us in the challenging moments when we, together, confront their pain and suffering.

Many people begin to feel uncomfortable when they reflect on the benefits they receive as helpers. They often reluctantly say something like, "I get more from this work than I give." Their hesitancy stems from believing egoistic and altruistic motivations must conflict. However, the reality, and a remarkable paradox, is that we grow most through caring for others. We saw this implicitly expressed in the mission moments shared earlier. In later chapters we will explore how working with grief, loss, and trauma can spark tremendous personal growth. One nurse put it this way: "Since working for hospice, I have a profound appreciation—greater love and zest for my life and my loved ones. I treasure the moment more often. I'm more aware of the wonders of life and the bountiful gifts I've been given."

The benefits of caring present a paradox. It's reflected in the responses of more than 2,000 members of the Presbyterian Church surveyed about helping others. For these church members, giving help to others was a more important predictor of their reported mental health than was receiving help.[63]

The emerging field of positive psychology has included intensive studies of empathy, compassion, altruism, and other prosocial phenomena. For example, positive psychologists instruct subjects to practice the loving-kindness meditation in the Buddhist tradition, or to engage in acts of compassion (e.g., interacting with someone in a caring and supportive way). We find that these prosocial actions increase positive social emotions, happiness, and self-esteem.[64; 65] These are heartening findings, since practicing compassion, and interacting in caring and supportive ways, lie at the core of your work.

Other recent findings also confirm this linkage between doing good and feeling good. If you find your work meaningful, you are likely to have greater life satisfaction, positive affect, self-determination and life meaning, together with less hostility, work stress, and depression.[66] A general sense of meaning (feeling one's existence is significant) and purpose in life (working toward and achieving goals aligned with one's values) are found to be associated with better psychological and physical well-being, and even reduced risk for cardiovascular events and all-cause mortality.[67; 68] However, sometimes we are so busy that the significance of the work doesn't even register with us. As a colleague once joked, "There's a lot of meaning in this work. I just don't have time to find it." But when we do find meaning, significant benefits can come with this awareness.

Scientists interested in quality of life issues are seeking even more answers to the benefits accrued from striving toward meaning and purpose beyond self-gratification. Some of this work rests upon a distinction philosophers have long made between two basic kinds of happiness. One consists of basic self-gratification (pleasure and satisfaction in life). The other, eudaimonia, is a deeper form of happiness consisting of the search for meaning and purpose in life beyond self-gratification. Eudaimonia is seen as including many virtuous, even noble, elements, including expression of the best within oneself, growth, authenticity, and flourishing.[69; 70]

Preliminary evidence even suggests possible immunological benefits of eudaimonia. A UCLA study examined these two forms of happiness, and found subjects who scored higher on a measure of eudaimonia had more favorable gene-expression profiles in their immune cells than subjects who had relatively high levels of hedonic well-being. The eudaimonic group showed low levels of inflammatory gene expression and strong expressions of their antibody and antiviral genes. Hedonic subjects had exactly the reverse profiles.[71]

In another study of the relation between immunity and other-oriented motivational states, Harvard psychologist David McClelland found that merely watching a film of Mother Teresa engaged in selfless acts of caring for abandoned babies, the sick, and the dying, had a positive effect on the immunological functioning of student subjects.

It worked even for those students who claimed a conscious dislike for Mother Teresa.[72]

CONCLUSION

How can we explain these phenomena? Perhaps we are part of a social body, a social organism which reinforces altruism and caring. Authors Robert Ornstein and David Sobel assert that our connections to the larger social environment are vital to our health.[73] They point out that all societies and religions have understood this relation between social connectedness, altruism, and immunity, and thus emphasize the importance of caring for others, generosity, and service. Although barriers of they-ness can disrupt this connectedness, our collective health may ultimately depend on our ability to see ourselves in others.

Even "one-way giving," that so frequently characterizes helping, may be healthful to the donor. That's because it nourishes connection to the social organism. In earlier times, helping was more of a reciprocal event. You used your nursing skills to help me heal my broken leg, or you compassionately supported me in a loss. I, in turn, helped you to raise your barn. Though the earlier forms of reciprocity no longer exist in professional helping situations, the psychological and physical benefits of helping—these brilliant evolutionary quid pro quos—continue.

It makes perfect sense that, for us to survive as a species, acts of helping are rewarded both psychologically and immunologically. What if each act of caring and helping depleted the helper, decreased his or her immunity and mood, and lessened the chances of survival? The view of caring and helping as being natural and good for us is intuitively and scientifically more accurate. When we help another person, we take part in an exchange, one that is shaped and finely tuned over the eons to ensure that when we help others we also help ourselves.

2

Burnout does not result from a genetic predisposition to grumpiness, a depressive personality, or general weakness. It is not caused by a failure of character or a lack of ambition. It is not a personality defect or a clinical syndrome. It is an occupational problem.[1]

Christina Maslach and Michael Leiter

I don't think I can do this anymore. It hurts so bad. No one cares. I think I would make a great florist or meat cutter.

Helper

Sometimes I ask, who cares for me?

Helper

The Challenge of Caring: Emotional Involvement in Helping

A t this point, you might consider the discussion on helping in the previous chapter to be somewhat one-sided, presenting a picture of happy, saintly beings fulfilling themselves through selfless devotion to others in a stress-free environment. Although a significant body of research and theory supports the positive aspects of helping, we need to pay equal attention to its more difficult side, a subject we address here. In particular, we examine in more detail why helping suffering persons doesn't always unfold naturally, if it happens at all, and how it can often lead to burnout, vicarious traumatization, and moral distress. However, as we will discover, these instances of emotional distress can be minimized or avoided if we maintain our emotional equilibrium and sustain our empathy-induced altruistic motivation. Finding a way to be emotionally involved in your work, to maintain your helping motivations, empathy, compassion, and commitment as you courageously—yes, this work is courageous—help people live with hope in a world where loss is inescapable, is perhaps the central challenge in this work. It is the challenge of caring.

Meeting this challenge is a complex psychological task requiring an awareness and understanding of one's emotional reactions and involvement as a helper. Fortunately, extensive research and clinical practice now offer key insights to guide our thinking and practice. One important observation, almost a truism, is that a deep commitment to caring is not without costs; the flame of caring can flicker or extinguish. When it shines brilliantly, it can inspire great acts of caring, lead to self-fulfillment, and actually buffer stress. However, a bright flame, by virtue of its intensity, is more likely to burn out.

In fact, we find the most idealistic, altruistic, and committed help-ers are among the first to burn out.[2] Failures to accomplish specific helping goals—when pain is not controlled, when suffering does not abate, when a grant proposal isn't funded, or when bureaucratic rigmarole interferes with the delivery of care—are most stressful to those caregivers who are particularly sensitive to their clients' needs. The difficulties of the work tend to frustrate their idealism, under-mine their sense of personal accomplishment, and exhaust their emotional reserves. For these dedicated helpers, burnout is, as Chris-tina Maslach has described it, the *cost of caring*.[3]

High empathy and helper stress also often go hand in hand. Using some of the same empathy statements you responded to in Chapter 1, Ezra Stotland and his colleagues found novice nurses who scored the highest were the first to leave the rooms of dying patients: They did a U-turn at the foot of the beds of the patients they cared for. The high-empathy nurses, imagining what it would be like to be in that bed, became distressed and left the room. Yet after receiving support and advice on how to relate to patients more effectively, the same nurses eventually spent the greatest amounts of time with patients and were highly successful.[4] Empathy, like your passion to make a difference, is a double-edged sword; it is simultaneously your greatest asset and a point of real vulnerability.

The Continuum of Emotional Involvement

As helpers, we are constantly moving back and forth on a continuum of emotional involvement, ranging from underinvolved to overin-volved. This continuum has distant and burned-out experiences at one pole, emotional overinvolvement at the other, and a more sus-tainable balanced stance between those two extremes.

Continuum of Emotional Involvement

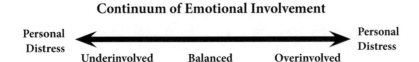

Personal Distress ← Underinvolved   Balanced   Overinvolved → Personal Distress

The two poles of this continuum are vividly described by a clinician who said, "I feel either as if I am encased in steel (the distant, uninvolved position) or as if my skin has been ripped off" (the overinvolved position). Most veteran helpers have been at both ends of the continuum. All caregivers shift their involvement frequently. They become more or less involved in response to external and internal demands.

You can think about the intensity of emotional involvement in two ways. First, there is the level of involvement you have from moment to moment as you help others. Reflect on some of your recent helping situations. What was your degree of involvement in each? Second, your emotional involvement in the work will vary at different points in your helping career, even at different points in the same week or day. Has your general degree of emotional involvement in the work changed since you finished your training and first began to work in this field? When you think about your current relationships with the people you care for, where would you locate yourself on this continuum, from emotionally distant and burned out to overinvolved?

The more distant, less-involved positions on this continuum can be momentary stances taken in response to a personal need for emotional distance. You might pull back for a moment or a day for some respite and to regain your sense of emotional balance. Or, something in a helping situation might push an emotional button in you. Then, your empathy and compassion take leave of you as you quickly move to a less-involved stance.

In these moments, it is common to have doubts about yourself and your caring, as these health professionals shared:

✧ Maybe I don't have the real capacity to love, to be truly close to people. I deal with people every day and compare myself to people who become so emotionally close. Is this distance professionalism, or a flaw in my ability to love?

✧ I feel guilty. I sometimes try to avoid families of dying patients when I feel inadequate to help them in the situation. I try to stay detached and come across as uncaring.

At the overinvolved pole of the continuum, emotional involvement is at a high pitch. Emotions here often include feeling out of control or "in over your head." You also might think, "What happened to my life?" The distress of the overinvolved helper is consuming:

✧ When I wake up at 3 A.M., I start to panic, thinking, "How am I going to manage the next problem?" It's not always a real problem. I don't even like to think about how I feel.

✧ Sometimes I feel no matter what I do, I'm hitting my head against a brick wall. At times I wish I owned a Polynesian island to which I could escape for rest and quiet. Yet there always seems to be another crisis needing my fixing, and my island retreats once again into my subconscious.

✧ I hate coming to work because I feel once I'm here it engulfs me like fire.

✧ I hated my patient at times because her emotions hurt me. The negative feelings toward her made me feel guilty, and I would hate her even more, and yet I loved her. She was a central part of my life for 6 months. Toward the end, I thought she would never die.

These distressing experiences can usher in burnout, and you find yourself taking a defensive and self-protective stance, relinquishing caring connections with the people you assist. The over-aroused position can also include a sense of exhilaration and getting something important accomplished. This intensity of feelings is exciting, but also exhausting. You think, "Nobody can do it as well as I can." Or, "Why aren't my colleagues more involved?" When the intensity becomes too great and your coping resources are strained, you may try to reduce your involvement, either (ideally) by setting healthy limits, or less adaptively, by withdrawing emotionally or physically.

The midpoint of emotional involvement has a paradoxical quality: the state of being emotionally involved while simultaneously maintaining a certain emotional distance, of being united but also separate. Ideally, this is a flexible and balanced stance. You are able to become more emotionally involved when the situation calls for it, and ready to pull back if necessary.

Frequently, however, the midpoint position is inhabited instead by helpers frantically moving back and forth between the two poles of emotional involvement. They might have been underinvolved, felt guilty, and decided to reinvolve themselves; or perhaps they were overinvolved, saw their personal lives were beginning to suffer, and decided to take a respite and become less involved.

Shifting degrees of emotional involvement also characterize our everyday personal relationships. We all want to find a comfortable distance between ourselves and others. Some people have extreme problems with intimacy. They get emotionally close to others only to withdraw again immediately.[5] This struggle between running toward and running away is often precipitated by early attachments fraught with anxiety, but we all act this way to a certain extent. Like the proverbial porcupine huddling on a cold night, we initially test the emotional climate, and then become more involved. When things get too hot for us, we pull back. So too, we constantly adjust the extent of our emotional involvement in the helping relationship.

Empathy, Compassion, Personal Distress, and the Helper's Pit

The metaphor of the *Helper's Pit* illustrates the varieties of emotional experience possible for you as a helper. Imagine the person you are helping is in a pit and you are standing on the edge. If you identify with this person, what happens? You fall into the pit!

Identifying with the other person and falling into the Helper's Pit can limit your ability to help. You don't accurately perceive the other and are unable to think objectively about what course of action might be best. You are caught up in your own emotional and cognitive reactions to the person's distressing situation, and experience *personal distress*. Most important, people stuck in pits don't want their helpers in the pit with them; it can be terrifying, and deepen their feelings of hopelessness and helplessness.

If you empathize, you *feel with* the person in the Pit, getting inside his or her experiential world. Empathy involves both cognitive role taking and an emotional responsiveness. In other words, you imagine being in this person's shoes, inside his or her predicament, and then you have a vicarious emotional response, based on your sense of this person's state or condition.

Empathy is not limited to the difficult and painful emotions associated with human suffering. We can—and must—empathize with the full range of human emotions if we are to be effective. These feelings can include joy, pride, courage, and caring, to name just a few. Although these empathic connections might not be as integral to the empathy-compassion-helping connection, they play a vital role in our helping. They enable us to respond to and facilitate our clients' forward moving, constructive aspects.

Mirroring the client's subjective reality does not, by itself, necessarily lead to helping behavior. To actuate empathy-induced altruistic motivation, there must also be the other-oriented experience of compassion or empathic concern—*feeling for* the person in distress. (I use the terms compassion and empathic concern interchangeably). In this state, you feel moved, compassionate, tender, or warm, but this state doesn't necessarily match that of the other person.[6]

Compassion can be defined as, "the feeling that arises in witnessing another's suffering and that motivates a subsequent desire to help."[7] You are moved by another's suffering and you want to help. Most theorists describe this as a sympathetic response. They see sympathy as aligned with empathic concern.[6; 8; 9] This is the meaning of the term as used here. Patients, however, view the term sympathy as connoting a feeling of detached pity and not as a core feature of compassionate care.[10]

In *Altruism in Humans*, Daniel Batson details how empathic concern produces altruistic motivation.[11] In his view, empathic concern can include a variety of emotions, including sympathy, softheartedness, tenderness, and grief. It is important to note that these are feelings for the other. They are not, for example, instances of personal sadness, personal distress, or personal grief. However, feeling with and feeling for others in distress are predicated upon an openness to our inner life, particularly to loss-related feelings. My view is that it is a sense of loss—the universal human experience we carry within us at varying levels of awareness—that primarily guides and energizes our empathy and compassion. It is the inner compass that guides us to the suffering of others and provides the foundation for the empathy-compassion-helping connection.

Empathizing can also lead to differing forms of personal distress. As we shall see, this can short-circuit helping and steer us toward several kinds of avoidance. The challenge is to convert your initial empathic response and understanding of the suffering or distress of the other into a compassionate reaction motivating you to do something about it. Empathy and compassion work together naturally to motivate you to help the person in distress, but in doing so, you must find a way to reach down and assist the suffering person to climb out of the Pit—without falling in yourself.

Findings in neuroscience and positive psychology are greatly advancing our understanding of the dynamics of helping and the Helper's Pit. The emerging model views empathy, compassion, and personal distress as three distinct responses helpers can have when confronting suffering. An additional distinction is made depending on whether the caregiver's attention is self-focused or focused on the distressed other.

Upon encountering someone who is suffering, the initial critical event is whether you attend to this person's distress. Do you even look into the Pit? As mentioned previously, your feeling state, your sense of connection with the person, and other elements affect what happens at this point in helping. If you do extend yourself, overcome all potential barriers of they-ness, and open your heart to the other person, you begin to empathize with and possibly have concern for his or her plight.

When you are experiencing empathy, your attention is markedly focused on the other: You look outside yourself and feel connected to the other. You observe someone suffering, and your initial empathic responses can then develop into feelings of concern or compassion for the other. A conscious desire to help accompanies this empathic concern or compassion.[12]

Personal distress, a central feature of burnout, differs significantly from empathy and compassion. When you are personally distressed, you lose your equilibrium and fall into the Pit. This distress occurs at both ends of the continuum of emotional involvement. Personally-distressed caregivers can feel drained, troubled, angry, worried, or grieved. They "go to pieces," feeling helpless in emotional situations, and losing control during emergencies.[8] When we are personally distressed, we focus on ourselves, and our caring connection with others becomes weak or nonexistent as we dwell on our own pain, sorrow, sense of failure, or other emotional reactions.[13]

The intensity and nature of your emotional responses contribute to determining whether you feel empathy and compassion, or personal distress, as a helper. Your arousal can be so high, personal distress results. For example, if your empathic sadness becomes too great, overarousal can occur, bringing about a more self-oriented, distressed response. If you believe you must continue to witness the other person's suffering, and think your intervention will not significantly ease it, overarousal is likely. Reviewing work in this area, Martin Hoffman states: "Perhaps there is an optimal range of empathic arousal—determined by people's levels of distress tolerance—within which they are most responsive to others. Beyond this range, they may be too preoccupied with their own aversive state to help anyone else."[14]

Thus, you can begin with empathy and end in personal distress. We can speculate that the nurses in the Stotland study described earlier were overwhelmed when they walked into the rooms of dying patients. Their empathy rapidly led to personal distress, overriding their compassion and desire to stay and help.

Balanced Emotional Involvement: Staying Within the Constructive Zone

Anthony Back and colleagues recognize the perils awaiting the helper at both poles of the continuum of emotional involvement, and offer suggestions for staying within a *constructive zone* of clinical work:

> Our approach to helplessness involves reading one's unintentional reaction to helplessness as a barometer of one's own engagement, then deliberately shifting from hyper- or hypo-engagement toward the constructive zone, and finally

working directly with the patient's suffering. When a clinician is working in his constructive zone, he can evaluate the situation for what it is, empathize without getting overwhelmed, draw on his wisdom and expertise, all the while experiencing moments of effectiveness and moments of disappointment.[15]

When we stay in this constructive zone, we are emotionally regulated, and can adopt an accepting stance toward our inner thoughts and feelings. There is emotional balance.

Harrison and Westwood asked therapists treating traumatized clients how they could be empathically engaged with clients without becoming personally distressed. The therapists described a form of empathic engagement the researchers termed *exquisite empathy*. When in states of exquisite empathy, the therapists were able to maintain clarity about interpersonal boundaries. They could get "very close without fusing or confusing the client's story and perspective with their own."[16] Practicing with balanced empathy—empathy not acting as a direct conduit for trauma from your patient to you—can prevent burnout.[17] A trauma clinician interviewed in the Harrison and Westwood study described this dynamic:

> I actually can find sustenance and nourishment in the work itself, by being as present and connected with the client as possible. I move in as opposed to move away, and I feel that is a way that I protect myself against secondary traumatization. The connection is the part that helps and that is an antidote to the horror of what I might be hearing. It's about working with the heart from a place of warmth and care and even love.[16]

Quite aptly, Jeremy Rifkin describes a kind of "empathetic extension" or "empathic embrace" in which there is "the awareness of the vulnerability we all share, and when expressed it becomes a celebration of our common yearning to live."[18]

Are there ways to help clinicians operate in the constructive zone and practice exquisite empathy? One answer comes from an fMRI study conducted by neuroscientist Olga Klimecki and colleagues. The researchers tested whether exposure to contemplative practices can reduce the excessive negative affect that results from empathy with distressed others. Subjects received brief trainings in empathy and in the contemplative practice of loving kindness, a compassion-enhancing technique emphasizing relating to one's own and others' suffering with friendliness, warmth, and caring. After compassion training, subjects had significantly less distress when exposed to videos depicting human suffering. They did so "without ignoring the presence of suffering or changing the negative reality."[19] Compassion training interventions like this could be widely used to reduce the likelihood of clinicians' empathic distress escalating into personal distress, and so enable them to work in the constructive zone, practice exquisite and balanced empathy, and avoid burnout.

In a different fMRI study, Singer and her colleagues found empathy for pain involves the affective, but not the sensory, components of pain. Neural responses for subjects were measured both when they felt pain, and when their loved ones, who were present in the room, felt pain. Empathic pain activated only the pain-related parts of the neural network associated with emotions, and not those involved with sensorial processing.[20] We can be engaged with the suffering of others without having the entire pain matrix in our brains activated.

Interpersonal Allergies: Emotional Buttons in the Work

Maintaining balanced emotional involvement in helping is challenging. For example, our empathy can be derailed by personal distress when our emotional buttons and vulnerabilities are triggered by events in the helping encounter. When this happens, we can instantly feel sad, angry, frustrated, detached, or a myriad of other emotions. Norman Kagan termed these emotional buttons *interpersonal allergies*—as with physical allergic reactions, a little bit of something can evoke a strong reaction in us.[21] When these buttons get pushed in us, we typically withdraw from our patients, become personally distressed, and preoccupied with our own emotional state. We fall into the Helper's Pit.

These interpersonal allergies are universal human experiences. They affect everyone some of the time, and some people all of the time, and are usually related to some basic fear or vulnerability. One common example of these emotional triggers at work is when we find it extremely difficult to work with a certain patient or family member. We are surprised when another team member is highly effective with the same individual. We can't even understand how he or she can even be in the same room with this "impossible" person. Then, we find ourselves easily dealing with a different patient, one with whom we work well, but whom our coworker can't tolerate. Our differing reactions to these people and situations can be traced to the emotional buttons each of us brings to these encounters.

The psychotherapy literature often discusses these highly individual reactions by helpers as countertransference phenomena. Countertransference occurs when we see and respond to something that isn't there, or don't see and don't respond to something that is there. It can involve overidentifying with clients, sometimes projecting ourselves onto them and their life situations. It's a pathway to ineffective helping and personal distress because we're relating most strongly to our own thoughts and feelings, not to those of the client. When this happens, we're not able to maintain a balanced position as helpers. For example, when a client reminds you of one of your family members or friends, or presents problems unsolved in your own personal life, you may be less effective with this person. Another example is when the grief of the person you're helping activates your own continuing grief reactions and you quickly fall into the Helper's Pit. The test then becomes how to use this sensitivity to deepen—not diminish—your empathy for the other person.

There are many situations where our interactions with clients can more overtly throw us off balance and challenge our capacity to remain empathically engaged. Our clients can be angry with us, refuse to stop harming themselves, violate our professional boundaries, displace the rage of grief onto us, and take other actions that can leave us feeling sad, angry, frustrated, or anxious. To transform our negative reactions in these moments into compassionate responses, we must remain open to ourselves, regulate our emotions, and have a compassionate perspective concerning the client's behaviors, as well as an acceptant stance toward our own reactions to them.[22] When these negative reactions create ruptures in the helping relationship, we need to contain our emotions and constructively and nondefensively process what is happening to restore trust and a solid alliance.

Our allergic responses are often unconscious and can catch us unawares: We suddenly find ourselves behaving in a way we might not have anticipated in our work with a specific patient or family member. We might either move rapidly to an extreme position on the continuum of emotional involvement, fall into the Helper's Pit, find ourselves withdrawing from emotional contact, or feel helpless, frustrated, or angry.

Here is an example of this phenomenon. Jan, an oncology nurse, found she had her greatest difficulty working with mothers. Her own mother died when she was 10 years old and she now finds herself feeling protective of the children of dying female patients. She is intensely interested in what it is like for the dying mothers to say goodbye to their children. By talking with the mothers about their experiences, and by supporting their children, she gets some insight into what might have been happening for her own mother when she had to leave Jan. Also, she can support the children in a manner she would have wanted for herself. The double-edged nature of Jan's deep empathy with these mothers and children is clear: She no doubt is profoundly caring in her interactions with them, but she also finds herself confronting personal pain in the process.

Four emotional themes that frequently appear in the interpersonal allergies of caregivers are fear of one's own mortality, fear of hurting, fear of being hurt, and fear of being engulfed.

Fear of our own death

Daily confrontations with lifethreatening illness can push perhaps our most core emotional button, the fear of our own mortality. We can work for long stretches of time without consciously feeling this. Then suddenly, we have a patient with our birthday, or who looks like our child, or our sister, or has our mother's name, and instantly we have an "ego chill" feeling. We lose our sense of "this is not me" who is suffering or dying. For that moment, we jump into the Helper's Pit .

How we handle our reaction determines whether or not we're able to continue providing help in an effective manner. This is a good example of a helper's moment when we need to maintain our balance, not let our empathy switch to personal distress, or allow ourselves to unconsciously distance ourselves emotionally to reduce this distress.

No matter how many times I ponder my own mortality, or however many dying patients I work with, I still have a hard time thinking about my own death. I'm not death phobic, but I have a "death button" that can get pushed. This often happens when I'm working with someone my own age who's a lot like me. As Freud noted, the ego cannot imagine its own dissolution. In one of his lighter moments, he is said to have told his wife, "If one of the two of us dies before the other, I think I'll move to Paris."[23] The fear of our own mortality is something we continually face. And our work forces us to look at it, or to work at avoiding it.

Regardless of how we cope with it, the pressure is still there. When this particular button is activated, you might find yourself making a referral, becoming emotionally distant while you're still physically present, or even leaving the helping field altogether. Hospice volunteers with lower scores on a measure of death anxiety continued working in their program for longer periods of time than did volunteers with high scores, suggesting the high death anxiety group had greater difficulty keeping their emotional balance.[24] Less fear of death has been shown to be a protective factor for burnout in nurses from internal medicine, oncology, hematology and palliative care departments.[25]

Fear of hurting

Another interpersonal allergy is the fear of hurting the person you're helping. This is not always an irrational concern. Indeed, so many necessary interventions entail bringing suffering with them, whether doing a spinal tap on a 5-year-old child, delivering bad news, or doing deep exposure work with a traumatically bereaved client. Your helping often hurts, and sometimes makes helping more stressful for you.

The fear of hurting others is compounded by the pressure to be perfect, and by often needing to make decisions based on ambiguous or incomplete information. Technological developments occur so rapidly it's almost impossible to stay current with medical facts. Mistakes can be costly, sometimes even life-threatening. Consequently, many health professionals can feel the *terror of error*. They fear making potentially life-threatening mistakes:

✧ I'm afraid of being caught in a crisis (life/death) situation of mother and/or baby when no doctor is around, and other staff are too busy to help me—I'll do something wrong or fail to do the right thing.

✧ Before a sick baby is born, I feel I will not do the right things to save the baby from dying!

✧ I'm afraid someday I'll accidentally say the wrong thing and take away someone's last hope.

Errors inevitably do or seem to occur, and the emotional consequences for the caregiver can be unsettling and persistent, as these clinicians' disclosures reveal:

✧ Sometimes I feel I've been careless, giving the wrong IV and rate to a patient. Instead of helping him, I'm making things worse. God! I feel so guilty and I have sleepless nights worrying what the consequences can be.

✧ I made an error once and never told anyone and have always worried about it. In my first nursing job, I was in a treatment room dealing with trachs and dressing changes. A patient was brought in who had trouble breathing. I went to help him, suctioned, and removed the dressing in the pharyngeal area. As I turned to do something, it seemed as if a small part of the dressing fell in the larynx, but I was never sure. The patient got worse after this and died later that night.

✧ If I would have been more knowledgeable and insistent about having a doctor come in for a late deceleration, the baby would be about 4 years old today.

Fear of being hurt

The fear of being hurt is also a frequent concern for helpers. The hurt we fear, and often feel, can take many forms. First, there can be direct physical and psychological aggression. Many, if not most caregivers have been kicked, spat on, sworn at, pinched, or mistreated in other ways I lump together as helper abuse. If we lose control and respond in kind, our self-esteem can be seriously eroded:

> I had a difficult patient who became angry at my attempts to help her. She spit in my face. Without thinking, I spit back in her face. I could have died with shame. I was there to make this more comfortable for her and I failed miserably. I don't think anyone else would have reacted so impulsively.

Second, displaced rage from patients and family members can be extremely difficult to cope with. For example, an oncology nurse related how she had struggled to provide excellent care for a patient with open wounds. The nurse was covered with blood and was standing near the husband, expecting him to thank her for her tremendous caring efforts. Instead, he slapped her face and said, "Even you couldn't save her!" This nurse was eventually able to see this outburst as displaced rage, yet, in the moment, the pain and hurt for her was all too real. The struggle to keep one's heart open in difficult moments like these can be fierce.

Third, we can feel hurt and grief when a patient dies. We grieve for them and for their families, and even for what we did or wished we could have done. Helper grief is an important issue for individual helpers and caring teams. If we work with dying patients, grief is a constant part of what we do, and it builds up if it's not confronted and worked through. In addition, grief from your personal life can be activated in helping encounters:

> The majority of people I care for have terminal cancer. I often feel anger, frustration and fear when dealing with these patients and their families. I, of course, try to hide these negative thoughts. My problem is I watched my father die a miserable death from lung cancer over a 10-month period. My new

patients and their problems bring up old feelings I felt when my dad died.

Fear of being engulfed

This concern is best captured by the thought "If I let myself become involved, I'll be sucked into the bottomless pit of the patient's emotional neediness." When activated, this emotional button can push us from a state of empathy to one of personal distress. These helper disclosures vividly convey what this can be like:

✧ When I was there Monday, she was very, very frightened. And it was like she was clinging, and there was so much power in that I had to just stand back. It became almost manipulative. I felt like I was going to get sucked in.

✧ I have a fear of becoming so attached to my clients I won't be able to detach myself when I go home to my family. I'm afraid of cheating my family out of having fun because I feel depressed over the client's situation. I can't turn my emotional state on or off easily, and I worry about my attitude toward my family and personal friends.

By blaming ourselves when things go wrong, or getting stuck in helplessness, we often make a difficult situation worse. Coping with our fears, vulnerabilities, and other emotional buttons adds to our stress levels. These internal stressors take their toll, but the toll often goes unnoticed. Maybe we start avoiding certain topics with patients or family members. Perhaps we just become emotional for no reason. We might get sloppy in our communication: interrupting more, questioning more, telling people how to act, think, or feel, or not paying attention to our real impact on others.

When the toll is too great, when we've ignored our own needs for too long, the result is we cut ourselves off emotionally from those we help—we tune out, stop listening, give pat suggestions, and disconnect. The remedy for interpersonal allergies is to recognize and understand our fears, and to retain our inner balance when our emotional buttons are triggered.

Emotional Involvement:
Necessary and Challenging

As we are seeing, finding a way to be empathic and emotionally involved without falling into the Helper's Pit is a central challenge for all caring helpers. Combs and Avila put it this way:

> Helpers must be able to find joy in bringing people through these dark places rather than take on their clients' problems as their own.... Helpers must learn to grow and increase their strength through wrestling with the pain of others rather than let that pain drag them down too.[26]

The alternative—to remain emotionally uninvolved—has burdensome negative effects on us as helpers, as Eugene Kennedy captures here:

> If we remain uninvolved, nothing much will happen, and the potential stress of emotional engagement will be transformed into a different difficulty commonly known by the reluctant counselor. Such helpers experience the problems of others as burdens or downright impositions; they struggle through relationships like a downed airman crossing a swamp with a parachute dragging behind him. There is nothing sadder than helpers who steel themselves against their tasks, who speak of "having to see all these mixed-up people," and who seem more grimly dutiful than interested in their work. The stress associated with noninvolvement is not very dramatic, of course; the heart does not leap with enthusiasm in these situations. It is like being caught between two grindstones which crush us slowly into a fine, dry powder. Few things are worse than working with people and not enjoying it.[27]

Because emotional involvement is essential, how can we tell when we are overinvolved? First, it is important to recognize we can have extremely strong emotional responses without falling into the Helper's Pit. Strong emotions are a natural part of helping people cope with grief, loss, and life-threatening illness. As Batson noted, our compassion can include grief and empathic (not personal) distress.

You can be emotionally centered, even as tears form in your eyes, as long as you are still focused on the other person, and your feelings don't shift from caring to personal distress.

An example from my clinical work illustrates this. A bereaved, usually unemotional client, was describing his final conversation with his terminally ill wife. She had told him, "Share your tears with our sons." He sobbed as he described this. I was deeply moved by both his suffering and the wisdom of his wife's final words. Some slight tears ran down my cheeks, and he saw them. We continued talking. Later, my client described the session as a breakthrough in his grieving process. Was I in the Helper's Pit in that key session? I don't think so, because I could still think about his situation as other than my own, although I resonated deeply with it.

Think of the times in your caregiving when you have had a tear in your eye while being present to great suffering. Did the distressed patient run from the room, or did the relationship and helping encounter deepen in some way? I like to think of it this way: If we are sobbing, our attention has turned inward and our empathic connection with the other is broken. We are in the Helper's Pit. If we have a tear in our eye, it can merely reflect our compassion in the moment and affirm our caring connection with those we assist.

Being close and helpful without being personally distressed can't happen unless we know ourselves and respect our own feelings. When we misinterpret, don't know, or cover up our genuine feelings and reactions, we risk the hazards of overinvolvement. Strong and sometimes irrational feelings are part of helping. They become troublesome only when we don't give ourselves time or permission to explore their roots, to reflect on why we are having these specific feelings at this particular time, and thus be able to regulate or manage our emotions. When you find yourself overreacting, clinging, rejecting, feeling possessive toward a patient, or saying this is the best or worst person you have ever worked with, it is time to look inside and try to make sense of what this relationship means to you.

We must also remain separate as we draw closer to the other person, a suggestion that may sound paradoxical. But it is only as a separate person that we can care for someone without our concern for him or her possibly pushing us into the Helper's Pit. Carl Rogers used the term *nonpossessive caring* to describe this relationship quality.[28] He also made a useful distinction in his definition of empathy. He wrote "to sense the client's private world as if it were your own, but without ever losing the as if quality—this is empathy."[29]

This definition fits perfectly with our earlier observation that if we identify with our client's experiences—if we lose the *as if* quality—we can fall into the Helper's Pit. Findings in neuroscience also support the importance of a self-other distinction in determining whether the empathic process results in personal distress or empathic concern. In an fMRI and behavioral measure study, Lamm, Batson, and Decety showed participants videos of medical patients (actors) receiving a painful treatment. In one condition (self-perspective), participants were told to imagine themselves in the place of the patient; in another condition (other-perspective), they were asked to imagine how the other felt. Participants were also told the treatment had been either successful or unsuccessful. The participants who imagined themselves in the place of the patient felt more personal distress and reported less empathic concern than the subjects who imagined how the patient felt. Furthermore, participants who were told the treatments had been unsuccessful evidenced the greatest personal distress.[30] We must have a real relationship with the people we care for. The greatest gift we can give is human presence, and with it, the feeling they are not alone in their struggles. We can give this gift only if we are willing to take the risk of becoming involved with this stranger who seeks our help. This necessitates a certain degree of vulnerability and courage. It challenges us to do this without becoming enmeshed with the other.

In both the intrapersonal and interpersonal realms, we want to be close enough to have contact, but not so close we lose our emotional equipoise and identify our whole selves with what we encounter. Whether it is your patient's pain, or the sadness you feel when a patient is suffering, you must befriend and acknowledge these feelings while also being able to step back and see the larger picture.[16] Without this skill, your potential for caring and compassionate helping, and possibly your longevity in the field, will be severely limited.

Within the Helper's Pit metaphor, we might think of multiple resilience-enhancing external and inner resources. These include self-efficacy, mindful awareness, self-compassion, social support, communication and emotion regulation skills. These attributes support us in our helping encounters. They allow us to maintain a poised emotional involvement. And, they keep us from personal distress and the Helper's Pit. These resources and skills will be explored in greater detail in subsequent chapters.

Empathy-Driven versus Distress-Driven Helping

As we have seen, balanced empathic engagement supports the natural unfolding of helping behavior. Our empathic attunement with the suffering other generates a promotive tension that motivates us to reduce the other's suffering. However, in what I term distress-driven helping, the process and outcomes of helping are shaped instead by personal distress. Here, the caregiver is more self-focused, and the task of reducing personal distress begins to compete with that of reducing the other person's pain and suffering. Unhelpful responses, such as blaming the victim, distancing oneself emotionally, self-preoccupation, and other burnout-related phenomena, become more common. Our helping becomes more effortful and less effective, if it happens at all. Another way to say this is your empathic suffering with the other does not transform into other-oriented compassion; instead, it transforms into personal distress and activates more egoistic motivations.

Let's look at this phenomenon more closely. What does egoistic mean here? If our helping is driven by personal distress, we are more likely not to help if escape (e.g., physical or emotional withdrawal) is easy; that is, our helping is egoistic or "selfish" in the sense that our ultimate goal is to relieve our own, not the other person's, distress.[11] If escape is too costly (e.g., negative responses from a supervisor, coworkers, or oneself), we can still escape by distancing ourselves physically or emotionally. Examples might be to leave the scene or not answer phone calls. If we choose escape, we may try to discharge our guilt by blaming the patient, saying things like "He's totally impossible," or "She just won't help herself."

During the course of everyday work with patients and family members, there are often many opportunities to stop or diminish your helping. You can decide to spend less time with this person, or you might possibly refer the person to another agency or helper. If physical escape is not possible, you can pull back emotionally and do only what is necessary. However, we usually do not avail ourselves of these escapes from helping: Our empathy for the distress of others, although weakened, usually energizes enough compassion to keep us moving steadily toward a positive helping outcome.

However, the picture changes dramatically in distress-driven helping. Here the focus shifts to relieving our own emotional pain. True, unless you escape the field, you are still helping the other person, but the entire complexion of helping is different, and the features of burnout begin to overshadow the positive qualities of helping.

The distinction between empathy-driven and distress-driven helping raises a more general issue concerning our motivations for helping. Is altruism ever actually the motivation for our helping, or is our caregiving always primarily self-centered? Think back to the scene with the young woman who had fallen from her mountain bike. Let's assume you were empathically aroused when you encountered her and helped her. Did you help her to relieve her distress or to relieve yours? The more general question is, are "altruistic" acts actually egoistic? In other words, do we just help others to reduce our own negative feelings, helping being the most efficient way to do this?

This question receives much attention from research psychologists, who reason as follows: If we are helping for egoistic reasons (to reduce our own emotional pain), we won't continue to help if we can easily escape from the helping situation (assuming there are low costs of escaping). If these options are readily available, we will escape by avoiding being assigned this person, not answering the phone, or getting a colleague to replace us. We might also be physically present but withdraw emotionally. If, on the other hand, our motivation to help is truly altruistic, the ease or difficulty (costs) of escaping the helping situation will have no impact on whether or not we help because this will be irrelevant to our goal—namely, relieving the other person's distress.

There are real world examples of remarkable altruism, such as living anonymous kidney donors. These suggest the possibility of purely altruistic acts, but what does our science tell us? What we have learned from extensive and carefully designed research addressing this issue is that empathic emotion can, in fact, produce a truly altruistic desire to reduce the distress of others.[11] We act first for the other person. Relieving our empathic distress (different from personal distress) is a positive outcome, but it is not the motivation for our actions. This finding explains why we persist in helping in situations where giving up or leaving the scene could be a tempting alternative. It also supports the view of altruism and helping as core features of human nature.

Another intriguing finding is that for the empathy-helping connection to occur, we must personally interpret our arousal as empathic concern, not as private distress or some other aroused state. Consider the following study conducted by Coke and colleagues.[31] Undergraduate subjects listened to a fake newscast about "Katie Banks," a senior at their university whose parents had recently been killed in an automobile crash. Katie needed money. She also needed help with grocery shopping, chores, and babysitting for her two younger siblings. Subjects were told that because Katie was nice enough to let them use the newscast in the study, the professor in charge of the research wanted to do something for her and had a list from Katie of things the subjects could do. The measure of helping was the amount of time volunteered to help Katie.

Some subjects were instructed to imagine Katie's condition during the newscast; another group was instructed to identify specific broadcasting techniques. Both groups had some subjects who were given a placebo pill they were told would either relax or arouse them. The subjects who were instructed to empathize, but were also told they had been given an arousing placebo, did not help. It was the subjects who were told they had been given the relaxation pill and were told to empathize who helped the most. They knew their arousal was due to empathic concern, and they proceeded to offer the most help, often involving many hours of volunteer assistance. When we are empathically aroused in response to distress in others, and we perceive our arousal as empathic concern, we help.

Just as not all empathy leads to helping, not all helping is a result of empathy. Helping, spontaneous or otherwise, doesn't always require personal in-the-moment empathy. Many, perhaps most, of our interventions flow from a more cognitive understanding of our clients' needs. This can be based on diverse sources of information, from test results to predictions based on previous clinical encounters. For example, consider a routine phone call to a family on the first night of homecare. This intervention makes good clinical sense and might seem extremely empathic to the family. But, its motivator is not necessarily emotional empathy, although deep empathy might develop during the phone conversation. Indeed, most of our helping moments—whether in a counseling session or during a routine medical intervention—are imbued with a more general sense of empathy for the people we care for. We develop a picture of their suffering in the present and in the future. This larger sense of concern and empathy guides our actions. When we sit face to face with them and discuss emotional issues, more specific empathic reactions develop and add further impetus and focus to our helping.

Some of our helping, however, can be almost purely, cognitively driven. The cognitively-driven helper thinks, "I know what they need at this time, and I will do it." As a physician friend once told me, "Sometimes I am just being a doctor." Although this helping is often on target and essential, it can sometimes be somewhat routinized and not attuned to the unique needs of the people we care for. For example, after many years of working with patients and families, we often know what to expect. Even the most poignant disclosures—things said for the first time, words taking form from raw experience—can be similar, beyond the specifics, to what we have heard hundreds of times before. This can lead to a tendency to anticipate and not listen, to act before hearing the full story, or to slip into premature advice-giving as we leap into doing what our prior learning tells us will usually be helpful to people facing this circumstance.

Still, cognitively-driven helping has some unique advantages. This helping can get you through many difficult helping situations. You might not have empathy for, or even like, some of the people you are caring for. However, you know what they need, you are committed to serving them, and you go on to make effective interventions based on your understanding of their situation, and the ethical beliefs, skills, and goals you bring to your work.

Downward and Upward Social Comparisons in Helping

When people are suffering, they often find some relief in comparing themselves with other, less fortunate people. Psychologists know this as downward social comparison.[32; 33] For example, the people we care for, even in the worst circumstances, often comment others are worse off. Knowing things could be worse can provide a perspective that serves a self-protective function.

We also make downward social comparisons as helpers. The suffering of patients and family members, a source of deep concern and compassion for them, also deepens our appreciation of the health of our own families. Difficulties in our personal lives can pale in comparison, and this comparison can bolster our resilience and helping. We think, "If they have the courage to deal with this, I must have the strength to help them in this time of need."

When comparisons go in the reverse direction, however, the empathy-helping connection can be derailed. For example, in one study, subjects who were asked to empathize with the positive feelings of others were less likely to offer help to these perhaps more fortunate others. Empathic sadness promotes helping; empathic joy lessens it.[34] Yet, in clinical work, where we have an ongoing caring relationship, a slight tinge of envy usually quickly converts into shared good feelings. Nevertheless, there can be moments when upward comparisons cause us problems. This can occur if our own needs are not being met in our personal lives, and we perceive our sadness as outweighing that of the client; as a consequence, our attention shifts to ourselves, and our empathy transforms into personal distress. You find yourself feeling angry or thinking, "I need comfort and help," and then feel inadequate or guilty for having these thoughts:

✧ Last month I felt no sympathy for and was even angry at a man who had lost his wife after 50 years of marriage. He felt he had no reason to go on. All I could think was he had 50 good years with her, and I may never marry, and then I felt guilty.

✧ I get so angry when mothers of healthy term newborns use me as a babysitter, or refuse to care for their own baby, when I have been trying desperately to conceive a child of my own.

Even when you just have a bad day, one peppered with daily hassles or small misfortunes, you must work harder to help people who are having an easier time. When you need help, when you are in your personal pit, helping others out of their pits is much more difficult, and your vulnerability to burnout is heightened.

Guilt and Low Self-Esteem as Motivators

As we have seen, empathy-driven helping outcomes can be explained without invoking the influence of egoistic motivations. However, this does not mean everyday helping is not frequently energized—and healthily so—by egoistic motivations. In fact, altruism and egoism are often closely and positively related in helping. They co-occur. The intrinsic and immediate rewards of helping—the do good-feel good effects—and the more long-term benefits to well-being that accrue to us, serve as positive reinforcers for our helping behaviors. Still, many helpers are a bit hesitant to acknowledge these rewards, believing these "selfish" elements somehow diminish their helping motivations. However, such benefits are better celebrated as affirmations of help-ing as natural and healthful. Helping is often difficult and stressful, but it is also one of the most—if not the most—rewarding endeavors we can engage in.

A slightly different, yet informative, perspective on the egoistic versus altruistic dimensions of helping comes from Wharton School psychologist Adam Grant. In *Give and Take: Why Helping Others Drives Our Success*, Grant says self-interest and other-interest are independent motivations, and that successful givers are *otherish*: "they care about benefiting others, but they also have ambitious goals for advancing their own interests."[35]

Otherish givers are willing to give more than they receive, but don't lose track of their own interests and needs. Other-concern and self-concern must be balanced. This general hybrid formula for success in giving parallels what we propose here for optimal helper emotional involvement. In this situation, balanced engagement prevents personal distress. Intrinsic rewards in the work (enjoying it for itself and finding it engaging and fun), independent of social benefits, can be highly motivating and mitigate against burnout.[36] There is, however, a more complicated, if not problematic, form of egoistic involvement in helping. As already discussed, helping often gets derailed, and empathy-driven helping can be replaced by distress-driven helping. Here, guilt and low self-esteem often play a central role.

Guilt can induce us to help others. In laboratory experiments, if someone does harm of any kind (e.g., he or she hurts someone's feelings, breaks something, or administers an electric shock to someone), that person is likely to engage in helping behavior. Think about the times you have made a mistake as a caregiver and have immediately gone out and made up for it. I know each time I've said the wrong thing in a helping situation, I have subsequently redoubled my efforts to do something positive. We also know the absence of guilt reduces prosocial behavior. Churchgoers, for example, are less likely to contribute to charity following confession than before it.[37]

Existential guilt, a specific variety of guilt common in our work, can motivate our helping. It is easy, perhaps unavoidable, to see ourselves in an extremely advantaged position in relation to those we help. We witness their suffering and often tragic circumstance, whereas we, who are relatively happy and healthy, go home at night to our friends and families. This guilt persists, even though we consciously recognize our advantaged position is a fragile one. Avery Weisman, the noted psycho-oncologist, would tell his caring and highly altruistic trainees to not become crippled with guilt when they had to leave the bedsides of their seriously ill patients. He would point out that the only thing differentiating them from their dying patients was time, so there was no need for guilt.[38]

Low self-esteem is another uncomfortable inner state that sometimes drives helping behavior. Christopher Mruk describes self-esteem as "the compass that tells people whether they are on a good moral track in life and rewards them with a clear sense of purpose, meaning, and direction."[39] When our self-esteem is at a low point, the internal and external rewards of helping can serve to improve our reputations with ourselves. Then, the enhancement of self-esteem is no longer a fortuitous byproduct of helping; it is the goal. For example, studies of volunteers' motivations find volunteering can serve an ego-defensive function. It reduces guilt related to being more fortunate than others. It can also assist the helper in coping with concerns about personal worth and competence.[40] As one nurse shared: "I fear I excel at my work to compensate for my sense of failure in my family and in my personal relationships—a general sense of failure."

Although helping can be partially motivated by guilt and low self-esteem, distress-driven helping like this is not sustainable, and can ultimately block or severely strain your empathy and compassion. We will now look closely at burnout, secondary traumatization (or compassion fatigue), and moral distress, the troubling trio of distressed-helper conditions presenting perhaps the greatest challenges to our empathy, compassion, and moral commitments. They jeopardize not only our helping, but our health as well.

Burnout: The Cost of Caring

At the distant end of the continuum of emotional involvement, we find the more enduring and painful condition known as burnout. The burnout concept suffers from being used so loosely that nearly all signs of stress—from depression to headaches—are seen as signaling its presence. Despite these definitional problems, extensive research now establishes burnout as a real phenomenon especially significant for everyone working in the helping professions. There is also agreement that burnout, most frequently assessed with the Maslach Burnout Inventory, has three central, defining characteristics: emotional exhaustion, diminished caring or depersonalization, and a profound sense of demoralization or reduced personal accomplishment.[1; 3]

Exhaustion

Burnout theorists and most helpers I have known or interviewed emphasize a deep sense of exhaustion as a central component of burnout. This is emotional exhaustion manifested in low energy, chronic fatigue, and feelings of being emotionally drained, frustrated, and used up, as captured in these disclosures:

✧ Sometimes I feel I deserve more because I give more. I get tired of trying. I'm so sick of patients draining every ounce of energy out of me. Mostly, lately, I feel like I have no more to give anyone. I need all my energy for me. I can't get over being "tired" all the time. My mental acuity is poor. Recall is almost zero.

✧ I wear a mask. I work so hard at being "up" for others and getting others "up," and no one knows how tired I am. I want out.

✧ I feel like I'm drowning, and there are no more lifesavers to be thrown out! I suspected, I recognized a potential, I saw it coming, yet I closed my eyes.

Lowered self-esteem and depression are also often part of this emotional exhaustion:

I feel so inadequate and lose my self-esteem when people reject my caring for them. Statements like "Leave me alone," or "Don't touch me," make me feel like maybe I should not be doing this work. I take things like this personally and probably should not. I'm too sensitive and too concerned with my own feelings.

Diminished Caring

A second component of burnout, perhaps the most painful, is diminished caring—for the people being aided, for coworkers, and sometimes for family and friends. You feel apathetic, have more "problem patients" (even though your patient population hasn't changed significantly), and don't want to take on any new patients and families. Barriers of they-ness can lead you to treat patients callously, as impersonal objects, even to blame them for their problems. Cynicism replaces engagement. The dynamics of diminished caring or depersonalization can be seen in these helpers' disclosures:

✧ Sometimes I don't have any connection with patients' pain. On the outside, I know what to say, and on the inside I'm daydreaming or thinking about my own needs. I just don't care. Many times I've felt like complaining and bitching when

I'm stuck at someone's home during an active dying process. Inwardly I'm hoping the next time I reposition the patient, he will die and then I'll be free. I feel guilty I can't inwardly be filled with compassion, love, and patience. Sometimes it amazes me I pull it off and at least appear caring—in fact, I overcompensate and do it up pretty well. But I'm left feeling selfish and guilty.

✧ Sometimes I judge people I serve like leeches, wanting more and more of your time—not trying to help themselves. And when I pull away from being involved with them I feel judged, like I'm letting them down, I'm letting God down, by not always wanting to give. I have feelings of anger and sadness when these situations occur. Yet I put on my mask and smile.

✧ I've worked with dying patients so long it no longer holds any type of feelings for me. I don't even feel for friends or family when they lose loved ones. I sometimes wonder if I've lost my feelings for other people.

Demoralization

The third component of burnout, demoralization, is also reflected in the statements just presented. At the heart of this attitude is a feeling of, "I can't." For example, "I can't do well at doing good. I can't make a difference." The sense of efficacy and the intrinsic rewards of helping are missing. Instead, feelings of helplessness and reduced morale dominate. New demands become burdens, not challenges. We think, "My God, what do I do next?" or "Don't ask me for help. I don't have the answers!" There is an overwhelming sense of futility, personal failure, and lowered self-esteem. A loss of idealism and enthusiasm for our work follows. These aspects stand out in the following disclosures:

✧ I try to act strong and capable, someone with a bag full of answers. But I feel helpless—weak and helpless!

✧ I feel helpless when there is nothing positive to say or do about a patient's condition, when they and their families are wanting me to say or do something to improve the situation, and there seem to be no answers.

✧ Sometimes I feel so tired or useless I find I cannot believe in anything. Hopelessness and doubt are nightmares to cope with. Where is God?

✧ I feel like I've lost much of the compassion and enthusiasm I had when I began this work, and as a result I'm feeling sad and ineffective.

✧ Experiencing the pain in a patient's eyes as she searched for some meaning to her life and death. There are questions which have no answers and I am helpless. I touch her and hug her, and sometimes I cry.

These exhausting inner struggles can be accompanied by self-talk like this: "I got into this work because I'm a caring person and I wanted to make a difference. Now, I don't even want to see another hurting person, and I don't think I'm doing much good." Frustrated idealism, failing to move successfully toward important personal goals, guilt, shame, and self-reproach combine to create a downward spiral, deepening personal distress.

It is easy to see how burnout can undermine helping. Our empathy, our caring relationships with others, and our good feelings all disappear, weakening or severing the empathy-compassion-helping connection. Without the remarkable forces of natural helping to sustain it, caregiving becomes arduous, empty, or even nonexistent.

Burnout Levels: You and Other Helpers

Despite its pervasive and sometimes dramatic effects, burnout is often subtle and insidious; it takes myriad forms and is often easier to recognize in others than in oneself. In one study, interviews with colleagues of coworkers who had left their employment because of burnout found the coworkers retrospectively recalled many signs of burnout among their peers. These included struggling to manage alone, showing self-sacrifice, becoming distant and isolated, and attempting to achieve unattainable goals.[41]

Here are some questions to help you reflect on any personal burnout you might have: Do you find yourself feeling apathetic? Emotionally exhausted? Tired? Hopeless? Trapped in your duties? As if you just can't cope anymore? Resistant to change of any sort? That everything has turned negative? Do you have more "problem patients" than you used to? Do you frequently find yourself saying, "patients are complaining too much"? Do you have a conscious reluctance to go to work or to visit patients, insomnia or a lower resistance to illness, or an increase in your (less than adaptive) "need to relax" habits (e.g., more drinking and smoking)? Have you become more distant and detached from coworkers and patients? Experiencing one or more of these doesn't mean you are burned out. Your caring flame might just be flickering. But it does suggest you should do more to prevent things from getting worse.

You can systematically check your burnout level by taking the Self-Diagnosis Instrument for Burnout in Appendix A of this book. Although this measure doesn't systematically assess all three components of burnout, it does evaluate core features. A score of 4.0 on it is used as the burnout cut-off score. In other words, a score of 4.0 or higher is in the burnout range. What's your score? By taking this test intermittently, you can monitor your current burnout level.

Burnout is common in end-of-life professionals. A survey of 1,357 hospice and palliative care clinicians in the United States using the Maslach Burnout Inventory found 62% of respondents were high on either emotional exhaustion or depersonalization; emotional exhaustion was most frequently reported, and nonphysicians had the highest rates. Predictors of burnout included working in smaller organizations, working longer hours, being younger than 50 years, and working weekends.[42]

A European study of nurses working with terminally ill patients in internal medicine, oncology, hematology and palliative care departments found that burnout scores for palliative care nurses, although significantly high, were lower in exhaustion and depersonalization, and higher in personal accomplishment than those for nurses working in other departments. The researchers hypothesized that this might reflect greater support provided to nurses in palliative care departments. Nurses reporting a greater sense of purpose and meaning in life, a secure attachment, and less fear of death had lower burnout scores, indicating these characteristics played a protective role.[25]

Burnout has extremely adverse effects on physical health. A comprehensive review of burnout research found it poses an increased risk of incident myocardial infarction, stroke, and sudden cardiac death, highlighting the critical need for preventive efforts.[43]

Returning to your burnout score: If your score is high, don't panic. It is important to realize we can have many feelings like these and not burn out. Also, remember that to burn out, your caring flame must have once burned brightly. So, one might even look at burnout as a badge of honor indicating you had the courage to care.

Yet, however meritorious, burnout is neither fun nor healthful, and it can exact a great toll on you. And if we do burn out, it doesn't mean we can't return to personally satisfying and effective helping. Many helpers, myself included, are members of the "formerly burned-out club." But it is essential you pay attention to these warning signs—these wake-up calls—when they occur and look more closely at what is going on for you at work and at home. If signs of burnout go unattended, your problems will grow. If you heed them, they can guide you toward a more sustainable and healthy approach to helping. In the next chapter, we will explore the best antidotes to burnout, as well as its primary causes.

A personal example illustrates the need to be proactive toward burnout. Early in my career, I was emotionally overinvolved as a helper. The intense world of my helping encounters and the empathic sorrow and personal distress I felt during these encounters overshadowed everything else. The rest of my world receded into the background. Unfortunately, this included my friends, my exercise program, and other elements of a healthy life. Compared with the intense feelings of the work I was doing, social occasions seemed vacuous. I felt guilty going to parties when my patients couldn't even get out of bed, and when I did go, one part of me was tempted to shake people and say, "You won't be talking about your new car on your death bed. I've never heard people talk about any of this in their final moments, so go home and hug your family and thank God you can still do it." Then I would realize my loss of perspective and equilibrium, and retreat to a less-involved stance at work. This stance was also untenable. Guilt and lowered self-esteem quickly overcame me. Helping—and not helping—became agonizing; both included feelings of personal distress and withdrawal from my friends, family, and colleagues. Burnout was not far off.

Secondary Traumatization/Compassion Fatigue

Emotionally connecting with traumatized persons can sometimes lead to vicarious or secondary traumatization, adding a dimension to the stress equation different from the exhaustion, demoralization, and diminished caring that characterize burnout. Charles Figley, a pioneer in work on helper stress, included these effects under the rubric of compassion fatigue. He defined it this way: "Compassion fatigue is a more user-friendly term for secondary traumatic stress disorder, which is nearly identical to PTSD, except it applies to those emotionally affected by the trauma of another (usually a client or family member)".[44] Some researchers see burnout and secondary traumatization as separate components of compassion fatigue.[45] Other scientists believe compassion fatigue should be renamed as *empathic distress fatigue.*[46] Here, we will treat compassion fatigue as a phenomenon separate from burnout, and consider it interchangeable with secondary or vicarious traumatization, preferring to use the latter terms for conceptual clarity.

In a helping relationship, these reactions can lead either to avoidance, distancing, and detachment, or to tendencies to become overinvolved. Secondary or vicarious traumatization can include having intrusive thoughts, flashbacks, troubling dreams, and lost sleep in relation to work with clients.[47] The intrusion of client material is fairly common for frontline caregivers, even those not working exclusively with trauma. For example, 46% of participants in a national study of social workers reported being somewhat or greatly bothered by the intrusion of client material when not at work; however, more than 50% were not significantly bothered by these intrusions.[48]

Working with people facing grief, loss, and life-threatening illness will never be free of all distress, and all frontline helpers will inevitably encounter trauma in their work. Being emotionally present is going to arouse strong feelings in you, whether it's to a bereaved parent crying out in anguish, a sexual abuse victim, or a veteran reliving traumatizing battle scenes.

Our approach to vicarious traumatization will determine its long-term effects on us. As with our traumatized patients, we know suppressing these feelings, or ruminating on them, will not foster their abatement. Instead, we need to approach the feelings with full awareness and, by reflecting on them, understand their meaning. Adopting this perspective can reduce our stress reactivity by allowing us to view our trauma-tinged thoughts and feelings as echoes of our clients' pain and suffering, not our own. They are also emblematic of our positive, caring acts. Indeed, there is more than distress here: courage, healing, satisfaction, and growth. They are often present in the intense encounters that live on within us, as this oncology nurse's disclosure illustrates:

> Joan, my patient with ovarian cancer, had a fistula. It was so upsetting to her to have constant drainage of stool from her vagina. She was spending most of her time in the bathroom. She was filled with anxiety and tears. I went into the bathroom with her and sat on the floor in front of her and we cried together. "How could this happen to me?" she asked. I responded, "I don't know, but I'm with you, and I care." And she knew it. It was beautiful.

None of us can be on that bathroom floor every day, nor should we be, but sometimes our work asks more of us. The challenge of caring in these situations is how to emerge stronger and more alive from these moments of shared vulnerability and confrontations with suffering.[49]

Moral Distress

Moral distress is another widely recognized, pervasive, and deleterious helper condition with many definitions. All characterizations essentially describe moral distress as occurring when you cannot do what you believe to be ethically appropriate in a given clinical situation due to institutional or other constraints (including internal constraints).[50] Caught in this bind, constrained from taking action you believe is appropriate, you can feel frustration, anguish, guilt, shame, or powerlessness. You might believe your personal and professional integrity are compromised. Multiple studies show moral distress is associated with an increased likelihood of burnout and the intention to leave one's position.[51; 52; 53]

Myriad situations in modern health care can be sources of moral distress. For instance, having to follow a family's wishes to continue life support when you do not believe it is in the best interests of the patient; perceiving a lack of provider continuity leading to your patient suffering; believing colleagues are not competent in their care, perceiving staffing levels create an unsafe situation; and observing colleagues giving false hope to a patient or family.[54]

Moral distress can also develop when you sense your organization is valuing efficiency over compassion, and the mission statement that inspired you to join is somehow not guiding actual practices. Conflicts between the team and family members, or between team members themselves, can also contribute to a disturbing belief your organization is not morally habitable, engendering moral distress.[55] These caregivers' disclosures capture the suffering associated with moral distress:

✧ I feel like a hypocrite when my patient or family member deserves and needs to know the extent of their illness, but I cannot communicate reality because the physician is not being honest with the patient and family.

✧ I feel torn between time spent on paper work, thinking, "Money! Money!" and time I want to spend with support to patients and their families. I feel at times the reimbursement side of things is clouding our purpose.

✧ A patient is in pain. The physician is unwilling to prescribe more and/or different medication. What to do? You have tried nursing interventions—massage, heat, cold, relaxation, etc.— to no avail.

✧ A patient is eligible for a clinical trial, specifically, an experimental drug. When informed consent is attempted, the patient
says, "Whatever you want me to do, doctor," and you know the
patient does not understand potential side effects. What to do?

Moral distress is found to be correlated with the organizational
environment (poor ethical climate and collaboration), professional
attitudes (low work satisfaction and engagement), and psychological characteristics (low psychological empowerment and autonomy),
and to affect clinicians' well-being and job retention.[56] Moral distress is most frequently studied in nursing populations and critical
care settings, but a study of nurses, physicians, and other providers
(e.g., social workers, chaplains, respiratory and occupational therapists) found it to be a widespread phenomenon across the different
professions.[53] A combination of moral courage and resilience, team
and institutional support, and thoughtful examination of the ethical
issues raised are needed to transform moral distress into professional
and personal growth and improved patient care.

Conclusion

Helping relationships are personal relationships. To be successful
as caregivers, we must enter into meaningful emotional relationships with the people we assist. We must make room for them in our
emotional worlds. Why is this emotional involvement so necessary?
Research on helping confirms the old adage: "People don't care what
you know until they know that you care." We know prizing and valuing the other, a real interest and concern, and nonpossessive warmth
are essential elements of effective caregiving. In the highly personal
and intimate helping relationship, your empathy and compassion,
not the scalpel and prescription pad, may be the most crucial instruments for healing and growth.

Your effectiveness as a helper, and the personal and professional
growth you have in that role, can be threatened if personal distress
and emotional overload push you into the Helper's Pit. Your relationships with the people you care for are only one source of this distress.
Your relationships with coworkers, problems in your organization,

and events in your personal life also contribute significantly to your distress quotient. To meet the challenge of caring, you must somehow find balance on your helping journey—balance between the demands you face and the resources you have to meet them, between giving to others and giving to yourself.

3

People are often able to flourish in stressful, demanding careers if they feel valuable and appreciated and that their work has significance. They burn out when their work has no meaning and stress continuously outweighs support and rewards.[1]

Ayala Pines and Eliot Aronson

One cannot remain in this work for long without being wounded. Caregivers who function only as technicians, who do not instinctively offer their souls, hands, and hearts, will not thrive. Therefore, by serving well, they, by definition, operate from a position of tenderness and vulnerability. . . . Learning how to manage the accumulated sadness in growth-enhancing rather than destructive ways may be the central task.[2]

Hester Hill

Beyond Burnout: Finding Balance and Enhancing Resilience

W e all know stress when we see it or feel it. You see it in the eyes of the people you care for. You feel it within yourself when a child in your care dies, when you are emotionally drained, when you have conflicts with coworkers, when personal problems grind you down, or when you have a difficult case keeping you up at night.

We also know the stress we feel when working with highly-distressed individuals and families can sometimes lead to burnout, vicarious traumatization, and moral distress. However, a growing body of research and clinical wisdom tells us we can exert significant control over stress and its effects on us, and that we can often even wrest personal and professional growth from it. These positive outcomes are now linked to an array of coping styles and stress management practices that includes stress hardiness, cognitive reappraisal, self-compassion, mindfulness, social support, physical activity, and finding meaning in our work. Whichever coping styles or practices we adopt, the goal is resilience—the capacity to negotiate with whatever comes your way, adapt to change, handle unpleasant feelings, persevere toward your goals, even sometimes find humor in difficult situations, and not be easily discouraged.[3] Such attributes are the building blocks of your stress-coping ability or resilience.

While addressing the many challenges this work presents, you can reduce your distress and grow— intellectually, emotionally, and spiritually—by enhancing the attributes enabling you to persist in the face of adversity and enrich your immediate environment. Consider each of the ideas, techniques, and strategies presented here. See if any might help you achieve a better balance between the demands you confront (internal and external) and the resources (also internal and external) you have available to meet them, thereby strengthening your resilience.

You will need discernment and discipline to choose and implement the stress-related techniques and strategies that will help you most. The choices will be different for each of us—one size does not fit all—but some specific strategies and principles do seem to merit strong consideration by us all. However, these approaches must be put to use if they are to achieve the intended results. Unfortunately, when we are most stressed, we are often least likely to practice good stress management. "I don't have time" or "As soon as I get through this one I'll take care of it myself," are familiar refrains. This is why it is crucial to have a perspective and a set of routine practices firmly in place and unlikely to be dislodged by unexpected demands. Before discussing specific approaches, let's first get a snapshot of what stress is like for you, and then use the snapshot to illustrate some of the core events at work here.

Stress and You

Think of your current work as a helper and rate it on a 10-point scale, where 1 is "almost no stress," and 10 is "extremely stressful." Give the rating for the past 6 months, or whatever period seems appropriate to capture the emotional realities of the work for you. Now reflect on the events and situations flashing through your mind while you were making the rating, and jot down whatever emerged for you. These could be specific clinical situations, team conflicts, chronic hassles, or whatever raises your stress level.

Next, take a few moments and write down your goals for helping in your current clinical situation, remembering our discussion of these in Chapter 1. These can include your broader purpose or mission, such as the desire to give something back or to ease the suffering of others, or specific helping goals reflecting your personal vision as a caregiver—in other words, the things in your work giving you a sense of personal significance.

Now look at the list of stressors and the list of goals side by side. Can you see any relation between the stressors that trouble you most, and the blocking of the goals that correspondingly matter most to you? For example, there could be a link between a passion to foster trust and openness in your organization, and how disheartened you are by unresolved conflicts among your team members. Or maybe those perennially late referrals to hospice and palliative care are especially exasperating because you highly value the healing end-of-life conversations among family members and pain and symptom control you know are possible with more timely referrals. Can you see links like these between your stressors at work and these core aspects of yourself—your goals, values, and self-esteem?

These linkages can be explained by contemporary stress and coping theory, which suggests the way we appraise events, and the meanings we assign to them, determine our emotional reactions. The theory also identifies key factors at work here, including the degree of stress we are experiencing, the personal stake we have in an encounter, and whether or not an event threatens our ego-identity. If we have a significant stake or commitment (i.e., a goal) threatened, or if other core aspects of our identity seem jeopardized, and we feel we may not be able to deal with this outcome, a stress response can ensue.[4; 5]

We know from our personal lives and clinical work that we are vulnerable to loss and stress when we love because fate—an accident, an illness, or other negative life event—can take away what we love. We are similarly vulnerable if we love the work we do. Without loss, says Stevan Hobfoll, "change, transitions, and challenge are not of themselves stressful."[6]

A TRANSACTIONAL MODEL OF STRESS AND COPING

Richard Lazarus and his colleagues, who developed this way of thinking about stress, defined stress as "a particular relationship between the person and the environment that is appraised by the person as taxing or exceeding his or her resources and endangering his or her well-being."[7] They assert stress is not an objective thing, but the product of an ongoing relationship or transaction between a person and his or her environment (environment meaning other people and the situations in which we find ourselves). If we appraise the demands on us as taxing or exceeding our resources and endangering our well-being, stress ensues. What is stressful at one moment might not be stressful the next, and what is stressful for one person might not be stressful for another. The personal meaning of what is happening is most important; our appraisals of these meanings act as critical on-off switches in the stress response.

Primary Appraisal: Am I OK?

According to this transactional model, the first or primary appraisal we make concerns the personal significance of the stressor. In essence, we ask, "Am I OK?" or am I (my physical and emotional well-being) in danger? In other words, is this worth getting upset about? For example, if our goals, personal relationships, or beliefs and values are jeopardized, our appraisal is we are not OK at this moment.

This appraisal is the starting point for the stress response, and several different evaluations are possible. First, our judgment might be the event has no bearing on our well-being. Most of what we encounter in life is seen in this way, and the stress response is never initiated. Second, we might view the event as beneficial to our well-being, and feel good about it. A pay raise or a compliment from a colleague or patient would most likely be viewed this way. Third, we might see the event as possibly involving a threat or a challenge.

When we appraise a situation as a challenge, we view it not only as having the possibility of causing loss or harm, but also as offering some potential benefit if we are able to meet its demands successfully. When we make a challenge response, we are energized and excited, as opposed to anxious and possibly ashamed when we make a threat response.[8]

Some people seem more likely to see things in this light. We know, for example, some helpers will make threat appraisals, whereas others will regard the demands of a situation as challenging.[9] In a series of studies, Kobasa and her colleagues looked at different groups of professionals undergoing high levels of stress. They found specific characteristics differentiated high stress/healthy people from high stress/ health problem groups. The high stress/healthy were more likely to be characterized by what Kobasa labeled stress hardiness. One defining characteristic of stress hardiness, as it is now conceptualized, is a sense of challenge.[10] Stress-hardy persons tend to see a challenge in potentially tough situations, while others see a threat. It is easy to understand how this somewhat optimistic stance can prevent many unnecessary stress reactions. For example, an individual who is always waiting for things to settle down, and is threatened when things don't, will become more stressed than someone who knows change is constant, and that the current crisis will only be replaced by another. If we can see a potentially stressful event as an opportunity for growth rather than as a threat, we are likely to cope much better with the demands confronting us. However, some stressors, particularly life's greatest tragedies, have no redeeming characteristics. To tell a mother who has just lost her child to leukemia to regard this as a challenge is cruel, and trivializes her distress.

For us as helpers, the advice to turn threats into challenges contains unmistakable wisdom, but this modern homily can also lead to self-blame if we interpret it as meaning fearless hope and mastery are always possible—if only you have the right attitude. We all know it is not easy to change the way we look at things, and even traffic jams, small losses, extra workloads, and other daily hassles can be alarming at times. Similarly, when we say of a situation, "That was a good learning experience," the unspoken message is often we would have gladly skipped the learning if we could have avoided the situation in the first place. However, if we can understand change is part of life, and we can embrace it rather than react to it with fear, we are more likely to move adaptively into the future. Our work with patients and families dealing with enormous life changes offers us almost daily lessons on the wisdom of this principle.

When the challenges you face, and the skills you have to meet them, are both at a high and commensurate level, it is possible for what Mihaly Csikszentmihalyi has labeled *flow* to occur.[11] When in a state of flow, we are fully immersed in what we are doing, we are "in the zone," doing what we like to do for its own sake, and can feel being part of something larger. When this happens in a caregiving context, the resulting do good-feel-good effects can add to the rewarding nature of flow.

Our general mindset or attitude about the nature of stress is shown to also play an important role in determining the stress response. In a series of studies, Stanford psychologist Alia Crum and her colleagues have found subjects with a *stress-is-enhancing* mindset, in contrast to a *stress-is-debilitating* one, show moderate cortisol activity and a greater desire for feedback on their performance in a stressful condition.[12; 13]

Thus, our mindset in relation to stress, our interpretation of an event, and the way we react to it, play a central role in the way we manage stress. In other words, objective events in our personal and work lives are stressful only when we subjectively appraise them as harmful or threatening.

You are probably familiar with the feelings associated with appraisals of being threatened, harmed, or challenged. Stress is a mind/body response including a variety of emotions. Anxiety and anger, and their accompanying physiological arousal, are most often seen as core stress responses. Lazarus argued that if we make clearer distinctions among these different feelings, and move beyond a uni-dimensional concept of stress, we will begin to get a more complete understanding of what is going right or wrong for us.[14] Along these lines, Smith and Ascough suggest we think of the stress response as also including guilt, shame, depression, and other aversive emotional states.[15]

Like other emotions, these feelings are indicators, telling us something about our relationship with the circumstances we are in; they motivate us to act in particular ways to address the stressful event. For example, the sadness accompanying loss tells us we have encountered something harmful, and pushes us to seek help and support. The anxiety associated with threat stems from an ambiguous answer to the question, "Am I OK?," and motivates us to escape from harm. Shame can motivate us to work toward more positive outcomes in our relationships and life situations. Feeling challenged, which goes with an active and optimistic relation to our external world, is a sustaining emotion pushing us toward mastery. This perspective underscores the adaptive nature of our emotions: they are a rich source of information about our connection to the world and guide us toward specific kinds of actions, potentially motivating and guiding psychological adjustment and positive coping. Stress is an inner call to action, and if we listen to ourselves we will be much more likely to know what to do in response to it.

Smith and Lazarus describe how our emotions evolved as an adaptation system from the simpler and more rigid reflexes and physiological drives once dominating our behavior. In this evolutionary progression, our judgments of threat and harm became more reliant on how we appraised the meaning of events, thereby permitting a greater flexibility in response to them.[16] Unfortunately, there hasn't been a corresponding evolutionary updating of our stress response system to go along with this more sophisticated way of evaluating our environments, and this creates problems for us.

In prehistoric times, the potential harm of stressors was clear: predators and a harsh environment often jeopardized our survival. The stress response system dealing with those situations worked extremely well for much of our history, but it gets us into trouble today. The main problem is this system doesn't differentiate between, say, an insult to our self-esteem, a symbolic stressor, and a saber-toothed tiger chasing after us; in either case, we have the "fight-or-flight" reaction. In the civilized world, it is unlikely we will choose either of those two options. Then, because the stress hormones generated—the catecholamines epinephrine (adrenaline) and norepinephrine, and the glucocorticoid cortisol—aren't being expended through physical activity, they tend to make us sick and exhausted instead.[17]

These hormonal and physiological changes can be activated instantaneously when the amygdala, the emotional part of the brain regulating the flight-or-flight response, detects threats. The amygdala processes information milliseconds before our prefrontal lobe or rational brain has a chance to mediate our responses and generate logical and rational responses, even when emotions are still present. Termed *amygdala hijack* by Daniel Goleman, this sequence can lead to irrational behaviors and increasing distress.[18] The key to short circuiting this hijacking of our rational brain by an anxious amygdala is to be aware of our inner reactions in these moments, and to generate more adaptive responses, even while experiencing emotional discomfort.

Psychologists have also studied an alternative stress response, dubbed the *tend and befriend* response. Most frequently found in females, this stress response is seen as tied to the attachment-caregiver system and as involving the release of oxytocin and endogenous opioid peptides. In contrast to the fight-or-flight stress response, the tend and befriend response emphasizes affiliative and caring behavior, like relying on and helping others.[19] This tendency to affiliate in response to stress is conjectured to help explain why women live longer than men.

Secondary Appraisal:
Can I Cope With This?

If we appraise an event as harmful or threatening, we then make a secondary appraisal in which we ask ourselves, "Can I cope with this?"[7] Here we assess our ability to deal with the loss or harm, or to reduce the threat. We examine the balance between the demands of the situation and the resources—time, energy, skills, support from others—available to us. If we perceive a balance between these two elements, a stress response doesn't occur.

If we generally perceive ourselves as competent and skilled in a particular area, we are more likely to see our resources as capable of meeting the demands facing us. Albert Bandura has shown some people are more likely than others to respond this way and to perceive themselves as being able to perform successfully in a given situation, a trait he calls self-efficacy.[20] These beliefs about our capabilities, our self-efficacy beliefs, are critical determinants of the goals we pursue and the control we are able to exercise over our environments. Self-efficacy in any situation is a belief in our ability to take actions to manage prospective situations; it is confidence in our ability to execute the behaviors required to bring about desired outcomes.

People with a strong sense of personal competence or self-efficacy approach difficult tasks as challenges to be mastered, rather than as threats to be avoided. When our self-efficacy beliefs are weak, and we assess we cannot meet demands and cannot reduce the continued threats to our well-being, distress ensues, along with continued coping efforts and heightened physiological arousal.

Let's look at an example of this in the physician or nurse with a strong commitment to quality pain management. When they are not able to successfully manage a patient's pain, they will feel threatened because an outcome mattering greatly to them is jeopardized. If they don't find a solution, and perceive none in sight, their secondary appraisal—that they cannot address the demands of the situation—would initiate a stress response. At that point, their bodies would try to preserve homeostasis, or balance, through a variety of adjustments: increased perspiration and respiratory and heart rates, higher blood pressure, the release of cortisol and other stress hormones, and suppression of the immune system. This fight-or-flight physiology, particularly when it is chronic or of high intensity, can eventually lead to the development of stress-related symptoms and illnesses.[17]

The effects of stress include highly significant changes, even at the cellular level. Scientists have identified telomere length as a key psychobiomarker of aging, and it reflects the effects of stress and trauma.[8] Telomeres are nucleoproteins on the tips of our chromosomes serving as markers of cellular aging. Telomeres, like the aglets on the tips of our shoelaces, are protective caps that maintain cells' genomic stability. Our telomeres shorten with aging and predict disease and longevity; they also are known to shorten with chronic stress. Keeping our telomeres as long and stable as possible is a major health goal and a benefit of good stress management.

Our stress model also clarifies why cancer and other life-threatening illnesses are so tremendously stressful. In these situations, the appraisal process goes haywire as patients are forced to negotiate numerous uncertainties surrounding diagnosis, treatment, and prognosis. The appraisal of "Am I OK?" taps into a wide range of vulnerabilities associated with physical survival and quality of life. The answers in each domain are rarely clear-cut. Evaluating whether one can cope with these complex and profoundly demanding events is equally difficult, generating the threat response and tremendous anxiety. Anxiety is what happens when you are driving along a freeway and a car unexpectedly slows in front of you.

For a moment you think, "Did I get my brakes checked recently?" Fear is the feeling that occurs when you are in the same situation, you push on your brake pedal, and discover you have no brakes.[21] A diagnosis of cancer evokes both anxiety and fear, but the emotional reality is a painful blurring of the distinction between them. In addition, cancer is usually perceived as undesirable, uncontrollable, and unexpected—three especially troubling features of stressful life events.

Our struggles with time pressure illustrate these connections. A common stressor for everyone in the health professions today is work overload. Too much paperwork, understaffing, and unexpected problems create a situation in which there is no slack in the system and everyone is always rushed. When you are so busy, taking the time to talk with your patients and give them special care is difficult. Remember the hurrying Princeton theology students who didn't help the person in distress while on their way to give a talk on the parable of the Good Samaritan. Eventually, you realize you can't give quality help to those in need. Hurried circumstances deny you the opportunity to do what you need to do. Feelings of resentment, guilt, and lowered self-esteem—features of both burnout and moral distress—tend to replace your empathy and ability to care.

Perez and colleagues identified these dynamics in an interview study of palliative care clinicians.[22] The clinicians in the study reported time constraints as a key stressor. When asked what was stressful about this, they said time limitations meant they felt compromised in the quality of care they provided for patients and families. They also reported it meant they had less time to debrief with colleagues and to grieve their losses, thus limiting their social support and self-care.

You can apply this model of stress and coping to any helping situation, whether the context is everyday psychotherapy or medical practice, administering a counseling program, or volunteering. In each case, the outcomes of our primary and secondary appraisals are key determinants of our stress. Many, if not most, of the stress management or resilience-enhancing strategies we will discuss here exert their positive effects by modifying our appraisals.

They are stress mediators. For example, if we have good self-esteem, our primary appraisals are less likely going to be, "I'm not OK," because personal insecurities are not aroused by the event, and we are more likely to make a challenge response than a threat response. If we have solid social support in our lives, we are more likely to think we can cope with a demand because we know others can help us with advice, tangible support, or a comforting presence. If we are self-aware and emotionally resilient, we can tolerate uncomfortable feelings, not become alarmed, stay out of the Helper's Pit, and make effective interventions in the face of trying clinical situations.

Perspective Matters

If we evaluate the demands of a situation as less threatening, or our resources as adequate to deal with the demands, we can stop the stress cycle before it begins. We can also reevaluate the risks the event poses for us. This coping and emotion regulation strategy, cognitive reappraisal, has proven to be a highly effective approach to stress management.[15] We can change the course of our emotions by entertaining different perspectives on what we are facing. For example, we could shift from a threat response to a challenge response. Or we might think "Rather than being a huge stressor, maybe leaving my cell phone at home could actually give me a nice break from electronics." The trick is to slow down, examine the thought patterns to which we have become habituated, and then shift to less threatening or even positive thought patterns.

In *Doing CBT*, David Tolin offers a number of alternative cognitive reappraisals or self-statements—what he terms "stress busters"—that can be used to counter stress-producing automatic distress-generating thoughts.[23] The stress-busters include, "Okay, so I don't like this. It's not the end of the world"; "If I catastrophize about this, I'm bound to be upset"; and, "I don't have to be perfect. I can make mistakes too. I don't have to please everyone."

A good sense of humor can be another valuable resilience-enhancing psychological resource as we reappraise the meaning of events.[24] The ability to laugh at ourselves and see things from a larger perspective can take the sting of stress out of many of the daily has-sles we routinely encounter. It can help us avoid becoming overcon-cerned with minor annoyances and small worrisome issues. Laughter can bring us together, help us shift perspectives, and prevent an acute stress response from becoming a prolonged one.

How we appraise events is certainly key, but the nature and quantity of the objectively stressful events or conditions we encoun-ter play an equally, if not sometimes greater role in determining our stress levels. In numerous surveys, clinicians highlight many of these, for example: patient-care-related stressors, such as the intensity of cases (e.g., exposure to sadness, pain, loss, grief and trauma); patient and family expectations; team conflicts; and sys-temic or organizational stressors, such as workload, lack of clarity in job expectations, failure to receive support and rewards, absence of fairness, nonparticipative management, lack of control in deci-sion making, excessive electronic documentation, and a rapidly changing medical landscape.[25; 26; 27] No matter how dedicated and resilient you are, these features of your work environment can be enormously taxing, and possibly burn you out.

This reality reminds us to avoid the common error of attributing burnout to the person of the helper, rather than to the helper's envi-ronment, a point Maslach and other burnout theorists have empha-sized.[25] They say burnout results not from "bad apples" but from the "bad kegs" the apples are in.[28]

One conclusion this perspective yields is our first step in man-aging stress should be to make any changes we can in the objective stressors affecting us. We need to shift from asking, "What's wrong with me?" to asking, "What can I do about the situation?" If we have a boss who is impossible to work with, we need to examine strategies to change the situation. If our patient load exceeds any reasonable limit, we need to do whatever we can to ensure optimum health care for ourselves and our patients. This might require us to take a difficult and morally courageous stand. We will return to some of these exter-nal factors later, and what we can do about them. But let's now look at how we respond when we are stressed, and whether we choose to attempt to change the external environment or to focus on our reac-tions to it instead.

Problem- and Emotion-Focused Coping

Coping, like stress, is a process. It involves our ongoing efforts to manage stressful demands—that is, demands we feel are taxing or exceed our available resources.[14] Lazarus distinguishes between problem-focused and emotion-focused coping.[5] Problem-focused coping refers to efforts to change our relationship to our environment by changing either our behavior or the environment itself. In contrast, emotion-focused coping efforts aim to alter our emotional reactions to a situation, even though the situation has not changed.

Different people cope differently at various points in any stressful situation, and our responses to most stressful situations include both problem- and emotion-focused coping. For example, imagine you are working with an extremely difficult family with a suicidal member. Problem-focused coping might include reading up on the management of suicidal people and carefully planning interventions you can make with the family. Emotion-focused coping might involve exercising more frequently, seeking the support of a friend, avoiding thinking about the problem, reappraising the meaning of the situation, or meditating. We usually make problem-focused responses when our secondary appraisal is that we can do something about the stressful event. Emotion-focused coping becomes more likely when we perceive there is little we can do to change the situation.

The range of possible coping responses in any stressful situation is enormous. For example, psychiatrist Avery Weisman outlined some possible coping responses for people with cancer. These include seeking information, sharing concerns with others, laughing it off, hoping a miracle will happen, and staying busy. Some cancer patients might even put the thought of their illness out of their minds, confront the issue, or redefine the situation and take a more sanguine view. Weissman also noted some people with cancer become resigned, review the alternatives, do what is expected or advised, blame or shame someone, ventilate their feelings, or deny the reality of the situation.[29] Cancer-coping research identifies a similar diversity of possible responses.[30]

We can respond to and manage, or mismanage, our stressors in many of these same ways. We can seek out more information, share our concerns with peers or team members, try to forget the whole thing, focus on something good coming out of the situation, or examine what we might learn about life, and accept our limitations.

Pick the two most stressful events from the list of stressors you created earlier in this chapter. How do you typically cope with them? What do you do in response to them? Have your responses changed over time? Do you take any actions to prevent stress, or are most of your actions geared toward dealing with stress once it occurs? How effective are you currently in coping with these stressors? What is keeping you from being more effective in coping with or preventing similar stressful events from happening again?

Approach and Avoidance: Two Basic Responses to Stress

When you thought about how you typically cope with stressors in your work, did you notice any avoidance behavior? Maybe you avoided critical conversations with patients or peers about these issues, or tried hard not to think about the troubling situations. Throughout this book, we are exploring how difficult it is for us to approach discomfort and distress, both in patients and in ourselves. When confronted by a threat, we can either move toward it or away from it. The avoidance or denial of anything that triggers unpleasant emotions is a pervasive feature of human behavior.[31] This tendency underlies such diverse phenomena as the denial of death or illness, the avoidance of threatening thoughts or memories, emotional distancing from patients and families, and a reluctance to express negative feelings to our spouses or coworkers. Psychologists now consider avoidance—whether behavioral or experiential—as a key contributor to poor coping outcomes and psychological difficulties.[32]

How does this work? Avoidance is strongly related to lowered self-esteem. We know we are avoiding something that makes us feel uncomfortable or anxious. Even though we gain momentary relief from the avoidant behavior, this relief is eventually replaced by more long-term disillusionment with ourselves.

Try this experiment. Think of a chronic problem in your work you have avoided facing. Visualize this situation—the people, events, feelings—and your behavior in it. Take a minute to do this. Now ask yourself, "How do I feel about myself in this difficult situation?" Next, visualize the problem situation again. Imagine yourself acting as if you were the person you would like to be in this situation. What words come to mind when you describe yourself in this second scenario? Then ask yourself how you feel about yourself in this second scenario. What words come to mind?

Like Richard Bednar and his colleagues who created this exercise, I have found most people describe their avoiding selves with words such as weak, cowardly, shameful, and frightened.[33] In the second condition, these self-critical feelings disappear, and the self-descriptions portray instead a competent, proud, courageous, and often caring person. In other words, avoidance usually lowers our self-esteem.

The negative consequences of avoidance extend far beyond lowered self-esteem in the avoiding individual. When avoidance becomes a dominant theme for caregiving teams and organizations, it can severely impair the openness, trust, feedback, and creative problem solving essential for productive group efforts. People stop telling the truth to one another, manipulation increases, trust levels drop, and the group fails to do and learn what is necessary to ensure its future success.[34]

Given its strongly negative consequences, how can we explain the persistence of avoidance as a coping strategy? A well-known animal study illustrates the controlling nature of avoidance as a learned response. In this experiment, dogs were placed in a compartment equipped with a light and a metal floor attached to a device designed to administer an electric shock. A small, low barrier separated them from a second, shock-free compartment. The experimenters turned the light on and gave the dogs a strong electric shock, causing them to jump immediately into the other compartment. After repeating this sequence several times, the experimenters turned the light on but disconnected the shock device. What happened? In this new shock-free condition, the dogs continued to jump after the light came on until the researchers stopped the experiment more than 50 trials later.[35]

The experimenters then simulated reality testing by putting a glass barrier between the dogs and the second compartment, thus forcing the dogs to stay in the first compartment after the light came on and see that no shock was forthcoming. But even after many trials with this "reality testing" condition, the dogs continued to jump when the glass barrier was removed.

The key to the persistence of the dogs' avoidance was that when they jumped—even when there was no real threat—their anxiety was reduced, and thus avoidance was rewarded. Like the dogs in this experiment, we often "jump" when there is no objective threat. Although this strategy reduces our fears, we don't learn from these outcomes, and thus continue with our self-defeating behaviors.

Most neurotic behavior has this same puzzling quality: We can continue to engage in self-defeating behaviors even while recognizing the counterproductive nature of what we are doing: this is known as the neurotic paradox.[36] The general principle explaining such behavior is that the short-term gain (anxiety reduction) of avoidance is more immediate and thus seems to outweigh the long-term pain existing only in the future.

Avoidance of anxiety has been a central concept of psychodynamic theorists since Freud's times. All the defense mechanisms Freud delineated share a common function: reducing anxiety, primarily by avoiding threatening thoughts and feelings. Facing unpleasant thoughts and feelings, and confronting threatening information rather than engaging in experiential avoidance, are seen by nearly all contemporary therapeutic approaches as prerequisites for emotional healing and growth.[37]

In our stress model, avoidance is a product of our appraisal that we are in danger and cannot cope with a situation and thus must escape it. When a thought, feeling, object, or person becomes associated with a strong fear, avoidance becomes almost automatic.

Existential theorists see our evasive behavior as driven ultimately by our fear of death. In *The Denial Of Death*, Ernest Becker contends our avoidance of death-related anxiety is an element common to all psychological disturbances.[38] He argues our self is shaped in a way that diminishes and deflects anxiety. We find anxiety-free domains to move about in, however limited these might be, and we remain within them even when the limitations become painfully confining.

Similarly, psychiatrist Irvin Yalom asserts death-related anxiety is at the core of neurotic conflicts.[39] In his view, our defenses against death awareness lead to a neurotic adaptation where we engage in rigid patterns of behavior—a partial death. Yalom interprets Otto Rank's statement, that the neurotic refuses the loan of life to escape the debt of death, as meaning we buy ourselves "free from the fear of death by daily partial self-destruction." Approaching these fears, says Yalom, "can transport one from a mode of living characterized by diversions, tranquilization, and petty anxieties to a more authentic mode."[39]

The "terror management" theory of self-esteem proposed by Solomon and his colleagues offers an integrative framework for thinking about these and other issues we are exploring here. They argue self-esteem "consists of the perception that one is a valuable part of a meaningful universe."[40] It serves the defensive function of protecting us from anxiety, which is, as Becker, Yalom, Rank, and other theorists agree, ultimately and intimately connected to the fear of death. By meeting the standards of our parents, significant others, and culture, we acquire a feeling of safety, and also protection from the unsettling truth of our own mortality. We struggle to preserve this sense of security generated by healthy attachments in early life.

When we have had healthy attachments in early life, they can serve as excellent stress buffers. Investigators studying attachment styles and burnout in health and human service workers find attachment security to be associated with lower levels of burnout, and attachment insecurity with higher levels.[41] Direct threats to our self-esteem and the frustration of our helping goals create stress because they threaten our feeling of having a uniquely valuable and valued role in a meaningful universe. Correspondingly, organizational interventions that enhance meaning and self-awareness in our work are found to increase clinician satisfaction and to reduce burnout.[42] One example, Schwartz Rounds, a program now widely implemented in health care, offers a protected space wherein clinicians can reflect on their work and their purpose in helping.[43] Continually connecting to the significance of the work we do, and recommitting to it, can energize a sense of purpose. This connection carries us forward in the face of suffering and stress.

So, there is a consensus that avoiding anxiety, conflicts, and psychological threats play a major role in many of our psychological issues, and in our everyday helping as well. The alternative to avoidance and its many unhealthy consequences is a willingness to approach what we fear most. When we face difficult and threatening inner and outer events, new dimensions of personal growth and effectiveness become available to us.

I have asked many groups of clinicians and students the following question: "Have any of you ever had significant and lasting personal growth without feeling any pain or suffering as an essential part of the growth?" Over many years, not one person has answered yes to this question. When our core beliefs are challenged, and we respond with thoughtful, deliberate, reflective rumination (vs. intrusive rumination), and disclose positive loss-related growth to others, posttraumatic growth is more likely.[44] Extensive research now documents these changes as reflections of growth through adversity.[45] We have all seen the personal growth patients and families often have—along with their suffering—during and after times of crisis: deepening spiritual understandings, new priorities, closeness with others, and new outlooks on life. This is true for both our patients and ourselves. For example, psychotherapists and other clinicians working with trauma survivors are found often to have what is now termed vicarious posttraumatic growth.[46]

The changes in identity that are part of growth, and part of grief as well, include a loss of what was, and the birth of something new. If we face an uncomfortable inner thought or feeling, something not fitting our vision of who we are or want to be, and we move toward the threatening content, our self-concept gradually expands to include all we truly are. Self-actualization does not mean becoming someone or something you aren't; instead, it is simply becoming who you are, including those difficult aspects you have resisted—in the words of Kierkegaard, becoming "that self which one truly is."[47]

The consequences of avoidance are dramatic in our helping efforts. Because we have the option to turn away from the suffering of others, as well as from our own, the tendency to avoid has profound implications for helping. We might choose to avoid something when our emotional buttons are pushed, or when we have conscientiously stayed with the patient to a certain point, but know what lies ahead is frightening or painful. Isolated instances of avoidance such as these are fairly common in helping, but when our responses as helpers reflect a general pattern of avoidance, we can be of little real assistance to others. Emotional and physical avoidance and distancing, often a feature in the burnout syndrome, is familiar to many clinicians:

✧ I sometimes have patients who become very close, yet when they are getting close to "the end," I avoid them. Yes, I want to go and talk with them and tell them how special they are to me, but I just can't. I had one very dear lady I distanced myself from. After she died, I went back to the hospital room where she died, many times, over almost a year. I silently talked with her and told her how much I missed her. Why couldn't I do it while she was still alive?

✧ Sometimes, when caring for a critical baby, I shut myself off from the parents and avoid them at all costs. Sometimes I also avoid the baby if possible. I feel like I'm abandoning the parents and I'm dumping the baby on someone else, especially if it's a baby I took care of continuously when he or she was well.

These vignettes illustrate how the short-term relief of avoidance only sets the stage for long-term strain and personal distress. Being present to suffering is never comfortable, but if we can somehow find a way to remain open and compassionate toward what are often frightening and foreign thoughts and feelings—in ourselves and in those we care for—we can realize our fullest potentials as helpers.

As we now review a variety of approaches to stress management and enhanced resilience, keep these dynamics of approach and avoidance in mind. Ask yourself whether avoidance in some form might be contributing to your struggles. It usually does, but just noticing how it does so requires we approach and accept these often invisible stress-multipliers—whether they are conversations we don't have, troubling thoughts we work to suppress, or clinical encounters we anxiously avoid. In each instance of avoidance you identify, imagine yourself instead behaving the way you would like to, and then envision how you would then feel about yourself if you acted this way. You might then take the next step, cautiously and courageously experimenting with these new ways of being and behaving in your everyday work and life.

STRESS ANTIDOTES: ENHANCING
RESILIENCE AND GROWTH

Take Action, Take Control

A first principle of stress management is to take action! It is essential to take an active stance and do something, whether you change your environment or change yourself. Never fall into the trap of believing you can do nothing about stress. That stance quickly leads to passive or minimal coping efforts, avoidance, demoralization, and increasing stress. An extreme instance of passive coping is the alcohol or drug use of the impaired caregiver.[48]

The model of stress presented here reveals the many negative consequences of avoidance, and, as a rule, the best antidote to avoidance is to approach: approach the problems you are confronted with, practice stress management skills, look for places where you can effectively take control, and do it. Because burnout usually results from the kinds of environments we are exposed to, it is critical always to begin stress management during the first stage of the stress response, and to look for ways to change the actual demands or problems we face. This can include trying to affect organizational elements such as staffing, job design, training and support, the mix of less demanding and more stressful work, and so forth. Ask first, "Is there anything I can do to change this situation?" Try to focus on things you can change. In this regard, many stress experts have recognized the deep wisdom of theologian Reinhold Neibuhr's serenity prayer:

> *God, give us the serenity to accept what cannot be changed;*
> *Give us the courage to change what should be changed;*
> *Give us the wisdom to distinguish one from the other.*[49]

It is often difficult to discriminate between those situations when problem-focused coping might eventually yield positive results and those when it will not. If we think change is possible when it isn't, we persist too long in our efforts to change the situation, and growing frustration pushes our stress levels even higher. However, as the prayer says, there are times when we must courageously work to change what we cannot accept.

Although generally counterproductive, avoidance has real merits when a stressful situation is overwhelming. Sometimes it is most helpful to retreat psychologically while attempting to come to grips with an event of great magnitude. In the case of grief and serious illness, avoidance can help maintain hope and courage. The ability to flexibly adjust our levels of denial when faced with these situations is an indicator of good, rather than poor, coping skills.[5] This adaptive coping pattern is also found in the dual-process model for grief developed by Stroebe and Schut, who see a flexible back and forth oscillation between loss- and restoration-oriented coping as most desirable.[50]

The other error we can make is to think no change is possible, when it is. Then, we give up too soon and remain stuck in the stressful situation. Here is an exercise to help prevent you from making this second error. First, look over the list of stressors you generated earlier in this chapter. Next to those you consider beyond your control write a "B." After this, go through your list a second time and put a "W" next to all the remaining stressors within your control. Now try to think of reasons or strategies for changing as many "Bs" to "Ws" as possible. Explore all the ways you can possibly gain control, even though your stressors may initially seem beyond your control.

We often equate having control over an outcome with having total control, when in fact having even an extremely small influence can significantly enhance our feeling of control in the situation. Look for small things you can do to help overcome the feeling of powerlessness, even though these actions might not bear fruit immediately. The key is to do something actively. If you can't change the situation, do something to improve your response to it, like exercising, talking to a friend or colleague, meditating, hiking in nature, or writing in a journal.

Consider, for example, how your sense of control and efficacy as a helper buffers you against stress. Our confidence as helpers usually increases with experience and training. If we have been helpful in similar situations in the past, or if we have learned specific skills for this situation, we will probably expect to be successful this time. The veteran helper thinks, "I've been here before and I've always been able to make something good happen, so the chances are, I can do it again." A novice helper may not have had enough successes or training to have this confidence, and might avoid even trying. For example, physicians and other health care providers are less likely to initiate end-of-life discussions if they believe they lack the interpersonal skills. Scores on an "advance care planning self-efficacy" scale (ACP-SE) predict the likelihood physicians will engage in these important conversations with their patients and patients' families.[51;52]

A sense of control is an excellent buffer against stress. Believing and acting as if life events are controllable and predictable can—within limits—markedly decrease stress. Having an optimistic outlook, believing your world and its demands are comprehensible and manageable (a sense of coherence), and thinking you can perform successfully in a given situation (self-efficacy), can buffer your stress.[53] Sometimes, however, these stress buffers are overwhelmed by harsh realities and unresolved adversity. When this happens, our best, and perhaps only, coping strategy is to reach inside, work hard in the presence of setbacks, persevere, and fulfill our mission with resolve and grit.

Set Limits

Many helpers report that setting clear limits concerning their time and involvement with the people they help is essential to their well-being. Doing this is often difficult because your contacts with clients and families can evoke your deepest sensitivity and empathy. You often fear that if you were not there for these people, probably no one else will be. In an effort to help, you can easily lose sight of your own needs, so it is critical to monitor yourself and be keenly attuned to whether you have gone too far. Try to keep the demands you face and the resources you have in dynamic balance. It can help to regard yourself as a choreographer who makes things happen for others, rather than as someone who is always in the spotlight. You can't be the number one psychosocial caregiver for everyone you work with.

Taking the choreographer role also means you must sacrifice some of the gratification from being perceived as the principal care provider. But there is no other effective strategy if you want to continue doing this work for an extended period. If you don't set limits, you will find that emotional and physical overload will ultimately make you less available emotionally to the people you care for. My observation is that many idealistic helpers come into the work of caregiving, try to be the principal support person for everyone they work with, and then leave the field in a year or less because they are overwhelmed and emotionally drained.

Stress from work can easily spill over into your personal life, and, conversely, stress in your private life can intrude in your work life. Conflicts between career and family can be enormously stressful, particularly for women. At the same time, success in both roles can lead to tremendous satisfaction. To achieve this success, it is important to put psychological and physical distance between your work and home life. One useful way of setting such limits is not to bring your work problems home. The way to do this is to create an environment and a routine wherein you can decompress. Sometimes a small symbolic act or cue—listening to a favorite song or reading a note to yourself on your door—can help demarcate leaving one world behind and entering another. When you are at home, keep your mind off your work life; when you are at work, avoid thinking about problems at home.

Although not easy, coping with the conflicting demands of work and home, and preventing difficulties in one arena from disturbing success and happiness in the other, are essential to effective stress management. Finding the right work-life balance is a significant challenge for us all, and is more likely to be achieved when we believe we are making progress toward goals that matter to us.[54; 55; 56]

Practice the Art of the Possible

Stress may be strongly related to the level and kinds of demands we face as helpers, but its origins are also firmly embedded in how we relate to ourselves—in the unrealistic expectations we have of ourselves, in a tendency to self-blame, and in the belief we alone have these issues. Do you ever think you must be successful with everyone with whom you work? Or that if other people were aware of how much you didn't know, they wouldn't want you as their caregiver? Do you occasionally think, "Nothing I do will even begin to make a difference in these awful situations," or find yourself wanting everyone with whom you work to enthusiastically appreciate and like you?

It is easy to see how irrational and self-defeating beliefs and perfectionism can affect our stress levels. Higher levels of perfectionism are shown to predict burnout in nurses, psychotherapists, and other clinicians.[57] However, it is important to note perfectionism is not all bad. There are both "good" (adaptive) and "bad" (maladaptive) types.[58] Having high standards and striving to meet them is an adaptive form of perfectionism. Having high standards and constantly noting discrepancies between your performance and your expectations—and then berating yourself for those differences—is a maladaptive form. Adaptive perfectionists score higher than maladaptive perfectionists on nearly all indices of well-being.

If you believe you must be successful with every one of your patients, any helping intervention you perceive as an actual or potential failure will threaten you and jeopardize your self-esteem. If you need everyone you help to be grateful and sing your praises, a small rebuff or an angry response can be particularly difficult for you, no matter how displaced or unfair this anger might be. Over and over again, your primary appraisal in these situations will be, "I am not OK."

This self-dialogue also ensures the *on switch* will activate when you evaluate your ability to cope with these threats: How can you ever have enough resources to balance the demands for perfection by you and your professional culture? Imagined failure accounts for a much greater share of our stress than real failure does.

The enormous range of skills required in this work fuels the pervasiveness of these kinds of internal stressors. For example, regardless of your training or profession, you are likely to confront suicidality, substance use, child abuse, uncontrolled pain, highly disturbed couples and families, trauma and complicated grief, disordered eating, and other challenging clinical situations. How many of us have received— or even could have received—thorough training for addressing each of these issues? Not very many. For this reason, it is important to differentiate between healthily recognizing one's skill limitations and unhealthily judging one's efficacy as a helper. We must accept sometimes not knowing what to do and then go on from there to do something. This could mean making a referral, getting more support, or learning new skills. The key is to have a clear idea of what you cannot do, and then go on to practice what is referred to in politics as *the art of the possible.*

Our unrealistic and idealized images of ourselves as helpers, and of what we can and should accomplish in this role, are shaped by our culture. Female caregivers, in particular, are trained in being over-responsible, and are conditioned to accept an imbalance between care for others and care for the self.[59] Women are taught from an early age to be responsible for managing relationships and making them work; this training can make female helpers more vulnerable to overextending themselves and blaming themselves when their helping fails. But this over-responsibility should not be pathologized and given labels like codependent caregiving; rather, as Krestan and Bepko put it, it is a positive impulse gone awry, and simply needs to be balanced with responsibility to self.[60]

We all had parents, teachers, and other helper role models in our lives who shaped our idealized image of self as helper, often in very positive ways. But some of the helping heroes we have been exposed to in our popular culture have shaped our schemata or mental blueprints for helpers and helping in less useful ways. As a child, my favorite fictional characters were Superman, Batman, and the Lone Ranger. Vicariously participating in the adventures of these valiant helpers always made me feel good because, in retrospect. It affirmed my developing altruistic self, and bolstered a belief I could act heroically in some ways.

As helpers, these fictional characters had several striking features in common: First, their true identities were hidden from others. Second, a traumatic loss preceded each of their careers as a helper: Superman lost his entire family and was orphaned; as a young boy, Batman witnessed the brutal murder of both of his parents; and the Lone Ranger was left for dead in an attack by bandits killing his brother. There was a profound connection between these painful events and our heroes' passionate commitment to doing good. They are *wounded healers* whose own traumas motivate and inform their helping, like the shamans who return from the underworld of suffering to heal others.[61] However, these iconic, wounded healers are not entirely recovered from their traumas, and the boundary between empathic distress and impairment is often blurred for them. Third, their helping was, it seemed, purely altruistic. These were people who selflessly did good for others. They rode, flew, or drove off before anyone could even thank them, let alone ask about their own needs: Who was that masked helper? Fourth, each seemed, in the end, invulnerable. Although there were some close calls with kryptonite, we knew when we looked up in the sky, Superman would always be there. Fifth, these super-helpers all had unhappy personal lives: they were helpers lacking a good work-life balance. Bruce Wayne had an unending string of failed relationships: Julie Madison, Vicki Vale, and the Batwoman. Clark Kent desperately sought real intimacy with Lois Lane, but was brutally beaten by a bully when he shed his super powers to attain it. Finally, they never failed: They always came through, no matter what the odds were against them.

During the endless hours I watched and read about these helping icons, I had many good feelings while witnessing their acts of helping—a vicarious version of the do good-feel good effect. Unfortunately, I also learned that helpers can't be fully authentic, don't seek help in dealing with their traumatic pasts, are virtually invulnerable, never accept any appreciation for the good work they do, have miserable personal lives, and always succeed. Now, when I sometimes fail or feel vulnerable, or have a need for appreciation or greater authenticity as a helper, I feel uneasy because these feelings and needs don't match with my mental blueprint of the "great helper." A key antidote to these influences is to develop a more balanced, less perfectionistic, and more realistic ideal image of helping and of yourself as helper, and to do this without sacrificing your vision for yourself doing this work.

Practicing the art of the possible as a clinician requires keeping an open mind as you deal with your work stressors. If your client doesn't respond positively to one intervention, try something else. If your coworkers don't meet your expectations, give them some feedback or try changing those expectations, and be willing to change your own behavior in ways to help your colleagues achieve their goals. We will discuss team communication issues in Chapter 7, but the important principle here is be patient and creative.

We tend to blame ourselves when things go wrong, and so add to our stress. It is also important to recognize and acknowledge our mistakes and real behavioral deficits. This association is associated with better stress management. When we make a mistake or don't know how to do something others in our position do know, we need to engage in honest self-confrontation, without blame. Questioning ourselves and our work is inevitable. Self-examination is an important skill, but self-blame and guilt can corrupt it. This leads to troubling thoughts and feelings undermining our well-being and ability to care. When we keep these thoughts and feelings hidden from others, they can corrode from within.[62] If instead we enlist the support of colleagues who understand our struggles, and practice self-acceptance while bringing the art of the possible to life, a positive and energizing quality can take hold, sustaining us on our helping journeys.

How can we tell when we are engaging in self-blame? One telltale sign is thoughts beginning with, "If only I were…" We think, "If only I were a better listener, or less selfish, or more skilled, then everything would work out well." I call the "if only I were" phrase a burnout mantra: repeat it to yourself often enough, and you will achieve a state of not-so-blissful burnout.

This helper's disclosure reveals this self-incrimination and negative self-talk:

> I can't accept that there is no humanly possible way to constantly meet every need of every patient/family, my spiritual needs, family, health needs, etc. After all, with God guiding my life, I should feel good about what I am able to do. But it's never enough.

Mea culpa reactions such as this are fostered in several ways. First, burnout usually results from lengthy exposure to chronic stress. When burnout is reached, there are often no distinctive external events to adequately explain our feelings of burnout.[63] A second reason we attribute our difficulties to something inside us is we don't know others are having the same or similar reactions. If we did know, we could overcome the *fallacy of uniqueness*—the belief we are uniquely experiencing this issue. We would see our stress has more to do with our situation than with some defect in ourselves.

This emotional, pluralistic ignorance reflects an underestimation of others' struggles, leading to loneliness and rumination over depressive feelings, as well as overestimations of others' positive experiences.[64] Rather than seeing our problems as part of a shared stressful situation, we attribute them to our character flaws or personal inadequacies. We may think, "I'm lazy...selfish...needy...unskilled...too angry...impatient...insensitive...codependent." Then, unable to share this negative view of ourselves, we try to look composed and confident, and work even harder. When this doesn't help, we become confused and further avoid any examination of what we feel inside. This oscillation between self-blame and emotional suppression only speeds us along the path to burnout.

Managing self-blame and other inner reactions in stressful situations requires knowing yourself. This means being aware of your moment-to-moment feelings and catching important issues or conflicts as they develop. We react to people and situations physically before we recognize our feelings or thoughts about them. When you are in difficulty or some feeling isn't clear, pay attention to your bodily sense of it all. Surprises may result. These surprises can present clues into what is stressing you, and what you can do to make the situation better. The focusing technique developed by Eugene Gendlin offers an empirically validated, step-by-step guide to accessing the important messages in these nonconceptual bodily felt experiences, what he termed *felt senses*—the not yet identifiable thoughts or feelings.[65]

The recommendation here is we must relate to ourselves in a gentle manner, similar to the way we strive to relate to the inner lives of the people we help. This means knowing and admitting when we are scared, or recognizing when our inner critic is activated. Agreeing with this notion is easy; doing it is tough. Stress-resilient helpers look at potential danger spots, trying to understand what they mean in their work and in their personal lives. They stay current with themselves. Having a supportive and insightful supervisor, keeping a journal, or being in a support group or personal psychotherapy can all help you develop this self-awareness and integrate your learning.

Be Compassionate with Yourself

This self-aware and accepting stance toward ourselves and our inner life is captured in the concept of self-compassion introduced by Kristin Neff and her colleagues. The three central features of self-compassion are self-kindness versus self-judgment, a sense of common humanity versus isolation, and mindfulness versus over-identification when relating to our painful experiences.[66] The thinking is that you are self-compassionate if you are not consumed by feelings of inadequacy and can be caring and tender toward yourself (self-kindness); do not feel alone in your failures but see your troubles as part of the human condition (common humanity). You are inherently self-compassionate if you can keep your emotions in balance without being consumed by feelings of inadequacy (mindfulness).[67] Self-compassion is possible whether you succeed or fail; it is kindness and acceptance of oneself and differs from self-esteem, which is more related to inner judgments about ourselves or our performance.

Self-compassion—or "compassion directed inward"—is a corrective to many of the stress-enhancers we have already identified, including self-blame, the fallacy of uniqueness, unrealistic self-expectations, and loss of emotional equilibrium.[66] Self-compassion is shown to moderate our reactions to negative events. It's associated with lower levels of depression, anxiety and stress.[68] Self-compassion also seems to deactivate our threat system while simultaneously activating the caregiving system, an ideal combination for helpers facing challenging situations.[69] In one experiment, a brief self-compassion intervention lowered levels of the stress hormone cortisol.[70] Thus, self-compassion is proving to be a valuable psychological tool for strengthening emotional resilience.

Be Mindful

Are there even more basic, teachable psychological skills to help us become more compassionate with ourselves and downregulate our nervous systems when we are caught up in the fight-or-flight response? Two such psychological resources are the relaxation response and the practice of mindfulness. Herbert Benson developed and tested the relaxation response method (a Westernized version of transcendental meditation), a stress management procedure now taught in a multimodal treatment program for coping with chronic stress.[71] The practice of the relaxation response creates a state of lowered arousal incompatible with the stress response. The sympathetic nervous system is quieted, muscle tension decreases, the heart rate slows, and a feeling of well-being occurs. The method also emphasizes an accepting, non-evaluative approach to immediate thoughts and feelings.[15]

Jon Kabat-Zinn also drew upon Eastern meditation practices when he developed the popular Mindfulness-Based Stress Reduction (MBSR) program. Kabat-Zinn defines mindfulness as "the awareness that emerges through paying attention on purpose, in the present moment, and nonjudgmentally to the unfolding of experience moment by moment."[72]

Garland and Thomas explain how mindfulness can enhance cognitive reappraisal as a coping strategy.[73] Mindfulness, they say, allows us to "step back" from stress appraisals into an observing state where transitory negative thoughts and feelings are not taken as veridical reflections of reality. You as your observing self can simply notice— "Oh, I am criticizing myself for not saying the right thing," or "I'm regretting not saying what I wanted to at the team meeting," or "My eyes are watering as I listen to this bereaved mother describe her final moments with her son." The point is to not let those thoughts and feelings lead to personal distress. Instead, there can be awareness, acceptance, deepened empathy, and compassionate action.

Shauna Shapiro and colleagues describe this psychological stance as "reperceiving," whereby mindfulness allows us to move from a subjective perspective to a more objective perspective, so what we are observing is separate from our observing self.[74] As a consequence, we can feel relief from distress (although uncomfortable feelings can remain) and do less catastrophizing. This can make finding meaning more likely, Garland and Thomas argue, because you are able to "reappraise the stressor in a more positive and adaptive way," and this makes possible "the selection of new narratives or life stories that engender eudaimonic meaning, resilience, and the sense of purpose in life."[73]

Thus, mindful awareness can be a key to transforming our stress, allowing us to see our stressors more clearly, and to act more adaptively in response to them. Even shown to have salutary effects on telomere health,[75] mindfulness supports us in connecting with our deepest values and what matters most to us, giving us access to the wellspring of empathy and compassion energizing our helping journeys.

Mindful awareness of our inner life has the same qualities we identified earlier as essential to emotional balance in helping encounters. When we deeply empathize with our clients' suffering, we will feel unpleasant internal states. But if at the same time we have an observing self or witness not identified with the suffering, we can respond to our own and the other's suffering without debilitating personal distress. By accepting our inner responses in this way, we are paradoxically no longer controlled by them, and positive change in us and in our clients is more likely.

Because mindfulness can so greatly enhance both stress management and clinical practice, it is increasingly being incorporated into training programs for health professionals.[76] Chaukos found lower levels of burnout in those medicine and psychiatry residents with higher levels of mindfulness, indicating a need for promoting mindfulness and self-awareness coping strategies in physician education.[77]

Exercise

No matter what your coping strategies are like, stress is unavoidable. Thus, we often need to make stress management interventions at a more downstream point in the stress cycle. Once stress hormones have been released into your body, the best action to take is to get them out of your system. An analogy might be helpful here: The oil in your car constantly collects dirt and needs to be changed periodically, and we all do this rather dutifully. Physical activity is a proven technique for "changing the oil" in your stressed body.

Walk, swim, run, hike, or do whatever gives your body a chance to unwind. After a particularly difficult day, a long run or a game of basketball or table tennis palpably reduces the stress in my system: I feel less tired, and my head is cleared of the day's worries.

Stanford psychologist Candice Hogan and her colleagues summarize some of the many physical and psychological benefits of exercise, including greater positive affect, recovery from exposure to emotional stressors, a reduction in negative affect and other depressive symptoms, and enhanced brain health.[78] The authors underscore these remarkable benefits saying, "if exercise came in pill form it would be the most sought-after drug on the market."

The research is indeed convincing and fascinating. Physical activity that increases your heart rate and brings on a sweat (e.g., walking, dancing, biking, cycling, aerobic exercise classes) predicts lower levels of future job burnout and depression and moderates the burnout-depression relationship.[79] Exercise predicts better physical and psychological quality of life, and general ratings of quality of life.[80] It also enhances our *vigor*, a positive counterpart of burnout, defined as feeling you "possess physical strength, emotional energy, and cognitive liveliness."[81] Exercise is also shown to buffer the effects of high stress on telomere length.[82] Even more fascinating is a recent finding that, even after adjusting for actual levels of physical activity and other covariates, individuals who perceive themselves to be less active than others were up to 71% more likely to die in a follow-up period than those individuals who perceive themselves as more active.[83] Our level of physical exercise matters; so does our perception of it.

Indeed, myriad studies support these general findings for exercise, indicating physical activity boosts the brain's stress buffers and protects against depression and anxiety by strengthening the body's ability to respond to stress. The more sedentary we are, scientists say, the less efficient our bodies are in responding to stress. All movement counts. Whether you walk briskly, bicycle, play racquetball, jog, swim, or mow the lawn, these stress management practices can yield enormous benefits now and in the future. You will have more energy and stamina, making you better prepared to handle stress and recover from it. If you are like the person who said, "I tried exercise once, and that was enough," and you don't exercise now, first check with your physician, then develop a plan for experimenting with this approach to stress management. If you doubt its efficacy, just ask friends and colleagues who exercise regularly and get their testimonials about the benefits they perceive.

Most clinicians already recognize the value of exercise. When asked about their stress management strategies, exercise is usually at the top of their lists. Whitebird and colleagues asked hospice workers about their stress and how they cope with it.[84] Participants reported social support, physical activity, and "saying 'no' more often" were their favorite and most effective stress antidotes. When asked what they would suggest be changed in the workplace, they recommended, among other things, the provision of more opportunities to exercise and to connect with coworkers. Meldrum interviewed winners of the American Medical Association Foundation's Pride in the Professions Award to learn how they manage burnout.[85] Again, the same themes appeared: the physicians highlighted exercise, sharing issues with family and friends, and setting limits.

Strengthen Your Social Support

As the surveys just reported indicate, social support is widely identified by clinicians as a key component in their stress management toolbox. This is not surprising, since social support can be such a great buffer against stress, affecting many elements of the stress response. Strong social support can enhance your self-esteem and make difficulties at work seem less threatening. Encouragement, support, and feedback lead to greater optimism and confidence in the availability of the resources needed to meet current challenges. Sharing troubling feelings and self-doubts with others doing the same work helps in two ways: It helps us redefine these difficult thoughts and feelings as normal and human. And, it leads to the identification of other coping responses. This sharing can improve your self-esteem, self-compassion, and self-efficacy.

Receiving strong support from your coworkers, supervisors, counselors, friends, and family is sometimes as difficult as it is important to do. A secondary effect of not having enough time to do the work is not having enough time to offer and receive support for doing it. Stigma perceptions can also interfere with help seeking. In a large multi-institutional survey of medical students, only about 3 out of 10 students with burnout had sought help within the last year, and the burned-out students were more likely to see receiving help for an emotional or mental health problem as a sign of weakness.[86] Receiving inadequate psychological support at work was found to be a significant predictor of burnout among oncology clinical nurse specialists.[87]

Social support from friends can also be elusive. How do people in general react when you tell them what you do as a helper? If you work with highly distressed populations, such as terminally ill or traumatically bereaved persons, it is likely you will receive one of two reactions. Either people put you on a pedestal and tell you, "I could never do what you do," or they look at you with a critical eye, giving you the message there must be something seriously wrong with you. For example, "You must be depressed or have a morbid interest in human suffering to do this work." Such a dynamic can lead to you going from the intense, often one-way intimacy of the helping encounter, to a personal social life lacking intimacy and social exchange.

Family members can provide invaluable support, but they can also sometimes be an additional source of stress. For example, one end-of-life clinician shared: "Sometimes my family makes me feel morbid and creepy because they can't understand how working with the dying means the privilege of helping the living."

Stress at work can also affect one's home life:

> I feel I can be very caring and empathetic at work to the point when I get home I want to be left alone. This happens even on "good" days. In turn, I feel I neglect my husband and children in an emotional way. There are times I find it hard to initiate a hug with any one of them, making me feel guilty. My husband has so often said, "You care more for your patients than you do for me." Maybe that is part of the reason I'm like this: I've heard it so much I'm proving him right. Drained at work, drained at home.

When conflicts at home become too difficult, greater involvement at work can provide escape from them, though certainly not solve them:

✧ I would like to leave my husband in order to devote more energy to my work.

✧ There are times when I get more out of my work than I do from having sex with my husband.

These poignant and worrying disclosures reflect the need to maintain balance in one's life as a caregiver and illustrate the destructive consequences of avoidance as a coping style.

The key point here is an extensive support system is critical to preventing burnout. Unfortunately, many caregivers (like most other people) focus their emotional and support needs primarily on one person—usually a spouse or partner. Imagine a caregiver named Mary and her husband, John, a tax accountant. Today, Mary has just had an emotionally demanding patient encounter. Her patient died while holding her hand, saying, "I love you. Thank you!" Her husband had problems at the office and came home exhausted. He isn't interested in hearing any more "death and dying stories," as he calls them. When Mary struggles to get him to listen, he says, "Mary, let's not forget there are death, and taxes." So, they sit silently at the dinner table, both of them feeling discounted and ignored.

Many of us with our limited support systems turn problems such as these into catastrophes; we take them as just another sign our partner doesn't love us, or that we are simply incompatible. Although some interest and concern in our work can be expected from those we love, when we look for it only there, we are stressing these relationships and probably keeping ourselves from other sources of support.

The encounter between Mary and her husband can teach us an important lesson about social support and how we should approach the task of increasing this important resource. People commonly think of support in a narrow way (e.g., as someone who listens and agrees with you). Although having someone agree is important, support is actually multifaceted.

Here is a list of six different kinds of support experts consider important.[1] As I describe each, think about the people who give you these kinds of specific, helpful input. Picture their faces. If no one comes to mind, think about someone who could do so.

The first category of support is our commonsense version: having a good listener. It could be someone at home or at work—someone you can always talk to about anything. The second sort of support is technical appreciation. It comes from an expert who gives helpful feedback on your performance and appreciates what you are doing. This most often comes from a colleague or supervisor. A third form of support is technical challenge. A colleague or supervisor who challenges your ways of thinking and working is providing this support.

Good clinical supervision is a frequently recommended and highly valued resource in our work.

Another variation is emotional support. This comes from someone at home or work who is there for you, whom you don't have to pretend with, who knows you well, and whose support is unconditional. Emotional challenge is a form of support from a friend or colleague who can catch you when you are sloughing off or working aimlessly, someone who can comfortably say, "Are you sure you're doing everything you can?" Or, "Aren't you pushing a bit too hard and trying to do too much?" The last type of support—shared social reality—is simply having a person who agrees with you. He or she has similar values, views, and priorities. This form of support can be as simple as two people exchanging a knowing glance when they both encounter someone or something at work that is troubling them. Review the different components of your support system, and look for new ways to strengthen and enhance them.

Find Compassion Satisfaction

As you review the events associated with stress for you as a helper, do you find most of those stressors involve difficult interactions with others—whether they are patients and families, coworkers, or administrators? I often ask people with whom I come into contact in everyday situations, from the supermarket to the photocopying store, the same question: "What's the biggest source of stress for you in your job?" The answer has most often been other people.

People are also a major source of stress for professional caregivers. Coworkers, not patients and their families, can be a main source of helper stress. In their study of 1,800 intensive care nurses, Claus and Bailey found interpersonal conflict (with physicians, supervisors, or other staff nurses) was the most commonly reported source of stress.[9] Vachon found the most frequently cited stressor of caregivers working with critically ill, dying, and bereaved populations involved team communication problems, not direct patient care.[88]

In a related nursing study, Claus and Bailey found patient care rated as the major source of satisfaction, as well as the third-greatest source of stress, behind interpersonal conflicts with other staff and management of the unit.[9] At the same time, interpersonal relationships at work were cited as the second greatest source of satisfaction.

A paradox emerges from these findings: People can burn you out, but at the same time, people can keep your caring flame burning. Interpersonal relationships are a crucible where caring is either nourished or transformed into personal pain and burnout.

Recent studies of *compassion satisfaction* support these views. Compassion satisfaction, a construct introduced to study the positive aspects of compassion and caregiving, is conceptualized and measured as the ability to feel gratification, even joy, when helping others.[89] If working with those you help brings you a great deal of satisfaction, you have happy thoughts about those you help and how you could help them, and you enjoy and trust your coworkers, you are high on this dimension.[90]

In a large study involving hospice and palliative care workers, compassion satisfaction was strongly negatively related to both burnout and compassion fatigue as measured.[91] Like the family caregivers who report benefits from caregiving and see it as a positive event, professional caregivers are also buffered from stress by the rewards of the work they do.[92] And although relations with coworkers (and patients and families) can be a major source of stress, they can also be a major source of satisfaction and a stress buffer, as we have seen in our discussion of social support as a key resilience factor.

Follow Selye's Recipe

Based on his half-century of pioneering research, Hans Selye offered the following recipe for reducing the stress of life:

> The first ingredient... is to seek your own stress level, to decide whether you're a racehorse or a turtle and to live your life accordingly. The second is to choose your goals and make sure they're your own, and not imposed on you by an over-helpful mother or teacher. And the third ingredient to this recipe is altruistic egoism: looking out for oneself by being necessary to others, and thus earning their goodwill.[93]

Selye's early recommendations still seem wise. We all need to carefully determine our own speed and work level. If you are one of those people who thrive on work, don't worry. If your goals and your energy levels lead you to be extremely active, don't create stress by worrying about being this way.

Selye's advice to work toward your own goals, and not those of anyone else, is closely related to the view of stress and personal growth in helping developed here. Fulfillment and meaning in your work are most likely when your helping goals express your deep values and vision for yourself as a helper. But setting realistic personal goals both in work and in private life is not easy. It is often difficult to develop a clear image of where we would like to be, and what specifically we must do to get there. Small positive steps are what eventually will lead to success in achieving your goals. As the ancient Chinese proverb advises, "A journey of a thousand miles must begin with a single step." At each step we need to be clear about whether our efforts are helping us make tangible progress toward our goals. This principle applies in our helping work as well as in our personal lives. Avoid setting goals so big and so general you are never able to give yourself credit for meeting them, and regularly monitor your progress.

Selye's third recommendation is to practice altruistic egoism, by which he means we should try to earn the goodwill of the people around us, because if we do, we will have more support and thus less stress. This reminds us our caring connections with others are at the heart of our helping journey.

Integrate and Transform Loss

All stress management might be considered loss management; however, the loss-related features of stress are dramatically intensified in working with people facing grief, loss, and life-threatening illnesses. They can take many forms. For example, you might support a dying mother as she says good-bye to a daughter too young to understand what Stage IV melanoma means, or how the events of this time will shape the remainder of her life. You might listen to a bereaved mother as she struggles to understand how the God she always devoutly believed in can take her infant son away from her. You might sit with a sobbing veteran as he recalls wartime losses. Or, care for a child with cancer, living through remissions and recurrences, and then grieve the child's untimely death.

The adaptational challenges of being exposed to such mortality, morbidity, trauma, and often overwhelming tragedy are daunting, but can be met if you first acknowledge their presence, accept them as part of the work you do, and find supportive colleagues with whom to safely confide. If we attend to these losses, we can integrate and transform them, and this personal grief work, though not without pain and difficulties, can be a source of growth for us.

Like our patients and families, we can reshape our assumptive worlds so we too can live with hope in a world where loss is inescapable. Like them, we can become sadder, but wiser.[94] Like them, we can grow through adversity and become more emotionally resilient. And if we maintain our emotional balance, practice solid self-care, and draw upon the sources of caring continually opening to us, these confrontations with life's ultimate stressors can, as Norma Haan puts it, make us more tender, humble, and hardy.[95]

Find Meaning

Think back to Chapter 1, where we discussed eudaimonia, a word meaning achieving individual indwelling happiness through virtue, morality, and meaning in life. Achieving happiness in this way unlocks the potential for personal growth. It might even offer immunological benefits. Remember Ernest Becker urging us to discover our unique talent and then express it and "dedicate it to something beyond" oneself.[38]

It is becoming clear that connecting to real purpose in our lives, and committing ourselves to something beyond our own gratification, provides a tremendous buffer against stress. Remember the study of nurses in internal medicine, oncology, hematology, and palliative care departments mentioned earlier, where it was found meaning and purpose in life, less fear of death, and secure attachment style were factors in preventing burnout.[96] Recognizing this, interventions for burnout are aimed at enhancing a feeling of accomplishment, purpose, and engagement in work.[42; 97] My colleague Ayala Pines captured these connections when she said burnout is a failure in the search for meaning.[98]

Conclusion

Working with people confronting grief, loss, trauma, illness, and tragedy in all its forms is an intensely personal endeavor, bringing us into contact with the deepest parts of ourselves. To negotiate the demands of work, we must be tough and tender, strong and vulnerable. We can best meet these challenges by strengthening our inner resources and developing habits promoting resilience to stress.

We've reviewed many resilience-enhancing strategies, from taking charge to connecting with meaning in our work. No doubt, you are already applying many of these strategies to strengthen your resilience. Which are most helpful? What additional strategies can you now employ to enhance your resilience? If the lengthy list of resilience enhancers is a bit overwhelming as you consider making changes, it is important to remember simple, restorative self-care activities such as sleep, relaxation, vacation, social interaction, and time in nature can significantly reduce stress, promote better physical and emotional health, and open the gateway to positive emotions.[99]

Your new stress management program might be as simple as taking all your vacation time, debriefing with a colleague over lunch each week, pausing for a minute or two to reflect on and absorb fulfilling moments in your everyday helping, or discovering a scenic hiking trail where you can reflect on the week's events. You can make changes in small steps, one thing at a time. The key is to recognize that building your resilience is essential, not optional.

No matter how many resilience-enhancing forces we employ, stressors at work will still sometimes challenge us to our limits. We will inevitably be weary at times, but if we counter exhaustion with vigor, moral distress with moral courage, and our suffering as helpers with its restorative meaning, we can transform and transcend stress, fulfill our purpose in our work, and live a life aligned with cherished values.[81]

To thrive and not just survive in this work, some of the same openness and compassion we extend to the people we care for must also be turned inward. And then, somehow, we must find the courage to bring the resulting insights and self-awareness back into the world with us, and to share them with others. Our clients face this same challenge: how to confront and talk safely about troubling thoughts and feelings. We will now turn our attention to this universal decision—whether to conceal or to reveal—and to its profound implications for health and healing.

4

Everyone has three lives: a public life, a private life and a secret life.[1]

Gabriel Garcia Marquez

The desire to share one's secret, to confide, to unburden, to reach out for greater intimacy, often conflicts with the desire to keep the secret to oneself and to draw protection or power from its preservation—at times in obedience to the forces of resistance that bespeak the risk of "betraying oneself."[2]

Sissela Bok

Nothing makes people more lonely, and more cut off from the fellowship of others, than the possession of an anxiously hidden and jealously guarded secret.[3]

Carl Jung

Love takes off the masks that we fear we cannot live without and know we cannot live within.[4]

James Baldwin

Secrets: Concealment and Confiding in Helping and Healing

Working with people facing grief, loss, and life-threatening illness ushers us into a veritable world of secrets, secret keeping, and secrecy. We encounter the tightly held and painful secrets of patients and families—abuse and traumas, self-hatred and suicidality, extramarital affairs and marital unhappiness, unfulfilled dreams and unexpressed love, disenfranchised grief and concealable stigmatized identities—all often revealed to us in times of crisis and in deathbed conversations. We are surprised and saddened by perturbing cutoffs between family members and across generations, unfinished business with deceased loved ones, and shocking postmortem discoveries that can complicate treatment and mourning.

We also confront our own secrets, the self-doubts and unresolved feelings about difficult clinical situations, and warning signs of burnout, vicarious traumatization, or moral distress we are concealing to avoid possible judgments by colleagues.

Confronting this wide range of secrets, and seeking to implement quality person-centered care, we must, as philosopher Sissela Bok advised, "navigate in and between the worlds of personal and shared experience, coping with the moral questions about what is fair or unfair, truthful or deceptive, helpful or harmful."[2]

Early in life, I learned a basic truth about secrets and secret telling. I have spent most of my adult years trying to understand this reality more fully. My efforts taught me that keeping distressing personal information concealed from others can often damage your health. Confiding these secrets to people who care about you can have an opposite healing effect. I found this true when, as a young Catholic boy, I negotiated secrets in the dark confines of the confessional. I struggled a bit with what to tell and what not to tell. I didn't, for example, tell the priest what I considered my more shameful acts. Instead, I recited the same litany each week: "I used bad language five times," or "I didn't obey my parents three times." The litany was carefully calculated to elicit an optimal penance. If I got into real trouble (nothing serious) during the week, I usually confessed it, and on those days my penance skyrocketed. Despite my ambivalence toward full and honest disclosure, confession usually felt good. I could share some of my secrets with a listener who didn't make harsh judgments about my everyday life (although he did invoke some retribution).

Many years after my final confession in a church, I found myself in graduate studies being trained to listen to confessions, not as a priest, but as a psychotherapist—a professional confidant who would, for the next several decades, sit with suffering clients disclosing shame, self-blame, mistakes in life, and transgressions. In this role, unlike the priest in the confessional, my job was not to administer penance or forgiveness, but to understand, analyze, empathize, and provide unwavering support for the client in unraveling his/her blame or shame, and enabling them to unearth or unveil the secrets that had often immobilized them for years. I have continued to learn about secrets through my clinical work, research, and teaching, and am increasingly amazed by the power and ubiquity of these psychological phenomena.

The Johari Window

To better navigate this terrain, we begin with a look at (or through) the Johari Window, a helpful tool for thinking about secrets, our degree of openness in revealing ourselves, and the distinction between private and secret personal information.[5] This simple and elegant graphic model identifies four different kinds of information about yourself. Think about the diagram as representing your total self as you relate to other people. The four panes or quadrants of the window represent different aspects of your total self in relation to others and reveal several facets of what is happening at individual and interpersonal levels.

The Johari Window

	Known to self	Not known to self
Known to others	**I** **Open**	**III** **Blind**
Not known to others	**II** **Hidden**	**IV** **Unknown**

Quadrant I represents those behaviors and motivations known to you and others. This is your public self. Quadrant II is the hidden area of the self. This area includes all the personal information you are aware of, but others aren't. If you are just meeting a new person this quadrant is very large, and it shrinks as you share your feelings and other information about yourself over time. Quadrant III is a blind area, representing behaviors and motivations that you don't know about but are apparent to others. For example, you may have a mannerism or a bad habit that you are not aware of but is perfectly obvious to other people. (This quadrant is sometimes called the "bad breath" quadrant.) Quadrant IV, the unknown area, includes information that neither you nor other people are aware of. Our unconscious motives and feelings reside in this quadrant.

The Johari Window can also help us chart our personal growth and change. Luft and others argue that personal growth and psychological health are achieved as Quadrant I expands and the other three quadrants become correspondingly smaller, although little systematic work has been done using the Johari Window to test that hypothesis.[5] Although the categories are not truly mutually exclusive, the tool nevertheless has heuristic value for our discussion. For example, in grief counseling, a bereaved client might become more aware of her feelings and changes in identity and share those with her counselor and others, thus expanding her Quadrant I. In this process, Quadrant II also shrinks because fewer of her thoughts and feelings are concealed. As her counselor and others continue to give her feedback, her blind area (Quadrant III) also shrinks as she learns new things about herself that others can see but she cannot. Once these are in her awareness, they can move into Quadrant I, expanding it even farther. As she continues her self-exploration, the extent of personal information formerly unknown to her and unknown to others (Quadrant IV) also shrinks as she grows and learns more new things about herself.

Try this experiment: Imagine that 100 points represent your total self. How much of this total self would you say is public—that is, known to others—and how much is private, or unknown to others? Distribute your 100 points in Quadrants I and II. Be sure your total adds up to 100. In this exercise, people typically assign about 60 points to the public area and 40 points to the private area. How do your figures compare with those?

Now look at the number you assigned to the private category. This category would include your secrets because your secrets are unknown to others. What percentage of your private self is currently represented by your secrets? Most people say that about 20% of their private selves is secret. What is your rating? What thoughts, feelings, and images came up as you tried to estimate your secrets percentage? How many of these are work related? Who have you shared those with, if anyone? What was sharing them like and how did it affect your relationship?

We know that secret keeping is quite common. Michael Slepian and colleagues developed a questionnaire with 38 categories of common secrets, ranging from telling a lie and sexual infidelity to trauma and sexual orientation. They found that participants in an anonymous online study report having had secrets in 20 of the 38 categories at some time, of which 13 are currently secret.[6] In my own survey, I found the most common topics were sex and sexuality, secrets about others (e.g., "My husband is alcoholic"), physical and emotional abuse, difficulties in a marital relationship, failure or feelings of inadequacy, and illness or substance use, but a much wider range of secret topics were endorsed.[7] Some people have more, and some people have fewer than what we are finding to be the average number of secrets kept in a lifetime. How many secrets do you have now, or have had in the past?

On Secrets and Secret Keeping

I am not alone in my fascination with secrets; indeed, the idea has captivated the interest of humankind throughout history. The works of countless poets, playwrights, and philosophers have explored the psychological significance of secrets. Some maintain the view that humans aren't very good at keeping secrets. In *Poor Richard's Almanac*, Benjamin Franklin remarked, "Three may keep a secret if two of them are dead," and Petronius, the Roman satirist, observed, "Sooner will men hold fire in their mouths than keep a secret."[8] The enormous response to the popular PostSecret blog, on which people can anonymously disclose their secrets, supports the view that we long to disclose our confidences.[9] Modern technology, for better or worse, also facilitates the revealing of secrets from our pasts; for example, as people discover their true origins later in life though DNA ancestry testing. Yet when we consider personal secrets, particularly those concerning information that threatens our self-esteem or well-being, the Latin saying that "small sorrows speak, great ones are silent" seems more accurate and more familiar to those who work in the contexts of grief, loss, and trauma.

Psychological Theory and Research

Psychologists have long addressed the act of keeping distressing thoughts and feelings secret from others and the psychological price to be paid for secret keeping. William James, the father of modern psychology, stated, "One would think that in more men the shell of secrecy would have had to open, the pent-in abscess to burst and gain relief."[10] James' contemporary, Sigmund Freud, and his followers, have persistently pursued their patients' pathogenic secrets.[11] Freud proclaimed, "Disclosure of the secret will have attacked, at its most sensitive point, the 'aetiological equation' from which the neuroses descend."[12] Erich Fromm considered the inability to disclose oneself to be a core reason for the alienation of the modern individual from the self and others.[13]

These early thinkers set the stage for contemporary research and theory regarding concealing and revealing aspects about ourselves and its effect on our well-being. Sidney Jourard led the way, his writings underscoring the negative health consequences of hiding significant details of the self, noting that it includes an active struggle to avoid becoming known:

> Every maladjusted person is a person who has not made himself known to another human being and in consequence does not know himself. Nor can he be himself. More than that, he struggles actively to avoid becoming known by another human being. He works at it ceaselessly, twenty-four hours daily, and it is work. In the effort to avoid becoming known, a person provides for himself a cancerous kind of stress which is subtle and unrecognized, but none the less effective in producing not only the assorted patterns of unhealthy personality which psychiatry talks about, but also the wide array of physical ills that have come to be recognized as the province of psychosomatic medicine.[14]

Following Jourard's lead, social psychologist James Pennebaker and colleagues launched a series of groundbreaking studies examining what they called the confiding-illness relation or the inhibition-disease link. They found that the lack of expression of thoughts and feelings about traumatic events (the divorce of one's parents, death of a spouse, death of a parent, and sexual traumas) leads to long-term negative health effects.[15] Pennebaker initially explained these effects much as Jourard did, seeing them as resulting from the increased physiological and psychological work required when one conceals such personal information.[16] The failure to confront traumas, they argued, forces us to live with them in an unresolved way, and the act of avoiding them—accomplished by inhibiting and controlling our thoughts and feelings—increases our stress and chances of becoming ill. Surveying his own and others' findings, Pennebaker arrived at the extraordinary conclusion that, "The act of not discussing or confiding the event with another may be more damaging than having experienced the event per se."[17]

To study the effects of disclosure, as opposed to concealment, of traumatic memories and emotions, Pennebaker devised an experimental paradigm known as expressive writing. During expressive writing studies, subjects are typically asked to write for 20 minutes on 3 to 5 consecutive days about an important personal and emotional topic that has affected them and their lives. Often the participants write about traumas and personal secrets. Meta-analyses of expressive writing as a therapeutic intervention have revealed quite positive outcomes from these minimal interventions.[18] The written disclosure of stressful or traumatic events appears to promote physical and psychological health and subjective well-being, including improvements in immune function, mood, life satisfaction, perceived stress, physical symptoms and health care visits.[19]

These results have led expressive writing interventions to become known as the *writing cure,* and have given impetus to journaling as a widely used therapeutic and self-help modality. Today, many helping professionals recognize the value of journaling; they record the joys and sorrows of their helping journey and use journaling as a therapeutic tool with their clients. Provided it does not lead to increased rumination and obsession about situations or events, journaling seems to be an excellent resilience-enhancing practice.

Recent explanations for such salutary effects of expressive writing focus on how translating these traumatic memories and emotions into language facilitates their integration into a coherent narrative and, in turn, reduces thought suppression and autonomic arousal.[19] Expressive writing can lead to the reappraisal of events and our responses to them, the development of new perspectives and their associated benefits, and changing of life stories. This interpretation is consistent with our model of stress and coping, which views reappraisal and cognitive restructuring as key processes. It also supports experimental findings that cognitive work like this facilitates emotional recovery extending beyond temporary emotional relief.[20] We see many of the same beneficial psychological processes at work in everyday grief and trauma counseling, where clients wrest new meanings from their painful life events, integrate their losses, and often achieve significant personal growth. Also, following the expressive writing intervention, participants can take advantage of whatever social support is available to process the trauma more deeply.[21]

Recognizing the benefits of expressive writing, clinicians are now incorporating expressive writing in E-mental health applications. For example, the practice of writing about trauma is being integrated into online structured writing therapy, an Internet-based therapist-guided treatment for posttraumatic stress disorder and complicated grief which is delivered without face-to-face contact between the patient and therapist.[22] However, while the longer-term outcomes of expressive writing are consistently positive, in the short term, subjects often report increased anxiety. I have found that when clients disclose troubling secrets in therapy, they at first feel heightened anxiety and shame, but once these initial concerns subside, psychological growth and healing advance. No matter how disclosure works, it seems the simple act of revelation can often stimulate positive change. William James put it this way: "For him who confesses, shams are over and realities have begun; he has exteriorized his rottenness."[10]

Another major contribution to the study of secrets and secret keeping came from psychologist Daniel Wegner's Harvard laboratory. Wegner and his colleagues examined thought suppression in the context of secrecy and secret keeping.[23] Their preoccupation model of secrecy suggests that secrecy plays a significant role in the etiology of psychopathology: "Secrecy sets into motion a self-sustaining cycle of obsessive preoccupation with the secret. Attempts made to suppress the secret thought are responded to with intrusive thinking of the secret, which in turn engenders further efforts to eliminate the secret thought."[24] To test this theory, Wegner conducted the well-known "white bear" studies, in which subjects were instructed not to think about a white bear; not surprisingly, they couldn't.

Secrets can lead to a self-perpetuating cycle of suppression and intrusion, during which the secrets become the focus of ruminative thoughts, which evolve into an obsessive preoccupation with the concealed personal information, leading to increased distress. The ironic outcome is that the struggle to keep a secret can result in the secret becoming hyper-accessible and even more pronounced. This leads the secret keeper to engage in a pattern of silent self-torment, not unlike the struggle Jourard described. Dostoevsky brilliantly portrays this inner struggle in the character of Raskolnikov, the murderer in *Crime and Punishment* who is driven mad by his terrible secret before finally confessing it.

Wegner and colleagues extend this etiological argument and suggest that secrecy and thought suppression play an important role in diverse psychopathological conditions. Suppressing sorrows, they believe, can lead them to develop into psychopathologies, and the obsessional behavior associated with secrecy can create vulnerability to anxiety issues."[24] The clinical implication for this identified role of secret keeping in psychopathology is, they argue, that breaking secrecy may be the first step toward achieving successful treatment of several psychological disorders.

Research teams at Columbia University led by Michael Slepian and Barry Farber are undertaking major studies of secrets, health, and psychotherapy. Slepian and colleagues find that when subjects are instructed to recall a big secret, their estimates of the steepness of a hill and distance increase, thus representing a physical burden.[25] This effect disappears when subjects are also instructed to reveal the secret by writing about it. The degree of preoccupation with the secret also predicts estimates of slope.[26]

In *Secrets and Lies in Psychotherapy*, Farber, Blanchard, and Love present some surprising findings.[27] For example, 93% of 547 psychotherapy clients surveyed reported lying to their therapists; only 7% reported having told zero lies in psychotherapy. The percentages of respondents acknowledging ongoing lying or secret keeping about specific topics were high and clinically significant. In decreasing order, the most frequently reported topics were: sexual desires or fantasies (34%), details of sex life (33%), suicidal thoughts (21%), real reactions to therapist's comments (20%), sexual orientation (17%), times treated others poorly (16%), family secrets (16%), whether therapy is helping (16%), trauma or abuse experiences (15%), self-harm (13%), feelings of despair or hopelessness (13%), and eating habits or eating disorder (13%). In a study of 754 adult patients by other investigators, more than one third admitted to lying to their physicians about information relevant to their care.[28] Clearly, patients often carry important secrets of which their helpers remain unaware.

Patients' concealment of treatment-relevant information is also pervasive in hospice and palliative care. In a British study, hospice nurses were asked to write down their patients' current concerns. Then, a research nurse used a semi-structured interview and Concerns Checklist to elicit input regarding their patients' concerns.[29] The striking discovery was that over 60% of concerns remained hidden and not registered by the nurses. Concerns about the future, appearance, and loss of independence were not disclosed more than 80% of the time. The researchers concluded that hospice patients selectively disclosed physical symptoms and their nurses did not bring out or record patients' concerns accurately. Focusing specifically on patient reluctance to admit pain, Cagle and Bunting developed a practice-oriented conceptual model highlighting six key factors promoting concealment: stigma, stoicism, cautiousness, fatalism, bother, and denial.[30]

Self-Concealment: What You Don't Say Can Hurt You

The early work by Jourard, Pennebaker, and Wegner linked the concealment of distressing personal information to negative health effects. Their work validated the established clinical wisdom and raised the question of whether individual differences arise in the propensity to conceal negative personal information. These possible individual differences became the focus of our early work on self-concealment (SC) and the development of the Self-Concealment Scale (SCS).[31] The 10-item Self-Concealment Scale is included in Appendix B. Data from more than 41,000 subjects are now reported and surprisingly show no differences in scores for men and women.

We conceptualized self-concealment as a predisposition to actively conceal from others personal information—thoughts, feelings, actions, or events—that are highly intimate and negative in valence. We noted that the most painful or traumatic events, such as grief, childhood abuse, rape, strong negative thoughts about oneself or unhappiness in relationships, and serious medical conditions are often concealed. This concealed personal information is consciously accessible to us, in contrast to "unconscious secrets," which result from repression or denial. We actively keep conscious secrets from others; sometimes we tell them to only one or two persons, and sometimes we don't share them with anyone at all.

SC is not the same as a low level of self-disclosure; in fact, the two constructs, although related, are empirically and conceptually distinct. A person can be a high discloser and a high self-concealer, freely revealing many aspects of oneself, while at the same time tightly concealing other self-information that is personally distressing or perceived as shameful.

We now conceptualize SC as a trait-like motivational construct, with self-concealing behaviors and a patterned set of maladaptive emotion regulation strategies acting in service of the motive to self-conceal.[32] In other words, the urge to conceal activates a wide range of external behaviors and internal coping processes that in the short-term accomplish this self-protective goal. These factors then negatively impact health and well-being on many levels unless disclosure affords relief. Psychoanalyst Donald Winnicott captured these dynamics when he wrote, "It is joy to be hidden but disaster not to be found."[33]

Self-concealment, much like resilience, is not a fixed, unchangeable personality trait. Although our personalities contribute to each, many other factors can increase or decrease self-concealment motivation and resilience. For example, if you suddenly develop a concealable stigmatized medical condition (e.g., lung cancer, HIV/AIDS) or are a victim of abuse, your SC motivation is likely to arise in protection of yourself from the blame and judgment of others. Heightened social constraint levels could also act as a promotive force that affects SC motivation. For example, we know that gay men living with HIV in metropolitan areas report lower levels of social constraints on disclosure than do their counterparts living in less metropolitan areas.[34] Such decreased perceived social support among LGBTQ individuals is associated with increased self-concealment.[35]

Our integrative review of SC research found investigators across a wide spectrum of research areas and populations as recognizing the relevance of SC in their work.[32] Their studies report the significant role of SC in emotion regulation, disordered eating, help seeking, suicidality, perfectionism, romantic relationship health, LGBTQ issues, cultural differences, therapeutic processes and outcomes, loneliness, coping with trauma, among others in different contexts. Since our review, subsequent studies have explored SC's role in social network activity and technology addiction,[36; 37] couples coping with cancer,[38; 39] parenting styles and impaired control over drinking,[40] and obsessive-compulsive disorders,[41] to name a few.

Our review identified many potential precursors or antecedents of SC, as well as the negative consequences of SC for mental and physical health, relationships, and other significant outcomes.[32] Traumatic events, (attachment) insecurity, the tendency to feel shame, and perfectionism seem to make a person more prone to self-conceal.

We also determined the key psychological processes and outcomes associated with SC, and within the findings, found a consistent portrait of the high self-concealer. High self-concealers are much more likely to be depressed and anxious, have physical symptoms, and register lower scores on a host of measures assessing dimensions of well-being. High self-concealers tend to employ more suppression-related emotion regulation strategies and score lower regarding mindfulness and psychological flexibility. They also have less social support and more difficulty in close relationships and are more likely to keep secrets and disclose less. Negative attitudes toward counseling are consistently found. In addition, individual studies indicate a relation between SC and a wide range of other health and counseling related phenomena, including suicidal behaviors, disordered eating and bulimia, self-silencing, physiological reactivity, pain, and undesirable psychotherapy processes and outcomes.

Pathways for the Negative Health Effects of Self-Concealment

What do we know about the active mechanisms of action for the negative effects of SC? Within our working model, the pathways for the effects of SC on health include several of the factors just mentioned: a greater reliance on suppression- or inhibition-related emotion regulation processes (e.g., higher levels of suppression of emotional expression and lower levels of healthy emotion regulation strategies such as mindfulness and psychological flexibility), decreased social support and health in close relationships, reduced openness and authenticity, and less help-seeking behavior when coping with distress.

Together, these dysfunctional avoidance-based behaviors and emotion regulation strategies prevent the high self-concealer from effectively tolerating and regulating emotional distress and integrating difficult life events and changes in identity. These behaviors and processes, not secret keeping per se, appear to account for the negative effects of SC on psychological and physical well-being, because they increase distress and prevent the adaptive resolution of concealed traumas, stigmatized conditions, and other distressing experiences.

A closer look at some of these variables helps explain their role in the negative health effects of self-concealment. Key SC-related variables are widely recognized as maladaptive emotion regulation processes. For example, Aldao, Nolen-Hoeksema, and Schweizer list suppression (including expressive suppression and thought suppression), avoidance (including experiential avoidance and behavioral avoidance), and rumination as three emotion regulation strategies most consistently associated with psychopathology.[42] Suppression and rumination can also be viewed as instances within the broader construct and phenomenon of experiential avoidance.

This constellation of dysfunctional strategies and processes appears to act in unison in the service of SC motivation. Other toxic components—shame, inauthenticity, mind wandering to secrets, and undermining of basic psychological needs—seem likely to also play roles in producing SC's negative effects.[6; 43]

We think of inhibition and suppression of emotional expression as particularly toxic aspects of SC. There is direct evidence of the link between the two,[44] and studies have confirmed that emotional inhibition or suppression leads to increased sympathetic activation of the cardiovascular system,[45] more rumination, less positive affect, more depressive symptoms, [46; 47] and higher levels of inflammation,[48] a biological state associated with stress and coronary heart disease.

Inauthenticity appears to play a role in producing such effects. Gross and John make the connection between emotional suppression and feelings of inauthenticity, confirming the incongruence between inner experience and outer expression described earlier by

Rogers.[46; 49] SC is negatively related to authenticity and openness, and inauthenticity is independently shown to be a mediator of the social effects of emotion.[50] High self-concealers also indicate the belief that they would be rejected if they revealed their true selves and thus conceal their genuine thoughts and feelings.[51]

Shame also appears to play a significant role as a precursor or antecedent of SC. It is also an active component in its emotional and behavioral regulation processes. Nathanson wrote, "shame…is what keeps things hidden."[52] The basic action tendency of shame—the desire to conceal undesirable aspects of the self from social view— is closely aligned with motivations for SC behaviors, and shame is independently linked to a variety of psychological symptoms and significant immunological impairments.[53; 54] Threats to one's social self, like those encountered in moments of heightened SC, lead to specific psychological and physical responses, including shame and other negative self-evaluative states, increased cortisol and proinflammatory cytokine activity.[55]

These combined features appear to be activated and directed by the struggle between the motive to conceal and the motive to reveal, identified earlier by Jourard and later confirmed by many others. Within this dual-motive conflict, the high self-concealer struggles to manage and tolerate negative thoughts and emotions and applies suppressive and other avoidance-based strategies to avoid experiencing and expressing them. In line with the neurotic paradox dynamics discussed in Chapter 3, these dysfunctional processes are reinforced by short-term reductions in anxiety but lead to long-term chronic stress and decreased capacity to self-regulate.

SC can also affect health when the suffering person disconnects from whatever help family, friends, and caregivers might offer. Negative attitudes toward counseling lead to greater social isolation and reduced help seeking.[56] When we are distressed, other people won't necessarily offer assistance if they don't know we are suffering. In this way, self-concealment obstructs help by blocking it during the first stage: a potential helper's awareness of distress. Because no help is offered, distress increases, and psychological and physical health worsens.

Thus, we, like Wegner, can think of SC as a contributing factor to negative health effects across a spectrum of disorders and conditions, and in that sense, it is transdiagnostic. These transdiagnostic effects are likely present in the majority of clinical situations we encounter. For example, SC's associated features (rumination, thought suppression, and negative attitudes toward help seeking) could contribute significantly to emotion dysregulation in cases of complicated grief and the underutilization of mental health services among individuals suffering from this condition.[57; 58; 59] Self-concealment is also likely to play a key role in disenfranchised grief, for which concealment is often a central coping behavior.[60] Indeed, SC is relevant to nearly all clinical work, whether everyday psychotherapy or treating trauma and medical conditions, as it can undermine resilience, interfere with treatment, and increase personal distress.[61] In its most extreme forms, the perfect storm of self-dysregulation that SC generates sustains human misery, emotional isolation, unmet psychological needs, inauthenticity, and ill health, as explored in the works of countless authors, playwrights, philosophers, and more recently, psychologists.

Positive Secrets

But not all secrets and secret keeping have negative effects on our well-being. My clients have shared many positive secrets with me, such as wealth or an inheritance, a high IQ, an award, or an anonymous act of kindness. These secrets are unlikely to have adverse health effects. Secrets can also fulfill a vital protective role in our lives. They can prevent the harmful effects of confiding delicate information to the wrong person or persons, which could destroy reputations or relationships. Perhaps most important, they provide critical information to us, guiding our attention to our greatest pains and conflicts, often key areas for our personal growth and healing.

So, there are some secrets that we posess healthily and other harmful secrets that possess us. If you are preoccupied with a very painful secret and feel the need to disclose it, finding a trustworthy and compassionate confidant is the healthiest course of action. According to

more than 100 years of psychotherapy practice and extensive empirical research, we should find a confidant when we need one, and be
one when needed by others.

Villains, Victims, and Intentions
for Secret Keeping

The world of secrets and secrecy can be roughly divided into two
realms—the nonpersonal and personal. In the nonpersonal realm,
we find secrets such as those held by corporations, the military,
sports teams, politicians, and others. These secrets are usually kept
to ensure a competitive advantage, retain power, or thwart an enemy.

In the personal realm, I think there are at least two categories of
secret keepers. There are villains and victims. In the villain category
resides the abuser, thief, murderer, and psychopath. These individuals keep tightly held secrets to exercise control and power and avoid
retribution. A sort of villainous secrecy is even found at the cellular
level: cancer cells "conceal" their identity and become invisible to our
immune system.[62]

In the victim group are those who suffer abuse, trauma, illness,
transgression, and other forms of harm. Secrets are held by these persons, and is our focus in these pages. These are also kept to protect
the self, but not to exercise power or to inflict harm. Some secrets,
such as those ostensibly kept to protect someone, can occupy the
penumbra between the two categories. In these cases, it is usually
easy to identify the intention behind keeping the secret.

Investigation of the motives to keep personal secrets raises an
intriguing question: Are the secrets of psychopaths, people incapa-
ble of guilt and remorse, as injurious to their health as they are for
those who are more morally grounded? No study has yet assessed
this, but our working model and clinical observations suggest that
without the activation of shame and painful preoccupation with a
secret, negative health effects will not be present. Dictators, tyrants,
serial criminals, and other patently evil characters seem unboth-
ered by their secrets; on the contrary, they seem to relish the power
that secrets afford. Secrets of both villains and victims can serve
self-protective functions, but villains keep secrets at the expense

of others, unaffected and unimpeded by the suffering such secrets may cause.

To Tell or Not to Tell

In a series of seminal psychology experiments, Stanley Schachter found that, when people are told they will soon be subjected to frightening experimental conditions, they prefer to wait with people who are going to share a similar fate. But when other researchers later added a condition in which subjects were told they were about to perform an embarrassing task, such as sucking on rubber nipples or holding baby bottles, they found their subjects tended to avoid people in the same circumstances.[63]

A person in distress who must decide whether to reveal or conceal his or her difficulties may feel conflicting motivations. On the one hand, a voice inside cautions against doing so, asking "Will others think less of me and perhaps reject me if they know this about me?" The natural human inclination or motivation to disclose distressing thoughts and feelings propels the other side of the conflict. Mac-Ready and colleagues describe this as *ancestral plain behavior*: We let others know what is happening so they can assist us, and we are not left alone, isolated, and helpless, and confiding secrets is a key way we reach out to others.[64] William Stiles' *fever model* of disclosure articulates this same view: the amount of disclosure tends to increase with the intensity of a person's distress.[65] Here, disclosure is to psychological distress as fever is to infection; both indicate a loss of health and point to the keys for restoring it.

At the core of this distress-disclosure conflict is the desire to maintain one's esteem in the eyes of others. Our fear is that we might present people with an image of ourselves we don't want to project. Although we long to be recognized and cared for by another, self-protective urges caution us not to increase our vulnerability beyond a level we can tolerate.[66]

Ultimately, these self-esteem concerns link up with anxiety over death and survival. We fear rejection as infants, and for good reason: if our caregivers don't show us affection and attention during such a vulnerable period, we are doomed. This primordial fear continues throughout our lives, shaping the contours and vicissitudes of our attachments to others close to us, and motivating our deep need for belongingness. Paradoxically, our need to belong ultimately leads us to demonstrate the behaviors that isolate us. We conceal ourselves and the parts of ourselves we see as unlovable and thus cut ourselves off from those around us. We seek connection, but fear rejection.

The concern that others will evaluate us negatively and withdraw their support if we talk about our problems is not unfounded. A great deal of evidence confirms that distress disclosure can lead to unfavorable reactions, rejection, and the loss of social support. One kind of inhibiting response is now extensively studied as social constraints. These responses can take many forms—avoidant, critical, unhelpful—and although usually well-intentioned, they are often associated with increased psychological stress for the suffering discloser, and help explain why distress is so often concealed.

Social constraints are studied in many different clinical populations, including cancer, bereavement, HIV infection, and sexual assault.[34; 67; 68; 69] For example, when cancer patients reveal the truth of their disease, they often find friends and family members misunderstand them and explicitly or implicitly encourage them to avoid such a difficult topic, with the rationale that focusing on it is a sign of poor adjustment.[67] In another example, the majority of childhood sexual abuse survivors who disclose the abuse are often further traumatized when others blame or do not believe them.[70] Although approximately 5 percent of college women are sexually victimized each calendar year, fewer than 5 percent of these victims report their victimization either to police, campus authorities, or counseling services.[71] The victims are silenced by shame, self-blame, a fear of recrimination, and a concern about not being believed. Bereaved parents I work with often share how much they feel the need to keep their feelings about their child's death to themselves because it makes other people uncomfortable, and they perceive that others don't want to hear about it.

The general solution to this *distress disclosure dilemma*, according to Coates and Winston, is to surround ourselves with people who can continue to be supportive, while allowing us to fully reveal our troubles.[72] The decision to conceal or reveal a particular secret reflects feelings about the other person and the relationship, the degree of trust in the other's discretion, the level of intimacy and empathy that already exists between the two people, and personal proclivities concerning self-disclosure. Such assertions make intuitive sense and fit with the finding that secrets are most likely to be confided to others who are compassionate.[73] However, intriguingly, politeness in a potential confidant is associated with confiding fewer secrets to that person.[73]

These patterns begin at an early age. An interview study with preschoolers showed that children as young as three can understand the concept of secrecy and typically disclose their secrets to their "best" friend.[74] At any point in life, when a trustworthy and compassionate confidant is found, disclosure can lessen the burden of secrecy and open new possibilities in our relation to the self and the other.

The health protective functions of having a confidant following a stressful life event are well documented. For example, women who had severe life events and who lacked a confidant (defined as a person with whom the woman had a close, intimate, and confiding but not necessarily sexual relationship) were roughly ten times more likely to be depressed than women having such a relationship. Women reporting the lack of an intimate confidant had more psychological symptoms than those who did report such a relationship.[75]

The Burden of Painful Secrets

What is your biggest, most difficult, or painful secret? I once asked this question of more than 300 human services workers and graduate counseling students participating in a questionnaire survey.[7] I also challenged this mostly female group to describe what keeping this secret was like for them. Because of the highly intimate nature of the questions asked, extreme care was taken to protect the respondents' confidentiality. All of the subjects were instructed not to indicate their names anywhere on the questionnaire. The depth of the disclosures was remarkable, and responding to the survey seemed to act as an expressive writing intervention for them, allowing many of them to share what they had never shared before. I was stunned to learn that 20% of my subjects had not confided their biggest personal secrets to a single other human being. Some of the heart-rending disclosures of the people whose biggest secrets had never been shared were as follows:

A secret kept for 15 years, not confided to anyone, including her husband:

> I had sex with my younger brother when I was 17. I was drunk. I have never talked about it since, nor have I talked to him about it. It's terrible. This is the first time I have been able to even come close to talking about it. It has tormented me for years. There is so much guilt. I can't begin to describe it.

A 67-year-old married man struggles with a sense of not realizing his purpose in life:

> I have this very strong feeling (always present, in retrospect) that I am not fulfilling my purpose in life, that when the record is written, I will not have been all that I could and should have been. Causes me to be dissatisfied with myself, regardless of what others might consider my contribution to life to be.

This middle-aged married woman would like to share this secret with her husband, but fears judgment:

> A homosexual experience when I was 26 or so. It lasted for 6 months or so and was a very rewarding relationship which filled needs I had at that time. I then moved back to heterosexual relationships and remarried. At the time the relationship was going on, I was very concerned that coworkers and friends would find out. A lot of guilt feelings since my family would have had a very difficult time understanding the relationship. Now that it is long past, it's no problem, except that I sometimes would like to share it with my spouse, but know he'd never understand.

Sharing her secret of 20 years for the first time, this woman hopes that she can relieve her burden by doing so:

I have something to share, for which I require no response from you, except for you to listen. Maybe by your listening and my telling it, it will help me get rid of the guilt I carry. When I was 21 or 22, I allowed my father to fondle and caress me. I didn't let him have sexual intercourse; I feel that God stopped it before that. I don't think of it much. I've buried it. It just reminds me of the humanness we all share (weak spots in our personalities).

Marital disappointment brings continuing pain for this 68-year-old man:

Failure of marriage. I feel rejected, denigrated, demeaned. I feel that it must be my fault, but can't put together the whys. It is a loss that fades slowly but will never go away entirely. It imposes a feeling of sadness. I can compensate for it by making others feel happy. My job and clientele make this possible. I have lost any confidence that I might have any future meaningful relationship with another, and so I don't try. I don't want to. I feel lonely and try to assuage the feeling by working and reading.

A mother fears that her emotional distance from her son has permanently harmed him:

Concern that I was an inadequate parent to one of my children because I seem to have few feelings about that child. I don't like to have him around me. Scary, mostly in terms of the damage I might have caused to his emotional health.

Another respondent in the same survey happened to write a corresponding childhood secret:

Have never been sure that my parents loved me. At times, I feel my father has cared for me. I never will know about my mother, as she died 21 years ago. Can't remember ever hearing her say, "I love you" to me. Feel like a baby to be 40 years old and so insecure about this.

The respondents' explanations for why they had not disclosed these secrets included regarding them as too personal or embarrassing, fearing others' reactions, and being afraid of hurting or burdening others.

Secrets at the End of Life

When secrets like these are shared with us helpers, either in everyday counseling or in end-of-life care, it is a profound and sacred moment. However, deathbed disclosures, in particular, can sometimes leave us in an awkward and even untenable situation. For example, a disclosure shortly before death, such as, "Our son is not my husband's. Please tell our son. He needs to know for medical reasons," would probably lead us to swiftly seek advice from a supervisor or an ethics committee regarding the best course of action. After death, postmortem discoveries—affairs, cyber relationships, disinheritance, parentage, substance use, and other disturbing secrets—can also complicate care and lead to major issues for surviving loved ones, who are left to ask, "Who was this person?" It becomes difficult to construct a meaningful narrative for a loved one and a relationship that, in hindsight, seems cruelly counterfeit.

Many deathbed disclosures reflect regret and a need for forgiveness. In an international survey, Betty Ferrell and colleagues gathered narrative descriptions of bedside disclosures made to nurses by their patients.[76] Clinical practice has shown that end-of-life conversations often include "unfinished business" related to the theme of forgiveness—either a need to forgive, or to be forgiven.[77] Disclosures related to forgiveness reported in the survey often reflected a transgression or conflict, most often between a parent and child, but also between spouses, between oneself and God, or with extended family or siblings. Many of the disclosures could be described as confessions, and these included homicide, failures as a parent, and military experiences.

Nurses' responses to the disclosures were also documented, capturing the often-intense emotion evoked in them and the challenges they confronted while responding to forgiveness issues. Instances of healing, reconciliation, and peaceful deaths were also described, many highlighting the importance of the spiritual component in palliative care. This study of forgiveness provides a unique in-depth view of secrets shared at the end of life: the burdens and suffering they reflect, the challenges they present for end-of-life caregivers, and the opportunity for healing they afford, which one nurse described as "miraculous."

In end-of-life care, when faced with life-threatening illness and loss, family members sometimes make a bad situation worse by adding the burden of secrecy. Usually well-intentioned, they seek to prevent suffering, but their actions often increase it. I worked with a Chinese American family in which the patriarchal grandfather prohibited the family from telling his enfeebled 94-year-old wife that her daughter had died. Younger members of the family refused to attend the family's Chinese New Year party—a very serious statement in their culture—because they were not allowed to acknowledge her death. In their words, "To deny her death was to deny her."

One common source of moral distress for end-of-life workers occurs when family members insist on keeping diagnoses and prognoses from their ill loved ones and actively conceal medical information from them. A nurse once described the following scene: She and the rest of the medical team were at the door of a patient's room. Inside the room, the patient looked up from bed and said, "What's this?," pointing to the large tumor protruding from his abdomen. At this moment, the patient's wife stood behind him, waving her arms, indicating to the medical team that she did not wish her husband to know about the tumor. In such moments, there's a proverbial elephant in the room, but no one feels comfortable directly addressing it. These family dynamics can interfere with end-of-life conversations essential for better care and outcomes.

Many other factors contribute to the frequent concealment of diagnostic or prognostic information from cancer patients; for example, the avoidance of the emotional reactions that truth-telling can precipitate. Panagopoulou and colleagues tested whether concealing bad news by health providers is less stressful for them than disclosing it.[78] They created laboratory conditions simulating disclosure or concealment of information to a 26-year-old woman with an inoperable brain tumor. In multiple contexts, medical students in the concealment group were less stressed than those in the truth-telling group. The authors conclude that people likely conceal bad news because of the reduction of short-term anxiety provided by concealment, and they recommend stress management as an integral part of clinical skills training to address this dynamic. In this case, the secret does not include distressing personal information for the physician. However, if the act of withholding care-relevant information from patients becomes a source of internal conflict for the physician or for other professionals on the health care team, and this reaction becomes a stress-enhancing secret, the act of concealing diagnoses and prognoses from patients could add to their long-term stress.

When clinicians are thrust into family conflicts concerning whether or not to acknowledge the reality of advancing illness, determining what to say or do is a difficult task, but sometimes we are certain we have done the right thing:

> A dying patient's wife said, "Don't talk to him about dying. He's a private person, doesn't talk much and doesn't want to talk about death." I went into the room without the wife, and he seemed so in need of talking, I asked, "What would you like to share in the time you have left?" He held my hand and poured out his heart for 2 hours and talked of fears of dying.

Sometimes secrets—large and small—naturally emerge simply because we are there to hear them:

> One patient opened up and told his family through me about a whole lifetime of experiences which he had never shared before and wanted his family to know. I had wondered when I first saw him how I could possibly help him. He was followed for months by other nurses, and there had been no changes and no real problems to solve. Shortly after he shared his secret stories he died, his work done. I felt overwhelmed with gratitude that I could be the helper for this final work of his.

A social worker related a similar story. An elderly dying woman was visibly agitated, and he stopped to talk with her. After several minutes of solid attention, she began to tell him a secret from her childhood. She had stolen her parents' silver setting and had never told them. This secret had haunted her throughout her life. My friend stayed with her for a bit longer. She seemed much relieved, having shared her burden. Late that night, she appeared at the nurses' station and handed the nurse her Bible and false teeth, and said, "I won't need these anymore." She went back to her room and died in her sleep.

In this deathbed scene, a daughter's puzzling ambivalence toward her dying mother is explained through her lifelong secret:

> We cared for a 65-year-old mother who was dying. A very pleasant, jovial daughter who was caring for her seemed so unsure of what she wanted to do for her mom. Her feelings swung from one day wanting to do a great job (which never quite happened), to the next day seeming disinterested. It was easy to wonder what kind of daughter she was. In the last few hours of her mom's life, she disclosed that she had been sexually abused as a child by her mom's boyfriends, and her mother had just looked the other way. I wondered how often I had come to conclusions about people and situations. I realized how little we know about some of the people we care for, and I felt guilty because I sometimes judge them even when I try not to.

In the next vignette a social worker in the Midwest describes her conversations with a dying man as he disclosed a lifelong secret to her. We see how her caring and patient presence allowed him to release a long-held and anguishing secret, bringing them to tears:

> This was the beginning for me as a social worker. I had just started working at a nursing home. I had not worked with this population before. I had a new patient, an older gentleman. He was very weak, dying of cancer. I was told to see him, went in and sat down, introduced myself, and told him a little bit about what I do. During this entire time he just stared at me. He was weak, not to the point of being emaciated, but very close. His eyes were burning alive and it scared me, very much

so, because I didn't know if it was something I had done. I just didn't know. And then he looked at me and asked, "Are you Korean?" My jaw dropped, and I said "Yes, I am Korean. I said "Is there a concern?" He answered, "I was in the Korean War." "Well, would you like to speak to somebody else?" I asked. Looking straight at me, he said, "No." So I continued with the rigmarole of, "What's your name? What's your past? What are some of your concerns?," and he continued to stare at me and didn't answer. He was not interested in this conversation, and then, out of nowhere, he said, "It was a waste." I stopped and asked if it was what we were talking about that was a waste, and he said "No, the war was a waste." I realized I needed to stop right then, and allow this gentleman to talk, and said, "Go on." He continued, "It was a waste. I let my men get killed. They died. There was so much death on both sides, and it was pointless." There were tears coming down his face. "It was a waste; too many people died. I don't know why I'm here." I moved closer and took his hand, and he squeezed mine. He kept repeating, "It was a waste." I let him talk, I let him cry, I let him squeeze my hand until it was sore. He started to sleep, and I left. In the days that followed, I would always stop by and just say, "Hi, how are you doing?," and he would smile. When I was told that he had died, I went to his bed. I was upset because he had died that morning and no one had told me. I went to his room and his son and other family members were there. They were silent. I was crying, but they had blank looks on their faces. I went to him and I leaned over and kissed him on the forehead, and said goodbye. I was crying when I left. Later, I spoke with the son when the patient was being taken to the funeral home. I said, "He was a special man. We had some special talks. He told me about being in the Korean War." And the son, startled, looked at me, saying "What? My father was in a war?" Startled myself, I responded, "Yes, you didn't know that?" "No, he never told me that," he said, and went on: "Our father lived with my family for 2 years before he came into the nursing home. He never mentioned the war while he was with us, or when I was growing up." I went home and thought, there are secrets. There are episodes in our past that are so emotional and damaging that all we can do is just shove them down, shove them down so we can function. But, at the end, it can't be shoved down anymore—it has to be released.[79]

This poignant story reminds us that a caring presence can facilitate release of a burdensome secret, and a life can find closure. Furthermore, it motivates us to extend the utmost compassion to our military veterans who carry the burden of their war-time traumas when they return from battlefields around the world.

HELPER SECRETS

The demanding and emotionally complicated nature of our work can trigger self-doubt and arouse strong emotions that may be embarrassing. All of us probably harbor some troubling thoughts and feelings related to our work that are difficult to share with others. However, professional self-doubt is not in itself bad. Effective psychotherapists are often reflective about their professional practice and question their ability to help patients.[80] However, a problem develops when these self-doubts are not kept in perspective and develop into what I call troubling helper secrets.[81; 82]

Helper secrets are invisible, internal stressors that can intensify the personal distress associated with burnout, vicarious traumatization, and moral distress. They are fueled by our fears of accepting and disclosing our limitations, vulnerabilities, ignorance, anger, and ethical quandaries. We expect ourselves to be knowledgeable, strong, successful, and in control, and when those attributes appear to be absent, it is easy for us to believe we are at fault and hide the problem from others. The fallacy of uniqueness we discussed earlier comes into play, and we assume that everyone else is coping effectively and that we alone are failing. However, in reality, these secrets have a universal quality—the specifics change, but the larger themes they reflect are repeated over and over, within and across helping organizations. As Rogers observed, "How does it happen that the deeper we go into ourselves as particular and unique, seeking for our own individual identity, the more we find the whole human species?"[83] My research on helper secrets confirms this view, as certain themes and issues appear repeatedly in the disclosures I have gathered.

As you encounter the helper secrets that follow, keep in mind that these are, in fact, secrets—they include uncomfortable and embarrassing personal information. Only some serious soul searching, and the assurance of anonymity, permit their disclosure. So, approach these self-revelations with compassion and respect, and let them resonate within to see if they touch you in any way.

I've Distanced Myself From Patients and Families

In a study of helper secrets I conducted involving nearly 500 nurses, more than 1 out of 5 responses contained descriptions of participants wanting to, or having actually emotionally or physically distanced themselves from patients, patients' families, staff, or their own family members.[82] This distancing took many forms: "becoming emotionally distant," "ignoring patients' needs," "avoiding visiting the difficult patient," "holding a part of myself back," and "feeling cold and unsympathetic," are just a few examples. This theme is also pervasive in the helper secrets of other helper populations as well.

Can you think of a way in which you have emotionally or physically distanced yourself as a caregiver? How did this make you feel about yourself? Chapter 3 offered a close look at how avoidance leads to lowered self-esteem and gave some examples of avoidance in caregiving. These acts might be placed at the low-involvement end of the continuum of emotional involvement.

The difficulty for the helper in attempting to achieve emotional or physical distance is that these efforts actually raise, rather than lower, stress levels because they lead to feelings of self-doubt, guilt, shame, and personal and professional inadequacy. They increase distress and in doing so make this an untenable long-term stance. This stress-avoidance-guilt sequence is reflected in the following disclosures:

✧ I have "distanced" myself deliberately from some patients and families as a form of self-protection when I've felt emotionally overloaded, even though I felt they needed emotional support themselves.

✧ I had called the caregiver at 9:30 A.M. The patient was within minutes of dying, and I could hear her whining and shrieking agonizingly with each breath in the background. She was 39 years old and there was nothing peaceful about her disease or dying. I was asked to come right over. I was reeling from the horror of the scene, and took 15 minutes extra to get there so I wouldn't have to confront her death. When I arrived she had died 5 minutes earlier. I was relieved.

✧ I feel guilty that my caregiving has become more emotionally distant. Seems I'm protecting myself. I don't want to give so much of my energy to others' lives or my work.

✧ I feel cold and unsympathetic when a coworker tells me the same old problem.

✧ I often say I'll be right back when I have no intention of coming back.

✧ I have always tended to avoid saying good-bye to my patients. I sometimes make myself do it, but am glad if they slip into a coma before I make the time to tell them how I feel about them.

I Feel Inadequate

Concern about one's competence and effectiveness is another frequently occurring theme in helper secrets:

✧ My inadequacy is my most personal secret, and it is very frustrating to be constantly in the company of so many talented, capable people.

✧ I often feel inadequate to say those wise and empathetic things that can be so comforting. I wish I could say those special words/phrases that are "just right."

✧ I'm always scared I won't have the technical skills to handle the patient's needs. This makes me feel like an incompetent, bad nurse. Everyone sees me as capable, but I am afraid. I seem to do OK when faced with new situations, but I panic inside. I'm afraid of being seen as incompetent by patients. That's where it hurts most.

The prevalence of this type of helper secret is not surprising. Feelings of inadequacy and incompetence are frequent themes in the secrets of nonhelper populations as well.[84] These kinds of concerns and self-doubts seem to be invisible stressors affecting all helper populations. In one study, for example, psychotherapists reported that doubts about the efficacy of their helping were their number one stressor.[85] Also, feelings of inadequacy and strong self-doubt are understandable, given the relentless demands of ever-changing technologies, treatments, and psychosocial complexities of modern health care.

I'm an Impostor

Feelings of inadequacy and self-doubt can often take the form of feeling like an impostor, as someone who is posing as a competent caregiver but who lacks the expertise to do the job. There is a strong fear of being exposed as a fake and a fraud:

✧ I am a fraud. People think I am an expert, but sometimes I don't know, and I should.

✧ Deep down inside I feel that I am fooling everyone. I'm not as bright or competent as people think I am. What if I fail? What should I do?

✧ I work in spiritual care on a palliative care ward. People think, assume, I believe in God and an afterlife. I'm at the point I don't really believe in God or the afterlife. I feel a fraud.

✧ I feel that I'm a fake. Someone else would be more effective. I frequently feel like I'm flying by the seat of my pants.

✧ I feel like I am an impostor. At work everyone looks up to me for the "latest" or "how to do it best" information. So far,

I have been able to wing it or come up with an acceptable answer, but I live with the fear of making a big mistake in front of everyone.

✧ I am uncomfortable. I've been put in charge of developing a hospice program. I don't think I know enough about it. I feel like a fake trying to pull off a bubble about to burst. On top of that, if the bubble did burst, and I was exposed as a fake, I would deserve to be ridiculed, laughed at, scorned, fired, burned at the stake.

✧ I'm afraid that if anyone found how much I don't know, they'd head for the door.

I'm Angry!

Unspoken anger, frustration, and impatience—with patients, family members, coworkers, and administration—is also a frequently occurring theme:

✧ There are times when I'd like to shake some of the people I work with until they scream and cry. I hate detachment as a coping mechanism. I can't reach them, and I don't feel like they can hear me. So how on earth can we deal deeply with patients, family, and each other?

✧ There are times when I feel like screaming or kicking or hitting something, like I'm about to lose control. But I usually just make tight fists, breathe, and then return to the situation, looking and hopefully acting calm, in control, and like a nurse.

✧ A couple of weeks ago, I was feeling burned out and I had a newborn who wouldn't eat, and when I gavaged (tube-fed) him, he spit all the formula back up. I gritted my teeth and became so angry at the baby it scared me, because I felt like I could have hit him for not eating. I waited 15 minutes and then tried to feed him again, feeling much better, but I felt guilty for a long time.

✧ Sometimes I feel like I'd like to tell a few arrogant doctors to stop feeding their egos through their ill patients, and that their patients aren't the only sick patients in the hospital.

✧ I hated the husband of a patient because he wanted her to die and did not want to care for her or be with her. I couldn't be totally effective because of my antipathy. He was selfish, and I didn't help him through the crisis as I should have.

This disclosure reminds me of conflicts I had while working with a family. The patient was a 50-year-old woman with metastatic breast cancer. As she became more seriously ill, I met with her and her husband. She didn't want to be told how long she might live. Although she was aware that her condition was terminal, and agreed to be admitted to hospice care, she preferred not to have a "death sentence" hanging over her, and she expressed this desire clearly to me and to her husband. Her husband separately met with the hospice physician and insisted on being given an estimate of how long his wife would probably live, which was less than 2 months.

After extracting the prognosis from the reluctant physician, he immediately delivered the information to his wife, something akin to passing her an emotional hand grenade. Later, at their home, with me present in the room, he pointed to a drawer in a dresser, and told his wife that if he were her in her situation, he knew what he would do. He opened the drawer, and it had his loaded handgun in it. The husband also refused to comply with his wife's request that her deathbed be moved to the room looking out on the flower garden she so dearly loved, saying it would "obstruct traffic flow" in the home.

Knowing the agony her husband was causing this wonderful woman, I hated him, and I often thought that if the world had an ounce of fairness in it he would be in that deathbed, not her. I somehow persevered and helped with my patient's dying, but I could not bring myself to have any further contact with her husband after her death. I didn't help him with his grief and felt guilty about it for a long time.

What About Me?

One-way giving is built into caregiving. Of course, there are moments of reciprocity—a deeply felt thank-you, an award, unsolicited caring from a coworker—but these events do not change the fundamental reality that in caregiving, the focus is on your patients or clients, and there is no guarantee that you will receive anything more in return for your services than a paycheck (if not a volunteer), the intrinsic satisfaction of helping others, or both.

A small but significant group of helper secrets contain direct expressions of a desire to receive—as well as to give—caring and appreciation. There is often an inner voice that is asking, "What about me?" and sometimes critical feelings toward oneself for not being assertive enough in getting one's own needs met.

◇ Sometimes I wish I weren't a nurse because I don't want to give anymore, and don't want to have to keep constantly learning. I resent it. I want to be taken care of—me.

◇ Sometimes I get angry and disgusted with myself for being afraid to discuss my feelings or communicate intimately and effectively about things in my life that bother me. I always give in and never insist on being heard and cared about. I never think my feelings are as important as those of other people.

◇ There are times when I want to stop all that I am doing and say, "Hey, what about me." I want and need someone to listen to me, to my needs. It feels like I am giving, and it is not coming back. I feel guilty about this. I'm not selfish, am I?

◇ I sometimes get to the point where I can't pick up a baby and hold him/her because I can't "give" any more. I'm the one that needs to be held and rocked!

This next rather ominous secret reveals a desperate need for more nurturance and self-care:

Sometimes I wish that I would come down with a semi-serious illness so that I could be taken care of for a while.

I'm Overwhelmed

Another theme, one closely related to that of one-way giving, focuses on difficult feelings associated with emotional and physical demands at work and at home:

✧ I resent being the everlasting, strong cheerleader and eternal caregiver, and having the staff think that when I call for help, verbally or through body language (drooping posture, face), I'm doing it to be one of the gang. Short version: I feel misunderstood. I'm human, too!

✧ Too many demands are killing me.

✧ I had a patient who I felt was very selfish and demanding, and the family also seemed very selfish and demanding, and I gave in to their demands when it didn't seem necessary. But I had demands in my life that didn't get taken care of, so some important things in my life fell apart (I lost a lover), and I'm still mad at myself and them.

✧ Trying to be supermom, supernurse, and superwife sometimes burdens me so. When I fail in one area, there is a domino effect. I hate to fail.

These self-disclosures reveal that even the most common stressors encountered by helpers, such as being overburdened by multiple roles at work and at home, have the potential to create a sense of inner turmoil that is then concealed. Most helpers would probably feel relatively comfortable confiding in someone about the excessive demands they face, but they still might hide some of the deeper feelings related to those demands, and those feelings of demoralization can foster burnout.

I Hope Death Comes Soon

Life isn't tidy, as Herman Feifel once observed, and death doesn't come at exactly the right moment. Caregivers working with the terminally ill often confront situations in which their deep caring and compassion lead them to wish for the death of a patient. Patients who are suffering greatly, and who ask for assistance with their dying, can trigger many difficult feelings in caregivers. A common secret of caregivers working with the terminally ill is the unspoken wish that a patient would die to end that patient's agonizing suffering:

✧ Sometimes I pray that God takes this patient because he's suffering so much. I hope he dies soon. I feel guilty.

✧ I wish I could pull the plug on someone I know will have a poor quality of life.

✧ He was in constant pain, unable to move, unable to control bodily functions. I straightened his bed and I held the pillow. I wanted to cover his face. I didn't. He died four painful days later.

By controlling symptoms and reducing suffering for dying patients, quality hospice and palliative care can certainly reduce the frequency of these morally-distressing situations. However, vast numbers of patients are dying without hospice and palliative care, and are dying poorly—with pain, dyspnea, lengthy stays in intensive care units, and futile aggressive treatments—so these moral problems will continue to distress nurses and other health providers.[86]

I Acted Inappropriately

Self-perceived unethical behaviors or mishandled clinical situations can generate great shame and distress:

✧ Some 25 years ago, when I was in training as a counselor, I worked with a female client who had lots of separation anxiety and abandonment issues. I found myself touching her (reassurance), and in another session holding her in my lap and rocking her. Later I saw the inappropriateness, and had a hard time correcting my therapy with her.

✧ Gave "sexual" comfort to a patient at the patient's direction. Done by patient placing my hands in or upon erogenous areas.

✧ I had a difficult patient who became angry at my attempts to help her. She spit in my face. Without thinking I spit back in her face. I could have died with shame. I was there to make this more comfortable for her, and I failed miserably. I don't think anyone else would have reacted so impulsively.

✧ As his mental health worker, I didn't have a clue this person was going to hang himself. I had put a lot of his behaviors down to "attention seeking." How wrong could I be? And I didn't like him.

Every veteran helper has, at some time, "said the wrong thing." This social worker lives with guilt from one of those moments:

> Many years ago, I worked as a social worker in ICU. I had worked for many hours with a family whose son had attempted suicide. I was mortally embarrassed, when leaving, I told the dad to "hang in there." It was totally inappropriate, as the boy had tried to hang himself.

Secret keeping heightens the burden of committing what are unambiguous medical errors. Medical errors are underreported and disclosed in fewer than one in three cases, with descriptions of what happened provided in only about half of such disclosures.[87; 88] Patients suffer in these situations, and so do the health providers who are severely limited in whom they feel safe turning to for help.[89]

Psychotherapists report a wide range of things that they find themselves reluctant to talk about, including fears that clients may commit suicide, being angry with clients, or being sexually attracted to them.[90] Therapists in training have anonymously shared a wide range of doubts and fears that they keep tightly locked away, like these:

✧ I work in a setting with many very angry individuals. Sometimes their anger paralyzes me. I am "supposed" to allow them to express the anger, but secretly hope they don't. I have one client that is so hard core that I have no idea what to do, where to go with him. I get so frustrated when I can't get through.

✧ I'm afraid that I don't or won't have enough patience to work with someone who is severely depressed. I worry that this is because I have a big depression of my own which I am avoiding dealing with myself.

The Helper Secrets Exercise

Avoidance, unrealistic expectations of self, weakened self-compassion, shame, and the fallacy of uniqueness all contribute to the genesis and maintenance of helper secrets. Perhaps the best way to counter these influences and restore resilience and emotional balance is to disclose those troubling thoughts and feelings to a trustworthy confidant.

Before I explain why this is helpful and how best to do it, let me emphatically state what not to do with your helper secrets, and with all other significant personal secrets as well: Do not indiscriminately share them. Nothing could be more hurtful to yourself. Research and our informed intuition suggest that the choice of confidants and the context for this self-disclosure are critical considerations. You need to find a trustworthy and compassionate confidant who is able to respond openly and nondefensively to your inner world. Friends, family, and other members of your social support network can often hear and respond well to these disclosures, which serve as markers of relational immediacy in our personal relationships. However, I believe helper secrets are best shared with a colleague who does the same work and who can have instant empathy with these difficult feelings. They are also less likely to feel burdened by sharing in them with you.

Revealing disquieting inner thoughts and feelings is not something you want to leave to chance and to the conversational patterns of everyday life, where interruptions, quick advice, veiled judgments, and other unhelpful responses are common. When I have conducted workshops or retreats, I have found that the following highly structured exercise can be an excellent vehicle for caregivers to disclose their helper secrets and get a caring, helpful response from others. In the exercise I ask participants to write their helper secrets on identical index cards or sheets of paper and to exclude any personally identifying information in their secret descriptions. The secrets are then gathered and randomly redistributed in the group. If someone gets his or her own secret, that's fine, because others in the group won't know this. Of course, if members of the group know one another's handwriting, extra precautions, like having a person outside the group type or transcribe the secrets, should be taken to preserve anonymity.

The secrets are then read aloud, and I ask the other participants to share thoughts, feelings, or actions similar to those expressed in the secret being read; in other words, to make "me-too" self-disclosures. These disclosures are directed toward the person who is reading the secret, and that person simply listens to the responses of others as a surrogate receiver for the actual secret holder. Here is a sample of the dialogue that can occur in these sessions. One helper shared:

> There was a young mother of three I cared for who was dying from ovarian cancer. We were giving her a big dose of IV morphine every 1 to 2 hours. After one of the doses I gave her, she quickly stopped breathing. One family member asked me if I killed her with that last dose.

After a minute or so another group member disclosed this:

> I was close to a family and followed the patient for 3 years. It was a baby, from birth. I gave him his last dose of morphine, and that's exactly what the mother said to me: "You've killed my baby." But to this day she still has contact with me and calls me. But it's still... it's right here (tears in her eyes as she touches her heart).

In dozens of instances leading this exercise, I have found that one or more listening group members can almost always find some part of the message conveyed in the secret that they can identify with and self-disclose in response to. Sometimes, the entire room is filled with nodding heads, but everyone is a bit reluctant to respond verbally because the secret shared is reminiscent of the participants' own carefully guarded secrets. Other times, nearly everyone makes an empathic self-disclosure. For the deeper revelations, it might take a while—certainly more than a minute—until someone does enough inner searching (I term it *inner googling*) to get in touch with a similar experience, so there is a need to give more time.

A tremendous sense of relief usually fills the room after we respond to all of the secrets. It comes from knowing that one is not alone in having these thoughts and feelings. Many people have said that what had been a well-kept secret became something that they could now freely discuss with others. Even though their secrets remain anonymous, they feel that a formerly secret part of themselves is now known to others (i.e., Quadrant II of the Johari Window has gotten smaller), and the responses they have received make them feel differently about these formerly secret parts: the burden is lifted. I believe that this profound change in stance toward one's inner world is a key element in helping and psychological healing.

You don't need to participate in a helper secrets exercise to have this shift. You might not even need to communicate these secrets to anyone else. The extensive research on expressive writing suggests that the simple act of writing about our secrets can have a positive effect on our stress levels. This is one reason I encourage caregivers to keep a diary chronicling their helping journeys.

What you can't fully achieve through writing, though, is that sense of "being in the same boat" with other helpers, the deeper knowing that others have some of the same difficulties with the stressful situations you encounter. You might know this at a cognitive level—for example, as a result of reading this book—but real knowledge at a deeper level can only occur when you actually hear and respond internally to the disclosures of others like yourself.

The best general antidote to helper secrets is to talk about our stress and to learn to see it as a common part of our work. When these difficult feelings are shared and worked through, they can be normalized, the natural bias toward self-blame can be corrected, and your energies can be directed toward developing better coping and problem-solving skills and strategies.

In your work, you naturally value and promote honesty, openness, and revelation; your courage and skill, applied in a timely and strategic manner, allow distressing thoughts and feelings to be safely confronted and the burdens of patients and families to be lifted. Yet in this role of midwife to open communication, you may sometimes forget that your longevity as a helper also requires maintaining an open and friendly stance toward yourself and the inevitable difficulties you have as a caregiver.

Helper secrets alert us to our inner crises as helpers. The Chinese pictograph for crisis is composed of two characters, one signifying danger, the other opportunity. Helper secrets have a similar twofold nature. Though frequently highly painful, they contain information vital to your survival as a helper and require your attention. When they are concealed, helper secrets can corrode you from within; when revealed to empathic others, they can strengthen your support and enhance your personal and professional growth.

Lifting the Burden

A central role we play as helpers is that of confidant. In my clinical encounters, as mentioned earlier, when a "big secret" is shared, often for the first time, a period of anxiety immediately follows. Clients often feel as if the "cat is out of the bag," as the saying goes, and they imagine that all the evaluations they have feared—often for years—will now rain down on them. Gradually, usually a few weeks after this anxious feeling has been exposed, clients begin to be freed from the inner judgments that the secret-keeping (and its echo chamber effect) has kept from new and healing information. It's like oxygen getting to a wound: there is a newfound sense of self, a more complete and authentic self in which the lid on self-esteem and self-acceptance is lifted. This shift is so profound that our psychological instruments barely begin to reflect and measure it—it's a discontinuous, quantum leap change.

Based on my research, my clinical work, and my personal life, I have concluded that we all need to have at least one—there can be more—significant other in whom we can confide all our troubling thoughts and feelings. If we don't, our self-concealing behavior will tend to influence our attitudes toward ourselves, leading to a conclusion that there is some part of ourselves that is in fact unlovable, or else we would reveal it. The only way out of this vicious cycle and echo chamber is through disclosure to a caring and empathic confidant.

Most counselors have witnessed how a client's disclosure of troubling personal information can often be a turning point in therapy, a moment demarcating a shift from shame to self-acceptance, authenticity, confidence, and pride. A study by Barry Farber and colleagues found exactly this pattern. They studied clients' emotions immediately after revealing something difficult to disclose to their therapists. Clients reported feeling more relieved, vulnerable, authentic, safe, and proud than ashamed following their disclosures.[91]

Most of us know that disclosure begets disclosure, and that sharing our secrets with others can deepen our relationships. One survey participant wrote:

> I told my best girlfriend that I had an abortion. Though she personally would never abort a pregnancy, she knew how devastatingly painful this was for me. She gave me total support. That was 7 years ago. We've gone through the deaths of both of our husbands since then. Our relationship has grown only stronger as the years have passed.

In one of my unpublished surveys of the effects of disclosing secrets, a positive effect on the relationship was described by more than 90% of respondents. They used phrases such as "our trust became stronger," "it brought us even closer," "it strengthened our relationship," "the best conversation I'd ever had with her," and "she knew my pain and still believed in me." One person wrote, "I remember being amazed that she could know the worst thing about me and still want to have me for a friend." Of course, you need the right confidant at the right time, but the search is worth it if a secret is troubling you.

In *The Great Turning*, Schindler and Lapid point out that the single-celled organism differentiates between "me" and "not me," and adjusts the flow of information across its boundaries accordingly:

> A primitive single-celled organism can be observed to move toward that which nourishes it and away from noxious stimuli that threaten it. In a nourishing environment, the organism becomes more porous and the flow across its cellular membrane is enhanced. In toxic or less supportive environments, the organism reduces its porosity and the flow across the cell

wall is diminished. The single-celled entity therefore spends a great deal of its life moving toward "friendly" environments and away from "unfriendly" ones.[92]

Creating friendly environments that facilitate a caring sense of connection and encourage the free flow and exchange of information crucial to the health of all living systems is a ubiquitous challenge in our work.

One unforgettable event on my own helping journey taught me a great deal about the healing connections that can rapidly develop when a friendly and safe environment is offered to people who are suffering and struggling with the distress-disclosure dilemma. Let me describe this situation as if we are there: We are at a rustic retreat site in California. Sunlight is streaming through tall cathedral-like windows, warming the chilly meeting room. I look out at the expectant faces of the retreat participants. The diversity of the group is striking. The many dozens of cancer patients and family members attending this weekend program span different ages, races, and nationalities. But, as we will soon discover, the differences among group members will be dwarfed by their common concern with cancer.

It is the first morning of our retreat. We have just completed some ice breaker exercises that helped us introduce ourselves. Now red, apple-shaped pieces of paper are distributed, and I am asking participants to write their secret fears on one side, and their secret hopes on the other side. Quiet fills the room. I begin to worry about what will happen. Perhaps this is too threatening for the group. Only hours earlier these people were complete strangers, and now I'm asking them to disclose some of their deepest feelings. When everyone finishes writing, the papers are exchanged randomly several times to ensure anonymity, and we slowly begin reading our fears:

✧ Being totally dependent on others.

✧ That I will not be there when needed most.

✧ I'll die a painful death.

✧ Giving up.

✧ Having to say good-bye.

✧ My dad dying.

✧ That I might get cancer when I grow up.

✧ The loss of my closest, most understanding friend and supporter.

✧ That I will die without coming to peace with my life.

Many participants are trembling as they read the secret fears. Others begin to cry. Tears fill my eyes, and my coleader has a look of awe. At the same time, a fear is touching one person, then someone else. A wave of compassion is also spreading through the room. Strangers are holding hands, offering solace and care. To an outside observer, it might seem that we have jumped into the Helper's Pit together. But for us, it feels more like we are scaling the walls of the pit together, reaching out to hold on to one another as we climb.

After a pause, they turn the papers over and begin to read their hopes:

✧ That I will be able to see my grandchildren.

✧ To be able to keep laughing at this.

✧ My brother gets well soon, and we can be a family together again.

✧ That my wife is successful in combating and overcoming her cancer. That she and I will remain together until the end of our lives.

✧ That I can give the emotional support that is needed throughout this ordeal.

✧ That I beat this.

✧ Communication, openness, forgiveness, patience, and that there is hope.

✧ That my mom will not suffer.

✧ I hope for courage, and lots of it.

The change in mood in the room was palpable. The connection between us—that almost sacred sense of we-ness—was something I will always remember. When things get tough, it is a real source of strength for me.

An extraordinary level of trust and openness prevailed during the remainder of the weekend. A group of strangers had become intimate and supportive friends, and many of these relationships continued long after the retreat.

Conclusion

It is often forgotten that in the Greek myth of Pandora's Box, after the Furies escape, one entity remains: Hope. Perhaps the key to our success was that we kept the lid open long enough for Hope to emerge. We might have closed the lid too soon, or never opened it, or tried to beckon Hope without her terrifying companions. The lesson here, one which applies to our secrets and those of our patients and families, and which is a major focus in the remaining chapters of this book, is that hope can emerge triumphant, replacing denial, avoidance, and fear, when it is sustained by empathy, caring, and support.

PART TWO

The Interpersonal Challenge

5

The question now is what have you known about being human that you can translate into usefulness to other people, to those you intend to help? How can you "relate"—which is to say, so act in the helping interchange—that the person you assist may experience some sense of being cared about by another human being and of being allied with him? He will not be asking you for a relationship. He is likely to be asking you for some plain, ordinary, necessary, life-sustaining thing like money, like medicine, like advice, like action in his behalf. But what he gets from you, whether in material or psychological form, will be "twice blessed" when it is conveyed in such a way as to affirm his personal worth and his social linkage.[1]

Helen Harris Perlman

When we honestly ask ourselves which persons in our lives mean the most to us, we often find that it is those who, instead of giving much advice, solutions, or cures, have chosen rather to share our pain and touch our wounds with a gentle and tender hand.[2]

Henri Nouwen

The practice of medicine is an art, not a trade, a calling, not a business, a calling in which your heart will be exercised equally with your head.[3]

William Osler

The Person-Centered Helper and Helping Relationship

We now shift focus from the inner world of helping to the communicated qualities of the helper and the nature of the helping relationship, the crucibles wherein our empathy, compassion, and resilience are tested in service to others. These components of care are now a major focus of theory, research, and practice in the medical and counseling fields.

Two very early, influential publications shaped the evolution of work in this area, one by George Engel, the other by Carl Rogers. In health care, Engel's seminal 1977 paper, "The need for a new medical model: A challenge for biomedicine," introduced a biopsychosocial model incorporating psychological, social, and cultural factors in addition to the traditional biological ones.[4] The biopsychosocial model became the foundation for a movement dedicated to a more *patient-centered* or *person-centered* (the terms are now used interchangeably) approach to care that emphasizes a compassionate, empowering relationship between health providers and their patients.

Health providers and patients alike have expressed the need for this change in clinical practice. A survey of 510 physicians and 800 recently hospitalized patients found general agreement that compassionate care is "very important" to ensure successful treatment outcomes. However, only 53% of patients and 58% of physicians thought compassionate care was generally provided.[5] The authors recommend

155

that compassionate care be measured, rewarded by payers, studied to determine its active ingredients, and be more comprehensively covered during medical training.

Person/patient-centered care anchored in the biopsychosocial model has continued to gain momentum since Engel's initial call to action. Laine and Davidoff confirm this trend, observing that American medicine is "in the midst of a professional evolution driven by a refocusing of medicine's regard for the patient's viewpoint" in patient care, health-related law, medical education, research, and quality assessment.[6] Person-centered care is now described as "a burgeoning social movement," "a mission statement for modern health care," and a "key concept in modern medicine."[7; 8] References to a "biopsychosocial-spiritual approach,"[9; 10] "person-centered palliative and oncologic care,"[11; 12] "person-centered social work,"[13] "whole-person care,"[14] and even "person-centered psychopharmacotherapy,"[15] are common, marking the growth of this movement.

New instruments now allow us to assess the level of compassionate care in clinical settings and its impact on clinical outcomes.[16] Accumulating evidence shows compassionate care is not just offering a more congenial approach to bedside care; it actually leads to better treatment outcomes. For example, Kelley and colleagues analyzed controlled trials wherein aspects of the patient-clinician relationship (e.g., improved communication skills, increased empathy, better attention to non-verbal signals, not interrupting, sitting down with patients, making appropriate eye contact) were systematically manipulated. Health care outcomes were either objective (e.g., blood pressure) or validated subjective measures (e.g., pain scores). The patient-clinician relationship had a significant effect on health care outcomes, with more compassionate and personally-attuned care yielding better results.[17]

Person/patient-centered medicine, and its view of the provider-patient relationship, have coevolved along with the person-centered model in counseling championed by Carl Rogers. Rogers' landmark 1957 paper, "The necessary and sufficient conditions of therapeutic personality change," directed the focus of research and practice to the qualities of the therapist and the therapeutic relationship, and identified core features of what has become known as the "person-centered approach."[18] In subsequent publications Rogers further elaborated on his model for the healing qualities of the helper and the helping relationship.[19; 20]

The person-centered counseling approach, as Rogers formulated it, emphasizes the qualities of empathy, respect, and genuineness, wherein the helper attends to the feelings and felt meanings of the client, communicates respect and positive regard for that client, and remains authentic and real in the helping relationship.[21] This approach recognizes it is the client who must ultimately make the decisions that determine the outcomes in that person's life, and it seeks to empower the individual to make the best choices, given his or her values and needs. Person-centered communication makes this possible because it leads to a two-way exchange wherein clients have a greater sense of control, play an active role, and perceive their counselors as interested in their problems and attuned to their personal situations. Rogers' thinking has profoundly permeated the culture and human services, including the medical field. Indeed, the central themes of the person- or patient-centered approach in health care correspond point by point with those of Rogers' person-centered approach to counseling. Other streams of research, theory, and practice, including positive psychology, health psychology, social work, and psycho-oncology, to name a few, continue to contribute significantly to the evolution of compassionate person-centered care in medicine and psychotherapy.[22]

Consistent with predictions made by Rogers' person-centered model, the literature on psychotherapy outcomes consistently shows that transtheoretical *common factors,* for example, the counseling relationship and its working alliance, and the person-centered core conditions of empathy, respect, and genuineness, appear to be as influential in determining therapy outcomes as specific factors such as therapeutic techniques or models.[23; 24] In their review of research related to therapist expertise, Clara Hill and colleagues conclude that the therapist's relational expertise is at least as, or more important than, his or her technical expertise.[25]

In *How Clients Make Therapy Work*, Arthur Bohart and Karen Tallman make a strong case, one supported by extensive research, that the client is actually the most important common factor responsible for making therapy work:

We believe that persons have a great capacity not only for physical self-helping but also for psychological self-healing. Therapy needs to mobilize that self-healing potential. The "interventions" that do this are not only the technological ones but also the therapist's ability to listen to and empathically understand the client and respect the client's own agency, creativity, ideas, and expertise. Technology is seen not so much as techniques that operate on clients but rather as tools for clients to use to help them utilize their self-healing capacities. What therapists do only works if it supports, channels, relies on, or mobilizes these capacities.[26]

Given these findings and viewpoints, a compelling case can be made for a person-centered approach as the foundation for psychotherapy, and perhaps all helping relationships.[27]

Clearly, Engel and Rogers boldly challenged the medical and counseling fields to consider the merits of a more person-centered approach. Their seminal works ignited a scientific and clinical revolution and paradigm shift in care that continues to this day. At the heart of this approach is the mutual-participation relationship, a relationship encouraging informed choice, patient autonomy, and joint decision-making between health care providers and their patients. In *Compassionate Person-Centered Care for the Dying: An Evidence-Based Palliative Care Guide for Nurses*, Bonnie Freeman captures the foundation of person-centered care:

This philosophical approach ensures that care is respectful and responsive to individual preferences, needs, and values, and that these values guide clinical decision making. It means that we ask questions to learn what is most important and what matters to individuals, making intentional efforts to begin interactions from that perspective and integrate those perspectives into all aspects of care through human connectedness.[28]

What Person-Centered Care Asks of Us

In person-centered care there is a broadening of the biomedical view that incorporates what is seen through the patient's eyes and appreciates and seeks to better understand the patient's perception of the illness by taking into account the web of relationships and contexts wherein each patient suffers. To achieve such understanding, health providers need communication and relationship skills that support positive relationships and compassionate connections with patients. These human connections enhance patient outcomes and also health care workers' satisfaction in their work.[29]

This mode of working with patients and families is familiar to most of us. For example, hospice care has been firmly rooted in a person/patient-centered, whole-person, biopsychosocial-spiritual model of care since its inception. Similarly, in psychotherapy, the influence of the person-centered model has been so pervasive that its core features—therapist empathy, respect, and genuineness in a reciprocally empowering relationship—are now universally viewed as essential for effective counseling.

Yet no matter where and to what extent person-centered care is practiced, it is always challenging for the provider. Person-centered care requires your whole person, particularly in end-of-life work and counseling with grief and trauma, where it can be most demanding. For example, in those contexts, it requires acknowledging intense emotional distress, providing understanding and care in the midst of life's tragedies, sustaining and expanding empathy and compassion in the face of great suffering, and having difficult end-of-life conversations with patients and families. It also requires you, as a provider, to integrate and transform your losses as you assist patients and families to do the same. Person-centered care necessitates being an engaged team member, sharing your own stories, and risking vulnerability with colleagues. It requires you to revise your assumptions and philosophy of life to accommodate the realities of life and death you witness, and to accept the limitations of your helping efforts. Finally, it calls on you to continually renew commitment to your work, despite any adversity you may encounter.

Great courage, compassion, resilience, and skill are needed to answer these calls to action. There is no painless path to follow in your responses to them. However, as I've maintained here, wrestling with these challenges and ultimate concerns on an almost daily basis can bring wisdom—and even a deep happiness and peace—to you.

QUALITIES OF EFFECTIVE HELPERS AND HELPING RELATIONSHIPS

If you needed to explore an unpleasant aspect of yourself, were contemplating a divorce, struggling with the loss of a loved one, or were suddenly diagnosed with a life-threatening illness, with whom would you feel most comfortable confiding? How would you describe the relationship you would like to have with this helper? Would this particular person be caring, empathic, flexible, a good listener, encouraging, friendly? Would it be someone you could trust and to whom you could impart your deepest secrets? Should he or she express interest in you? Believe in you? Would you like your relationship with this helper to be one of equality and mutual participation, or one where you are passive and feel inferior?

These are some of the helper qualities that would likely come to mind if you were considering seeking help for yourself. Notice too, that your first thoughts about your preferred helper are probably not about their professional training, credentials, theoretical orientation, or technical expertise. Although these considerations may influence your decisions later, your initial concern, and that of others in distress, usually will be finding someone who is caring, empathetic, and supportive. Of course, with more complex and threatening medical and mental health issues, we typically first seek out the greatest technical expertise available, and then sort out relational issues after we access the highest levels of care.

Recent scientific findings support the wisdom of this particular set of priorities guiding people when they seek help. We know that the therapeutic relationship consistently accounts for at least as much of the variance in outcomes as the actual therapeutic techniques employed. This largely accounts for the finding that generally, when different schools of therapy are pitted against one another, no one brand of therapy is more effective than another. This finding has become known as the Dodo bird verdict, mirroring a quote from the Dodo bird in *Alice in Wonderland*—"Everybody has won and all must have prizes."[30] A supportive and compassionate helper delivering a helping relationship, combined with technical expertise gained from solid training, is the ideal formula for successful helping and healing. However, no matter what the ideal ratio of technical and relational expertise is, the most efficacious approach is, as John Norcross has advised, to combine "the power of commonalities and the pragmatics of specificity."[31]

Can you say that most of your personal and helping relationships are characterized by feelings of mutual respect, acceptance, and liking or positive regard? Let's assume you do possess these engaging qualities, and then let's add to them your heightened idealism, altruism, and capacity for empathy, as discussed here in Chapter 1. What can you then conclude about yourself as a helper? You might correctly conclude you have valuable natural gifts as a helper, and that these qualities can be predictive of your success in that role. Yet, too often we come to the opposite conclusion and underestimate our potential for helping and our ability to impact the lives of others positively. I see this most often, and most dramatically, among volunteer caregivers who negatively compare their own helping efforts to those they imagine belong to highly trained mental health professionals.

Health care professionals can also underestimate the positive impact of even a brief, but empathic and empowering intervention with a patient or family. The therapeutic and healing value of these brief encounters is often dismissed with statements such as, "We just talked," or "I didn't really do anything." Often, we don't appreciate that in dealing with most emotional problems, simply being there with our clients can have a healing quality. Many of us have ruminated for months about not having done enough in a clinical situation, only to hear later from a patient or family member that our "not enough response" was immensely helpful. As Kennedy and Charles observed, it is often the case that "a little bit of help is a lot of help."[32]

Presence

Presence, or being fully in the moment with your client, is a critical component of care in all helping contexts. Presence is being with the person you are helping—being fully engaged, and having a real meeting that affirms the other's humanity and dignity. Shari Geller, an expert on therapeutic presence, describes it as "bringing one's whole self into the encounter"—as a state of "grounded, immersed, and expanded awareness" wherein you are "completely in the moment…physically, emotionally, cognitively, and spiritually."[33] Geller emphasizes that when evaluating the benefits of presence what matters most is not how you see yourself, but rather how your clients see you. Do they perceive your responses as being in harmony with what they are experiencing and see you as fully present and not distracted in the moment?

Presence can be communicated in many ways, often through simple acts like those Colosimo and Pos term "here behaviors."[34] Examples include giving tissues to clients when they need them and laughing when something funny happens between the two of you. However, the authors add that although presence can be communicated through simple behaviors, it is nonetheless often difficult to sustain. They note there are many barriers to being fully "here and now" with clients, including countertransference, hyper-intellectualization, fatigue, and distractions of all sorts. Work overload, multitasking, and time pressures can also undermine presence. Being fully present in mind and spirit when you are pressured to be physically present somewhere else in only a few moments can be daunting.

The revolution in information technology—telehealth modalities, electronic health records, virtual reality applications, and digital therapeutics flooding the helping professions today—also pose significant challenges to being present in a helping relationship. In "Tethered to the EHR," Arndt and colleagues find that primary care physicians spend more than half their workday interacting with electronic health records during and after clinic hours, instead of interacting with their patients.[35]

The caring qualities and behavior we bring to the helping relationship extend the therapeutic effects of simple human presence. However, simple presence alone can be helpful and healing. I believe our healing power is bolstered by the invisible contributions of simple human presence. The difference between no human contact and the presence of another is a significant, yet little studied, psychological phenomenon. However, physician John Kennell and his colleagues did look at these phenomena more closely. The researchers examined the impact of the continued presence of a supportive companion during labor and delivery for more than 400 women in labor in a Texas public hospital.[36] At the time when this early study took place, companions were not routinely permitted to be with a woman during labor and delivery because there was insufficient privacy in the ward to allow visitors.

The experimenters trained a group of *doulas* (the Greek word for a woman who guides a new mother in her infant care tasks) and assigned them to the women in the study's support condition. The doulas stayed at the bedside from admission through delivery, soothed and touched each laboring woman, and encouraged her. They also engaged in patient education and explained what was occurring during labor and what the women could expect to happen next.

Patients in the observed condition did not have a doula assisting them, but instead had an observer in the room at all times. The observer kept a record of what was happening in the patient's room but without speaking to the laboring woman, thereby remaining as inconspicuous as possible in the crowded and hectic labor ward. There was also a control group that was neither supported nor observed by anyone.

The three groups were later compared on a variety of medical outcomes, including oxytocin use, duration of labor, type of delivery, and neonatal outcome. The doula intervention significantly reduced Caesarian section rates, forceps deliveries, the need for oxytocin, and epidural anesthesia. Also, labor was shortened and the incidence of maternal fever decreased. For those who had spontaneous vaginal deliveries, epidural anesthesia was used in 8% of the women in the supported group, 23% of the women in the observed group, and 55% in the control group. In other words, the presence of the observer alone had a significant impact on many outcome measures, and when caring responses such as giving information and touching (the doula condition) were added, these effects were even greater:

Today, professional doula care (the giving of nonmedical maternal support) for pregnant and birthing women has become a feature in many maternity care services. Doulas or birth attendants are professionally trained in childbirth and provide educational, physical, and emotional support to women before, during, and after childbirth.

The benefits of the doula intervention include shortened labor duration, reduced rates of instrumental delivery, and fewer Caesarian sections.[37] At the other pole of life's passage, we now have trained end-of-life doulas who provide support and comfort to the dying and their caregivers, and also patient "navigators" in oncology.[38; 39] Doulas and patient navigators could be thought of as newly speciated person-centered interventionists emerging in response to identified gaps in service delivery.

In summary, simple and therapeutic human presence are integral parts of helping, indeed a part of the "social linkage" that, when directly felt, makes our helping others "twice blessed." The low-tech, high-touch aspects of caregiving are not merely components of a pleasant bedside manner. They are also critical to successful treatment and can even improve health care outcomes.[17; 40] Therapeutic presence provides the foundation for empathy, respect, and genuineness—core features of the helping relationship. In our clients' most challenging and vulnerable moments, when together we confront suffering for which there are no quick fixes, we must be with rather than simply do for. It is then that our full presence can communicate shared humanity, afford dignity to those suffering, and buoy their hopes for the future.

Empathy, Listening, and the Caring Connection

As effective helpers, we are primarily empathic. In Chapter 1, we saw how we are wired to be empathic, and how our empathy energizes our compassion and helping behaviors. In action, empathy requires freeing yourself from yourself—to see and understand life through another's being. The English word "empathy" is the equivalent of the German word *Einfühlung*, literally translatable as "feeling into." When it was first introduced, the term was used to refer principally to the aesthetic experiencing of art forms—the feelings you might have when listening to a work by Mozart or viewing a masterpiece by Michelangelo.[41] Being empathic means feeling your way into the consciousness of another person, and seeing the world through his or her eyes.

In psychotherapy research, empathy is consistently identified as the most important element in achieving successful helping relationships.[24; 42] Rogers described empathy this way:

> It means entering the private perceptual world of the other and becoming thoroughly at home in it. It involves being sensitive, moment to moment, to the changing felt meanings which flow in this other person; to the fear, or rage, or tenderness, or confusion, or whatever that he/she is experiencing. It means temporarily living in his/her life, moving about in it delicately without making judgments. It requires sensing meanings of which he/she is scarcely aware, but not trying to uncover feelings of which the person is totally unaware, since this would be too threatening. It includes communicating your sensings of his/her world as you look with fresh and unfrightened eyes at elements of which the individual is fearful. It means frequently checking with him/her as to the accuracy of your sensings, and being guided by the responses you receive.

To be with another in this way means that, for the time being, you lay aside the views and values you hold for yourself in order to enter another's world without prejudice. In some sense, it means that you lay aside yourself and this can only be done by a person who is secure enough in himself that he knows he will not get lost in what may turn out to be the strange or bizarre world of the other, and can comfortably return to his own world when he wishes.[43]

Rogers' empathic helper is aware of the client's private, inner world of perceptions, conscious and blocked feelings, and the meanings ascribed to those perceptions and feelings. Note also that Rogers' definition of empathy includes communicating your empathic understanding to the other person. For Rogers, empathy involves seeing the problems of the other person from his or her perspective, feeling those problems with that individual, and then delicately checking out the accuracy of your sensings by communicating them to the other person. Thus, empathy involves both role-taking and emotional responsiveness.

Empathy begins with listening. When asked to summarize the basic personality and professional requirements of a psychotherapist, the renowned psychoanalyst Frieda Fromm-Reichmann declared, "The psychotherapist must be able to listen."[44]

As listeners, we are always trying to get to the crux of what some-one else is saying. To do this, we must respond to the nonverbal and verbal aspects of their message. Good listening requires absorbing the other person's mood—noticing a puzzled look, hearing a small sigh, or seeing a hand becoming a fist. These nonverbal cues are often the best markers indicating that good listening will be highly produc-tive at that moment.

There is a sense of poignancy or possibility in these moments, a feeling that something important may emerge. Freud reputedly summarized his therapy in a single word: surprise. Theodore Reik, psychologist Clara Hill notes, emphasized that the insights clients achieve should have an element of surprise for both the therapist and the client.[45] Good listening does lead to surprise; it is an enriching process of discovery for the helper and person being helped.

Listening requires paying deep attention to our innermost thoughts and feelings. Reik also spoke of "listening with the third ear," stressing that our deepest understanding of the people we help draws on our own intuition as well as on logic and inference.[46] This intuitive listening is rooted in a deep desire to know the other, and as Robert Katz explained, it "depends on the wish to be of loving service and a readiness to be lovingly touched by the sufferings of others."[41]

What is listening like for me? Whenever clients discuss emotional issues with me, and seek understanding and involvement, I direct all my energies to the dual tasks of listening and responding to them. I begin by focusing my attention on exactly what my client is saying. What words is he or she using? Are there any feelings explicitly or implicitly being communicated in this message? I take the message in and replay it inside myself, mentally taking his or her position, and thinking what it would be like to say or feel this way.

I might recognize a connection between this current message and something shared with me at an earlier time. In this way, previous conversations inform my understanding and deepen the quality of how well I can approximate what this is like for him or her in the current moment. In a way, I take these feelings inside (a kind of iden-tification) and then relate to them, using my own feelings and understanding of them as they resonate with this internalized other. Then there can follow a phase when I step back from this inner dialogue and try to make sense of—and give words to—what is occurring. This is a creative activity, and it takes time. Saying the first thing that comes to mind, without even a moment of reflection, is unwise and unlikely to be as helpful as preparing a more considered response; that is, one I have allowed to reverberate inside me, and have imagined how it would land for the client.

When my clients rush from one topic to another, I try to return us to the present moment by reflecting my current understanding of their communications. As I attempt to capture their inner reactions, they take my reflected message and check it against their internal sense of what they are trying to say. If my message fits for them, they can then move forward in their experiencing. In a way, I am trying to facilitate a deepening of their empathy and connection with themselves. It is said, we listen to our clients so they can hear what they are saying.

One way of describing this is that you are helping a person process or experience his or her experience more fully. Perhaps this sounds like a tautology, but it makes good psychological sense. When we have problems, we often just feel stuck. We feel some aspects of our inner reactions are unacceptable or "not me," so we become hesitant to disclose or even acknowledge these parts of ourselves. In earlier chapters, we discussed how experiential avoidance and self-concealment can be seen as transdiagnostic factors deleterious to psychological and physical health. Therefore, reducing them can be a central feature of therapeutic action.

Deep empathy communicated by helpers enables clients to truly inhabit their inner life. They are free to have a different orientation toward their feelings, and to allow those feelings to serve them in a more constructive fashion. Essentially, they become more engaged in change, as Leslie Greenberg and Jeremy Safran explain here:

> The process of acknowledging previously unacceptable feeling is experienced as a stamping of that feeling as OK, as mine, as legitimate, and almost desirable because it is what I'm experiencing. One feels a type of relief or recognition, "Oh, this is

what it is"; allows it, "I feel really sad, lonely, ashamed, angry, or whatever"; and accepts it, "Yes, this is what I feel, and I accept this as part of my experience without censure or punishment."...Accepting these feelings as truly occurring tends to deepen the individual's awareness of what is occurring, and informs them of what they want, are missing, or wish for; that is, the feelings are information that tell them in a very direct fashion of their desires. The hitherto disclaimed is thus claimed as one's own.[47]

In these moments, empathy is not just an abstract understanding of the other's experiencing; it is part of having a caring connection, part of feeling and being with the other. There is the sense of the we-ness we discussed in Chapter 1, a kind of communal orientation toward the other. In Martin Buber's words, an *I-Thou* relation is established with the other wherein there is a sense of unity and, simultaneously, a sense of separateness.[48] Other sympathetic feelings not specific to the person, such as warmth, tenderness, and concern, become part of this caring connection as empathy awakens compassion.

The caring connection is your most indispensable tool as a helper. It sustains and guides your helping and connects the deepest and best parts of yourself with the person you are helping. In this way, empathy and caring become a bridge between your innate altruism—your own humanity—and your helping efforts. No matter what else you do for the suffering person, it will indeed be "twice blessed" if your actions are grounded in compassionate understanding and experiencing of the other and his or her communication.

It might be useful for you to think of helping as being analogous to driving a car. As the noted psychologist Eugene Gendlin once observed, listening and empathy are like watching the road while you are driving: You do lots of other things at the same time, but if you take your eyes off the road, you will never get to where you are going, and you might even have a major accident.[49] When you are similarly attuned to the person you are helping, you will also avoid making irreversible errors. Your helping will be guided to move in positive and creative directions, even in those situations where you don't immediately perceive what the best direction to go is at that moment.

Let me offer here one illustration of this point from my own clinical practice. Pamela was a client of mine who had died 18 months earlier. I was talking with her parents, Nick and Marge. Pamela died on Nick and Marge's wedding anniversary and was buried on her mother's 60th birthday. Nick and Marge felt their anniversary could never again be a happy day, and Marge doubted whether she could ever again feel happy. The thought of being reunited with Pamela in Heaven was her only respite from the deep pain of losing her beloved daughter.

I was Pamela's counselor during her treatment for Hodgkin's lymphoma. Her cancer returned on the eve of her 2-year remission milestone. Sadder still, that recurrence was diagnosed 2 weeks before her long-awaited wedding to the love of her life. She and her fiancé courageously decided to proceed with the wedding and had only a few months of married life together.

I deeply cared for Pamela and was awed by her incredible fighting spirit. I felt Nick and Marge's deep pain. As I listened to them, I recalled my own conversations with Pamela about life and her relationship with her parents. I remembered the deep feelings of love she often expressed for her parents. In the midst of our conversation, I began to tell Marge and Nick what Pamela had said. This wasn't a carefully planned intervention, and I don't know why I suddenly remembered these conversations from several years earlier. I had tears in my eyes as I spoke. I felt like a messenger delivering a gift from someone now far away. I saw the pain on their faces ease, and the guilt they felt about not having done enough lessen. Their healing was thus able to move one small step forward, toward what Robert Cantor termed "enriched remembrance," and being able to hold Pamela even more securely in their hearts.[50]

Empathy Rooted in Our Personal Sense of Loss

Considerable debate in the literature has centered on the origins of empathy and whether or not it is a teachable attribute.[51] The consensus is that empathy for our clients can definitely be taught, and our capacity for empathic learning can be enhanced. Much of our empathy—in helping contexts and in everyday life—relates to others' anxiety, anger, depression, and similar forms of emotional or physical distress triggered by separation, loss, illness, or everyday stressors that threaten the equilibrium and happiness essential to well-being. Irvin Yalom reminds us that, "A therapist who is receptive, who inquires deeply into a patient's concerns will encounter death continuously in his or her everyday work."[52] Importantly, our capacity for empathy is rooted in our own emotional knowledge of loss. This knowledge is an unavoidable part of the human condition, but, as psychiatrist Alberta Szalita observes, some individuals are better schooled than others:

> But it is perhaps through personal suffering that we learn most about empathy.... Suffering is not a guest we have to invite; it comes unasked and may even become an insepa- rable companion. Suffering per se does not lead to wisdom, as some people maintain. Wisdom is more readily acquired when we gradually emancipate ourselves from narcissis- tic preoccupations. Empathy becomes more accessible as we come to grips with fears of death. Confrontations with sorrow, grief, and bereavement are always painful, but often engender a more compassionate attitude toward others and a commitment to life.[53]

Rainer Maria Rilke might have also had this idea in mind when he wrote these words:, "Do not believe that he who seeks to comfort you lives untroubled among the simple and quiet words that sometimes do you good. His life has much difficulty and sadness and remains far behind yours. Were it otherwise he would never have been able to find those words."[54] Jackson notes Goethe made this same point in a poem when he wrote, "our own pain teaches us to share in the sufferings of others."[55]

There is little doubt that our sensitivity and compassion toward others is shaped by our own losses and suffering. The early loss of my brother Dickie surely shaped mine. One afternoon when Dickie was playing on a rope swing with a friend, he lost his grip on the rope and fell. Despite suffering a serious concussion, he managed to ride his bike home. My parents had forbidden him to play on the rope swing, so at first Dickie told them he had fallen off his bicycle. But when his pain became unbearable, he told my parents what happened. I can still see my father's hand opening the desk drawer and retrieving the Blue Cross card.

The following morning, I was at my grandparents' home, sitting alone on the porch, listening to the adults talking in the living room. Suddenly, their conversation ceased, and they began to cry. The wave of pain going through the room hit me, and I cried, too. I knew I had lost Dickie; I knew grief. The next thing I remember is reaching through the white lace of his casket to place a penny near his hand. Dickie was leaving me, and I wanted him to have candy in heaven.

Nearly 30 years later, I sat in a theater viewing the movie *Ordinary People*. This iconic film focuses on the grief of a young boy for his older brother, a victim of a boating accident. In one pivotal scene, the two boys struggle to hang on to a raft in rough seas. The younger brother holds his brother's hand but cannot hold his grip, and his brother slips into the stormy sea and drowns. During this emotional scene, an image of my brother's face seemed to appear on the screen, replacing that of the drowning boy in the story. Waves of sadness immediately overcame me. My wife and I went to our car and I sobbed deeply for half an hour as pristine memories related to my loss of Dickie flooded my mind: conversations between my grief-stricken parents, the way his room looked, and how I acted at his funeral. That day, I finally confronted my loss and became better able to hold Dickie firmly in my heart. Grief can be locked away for years until an event in our lives unexpectedly brings it to the surface.

Two weeks later, I spoke to health care workers at a seminar. I urged them to "help the sibs grieve," an exhortation I often included in my lectures. During our discussion of grief, I disclosed my reactions at the movie. Later, when I asked members of the group to describe what brought them into this work, one participant intuitively asked me if I ever considered how my brother's death might have influenced my career choice, perhaps even specifically to advocate for bereaved siblings. I had an immediate flash of recognition and thanked her for this insight into my helping journey.

Empathy Turned Inward

The idea that our own traumas and suffering can energize and inform our helping is captured by the concept of the wounded healer. The image of the wounded healer was initially inspired by the Greek mythological figure, Chiron, a healer with an incurable wound inflicted by a poisoned arrow. Reflecting on the therapy implications of the Chiron myth, Carl Jung said it is essential for therapists to draw upon their own inner work with pain and healing to be effective helpers.[56]

An extensive literature discussing the wounded healer concept often highlights the need not to confuse the recovered and efficacious wounded healer with the impaired or burned-out practitioner.[57] The wounded healer who has restored emotional balance can confront his or her old wounds and reflect on that suffering without being debilitated by personal distress.[58] Achieving such a balance can enable the recovered healer to bring the synergy of shared personal growth and healing to a therapeutic relationship.[57; 58]

In a captivating clinical case history, child psychoanalyst Selma Fraiberg and her colleagues illustrate how we cannot hear the pain of another until we have listened to our own.[59] A 5-month-old infant, Mary, was showing dramatic signs of a lack of care from her mother, Mrs. March. She rarely smiled, showed little interest in the outside world, and even when she was suffering, she didn't reach out for her mother. Mrs. March, described by some as a "rejecting mother," was depressed and "seemed locked away in some private terror, remote, removed." Clinicians who attended to Mrs. March and her child would incredulously observe how the former would make little effort to comfort Mary, even when she screamed hopelessly. The therapists' diagnostic question was, "Why doesn't this mother hear her baby's cries?"

Subsequent therapy sessions with Mrs. March revealed a troubled childhood in which she felt abandoned, unheard, and unloved. The therapists repeatedly broached the depth of her grief and intolerable pain and formulated a guiding clinical hypothesis and treatment plan: when the mother's own cries were heard she would hear her child's cries. Soon, something remarkable began to happen between the mother and her baby:

As Mrs. March began to take the permission to remember her feelings, to cry, and to feel...comfort and sympathy...we saw her make approaches to her baby in the midst of her own outpourings. She would pick up Mary and hold her, at first distant and self-absorbed, but holding her. And then, one day, still within the first month of treatment, Mrs. March, in the midst of an outpouring of grief, picked up Mary, held her very close, and crooned to her in a heart-broken voice. And then it happened again, and several times in the next sessions. An outpouring of old griefs and a gathering of the baby into her arms. The ghosts in the baby's nursery were beginning to leave....Within four months Mary became a healthy, more responsive, often joyful baby.[59]

Later in the treatment, Mrs. March revealed the origins of her suffering: Her father had exhibited himself to her when she was a child, and a cousin had sexually molested her. After confronting these issues during therapy, Mrs. March seemed to have achieved an optimistic outlook toward a promising future free of the terrible pain that crippled her and her mothering.

This is a pattern we often see in helping: The ability to care for oneself is made possible by the caring and validation offered in the helping relationship. Feeling cared for and valued in a helping relationship leads to a new sense of self and of the world—something such as, "I am a lovable and worthy human being, and there are people in the world who are sensitive toward me."[47] When Mrs. March felt the therapists' care, she started to care for herself. This allowed her attachment to her daughter to blossom. The message here for us as helpers is this: If we can't reach into ourselves with love and acceptance, we will not be able to reach out to others with care and compassion.

Respect

Counseling helped Mrs. March restore her sense of worth as a person, boosting her self-esteem dramatically. Almost everyone who seeks help faces different kinds of threats to self-esteem. We have already seen the central role self-esteem plays in the stress response, particularly within helping relationships. In *Feeling Good by Doing Good*, Christopher Mruk notes that in addition to buffering stress, self-esteem promotes psychological growth because it enables the client to take the risks necessary for that growth. He likens self-esteem to "going on a long journey through a desert while carrying a bucket of water. In this case the desert represents the trials and tribulations of life, and the water stands for the self-esteem that will sustain us through the difficult periods until we can reach the next oasis."[60]

Many different words can describe the qualities imparted by respect: acceptance, warmth, positive regard, interest, and rapport. Your undivided attention and empathy enhance self-esteem because they say to your clients, "You and your feelings are worth making this effort to understand you." Respect is a key interpersonal common factor that make therapy work, as Mruk highlights here: "Warmly and genuinely affirming an individual's worth as a unique human being turns out to be one of the more frequently identified relationship factors that appear in good therapy relationships."[60] You also enhance your clients' self-esteem and communicate respect by affirming each client's capacity to solve his or her problems.

True respect means we never lose sight of the dignity of the person we are helping. This moment of precious dialogue between a helper and an elderly dying man captures the essence of respect:

> **Man:** Why do you continue to hold my hand and listen?
>
> **Helper:** Just to get the blessing of one more of your smiles.
>
> **Man:** Thank you. I am glad I still have value.

It is difficult to trust and be open with a stranger, to share problems, and overcome the distress-disclosure dilemma discussed in Chapter 4. Just the act of accepting help can represent a threat to one's self-esteem because it can suggest a sense of inferiority and dependence. As the helper, you can often get things off to a productive and positive start by complimenting a new client for his or her courage and assertiveness in seeking help. I often say, "Just asking for help is a very positive step you've already taken." If appropriate, you can ask a client how his or her problem affects how they feel about themselves, and thus you can begin to look together at the self-esteem issues inevitably accompanying unsuccessful efforts to solve life's problems. Interventions like these can rapidly deepen the client's level of self-exploration.

Asking your clients to tell you about their past successes and positive personal qualities, such as perseverance, can enhance their self-esteem. You can always point to something an individual is doing right, or to the more positive side of an action or feeling, even when things are going poorly. For example, I often point out how much family members care for their loved ones: "This hurts so much because you care so much," or, "It really matters to you to do a good job because you care so much."

There will be times when your ability to appreciate and respect the people you help is severely strained. You do not necessarily feel a natural closeness to everyone, but in situations where it is difficult to side with the other person, your empathy can still inspire and guide your ability to help.

Authenticity

Learning how to be yourself is a great challenge you face as a helper. If you avoid role-playing, and conduct yourself in ways that are real, honest, and authentic in your helping relationships, you will have more success and less stress as a caregiver. The idea that being yourself as a helper can reduce your stress may seem somewhat counterintuitive. Isn't the detached helper who stays in a safe and distant role less likely to burn out than the helper who acts more authentically and is more personally involved? The truth is the inauthentic helper is more vulnerable to stress, as we saw illustrated in the case of helper secrets.

Suppressing verbal and nonverbal expression of our emotional lives as helpers comes at a cost. Emotional suppression, a common feature of inauthenticity, is generally associated with flawed interpersonal functioning: Suppressors are often unsure of their feelings, disguise their inner feelings, and are not comfortable expressing their emotions.[61] This way of managing emotions can have a dramatic and detrimental effect on the helping relationship in several ways.

First, because emotional suppression poorly manages self-oriented feelings of upset or personal distress, it does not support the balanced, other-oriented empathic state that energizes compassion. In a study of emotion regulation strategies, empathic concern, and helping behavior, Lebowitz and Dovidio found that induced suppression was indeed negatively associated with empathic concern.[62] The experimenters read a fictitious transcript from an interview with "Patricia," a highly distressed high school student. One group of subjects (the reappraisal condition) was instructed to change what they were thinking about while reading the transcript so they would feel more positive emotion and "stay calm." Participants in the suppression condition were instructed to control their emotions by not expressing them, to do their best to stay calm. They were asked to keep their emotions to themselves, "so that if someone were watching you, that person would not know you were having any emotions." Suppression was associated with decreased empathic concern, whereas the positive reappraisal strategy was related to enhanced empathic concern. Reliance on suppression was also associated with a reluctance to engage in helping behaviors. The authors concluded that relying on suppression to regulate emotions stifles empathic concern.

Second, clients need their helpers to reflect their distress and perspectives and show they understand and care about them.[63] Clients also benefit from the modeling of effective emotion regulation by their helpers. This modeling tells clients their difficult emotions can be approached safely, even mastered, and invites further exploration. The incongruent helper is unlikely to meet these multiple client needs.

Thus, an authentic sense of self is essential to the social connectedness and compassion at the heart of helping relationships. We need to maintain finely-tuned awareness of our moment-to-moment emotions and effectively regulate these. Authenticity or congruence, according to Rogers, means "the feelings the therapist is experiencing are available to him, available to his awareness, and he is able to live these feelings, be them, and able to communicate them if appropriate."[20] Your helping is more stressful, and less efficacious, when you deny perhaps the greatest single instrument of healing at your disposal: yourself.

Personal self-disclosure is a major component of being genuine. People want their helpers to be skilled *and* human, technically proficient and caring, and self-disclosure is a principal way we communicate our humanity to another. You might be thinking, "Just how open should I be? Does this mean I should express my thoughts and feelings on everything the client is talking about?" No, it doesn't. I will say more about appropriate and inappropriate self-disclosure in the next chapter, but the general rule is, you don't want to shift attention to yourself at the expense of the person you are helping. I often find it particularly useful to share how I am feeling at a particular moment. For example, I might be feeling sad because of someone's loss, or angry at their victimization. I might also feel confused or excited. If feelings like these are shared at all, they should be presented more as tentative hunches about what the client might also be feeling and in the spirit of deepening empathy, not sharing personal distress.

Self-disclosures create a two-way and potentially beneficial intimacy. However, significant self-disclosures should always be communicated with great discretion and only after considerable trust and rapport are established in the helping relationship. When wisely chosen and timed, self-disclosures can uniquely convey you are a real person involved in a real and caring relationship with the person you are helping.

Flexibility

Flexibility is another key attribute of effective caregivers. This dimension was identified by Hyman and Woog, who studied a sample of helping professionals including nurses, nursing supervisors, administrators, educators, psychologists, aides, and social workers.[64] They administered measures of eight personality variables thought to be attributes of competent helpers, and their analyses yielded a single factor: flexibility. The flexible helper, according to the researchers, "thrives in the complex and ambiguous," and "is governed more by internal cues rather than rules or authority." The researchers elaborate on the nonauthoritarian features of the flexible helper:

> Perhaps the most important characteristic of an effective helper is the ability to be freeing rather than controlling.... The helper cannot impose self as an authority and cannot be

oriented toward rules and regulations or place too much value on order, procedures, custom, or tradition. All of these may impede openness, which implies ability to perceive reality without applying preconceived categories.[64]

When you are open to the reality of the person you assist this way, your empathy will be more accurate and creative. You will help that person tell his or her, not your, story, and grow in the direction he or she elects. Behavioral adaptability or flexibility, the capacity to change nonverbal and verbal behavior in response to what each patient needs, is key to effective patient-centered adaptability or flexibility.[65]

Being flexible also means knowing you can't solve every problem or have an answer to every question you encounter as a helper. Most veteran helpers know this, but this awareness doesn't lead to feelings of helplessness or to being overly anxious or defensive. Instead, such helpers recognize that at these times they must be honest, let their intuition guide them, and, above all, communicate their intention to continue caring for the person they are helping.

Leading psychotherapy researcher Bruce Wampold and colleagues conducted an exhaustive review of the research-identified characteristics of effective therapists.[66] They found highly effective therapists shared specific qualities or capacities: They can form solid alliances across a range of patients because they possess facilitative interpersonal skills (e.g., they are fluent and can express their emotions appropriately; they communicate hopefulness; they are warm and empathic; they create strong bonds with their clients and focus on the clients' problems). They also have professional self-doubt and actively practice improving their therapy skills. Each of these qualities or capacities seems to reflect a high degree of flexibility in response to their patients and to themselves.

Cultural Sensitivity

As a person/patient-centered, culturally sensitive clinician, you need to be acutely attuned to how your client's race, ethnicity, religious views, sexual identity, and language shape his or her personal experience of illness, expectations of treatment, treatment adherence, mourning rituals, family decision-making, and personal and social resources to help in those circumstances. Issues of discrimination, cultural privilege, and health disparities must also always be considered. Here, Laura Brown captures the complexity we and our clients bring to the helping encounter:

Each of us is a creature of multiple and intersecting identities—with a sense of self arising from our gender, culture, social class, sexuality, ability and more—those intersectionalities and their meanings are an integral component of how we perceive and are perceived in the therapy relationship.[67]

Being culturally sensitive requires self-reflection on the personal cultural self, and an examination of your own possible biases and blind spots. Myriad differences between you and your clients can quickly create barriers of they-ness, like those discussed in Chapter 1, and they can challenge or even block real empathic responses.

The key to being culturally sensitive is the capacity to inquire nondefensively how a difference between you and your client might be affecting your client and the helping relationship. For example, you can ask your clients about their racial and ethnic background and whether they feel comfortable talking about it. When there are obvious significant cultural differences, it can be helpful to say that although this topic is something that can be difficult to talk about, you want to know how they feel about working with someone from a different racial or ethnic background.[68]

I find that the cultural differences I encounter in my clients give me tremendous opportunities to expand my understanding of people and life. I try to approach differences with a caring, curious, and open attitude, and an eagerness to understand the meaning each counseling event has for my client. If I can do that successfully, then our relationship can be enhanced, rather than diminished, by our apparent differences.

A Strong Working Alliance

Do your clients have a strong bond with you? Do they feel appreciated and know they are respected by you? Do they believe you will collaborate with them in setting goals for their treatment? Do they believe their treatment is helping them accomplish the changes they are seeking? If so, the likelihood of successful treatment is greatly enhanced because your clients are in a strong working alliance with you. They feel there is mutual agreement on the goals of treatment and the tasks required to achieve those goals, and have a positive emotional bond with you.

Working alliance models and measures are now widely used in research and clinical practice.[69; 70] The strength of the working alliance has proven to be a powerful predictor of psychotherapy outcomes across different treatment conditions, and it is perhaps the most robust of all the contributing common factors.[71] For example, a meta-analysis of 295 independent studies, including more than 30,000 psychotherapy patients, found a positive relationship between the alliance and outcomes across assessor perspectives, alliances and outcomes measures, treatment approaches, patient characteristics, and even countries.[72] Changes in the alliance can have immediate effects. One study showed that improvement in the quality of the client-therapist alliance in a given treatment session led to a decrease in clients' depressive symptoms by the next session.[73] Finally, in medical practice, an extensive review and the meta-analysis of empirical research on the physician-patient alliance found positive effects of the alliance for patient adherence, patient satisfaction, and improved patient outcomes.[69]

A strong working alliance between provider and patient creates a greater sense of safety. This promotes treatment-relevant client disclosure. Kelly and Yuan found that psychotherapy clients who were keeping more relevant secrets from their therapists scored lower on the Working Alliance Inventory (WAI). Their therapists also reported a weak working alliance. The researchers concluded that secret keeping either hurts the development of the therapy relationship or is the result of an already weak one.[74]

A similar finding was discovered in a study with advanced cancer patients. Patients with a strong working alliance with their physicians were more likely to share their concerns about their family's coping and their own fears of suffering. A strong working alliance with their nurses was associated with greater openness when discussing symptom control.[75] Thus, a robust working alliance is shown to promote

feelings of trust and safety in patients, and this sense of safety promotes disclosure of treatment-relevant information.

Each patient's capacity to participate in a collaborative and
empathic working alliance is an important clinical consideration.
An Italian study examined the relationship between the attachment
security of in-patient hospice patients, their perceptions of empathy
in the relationships they had with their caregivers (spouses or other
family members), and their working alliances with their physicians.
Patients with a secure, as opposed to an insecure, attachment style
had more empathic closeness with their caregivers and stronger
working alliances with their physicians.[76] The clinical implication is
that identifying the attachment orientations of end-stage patients (in
this case, cancer patients) could have great value as we respond to
their unique selves.

Ruptures often occur in working alliances. Because patients often
do not share their negative responses to treatment and to their therapist, detecting these ruptures can sometimes require considerable
clinical skill. When ruptures are detected, the therapist or medical professional must immediately attend to the alliance, respond nondefensively, change behavior when needed, restore trust, and explore what
might be keeping the client from sharing his or her negative reactions.[77]

A Mutual Participation Relationship

Clearly, a strong working alliance reflects a collaborative, caring, and
empowering relationship. Szasz and Hollender describe three basic
models of helping relationships, and only one, the mutual participation relationship, seems most aligned with these qualities.[78] Although
the models relate to physician-patient interactions, they can be
applied to any caregiving relationship. According to Szasz and Hollender, in the *activity-passivity relationship*, the patient's contribution
is small, and the physician's is paramount (for example, the physician
assumes an active role toward a passive patient, such as administering a treatment for an injury or anesthesia before surgery). Such a
relationship resembles that between a parent and a helpless infant.

In the *guidance-cooperation relationship*, the physician advises the
patient what to do, and the patient usually obeys. An example of such

a relationship would be a patient being treated for an infection in a clinical setting, where the patient becomes more involved in his or her own treatment by following a physician's advice. If the patient fails to cooperate with such advice, the physician could employ different forms of persuasion. This model has its prototype in the parent-adolescent relationship.

In the *mutual participation relationship*, the health provider helps patients to help themselves. In this scenario, the patient participates in a partnership by accessing the provider's expertise. The relationship is of one adult to another—human being to human being—and is predicated on a belief in equality. This type of helping relationship is perfectly suited for assisting people to cope with chronic illness, grief and loss, and other issues where the goals are to mobilize and support the individual.

Schillinger and colleagues argue that an essential component of person-centered care for serious illness is eliciting and supporting patients' self-identified physical and psychosocial goals.[79] Assisting patients to meet these self-identified goals can require creativity on your part, and might not be reimbursable—for instance, arranging the travel plans for a geographically distant family member to have a final visit with your patient—but addressing end-of-life tasks and goals like these exemplifies compassionate, whole-person care.

Of course, in different circumstances, all three of these kinds of helping relationships are appropriate, but in the modern world, where patients and families must make complex medical decisions, and chronic illnesses and difficult psychosocial problems are the rule, relationships based on equality and mutual participation are usually most effective.

On Directiveness, Control, and Responsibility

Who is responsible for change in the helping relationship? What control and direction should you provide as a helper? What are your basic assumptions about these important dimensions of the helping relationship?

As we have seen, a helping relationship based on mutual participation implies, or even necessitates, a less directive and controlling style of involvement by the helper. This is because when the helper relinquishes control, it has the desired and paradoxical effect of actually restoring control to the person being helped. This new sense of control can be a powerful antidote to the loss of control most people feel during negative and stressful life events. Loss of control is a central feature of dying and grieving, so it is not surprising the common purpose of many of our interventions is to reestablish a sense of control in the people we are helping.

It is important to clarify that there are many situations wherein you as the helper are highly directive and take control: you solve a practical problem, provide medication, do psychoeducation, share specific information, teach a skill, perform a medical procedure, give a psychological test, or massage a sore back. This active assistance is necessary and vital; sometimes it is all that is needed. But when we look at emotional difficulties, interpersonal dilemmas, treatment decisions, and other psychosocial problems, the appropriateness of the patient as problem-solver becomes more clear-cut. Here, even though you are active and may teach skills or offer educational input, the responsibility for change remains with the client.

The ancient Chinese proverb "Give a man a fish, and he has one meal; teach him to fish, and he can eat for the rest of his life" is a good rationale for this nondirective approach. The helper with a directive and controlling style is always giving people answers and ideas (i.e., giving them the fish). The nondirective helper teaches people to fish by helping them find their own answers and by teaching them problem solving skills they can use in the future. Educating people about their illnesses or disorders, training them in specific therapeutic techniques, and urging them to participate directly in the treatment, management, and prevention of their conditions are all examples of teaching people to fish.

Taking a nondirective approach as a helper requires basic confidence in other human beings. Without a deep belief in the people you are helping, you can't remain optimistic they will move in a positive direction. If you hold a cynical view toward other people and tend to see their bad choices and life problems as reflecting fundamental flaws in human nature, a more authoritarian and directive helping style may seem warranted (i.e., you think you just have to save people from themselves).

Many theorists have described a belief in a self-actualizing tendency in all humans as the basis for a more optimistic view. Rogers put it this way: "The individual has within himself vast resources for self-understanding, for altering his self-concept, his attitudes, and his self-directed behavior—and that these resources can be tapped if only a definable climate of facilitative psychological attitudes can be provided."[80]

In addition to having this inherent tendency toward growth and self-actualization, people also know more about the solutions to their problems than even they realize, certainly more than we often think they do. Our task is to help them check inside about the issue and allow different facets of the problem, and what they need in this situation, to become known. When they do this, the actions they need to take can become clear to them. A sense of relief often comes even before they take these actions; just knowing what they need brings some comfort. Gendlin calls this inner release a body shift.[81] The individual is then usually freed to decide when and how to take action in the world.

To successfully facilitate this inner problem solving, we must believe in the wisdom of the total organism, the mind and the body, the conscious and the unconscious self. Much of our journey as helpers is learning to trust ourselves and helping others to trust themselves.

I find it helpful to think of the appropriate helping stance as one of *controlled nondirection*.[82] You want your efforts to be freeing and facilitating rather than manipulative, but you also want to exert significant control. To achieve this twofold goal, you can employ a directive approach with regard to process in helping, but a nondirective one with regard to the content of helping. In other words, you can influence the helping interaction by structuring the conversation—by jointly defining what the problem is and how your client can begin to solve it—and by focusing and deepening his or her exploration of it. In a medical interview, you might simply begin with "How are you? What is your concern today," and go from there. You are being nondirective in that you exert little control over what your client says or does. You then respond to the forward-moving aspects and inner reactions of your client as much as possible instead of having him or her respond to your ideas and frame of reference.

This controlled nondirection is reflected in the kinds of communication skills you use. By using less directive interventions, such as paraphrases, reflections of feeling, and self-disclosures (*see* Chapter 6), you can provide structure without taking the initiative and control away from your client.

If people have a sense of responsibility over the outcomes in their lives, they are more likely to succeed in their goals. Instilling this sense of responsibility and an expectation of success is a key ingredient in helping. Another good reason to adopt this helping philosophy is it relieves you of the debilitating burden of the misguided belief that you are responsible for solving all the problems of the people you help.

I learned something about this from my professor and mentor, the late Sheldon Korchin. Shelly had polio as a child living in New York City. Franklin Delano Roosevelt, himself a polio victim, was Governor of New York State then. On weekends, he took Shelly and other children with disabilities on river outings. The children rowed the boats, and with Roosevelt's inspiration, they were able to expand their visions of what they could accomplish in life. I don't know what happened to the other children, but Shelly went on to lead an inspiring and dynamic life and became a luminary in clinical psychology. As one of my professors who taught therapeutic skills, Shelly told me he often said to his psychotherapy clients, "I can help you steer the boat, but you have to pull the oars." Shelly never mentioned this connection himself, but as he encouraged his clients to pull the oars in their lives and to overcome their hardships, he was sharing the lesson he learned from Roosevelt: If we take responsibility for improving our lives, we can overcome setbacks and achieve our dreams. I often share this metaphor with the people I help.

There is an element of paradox in this controlled nondirection approach. We need to inspire people to take responsibility, to pull the oars in their own lives, but at the same time, we shouldn't try to tell them what to do. Rogers once commented that the ancient Chinese philosopher Lao Tzu expressed this paradox and also his essential philosophy of interpersonal relationships in the following saying:

> If I keep from meddling with people, they take care of themselves,
> If I keep from commanding people, they behave themselves,
> If I keep from preaching at people, they improve themselves,
> If I keep from imposing on people, they become themselves.[83]

This orientation is part of the modern person-centered outlook in health care. It encourages us to be advocates for the people we care for and do everything possible to involve them in their own care. The emphasis is on the *activated patient* who is fully knowledgeable about his or her medical condition and your view of it, and is a full participant in any treatment decisions. The Patient Activation Measure (PAM) is now used to assess patient knowledge, skill, and confidence (i.e., self-efficacy) for self-management of one's health and chronic condition. Activation scores can inform patient care plans.[84] The PAM(MH) is a version of the PAM for use with mental health conditions.[85] This image of the activated patient is in sharp contrast with the "good patient" of several decades ago, who was compliant, unassertive, relatively uninformed about his or her medical condition, and did what he or she was told.

The problem is, many helpers have discovered that a more egalitarian relationship with an activated patient is not always easy to manage. It is often much simpler to have people just follow instructions and not ask too many questions about what you are doing and why you are doing it. The litigious atmosphere of our times can also fuel this ambivalence toward the activated patient. If you are a health care provider, what is your first reaction to "May I see my chart?" Most likely, it isn't "Wonderful, I'm glad you're so involved," but rather something more like "Oh boy, did we chart everything accurately?" or "What's she been told?"

Adopting a nondirective stance as a helper is also difficult because it requires us to relinquish some of the gratification we gain from giving clients our answers to their problems and from being seen in the flattering light of an advice giver. The best helpers get little recognition for much of the good they do.

An emphasis on personal responsibility presents yet another challenge to us as caregivers. Encouraging a responsible approach to the future without promoting blame for creating the problem can be difficult in our culture, where responsibility and blame are so conflated in our everyday thoughts and language.

This dilemma is particularly apparent in work with people with cancer and other chronic conditions. Exposed to the popular and simplistic views of the role of psychological factors in health and illness that appear in our media, these patients can tend to blame themselves, thinking, "I caused my illness." In other words, they assume they are bad or wrong for having done this to themselves.

As a counselor to people in these situations, I deemphasize the notion of blame while simultaneously accentuating personal responsibility for doing everything possible to enhance total well-being in the future. I also stress that positive coping and communicating suffering are not mutually exclusive. I do this because these highly distressed patients are often reluctant to share their suffering with helpers and family because it would reveal they weren't coping very well and were "making themselves sick again." Ironically, concealing these feelings only adds to the stress of the illness. By explaining that the expression of these difficult feelings is a normal and healthy response to their situation we can assist patients to accept their feelings and to develop more adaptive coping strategies.

Strengthening the support systems of people you help is a key aspect of effective, empowering interventions. Most people facing major losses and other negative life events feel the need to talk about the event and their reactions to it with others. In Chapter 4, we explored how the dynamics of self-concealment and social constraints can combine to lead people to withdraw from others and conceal their suffering. Disclosure could hypothetically break this vicious cycle and disrupt negative self-attributions accompanying concealment, but it is absent.

This is why it can be so important and helpful to ask distressed people how they might be keeping their suffering from others. I find it most effective to ask them first how they feel about their ability to cope, and then to listen carefully for critical thoughts such as "I should be doing better by now," or "I expected to be a bit farther along at this time." This self-reproach is usually accompanied by the concealment of suffering and social isolation. Then I assess their level of social support. Are they part of a community? Who is offering them assistance? Whom have they confided in? In whom could they safely confide? How can I help create or strengthen their social support resources? How can I foster additional companionship to make their lives easier?

In our best moments as helpers, we encourage clients to look inside for the wisdom to make healthy choices. We invite them to take responsibility for their lives without the onus of self-blame. And, we support an openness to additional support from their family and community. To do this, we must resist our impulses to (try to) provide them with all the answers, to point out what they are doing wrong, and to single-handedly meet all their needs. These principles are the foundation of successful and empowering helping relationships.

The Codependent Caregiver: A Dangerous Myth

We now have a clear picture of the effective helping relationship: It is a caring, empathic, authentic, and collaborative meeting of persons. However, as we have seen in earlier chapters, helping relationships are not always untroubled. Burnout, boundary issues, countertransference, and other difficulties can complicate caregiving. One unfortunate response to explaining these and other difficulties in helping relationships has been the emergence of codependence theory. The codependence literature invokes the specter of the "codependent caregiver," the helper who allegedly satisfies personal needs through the people he or she cares for. This concept has frequently been invoked to explain the difficulties of caregivers.

In an early critique of codependency theory, Edith Gomberg chronicles the expansion of the term *codependent* beyond its use denoting family members of the alcoholic or drug abusing person.[86] The first people labeled as codependent were wives of alcoholics in the 1950s and 1960s. These women, seen as dependent and frustrated, and as marrying their husbands to meet their own neurotic needs, were referred to as "Suffering Susans," "Controlling Catherines," or "Punitive Pollys." Other writers also critique codependence theory from a feminist perspective, arguing it pathologizes gender-associated female traits of caring and compassion.[87; 88] The "codependency epidemic" then spread to coworkers and friends of the addicted person and now is claimed to affect the relationships of virtually everyone to everything, explaining our dependence on food, religion, and even on the people we work with as helpers, although no scientific research supports any of these applications.[88]

The continuing proliferation of codependency is fostered by the unclear criteria for and vague conceptual boundaries of the concept. When we look at any of the myriad statements on codependency, we always find lists of characteristics easy to agree with, such as having a need to be needed, having low self-esteem and problems with boundaries, being afraid to express your needs and opinions, and growing up in an emotionally repressive family. Like the rest of the helper population of the world, you can probably identify with several of these characteristics, suggesting you have a mild or perhaps even a full-blown case of codependency. Or do you? In fact, we cannot reliably differentiate the codependent person from anyone else in the population. In psychology, we call this a lack of discriminant validity; in everyday life, it means you can never exclude yourself from codependent status.

But what could be wrong with this attempt to pay more attention to our difficulties as helpers? The reasons relate to some unintended and negative consequences of looking at ourselves and our helping this way. Viewing our difficulties in helping as symptoms of a disease is an unhealthy, self-defeating approach to these problems. Richard Lazarus cautioned against explaining our distress this way, arguing we should be wary of a pathology mystique that automatically relegates emotional distress and dysfunction to the category of sickness rather than seeing them as components of the active adaptational struggles of a person under stress who is trying to cope as best as he or she can.[89]

Research on the effects of different attributional styles demonstrates interpreting our difficulties this way engenders feelings of helplessness and depression.[90] We come to believe the source of our problems is internal ("It's me."), stable ("It won't change."), and global ("And it will affect all other areas of my life."). In our culture, as I've noted, the line between self-responsibility and self-blame is already thin. When we add the stigma of a disease diagnosis, the tendency to blame oneself is intensified.

As we discussed earlier, a key lesson of systematic work on caregiver burnout is the major source of problems is usually in the situation or context, not in the caregiver. Unfortunately, so often when the quality of care begins to decline, people and not the work environment are usually first to be blamed. The cause is often attributed to either "bad patients" or "lazy staff."

The tendency to explain negative events as reflecting something about the people experiencing them, rather than the situation itself, is a pervasive human phenomenon and follows from a more general bias known in psychology as the *fundamental attribution error*.[91] Viewing ourselves as codependent caregivers is a doubly dangerous error because, in addition to heightening self-blame, it shifts our attention away from the situational determinants of our stress and undermines our efforts to change them.

Perhaps the most destructive consequence of the codependent caregiver concept and others like it is the web of blame and cynicism it fosters. This can undermine your external support for doing this work. With the arrival of codependency in the popular press, your disclosures of distress associated with your work are more likely to be greeted with "Maybe you shouldn't be doing this work. By the way, have you read anything about codependency?" The message is clear: Caring for others must always stop short of personal inconvenience or distress. In the real world, it does not.

Support from administrators, coworkers, and supervisors can also be undermined by the codependency model. We already witness discussions about "codependent" employees and coworkers. Listen carefully the next time someone in your work setting uses the term to describe someone. Is it used with compassion? Is the message, "This person is hurting and we need to do everything we can do to help her," (e.g., add staffing)? Or is it tinged with blame, more resembling, "She's got a real problem."? Because of this negative aspect, helpers become even more likely to conceal their pain.

Finally, the codependency model makes us doubt ourselves. If we label our caring motivations as codependent needs, our altruistically inspired helping becomes a product of emotional instability. When we go out of the way for others—something part of everyday care-giving—we wonder why we are doing so. We ask ourselves, "Is this just a need to please?" Codependence theory makes caring an addiction. Codependency theorists fail to see the wellsprings of human caring run much deeper than dysfunction. What is most noble in the human spirit—and in caregiving—becomes suspect. These doubts about our helping motivations can erode what we have seen is an excellent buffer against stress in caregiving: your sense of purpose in the work. You jeopardize a precious resource, your love, if you view yourself and your caring as something less than what they are.

Each of us has a unique blend of motivations driving our helping efforts. Guilt, low self-esteem, personal distress, and "selfish" motivations are probably a small part of every helper's motivations. All caregivers must find a balance between responsibility to self and responsibility to others, between balanced helping and rescue operations. We need to closely examine all the ways we might land in the Helper's Pit and look at whether we are being overcontrolling, communicating ineffectively, not setting boundaries, or vicariously living through the lives of the people we care for. And when we identify these bad habits, we need to change them, but we don't need to have a disease to do this.

Conclusion

In a thoughtful and humorous article, Quentin Rae-Grant describes the art of being a failure as a consultant.[92] His guidelines for ensuring failure as a consultant are equally applicable to other kinds of helping and are consistent with the ideas presented here for ensuring success, only presented in reverse form. To guarantee failure, says Rae-Grant, simply present yourself as knowing all the answers; ignore the client's ideas, desires, and goals; insist upon complete reliance on your authority as an expert; and have lots of hidden agendas. Above all, he argues tongue-in-cheek, if you want to prevent success, avoid the development of a warm, trusting, and empathic relationship.

When we avoid these and other pitfalls in our helping relationships, like asking too many questions, or giving too much advice, a different scenario can unfold, one clearly revealing the value of our efforts:

✧ A 5-year-old child who was in isolation for months while undergoing a stem cell transplant asked (with obvious pride at his verbal mastery): "Are you a psy-chol-o-gist?" When I answered in the affirmative, he responded: "Every boy needs a psychologist to see his feelings!"

✧ We continually get phone calls from people who don't know what to do. They call me as a last resort when they find they have nowhere else to turn. In many cases, there is nothing we can do either, but invariably I hear "Thank you, you've helped so much. You're the first one who has listened and understood."

✧ A terminal patient with paralyzed vocal chords whispered to his son in his native tongue that he wanted me to come spend time with him, anytime. I had been uncomfortable with the communication problems and cultural differences, and I was not sure I was being effective. It made me feel very good to know he valued my presence.

✧ I gave time and presence and a caring heart to a child who was not permitted to grieve the suicide death of her very close uncle. The transformation of this intensely sobbing child into a giggling, alive, 6-year-old was profound and sacred.

This chapter has identified the qualities of helpers and helping relationships leading to successful and rewarding outcomes such as these. But what do empathy and other relationship qualities look like in action? What, specifically, does a helper do to convey respect or to develop an empowering helping relationship? In the next chapter, we will try to demystify the art of helping and identify specific communication and relationship skills essential to compassionate care.

6

This is the role of psychotherapy—a guided tour of the self in the company of a trusted other whose professionalism guarantees that the shame of self-discovery will be minimized.[2]

Donald Nathanson

Upon meeting a new patient, an elderly woman, small and frail, I was preparing to explain how I could assist her. Before I could begin my presentation, she lifted her hand slightly, and then spoke clearly, "So, you are to be my warrior."

Helper

Healing Words: Compassion in Action

O ur helping reflects, first of all, who we are. Our personal histories, attitudes, and beliefs all contribute to the quality of the helping relationships we establish. The distinguishing qualities of successful helpers—sensitivity to the distress of others, flexibility, presence, authenticity, empathy, respect—are not simply external behaviors we can assume at will. They are the product of a lifetime of learning shaping us into the particular kinds of people and helpers we are. However, to be healing, these experiences, attitudes, and beliefs must be brought to life through words and actions—they must be communicated.

There is a set of communication skills that make this possible, skills that set helping conversations apart from our everyday interactions and distinguish effective helpers from those who are less successful. These skills are the vehicles enabling you to express your caring, establish solid working alliances, facilitate emotional processing, and help people find solutions to life's dilemmas. This is true for a 5-minute medical consultation, or a year-long psychotherapy. By linking these skills with your empathy and helping motivations, you can become the confident, creative and caring helper your colleagues and clients immediately recognize, respect, and seek out. This chapter is intended to help you achieve these goals.

Exploring Your Communication Skills

Before learning the skills presented here, it would be useful for you to take some time to look closely at your current communication style and habits. Here is a quick opportunity to examine your communication skills right now. Imagine you have just walked into the hospital room of a young woman named Jenny, a 25-year-old with cancer who is not responding well to her treatments. She turns to you and says:

> I'm just sick and tired of being some kind of guinea pig. All these damn drugs. My hair is falling out. I feel sick to my stomach. And what good is it gonna do? Everyone knows I'm not gonna get better. You don't know what it's like. You get to go home every day. I don't. I'm stuck here. You don't care, anyway. How could you? Just get out and leave me alone!

Now take a piece of paper and write down what you would say or do with Jenny if you were with her in real life. Write your response exactly as you would say it.

Let's compare your response with those written by other clinicians who were presented with this vignette. One possible response might be to leave the room. Some helpers wrote they would say, "I'll be back whenever you're ready to talk," or, "Turn your light on when you want to talk." After all, this is what Jenny seems to be asking for. Still, simply to leave without meeting Jenny's implicit request for greater empathy and involvement wouldn't be very helpful to her. This distancing could also increase your stress level, as this nurse reflected:

> When a patient is difficult to care for, belligerent, or states, "Get out of here, leave me alone," I have sometimes done just that! I do only what I have to do and then tend to have limited contact with the patient. Later, though, I feel like I shortchanged the patient, and then I feel guilty, like I haven't done my best.

Like the nurses in the Stotland study (*see* Chapter 2), this nurse didn't know how to communicate in a way allowing her to stay in the room and maintain a caring connection with the patient. I believe most of the U-turns made at the foot of the bed of dying patients result more from a lack of communication skills than from a lack of caring. This is why it is so important to identify and learn these skills.

Another caregiver suggested the possibility of ignoring Jenny's feelings and trying to turn her thoughts toward more pleasant topics:

> I can empathize with all you are saying and how you must be feeling. Let's try to think together about a very special day when something wonderful happened to you. Who did you share it with? What did you do? Was it a beautiful day? Try to remember and tell me!

This caregiver added she would touch Jenny's hand as she said this. What would this response feel like if you were Jenny? Would you feel supported? Heard or not heard?

Jenny's confrontation with mortality could trigger the fear of death interpersonal allergy discussed in Chapter 2, leading her helper to make a response like this:

> I know I don't know what you're going through, but I want to try to understand. Can you help me? Someday I'll be facing death, too.

In this next response, the helper is detached, but simultaneously demands greater involvement from Jenny:

> I am here to share your human condition. You can give me the privilege of doing that, or you can reject me. I think together, our sharing of your suffering will help us all. If you refuse, we both lose.

The irony here is Jenny is already sharing her human condition. The problem lies in the helper, who is threatened by Jenny's demand she leave, and can't communicate her caring in a way that keeps her in the room. Instead, the helper holds Jenny accountable for whether they "win" or "lose."

When we are threatened as helpers, we are prone to making defensive, falsely reassuring, and disrespectful responses such as:

> It's all part of your illness. Don't be so angry. It will only make you feel worse. You know that what we are doing for you is for your own good in the long run.

Or,

> You may feel awful now, but you'll eventually feel much better.

In a similarly disrespectful way, we can find ourselves saying, "I know" or "I understand":

> I understand your feelings, but these treatments are necessary for you to get well.

> I know you feel that way. We shouldn't give up hope yet.

These responses suggest the helper is thinking, or is beginning to think, he or she knows more about Jenny than Jenny does. Few messages are likely to get you into trouble more quickly than ones beginning with "I know how you feel," or "I understand."

In *Zen and the Art of Helping*, social worker David Brandon explains why "I understand" and "I know how you feel" responses, even those based on similar life events, diminish our helping:

> "I know exactly how you feel" must be mistaken however good the intent of the speaker. How can it be possible to make any kind of accurate analogy, experiential or otherwise, between two persons' feelings, even about an apparently similar happening? When you tell me about the death of a friend, it is most probable that it is my pain I feel about the death of someone close to me. I cannot tell whether what moves inside my heart is similar to that which moves inside yours. I can share it but must be careful not to drown your grief and sorrow with my own.[3]

Another variation on this theme is the "I know where you're going, let me take you there" stance. A more helpful alternative message, one I frequently convey, is "I don't know where we're going, but I do know how to get there."[4] This more accurately matches the reality of the situation, and it also conveys confidence in your ability to facilitate a healthy and growth-producing relationship.

Effective helpers can admit they don't have an answer, don't know what to do, and don't understand yet, but they also don't run away. They communicate their caring and commitment to not abandon the person. Genuine and caring responses like the following ones can be extremely reassuring to someone in Jenny's predicament:

I wish I had the answer for why you have to lie here, and I get to go home at night, but I do care.

I know this is tough. I don't have the answers, but I'm here for you.

Other helpers see their major task as problem solving:

Jenny, you're right! I don't know how you feel, but you have choices. You can continue treatment and live here for as long as it takes, or you can stop treatment and go home to make each day a quality day for the rest of your life.

This response leaps into perhaps premature problem solving, what motivational interviewing experts call the *righting reflex*, but it also includes an elegant and disarming way of answering Jenny's cry. By saying to her, "You're right, I don't know," these responses neutralize her aggression and direct the interaction in a more constructive direction, similar to the way an aikido master disarms an opponent. In the following responses, we see this psychological aikido at work, plus some good empathy, personal sharing, and reassurance:

I can hear how angry and frustrated you are. I've never been in your situation, but I'm sure I would feel the same way. I admire you for hanging in there despite how difficult it is.

I don't understand everything you're feeling, but I understand you're mad. I'd be mad, too. I just want you to know that if you need me, I'm here. Just to hold your hand, or yell at, or anything.

I don't know what it's like to be in your situation, but I'm here and I'll do what I can to help.

I know you're feeling bad, and there's no way I can understand it fully, but I want to be with you and hear what you have to say.

Each of these last four responses avoids the conflict and misunderstanding possible if the helpers had instead attempted to convince Jenny they know how she feels. The interventions also reflect the capacity to be vulnerable, to not have a quick solution, and at the same time, to communicate caring.

Take another look at your response to Jenny. Did you stay in the room? Did you let her know you heard her anger? Did you acknowledge you don't know what it is like to be her, or that you do get to go home? If you were Jenny, how would you react to your own response?

HEALING WORDS: A MICROSKILLS APPROACH

Another way to look at your response to Jenny is to take a microskills approach, focusing on the specific communication skills you used or didn't use in the interaction. Did you respond with a question or a paraphrase of what Jenny said? Did you restate her feelings or disclose your own feelings or experiences? Did you give advice, make an interpretation, or stay silent? These possible responses are the communication microskills we use to convey our understanding, empathy and compassion.[5]

Skills are simply actions under voluntary control. Learning a new skill, whether it is empathic listening, problem solving, dancing, playing the violin, managing money, or being assertive, involves learning subskills that are then hierarchically organized in the execution of the skill. An intuitive model of skill development I like delineates four stages in the acquisition of a skill, with movement through stages of unconscious incompetence, conscious incompetence, and conscious competence, finally leading to consolidation of the skill in a state of unconscious competence.[6]

Initially, there is a state of unconscious incompetence: We don't know what we don't know. For example, many us—although the number is dwindling—remember the first time we tried to drive a car with a clutch. As the car lurched forward for the fifth time, most of us probably had a surge of newfound admiration for the way our parents flawlessly operated this recalcitrant machine.

We are all at a stage of unconscious incompetence with many communication skills essential to helping. This is true because our patterns of communicating have been strongly shaped by our social conditioning and are enacted automatically, with little awareness.

How many closed questions have you asked today? How many self-disclosures have you made? Few of us are aware of the pattern of communication skills we use every day. Yet these same patterns of communication significantly affect the levels of intimacy we have in our helping relationships, and our general ability to achieve positive helping outcomes. Because these communication patterns are largely outside our awareness, we can't map out alternate ways of reacting, and may feel helpless and stuck at times.

Some prevalent communication styles in our culture are an over-use of questions and quick advice by listeners, an extremely brief (1 second or less) pause between speakers, lots of verbal crowding, and an absence of quality listening responses sensitively reflecting the feelings and meaning the speaker has expressed. Carefully observe your own and others' conversations for the next week and see whether you notice these or other patterns.

Unfortunately, these culturally-conditioned patterns of communication are the reverse of the communication style demanded by the intimate encounters of the helping relationship. For example, to be effective as a caregiver, we must learn to ask fewer questions, give advice less often, allow more time before we speak, and mirror the feelings and content communicated by the people we are helping. When we begin to study our everyday styles of communication and attempt to change them in our helping encounters, we enter the unsettling second stage of skill development: conscious incompetence.

Conscious incompetence is a painful state wherein the subskills are not integrated and the learner is self-conscious and awkward. This phenomenon is a generic characteristic of skill acquisition. Returning to our driving example, in this stage you are fully aware of your limitations as a driver but haven't begun to learn the skills necessary for smoothly shifting the gears.

The third stage is conscious competence. In this stage of learning, you can execute the skill, but not without giving it your full attention. To use our driving example, now you can shift, but you can't talk with a passenger while you are doing so. With time and practice, the component skills will require less and less conscious attention, allowing you to devote increasing attention to higher level strategies for achieving your goals. When we are at this stage in skill acquisition, we can get excited by the successful execution of the skill in question, lose our hold on what we are doing, and make a next response significantly worse than our last one.

When a particular set of skills becomes automatic for you, you have arrived at the final stage of skill acquisition: unconscious competence. You already have many skills you use competently without thinking about what you are doing or why you are doing it: things like riding a bicycle, typing, or any of the hundreds of technical and clinical interventions you routinely make. The skills are automatic, and you draw upon them as situations call for them.

With new communication skills you are attempting to learn, the challenge is to make them your own and integrate them within your natural helping style. The goal isn't to become an obsessive imitation of the good helper and to make inauthentic, textbook responses. You need to discover what works best for you.

Becoming a master helper all at once simply isn't possible. Skillful performances must be broken down into their component skills, and then these microskills have to be learned and practiced separately before they can be combined in the execution of the larger task. It is common for beginning helpers to observe an expert helper in action and immediately want to duplicate the expert's helping style. This seems possible to the neophyte only because he or she isn't aware of the many component skills necessary to the expert's performance, whether the skilled act is a surgical intervention or a facilitative verbal response. This state of unconscious incompetence ends abruptly when the neophyte attempts to imitate the expert, and is disappointed by his or her much less effective results.

You can't learn all the skills you need in one fell swoop. However, you can be encouraged by knowing small, consistent changes in your communication style can lead to truly enormous changes in your helping relationships.

No skill can be learned, refined, and truly grasped without repeated executions. This saying of Confucius expresses the idea well: "I hear and I forget. I see and I remember. I do and I understand." It has been said a tourist in New York City once asked violinist Yehudi Menuhin for directions:

Tourist: Excuse me, how do you get to Carnegie Hall?

Menuhin: You practice! You practice! You practice!

However, we are learning not all practice is the same. Simply repeating a skill is not as growthful as practicing with focused attention and the specific aim to improve performance—what has become known as deliberate practice.[7] The deliberate practice (DP) model is being applied in the training of medical professionals and psychotherapists.[8; 9] Remember that a distinguishing characteristic of effective therapists is they actively practice improving their therapy skills. Skill acquisition and development is a lifelong endeavor.

Unfortunately, we frequently stop practicing a skill when we can successfully execute it just once. When this happens, the skill is still at the stage of conscious competence, and it will not be accessible to us in a wide range of situations with varying levels of complexity and demands. We can make the appropriate caring responses in an exercise with a peer, but put us in a room with a family, time pressure, and competing demands for our attention, and we will naturally revert to those behaviors most familiar to us.

Skill regression like this can also occur when our emotional buttons are being pushed and we are feeling some pain. As we struggle to get out of the Helper's Pit, we usually attempt to regain control, and find ourselves asking lots of questions, giving quick advice, and sometimes making inappropriate self-disclosures.

In our analysis of the responses to Jenny, we began to identify some general principles for effective helping communication. I would now like to suggest some additional guidelines for successful communication in the intimate process of helping. But I need to acknowledge writing on this topic is inherently risky. Any textbook solutions I might offer are at best mere guidelines for action in these difficult situations; at worst, they might lead to misapplications and failures. And, of course, I can only include a handful of the many skills necessary for effective communication. I cannot address the intricacies of therapeutic communication and strategy here. However, here are some suggestions you can experiment with.

Nonverbal Communication Skills

Much of helping communication is nonverbal and beyond words: your posture, the tone of your voice, the look in your eyes, the touch of your hand. These nonverbal channels of communication are probably as much or more important than verbal channels in determining what meaning others receive from our communications. They play an important role in creating presence and "being with" the person you are helping. Our extra-verbal behavior—fidgeting, or glancing at the clock—can significantly and often negatively affect how clients feel toward us and our relationship with them.

Our empathy is also dependent on how well we decode our clients' nonverbal behavior. A downward glance, rapid speech, or a clenched fist speak volumes, and affect us consciously and subconsciously. Mindfulness and self-awareness are needed to track these influences and messages—and respond accurately and empathically to them.

For empathy to develop, we must resist outside distractions and give the other person our deep, undivided attention. The way we attend to him or her plays an important role in fostering and maintaining quality attention. It is said empathic listeners develop big eyes, big ears, and a small mouth. Another adage is we have two ears and one mouth because we should listen twice as much as we speak.

A program (E.M.P.A.T.H.Y.) developed in the Empathy and Relational Science Program at Massachusetts General Hospital teaches medical professionals how to improve key dimensions of their helping behavior.[10] The program's title reflects the communication skills focused on: E (eye contact); M (muscles of facial expression); P (posture); A (affect); T (tone of voice); H (hearing the whole person); and Y (your response). The goals of the training are to enhance clinician empathy, increase patient satisfaction, improve health outcomes, and reduce malpractice claims. In a study of surgeons' voice tone and their malpractice claims history, tone of voice (dominant versus warm and concerned) was associated with the number of lawsuits filed by their patients.[11]

Another acronym for effective helper nonverbal communications is **SOLVER**. This acronym is based on a model devised by Gerard

Egan,[12] and is similar to the E.M.P.A.T.H.Y. teaching tool. The acronym helps remind us of some key elements of our attention to the other person:

Squarely Face the Other Person. Even if you are only making a brief visit or just stopping to talk for a minute or two, always turn your body directly toward the other person. If the person is in bed, sit near him or her and get at the same level. If you doubt the wisdom of this, try having a conversation with a friend while you are lying on the floor and your friend is standing over you. You will see how uncomfortable the listening position is and how it creates a passive-active, child-parent style of relating.

Adopt an **O**pen Posture. Don't cross your arms or legs or clasp your hands. These nonverbal behaviors signal defensiveness or unavailability, messages you don't want to communicate to the people you are assisting.

Lean Forward. This is a nonverbal behavior clients frequently cite as an important cue in giving them the impression their helper is genuinely interested in them and their problems. Of course, you don't want to lean forward compulsively in every moment of every helping encounter. But if you experiment with this behavior, you will find when you act interested, you will become more interested in what is happening. This happens in part because if you look interested, your client begins to notice this interest, and so becomes more engaged, open, and interesting.

Verbally Follow. Don't jump from topic to topic. Try to stick to the themes and content the client is bringing up. This is one way you can communicate respect to the other person. You are saying, "What you're sharing is important to me."

Maintain **E**ye Contact. This is an important way of saying, "I'm with you." The trick is to do it in a way feeling comfortable for you and for the other person. What this recommendation refers to is the kind of gentle and engaging eye contact (and not a fixed stare) we make in our everyday lives when we are in emotional contact with someone.

Be **Relaxed.** There are many distracting behaviors we can unconsciously engage in, like fidgeting with something, playing with a
pen or pencil, or rubbing our hands together. Videotape feedback
is extremely helpful in identifying and changing these habits.

Timing, Warmth, and Length of Responses

Plato gave us sage advice when he said, "Wise men speak because
they have something to say; fools speak because they have to say
something." We are often busy formulating our next response while
the person we are helping is still speaking to us, and so we don't
hear the last— and often the most important thing—the person
said. This interval between the time the other person stops talking
and you begin is crucial in helping. Unfortunately, we are usually unaware of our own tendencies to overtalk, crowd, or hurry
the other person. This crowding conversational style prevents the
development of intimacy in the helping relationship and hinders
self-exploration by the client.

If you give yourself permission to wait 1, 2, or sometimes even
3 seconds before you speak, you will most likely be pleasantly surprised by the results. Although you might think other people will be
disappointed with you for being slow to respond, in fact, they won't.
Because you will have an opportunity to be more fully immersed in
empathy and more delicately feel your way into what your clients
share with you, the accuracy, conciseness, and creativity of your
responses will dramatically improve. You will be more attuned to
your client and yourself. Once your clients hear your more thoughtful and empathic responses, they will start to enjoy waiting for them.
They will also find this small break gives them a chance to attend
more fully to their inner life, and they may jump in during this interval with another thought or feeling they have. Don't forget, empathy
takes time, If you are rushed, your responses will remain at a superfi-
cial and highly intellectualized level, and so will your client's. Remember you are there to listen, and when you respond, it is important to
take time to consider what you say. An ancient Chinese proverb tells
us we can chase butterflies all day, but only when we finally sit still
will one come and alight on our shoulder.

You can also dramatically increase the impact of your responses by shortening them. Long responses are difficult for clients to respond to. Keep your response to a single sentence or two, convey one idea, and have the response capture what is most alive for the client in this moment. Finally, deliver responses with modulation, accenting key words and consistently conveying a warm and soft quality. So, try out the habit of making "slow, soft, and simple" responses, and see what the effects are. Susan Johnson says these three qualities in our responses create safety for our clients.[13] These subtle but influential aspects of communication style lead clients to feel more understood, to share more, to deepen their experiencing level, and to enjoy a stronger working alliance.

The verbal skills we will now consider include the following: Minimal encouragers and repetitions; paraphrases; summarizations; reflections of feeling; additive empathy responses; client-frame-of reference responses; reflections of meaning; questions; self-disclosures; confrontations; interpretations; and directives or advice.

Minimal Encouragers and Repetitions

Let's continue to demystify the art of helping by looking at other basic elements of communication. Minimal encouragers, for example, are simple but key responses telling the other person you are right there and are interested in hearing more. Silence and the nonverbal attending behaviors already described—leaning forward, good eye contact, and focused attention—can be considered minimal encouragers. When you nod your head, say, "Tell me more," or utter "uh-huh" or "hmm," you are using minimal encouragers. These responses can maintain a smooth flow in the conversation.

We engage in repetitions when we restate some exact or almost exact words of the other person. We might select just a few words from several sentences and repeat them for emphasis, for example, "nowhere to turn," or "it feels like a dream." We can also add a questioning or interrogative element to the repetition: "at loose ends?" or "unglued?" Repetitions are useful because they highlight an important part of the message we are receiving and give our client an opportunity to elaborate on this theme.

Paraphrases

Paraphrases are real workhorses of helping, and mastering this talk tool will significantly improve your helping communication. When you paraphrase, you freshly state the content of the message and represent it. You will often use some of the client's exact words, and personalize the response by adding the client's name or by including "you" in the response. Although the paraphrase may include some of the client's words, its main job is to summarize the essence of what the client has said—staying true to his or her ideas without repeating them exactly, and trying to capture what is most alive and meaningful for them.

When done skillfully, paraphrasing can have an extraordinary impact. Paraphrases are reflections of content that do not include feelings. If feelings are included, the response is considered a reflection of feeling, to be discussed next. Here are some examples of paraphrases from interviews with two bereaved spouses. The first is from an interview I conducted with Anne, whose husband died 5 years earlier:

> **Anne:** I was totally unprepared to accept the fact he wasn't alive, and it took me a long time to come to terms with the reality of the fact he wasn't in this world in a physical way anymore. And...
>
> **Dale:** To come to grips with the finality of that.
>
> **Anne:** Yes, definitely. I remember initially thinking he'd still be coming home.

Although my response didn't use Anne's exact words, my words are close to hers in meaning, and mirror her initial difficulty accepting the reality of the loss.

Bill's wife died a year ago. Here he is describing his current reactions:

> **Bill:** I think that's what's been happening over the last year, going through the good...We'd been married almost 24 years. Going through all the good and the bad, and a lot of good memories.

Dale: You were able to go back to some of the good memories.

Bill: A lot of bad ones, too. I didn't realize they were there.

Dale: The complete picture of who you were together.

My first response wasn't totally accurate, and Bill corrected me by clarifying that the memories of him and his wife together aren't all positive ones. My "complete picture" response, also a paraphrase, gets us back on track, and adds a bit of my understanding as well. Good paraphrases require you to give of yourself: you synthesize what someone is saying and then share your best approximation of the essential message.

Listening and communicating are hard work, and we often think we are doing a better job at them than we actually are. Quality listening requires hearing the entire message being communicated by your client, not just the words. When we carefully study our actual responses in real-life helping encounters, we might realize we have repeatedly missed the essence of what someone was saying to us, or that our paraphrases have significantly detracted from the meaning communicated to us. We realize how much we still have to learn. At a conference honoring Carl Rogers' influence on health care, Rogers reflected on the hard work of becoming a good listener: "Listening seems such an easy word. I find it a lifetime task to achieve true listening, and a task well worth the effort."[14]

Summarizations

Think of summarizations as big paraphrases. Summarization responses usually reflect the content of more than just the previous exchange. Sometimes they reflect content shared earlier in the meeting or even days or weeks ago. Summarizations can also pull different contents together, identify themes, or recount what has happened up to a given point in a meeting. They are an excellent tool for making sure you and the client are on the same page. It is worth making a mental note to remind yourself to summarize several times in each helping encounter. Longer summarization responses can be made near the end of an intervention. For example, you might briefly summarize the understandings you and your client have arrived at, or an action plan you have developed together.

Reflections of Feeling

The reflection of feeling response is at the heart of empathic communication. These responses include a direct reference to the emotional part of the client's message and re-present the context of the feeling (i.e., why the person is feeling this way).

At its simplest, this response takes the following form: "You feel (feeling word or phrase) because of (source or context of feeling)." You can usually omit the word "feeling" in your response. For example, a reflection of feeling response to Jenny might be "You're angry and frustrated because of the illness and what you are going through." This response identifies her feelings (angry and frustrated) and their context (her illness and its painful effects on her).

You need to be careful, though, because sometimes we think we are reflecting feelings when we are actually responding to thoughts. A useful rule of thumb is feelings can usually be expressed in one word, whereas thoughts rarely can. Ask yourself, "How does he or she feel about it?" If you can formulate the answer in one word, chances are good you are dealing with a feeling, not a thought. The word "feeling" in a response does not guarantee emotions are being discussed. In fact, when the phrase "feeling that..." is used by you or the client, feelings are rarely being referred to or felt. For example, the statement "I'm feeling that you are taking advantage of me" is more focused on the behavior of the other person than on one's own feelings. A more direct feeling statement is "I'm feeling taken advantage of" or "I'm hurt by this."

Once you are sure you are reflecting feelings, a useful initial step is to distinguish whether what you are hearing is a positive or negative emotion. Positive emotions include love, caring, concern, joy, hope, confidence, delight, and relief, among others. Negative (does not mean "bad") emotions include inadequacy, fear, confusion, hurt, sadness, anger, loneliness, guilt, shame, victimization and others.

The next step in reflecting feelings is to identify the intensity level of the feeling. The angry person can be *furious* (high intensity), *resentful* (moderate intensity), or simply *put out* (low intensity). The depressed person can feel *hopeless* (high intensity), *discouraged* (moderate intensity), or *disappointed* (low intensity). A frequent error in reflecting feelings is misidentifying their intensity level.

Finding exactly the right word is the final step. You need to find a word or phrase the other person can relate to. For instance, some people can relate to feeling *impugned*, whereas I would relate better to the word *mistreated* or *exploited*. We all tend to overuse our favorite feeling words—words like upset, depressed, angry, hurt, and happy. These words don't adequately reflect the many nuances and contexts of our emotions, and when they are used too often, they tend to lose their meaning and effectiveness. Therefore, it is essential to develop a rich and differentiated vocabulary of feeling words and to put the vocabulary to work every day. An impoverished vocabulary of feelings can lead to uninspired and uninspiring responses with little emotional impact.

Good poetry has exactly the reverse effect: particular words or lines in poems touch some aspect of our experiencing in amazingly precise and affirming ways. In this sense, communicating empathy is a poetic process. You are painting a picture in words, a picture mirroring what you have heard or seen. As in poetry, metaphors and imagery are highly appropriate. Clients can speak in metaphors about things they could not otherwise find words for. For example, bereaved clients of mine describe feeling like they are "coming out of the fog," or "swimming in jelly." One client who was recovering from cancer and prided herself on a beautifully appointed home, said her inner emotional work and healing seemed much like "interior decorating."

Here are some examples of the reflection of feeling response. Linda's father died just 6 months before this interview, and she is describing the upsurges of her grief. I make a repetition response encouraging her to elaborate what "it" is, and then a second response reflecting the ambivalence she feels toward her emotional pain:

Linda: For me, just being with it was really hard, still is really hard, but it's getting better.

Dale: Being with the...

Linda: Being with the grief. It just comes. Everything's OK for a while, and then something just happens, you know.

Dale: It's a kind of ambivalent feeling about it. Part of you wants to go with it, and embrace it in a way, and say, this is a remembrance, and another part is saying, hmm, this doesn't feel so good.

Linda: Yeah, it's still uncomfortable, and I don't know when that changes, or if that changes.

In this next exchange, Anne describes being suddenly cast into the difficult role of single parent by her husband's death and her feelings of abandonment:

Anne: I mean, like I felt I had people dependent on me all the time, and I didn't have someone else sharing what I was feeling. This was a commitment we made to have these children, and that we would both raise them, and love them, and care about them, and I felt very abandoned. I felt like I was now the person responsible for these kids all the time. There was no one else really behind me in what I was doing or could give me a break and say, "You are doing a great job." It wasn't a team effort anymore.

Dale: Before that you couldn't, or didn't even realize, how much relief he did provide.

Anne: Exactly.

Dale: Or how important he was to you and the children. It's funny, isn't it? It was almost invisible, although you knew he was important. And

> also, it sounds like, maybe, with feeling aban-
> doned...I don't know...some anger at this—to
> be left alone to deal with this.

Anne: I don't think I allowed myself to get in touch
with how angry some of it made me.

My response to Anne's anger was intentionally tentative. I could hear the anger implicit in her statements and in her voice and expressions, but even though I was fairly confident in my perception of the anger, I didn't know if she was aware of it, or ready to explore it. Even though I hear anger, it doesn't give me license to tell her what she is feeling, because she is the authority on this. If I am correct, she might explore her feeling more deeply. If I am wrong, or if the feeling is too uncomfortable for her to acknowledge or fully confront, she might lead us to the areas of her experience she can safely talk about. However, if my response is insensitive in some way, she might conceal her inner reaction to it and our working alliance would suffer as a result.

Tentativeness is appropriate and helpful but shouldn't be confused with a timid and diffident interviewing style. The tentativeness must be the kind saying, "Does this fit?" or "Am I on track with this?"

One way to ensure greater tentativeness is to develop a large repertoire of *empathic response leads*. Beginning helpers often get into ruts by beginning each of their empathy responses in a stereotyped fashion. Stereotyped responses such as "I hear you saying...," " or "You feel...," " or "So..." repeated three or four times in a row draw attention to your technique and away from the content of your message. Having a large repertoire of different communication leads can help your client react to what you are saying and not how you are saying it. The best way to add these to your talk toolkit is to memorize them and then practice them in your everyday helping. Here is a brief list of some of these introductory phrases:

- If I'm hearing you correctly...

- To me it's almost like you're saying...

- So, you feel...

- So from where you sit...

- As I get it, you're saying…
- Sort of like saying…
- I'm picking up you…
- I wonder if you're saying…
- Sort of like feeling…
- In other words…
- I gather…
- It's like…
- I'm kind of hearing you say…
- What seems to be coming up for you is…

We also need to continually check out the accuracy of our response with the person we are helping. This doesn't mean we can never directly state what we see and say, for example, "I can see this is really painful for you."

The best measure of the effectiveness of any response is the client's response to it. With each response, ask yourself, "How did this response land with the client?" If the client doesn't negotiate in some way (e.g., look puzzled, ask a question) with the response and instead turns his or her attention inward, continuing with self-exploration, your response is likely facilitative.

Additive Empathy

Beyond the simple reflection of feeling responses are additive empathy responses. These responses reflect underlying or implicit feelings.[15] These responses add something by making the client's implied feelings explicit. My response to Anne's anger in the example just given was additive because, although her anger was implicit in what she said and how she said it, she didn't explicitly communicate it.

When you are reflecting implicit feelings, it is important to be somewhat tentative because you are inviting the person to openly explore what is going on for him or her, and to enter what might be uncharted and possibly frightening emotional territory. Often people will approach some of their more difficult feelings incrementally; for example, after clients first acknowledge and feel their frustration, then they can explore the full force of their anger.

The best advice is to approach feelings as a process and not to try to quickly categorize the feeling the client is experiencing. Feelings occur as part of emotional complexes containing a variety of feelings, and they change when they are exposed to the light of our awareness. Our affect is rooted in our biology; our emotions are rooted in and reflect our biography, our larger experience of life.

Beginning helpers often make the mistake of relating to feelings as fixed, unchanging entities inside the other person. But the reality is when clients turn their attention inward, and contact the problem they are having at a deeper experiential level, many different kinds of words and images might emerge. When trying to capture this emotional complexity, I often find it helpful to say, "Part of you is feeling... but the other part feels..." or, "It seems like several feelings are coming up for you. I'm getting a sense of both anger and hurt. Does that fit?"

As a helper, your task is not to tell the client what he or she is experiencing; it is to assist clients in bringing the unclear parts of their inner life into focus. If your responses are on target, and intersect with their experiential track in this very moment, your clients will receive them as congruent with his or her experiencing—as the next thing he or she might have said or felt. He or she can then continue in this process without having to stop and negotiate with your response. Elliott and colleagues describe what is happening in these moments:

> The art of empathic affirmation is to trust that clients' growth potential will emerge in response to the therapist's being able to see and validate the client as they really are in the moment and by providing safety and validating the vulnerability, clients will become more resilient.[16]

This process is analogous to a quarterback throwing the football down the field to a receiver.[17] If the quarterback throws the ball ahead of the receiver, the pass has too much "lead" in it. The same is true with our empathic responses. We have to estimate where the client's experiential movement is going next and throw the ball (our response) exactly there. If we are on target, the client catches the ball without missing a step and continues down the field. If we throw the ball behind the client, he or she must slow down or stop and back up to catch the pass. For example, if someone says, "I'm hurt my sister hasn't visited me," and we say, "You're feeling hurt because your sister hasn't visited you," we've thrown the ball behind her. She might think, "Yes, that's what I said, all right," and then hope our next response is better. If we continue throwing the ball behind her, she'll become irritated and probably not want to continue the interaction.

In this situation, sensing their clients' growing irritation, many helpers become threatened and decide they need to do something dramatic to get the interaction back on track. So they throw the ball all the way down the field (a "Hail Mary" intervention) with a response something like "This feeling of abandonment is like what happened with your father, isn't it?" The client dives for the pass but fails to catch it because it is way ahead of her. Seeing this, the helper then returns to responses with less lead, but the same problem recurs.

This sequence can repeat itself again and again. Inadequate, low-lead responses are followed by even less effective, high-lead responses, and then more weak, low-lead responses. The client feels alternately frustrated and confused or defensive. The key to preventing this pattern is to work hard at freshly phrasing what the client is explicitly saying to you, listen for the implied parts of his or her message, and capture the forward moving edge of experience reflected in this implicit message. Clients can then become more aware of their feelings and meanings, and the exchange can continue in a pattern much like the children's game, "warmer," "warmer," "colder," "colder." It is a process of discovery for you and your client.

Another metaphor for this is that of climbing a ladder. Visualize yourself and your client climbing a ladder together, with each new awareness moving your client one rung up. Your additive responses should be directed to the next rung on this ladder, but not beyond it.

Client-Frame-of-Reference Responses

Another advanced microskill is what I call the client-frame-of-reference or first-person response. This microskill is excellent when you are deeply empathically attuned to what the other person is experiencing and want to communicate your perception of that in the most direct way possible.

In the client-frame-of-reference response, you speak from the point of view of the client, using the first-person. Rather than replying to Jenny with, "I can hear how angry and frustrated you are about your illness and what you're going through," you would instead say, "What I'm hearing you say, Jenny, is, I'm angry and frustrated by this illness and what it's putting me through." This response mode can be used to paraphrase, summarize, or reflect feelings.

Here I make a first-person response to Anne, and she discloses the feelings of hopelessness she had after her husband's death:

> **Anne:** I guess the thing that comes most to mind is change. I mean phenomenal changes occurred after Chris died. Changes for me, it was who I was, what my role was, and how I was going to survive, initially, the first 5 years…
>
> **Dale:** So, for you, it was "Can I go on?"
>
> **Anne:** A tremendous amount of hopelessness initially. Chris died 33 days after an acute leukemia diagnosis.

My response to Anne is a prototypic client-frame-of-reference response because it includes the introductory phrase, "So for you it was," which told Anne I was reflecting what I heard her saying. This is important because things said in the first person can be mistaken as self-disclosures. If I had said only, "Can I go on?" Anne might have wondered if I was saying, "Can I [Dale] go on?" To avoid this confusion, it is best always to introduce first-person responses with a phrase like the following: "I'm hearing you say, for me…"; "It sounds like you're saying, I…"; "So for you, it's I…"; or "The way you see it is, I…" But be careful. Even if you become proficient at using the first-person response, resist overusing it. It is an ideal communication skill when your other listening responses have set the stage for this more powerful intervention. It is not such a good skill for getting on track with your client. Paraphrases, questions, and simple reflections of feeling are best for that purpose. But when you are already accurately empathizing, and want to deepen this empathy, a client-frame-of-reference response can be highly facilitative.

Examples of this first-person response with a bereaved client can be found in Carl Rogers' (CR) demonstration interview with Peteranne (P), who had miscarried twins 2 years before and was possibly pregnant at the time of the interview:

> **P:** ...I guess I question myself in a lot of ways too. If I had made attempts earlier, would it have been easier?

> **CR:** Uh-huh, uh-huh. Should I have laid aside my career a little earlier and tried to become pregnant?

> **P:** Yeah, because...I would have had two little kids 2 and a half years old.

> **CR:** And so, you're asking, "Did I make a mistake?"

> **P:** Yeah. And that's...a scary thought, to think that your whole life has been a mistake along the way.

> **CR:** Uh-huh, uh-huh. Did I make a very grave error in not having made the attempt sooner?[18]

HEARING AND RESPONDING TO GRIEF'S QUESTIONS

As we see in the Rogers interview with Peteranne, the client-frame-of-reference response is particularly helpful when responding to grief and loss. The person confronting grief and loss has more questions than answers, and asks these of us, of himself or herself, and sometimes of God. The questions often concern the following existential issues that now confront them:

Why me? Why did this have to happen? These are probably the first questions every bereaved person asks. Why did my loved one have to die? Existential questioning is common: Are we ants on the railroad track, or is there some reason for this suffering? We attempt to get secondary control over the loss: to make sense of it, to find meaning in it, and to prevent it from occurring in the future. At a time when our basic assumptions about the world and ourselves can be either shattered or transformed, these efforts to restore our psychological equilibrium make eminent sense and are a critical component of coping.

What is happening to me? The grieving person feels radically different from his or her former self and wants to know what is happening to him or her. Here I reflect Bill's questioning with a client-frame-of-reference response, and with a question checking out the accuracy of my response:

> **Bill:** I was at a retreat house this summer. It was something I found in common with some of the people there. You think you are going out of your mind. Everyone else is normal, thinking it's crazy. The feelings are so strong. They are so intense you don't have anything to relate them to.

> **Dale:** So, what is this process? What is this? What's happening to me? Is that how you feel?

> **Bill:** Is this normal, or am I just completely whacko?

How can I go on? Feelings of hopelessness are common in people who are grieving. In the exchange with Anne presented previously, I made a first-person response—"So, for you, it was a 'Can I go on?' kind of feeling?"—reflecting her struggle to continue on with life after the loss of her husband.

What can I do? The "problem" of grief has no easy solutions. The grieving person's course of action is unclear, and at the same time, a cascade of advice pours in. Friends advise the individual to go on, have another child, remarry, or find meaning in the loss. The problem is there is often a stinging discrepancy between these expectations and the inner reality of the grieving person.

Who will help me? The grieving person asks, "Who will be there for me?" "Whom can I count on?" There are often many unpredicted responses, some pleasant, some unpleasant, as the grieving person seeks out support from family and friends.

What do I need? A fog of ambiguity can envelop the grieving person, making it difficult for the person to tell us how we can be of assistance. The grieving person often just does not know what we could possibly do to be helpful, because they know their ultimate desire—to have their loved one alive again—is not attainable.

Will this ever end? The grieving person asks, "How long will this last?" "When will I feel better?" This question becomes more urgent when the individual feels as awful, or even worse, months or years into the bereavement. For many people, it is particularly upsetting when they feel no better at 13 months than they did at 11 months, because they expected things to change for the better at the 1-year mark. Other people think they should be finished grieving at 3 months or 6 months, or they are frightened when waves of grief are triggered by events in their lives. I label these upsurges "grief attacks" and explain they are normal and to be expected.

Who am I now? Our identities to a large extent consist of the images self-important people in our lives reflect back to us, and when we lose one of the mirrors that uniquely defines us in this way, we lose some of our identity and sense of self. Here Linda grapples with the change in her identity—the redefinition of self—that is part of grief and mourning:

I think, after the initial shock of it all, it's just been hard to figure out who I am now. I'm a daughter without a father. And that was the first thought that came to me after I settled a little bit. Who am I, now that I don't have my dad?

How will my life be? This questioning reflects the struggle to become an active agent for one's own well-being, and to reinvest in life. All grieving people have some uncertainty about this new future lying ahead, and how they will find their way in it.

As we are seeing, the client-frame-of-reference response is particularly effective in responding to the inner questioning and struggles of our clients. There are three ways it promotes therapeutic process. First, the response has the effect of deepening our empathy by having us more fully assume the client's frame of reference. When we say, "So for you it feels like, I'm different now," we are more able to feel this change in identity with the client than we are if we say, "So for you it feels like you are different now." Second, for clients, the first-person response is like a perfect mirror of their experience, not requiring translation from the second-person to first-person tense. They can take the response in and immediately resonate it with their current experiencing. Finally, it is a way to make perhaps the most valid and honest response we can when our clients struggle with grief's questions. We can't give easy answers to these questions, but if we hear them, and help the grieving person live the questioning process, the answers may someday appear, in a way described by Rilke in this beautiful passage:

> . . . be patient toward all that is unsolved in your heart and try to love the questions themselves like locked rooms and like books that are written in a very foreign language. Do not now seek the answers, which cannot be given you because you would not be able to live with them. And the point is to live everything. Live the questions now. Perhaps you will then gradually, without noticing it, live along some distant day into the answer.[19]

Reflecting Meaning

As the preceding discussion of the first-person response illustrates, we are often responding not just to thoughts and feelings, but also to the deeper meanings tying these thoughts and feelings together. Here we enter into the realm of values, beliefs, and the sense people make of events in their lives. These basic theories (schemata) about the world can be severely threatened by negative or unexpected life events such as loss, life-threatening illness, or pain. Assumptions of personal invulnerability, of a meaningful and benevolent universe, and of one's own self-worth no longer seem adequate to explain what is happening, leading to a search for a new set of personal beliefs to make these traumatic events more comprehensible.[20]

Reflecting meanings is similar to reflecting feelings. The reflection of meaning response can take many forms, but it is essentially an elaboration of a basic "You mean" message, similar to how reflections of feeling have "You feel" as their core message. You can reflect meaning and the search for it with a variety of microskills. For example, you might ask a question: "What does this mean to you?" or "What sense are you making of this?" You could also use a paraphrase to reflect meaning: "It looks like the world sometimes just isn't fair," or "It sounds like you value the closeness you've had during this time."

Many assumptions and beliefs people have about life and themselves are implicit and are only brought to awareness when they are threatened by events contradicting them. You need to listen carefully to people as they struggle with these often confusing and uncertain thoughts and feelings. As with grief's questions, there are no easy answers you or anyone else can provide. But if you recognize this search for meaning, and can find words offering comfort and empathy in this time of crisis, the people you help will be more likely, ultimately, to find positive meanings in these painful events.

Questions: To Ask or Not to Ask?

Questions, the kinds we ask as helpers, are the most overused and misused of all the helping microskills. In my graduate counseling classes, students participate in a skill-building exercise in which I instruct them to refrain from asking any questions for several 15-minute conversations. At first, they are either speechless because they can't imagine how anyone could converse without asking questions, or they are confident this won't be a difficult assignment for them. All finally do succeed in this task, but not without real difficulty and much valuable learning along the way. I encourage you to try this exercise sometime in the next week and see what you learn about your questioning skills.

My students frequently report after doing the question-free sessions that the impact on their interactions was dramatic and often surprising. There is usually one or more students in the class who report a communication breakthrough of some kind. For example, many students who are parents say they had the most intimate and revealing conversation with a teenage son or daughter they have ever had. No small effect for simply deleting one microskill!

Others also report refreshing changes in their interactions and describe a new awareness of the liberating effects of not asking questions, not just for the person with whom they were talking, but also for themselves as listeners. They felt they responded more sensitively and accurately to the content and feelings of their conversational partner because they had more time to think about what they heard and formulate their responses.

We usually think of questions as the best way to get people talking or gather information. We fail to see what most helping theorists do, namely, that questions are ineffective in helping someone explore thoughts and feelings and they often fail to gather the most helpful information. Asking questions creates the expectation we will do something useful with all the information we have collected. As helpers, our goal should be to assist clients to attain an increase in their understanding of their situation; questions tend to increase our understanding, not theirs. Of course, when specific information is needed in the care of a patient, questions can be helpful, even necessary.

In everyday conversations, questions can serve the function of keeping the conversation away from intimate topics and feelings, and this is probably appropriate most of the time. However, in the intimate communication of the helping encounter, these effects are undesirable and undermine our efforts. A rapid-fire series of closed questions is appropriate for an IRS audit or a courtroom interview, but in an intimate, egalitarian relationship, this communication style can be highly counterproductive. The advice of most helping experts is to ask very few questions and, if you do ask a question, don't follow it with a second or third.

There is a dramatic difference, too, in the effects of different kinds of questions. The two basic types of questions are closed questions and open questions. Closed questions can usually be answered with a yes or no and typically begin with *Are, Is, Can, Do,* or *Have.* For example: Are you feeling nauseated today? Is your sister going to visit? Can you understand what she's going through? Do you want to go there again? Have you had anything to drink this morning?

Closed questions can also be of the multiple-choice variety: "Whom do you want to see most—your father, your mother, or your sister?" Closed questions are highly directive because they drastically limit the possible range of responses to them. Of course, there is a place for them, for example, when you need specific treatment-relevant information.

Open questions begin with *How, What, Could,* or *Why.* They are less directive than closed questions because they permit a greater range of responses. If you visualize the helping conversation as a funnel, open questions expand the conversation into the large section of the funnel, and closed questions squeeze it into the funnel's narrow opening. This is why open questions are effective at the beginning of a conversation to "open things up" and why we often rely on closed questions to help us end or leave interactions (e.g., "Is there anything else I can do for you today?" "No." "Then I'll see you tomorrow.").

Different kinds of open questions have considerably dissimilar effects. *How* questions are best for eliciting feelings and exploring psychological reactions: "How is that for you?" *What* questions are better for eliciting less affective content: "What's been happening in the past week?" or "What do you think about that?" *Why* questions should be used sparingly because they are usually not easily answered and tend to provoke defensiveness. For example, "Why are you doing that?" might be a simple request for information, but it could easily be interpreted as including a veiled opinion about what the other person should or should not be doing.

There is another way to less directly ask a question that is useful because it is particularly effective in inviting the client to take an active role in the conversation. The indirect question requests information by stating your interest or curiosity about some aspect of the client's thoughts, feelings, or situation.

- I'd like to know more about how your chemotherapy has been going.
- I'm wondering how your husband is responding to all this.
- I'm curious about your plans for taking care of yourself.

- It wasn't clear to me what you meant earlier when you said…
- I need some information about any childhood illnesses you might have had.

This way of responding can keep you from getting into a flurry of questions when you don't understand what the other person has said and need something clarified. When this occurs, it is good to say something like, "I missed what you were saying about how…."

One way to decrease question usage is to transform questions into statements. We often observe or hear something and then ask an obvious question about it. For example, we might see someone in physical discomfort and ask, "Are you feeling more uncomfortable today?" We could instead say, "It looks like you're feeling more uncomfortable today." This makes for a more direct and engaging style of interacting, and puts less pressure on the client to accommodate to what he or she might perceive as a demand.

You can get more control over this central microskill by studying yourself to see what your current questioning pattern looks like. If more than 10 to 20% of your responses are questions, particularly closed ones, you can enjoy quick success by beginning to experiment with other ways of communicating. Of course, you will have to go through a painful period of conscious incompetence and conscious competence en route to a new helping style less encumbered by question asking, but it will be well worth it. As your questioning decreases, other microskills will take their place. These other microskills will soon become more natural to you, and you will begin to use them at increasingly higher skill levels.

Self-Disclosures

Most people think self-disclosures are the most natural and spontaneous of all communications. The reality is this communication microskill is usually either overused or underused, and not skillfully delivered. Few helpers have developed the skill of effective self-disclosure; they remain limited to a few basic ways of disclosing themselves as helpers. Usually, they offer a "me-too disclosure" that says, "I've encountered something like this myself."[21] These kinds of disclosures should be kept to a minimum, and should only reference issues in your life not currently troubling you. You might think disclosing a personal difficulty much like the client's issue will increase the bond between you, but it can instead backfire, converting the helping relationship into one of mutual support, with the client becoming concerned about your welfare, and perhaps more reluctant to share his or her struggles because they are seen as potentially being an additional burden for you. If you do a me-too disclosure, the important element of it is the empathy it conveys. If it is delivered effectively, the client's attention remains focused inward, and does not shift to you.

When there is a problem in the helping relationship, we need to address it immediately. It must become our number one priority, but how do we do this? One axiom I have always found helpful in these circumstances was advised by psychologist Gerald Goodman: "When in trouble, disclose on the double."[21] For example, we earlier saw self-disclosures used in many of the more effective responses to Jenny: "I don't know how you feel," "I've never been in your situation, but I think I would feel the same way," and "I sure wish I had the answer for why you have to lie here and I get to go home at night, but I do care." Note how important it is to convey your caring and desire to help her.

If you stumble in some way, such as forgetting something significant about a person or their problems, or make any other mistake clearly apparent to him or her, self-disclosure can put things back on track and repair momentary ruptures in the working alliance. We all make mistakes. Nondefensively acknowledging them, even almost beatifying them sometimes, can turn a difficult moment into a relationship-enhancing one. Few people can resist disarming and supportive self-disclosures at moments like these. Practicing openness and processing everything are key.

We often resist self-disclosing our stumbles or more major errors as helpers because this behavior doesn't match our internalized ideal helper—the helper who never makes mistakes. My argument is nothing inspires confidence as much as a nondefensive, truthful approach. However, once you have either disclosed personal content to convey empathy, or acknowledged an error, or the reality that you do get to go home at night, it is critically important to keep your focus on the person you are caring for, and to acknowledge you are going to continue working to help solve his or her problems. Self-disclosing in situations like these is a high-level skill some helpers acquire naturally, and others never do. When you are considering self-disclosing, always ask yourself, "For whom am I doing this?" The answer should always be "For my client." If not, don't self-disclose.

Confrontations

Confrontation responses are not what most people first think they are. Confrontation in this context does not mean attacking, or in any way, lowering the self-esteem of the other person. The most critical and defining feature of a confrontational response is it points to a discrepancy in what the client is saying, thinking, feeling, or doing. Because of this, confrontations can often be worded as follows: "On the one hand, you said, felt, or did this one thing, but on the other hand, you said, felt, or did this other thing." For example, someone might say, "I am all alone; there's no one to turn to." A confrontation response might be "On the one hand, you feel all alone, but you've told me you do have some friends who have come through in the past, and I wonder if they might do it again." A somewhat gentler confrontation would be "You've told me you have some friends, but even though you have them, you still feel alone."

The trick with confrontation responses is to deliver them in a way not lowering the person's self-esteem by denying the emotional truth of his or her statements. For this reason, I like to think of confrontations as *care-frontations*. Also, because confrontation responses are more action-oriented responses and sometimes bring attention to touchy topics like self-deception and patterns of avoidance, they shouldn't be used until a supportive relationship is firmly established.

Interpretations

Interpretations are responses wherein the helper offers an idea the client hasn't already (consciously) thought of. Nevertheless, the response should make immediate sense to the client because it captures meanings already forming in the client's awareness. For example, a client might be having a recurring problem in all her relationships, but not be consciously aware of this pattern. You might present your observation of this pattern with an interpretation: "You know, Jane, I see some of the same patterns in your relationship with your mother in your relationships with Karen and Joan. In each relationship, you're always the one who gets stuck in the caretaking role, and you're not getting your needs met." It is usually best to first invite the client to connect some of the dots by asking, "I am wondering how you make sense of these recurring issues in your relationships?" It is always best if the client feels the insight is their own, because this allows them to take full ownership of it and to more readily translate the insight into productive changes in behavior.

These kinds of responses are, I believe, best reserved for the more uncovering, and insight-oriented, work of psychotherapy. However, an occasional interpretation, if offered tentatively and in a way not lowering the person's self-esteem, or putting the person on the defensive, can be thought provoking and helpful in any caregiving situation. Making these kinds of responses without increasing shame and guilt is an essential therapist skill, particularly in the deeper realms of therapeutic action.

Advice

We work with people in highly stressful situations. This inevitably pushes some deep and frightening emotional buttons in us. When this happens, we and our clients are vulnerable and eager to solve the problem to ease our shared discomfort. Unfortunately, there are usually no simple solutions, only questions: questions about what we are doing, and how we might help in better ways. For example, we might ask, "How can I help Joan's family deal with their struggle around holding on versus letting go of her?" In a different situation, we might wonder, "Am I the only one around here who feels all this pain about Jimmy's dying? How can I get his family to tell him how they actually feel? Or don't they feel anything?" Faced with a young, terminally-ill mother who is trying to keep the truth of her condition from her children, we might think, "How can I get through to Sally? She has to make plans so her kids are taken care of. I feel like I just have to get her to talk about just how sick she is."

Such questions are inevitable and necessary to the work we do, and we sometimes feel almost desperate to find answers to them. This urgency makes us susceptible to quick advice. Trouble is, this advice doesn't usually solve our problems. As H. L. Mencken once said, "There's always an easy solution to every human problem—neat, plausible, and wrong."[22] Even when solutions are simple, carrying them out can be difficult. Quick advice often leaves the recipient feeling unsatisfied, misunderstood, discounted, or even angry and resentful. Listening carefully and empathically to someone without trying to solve his or her problem is an important form of skilled communication. Of course, an active problem-solving approach is highly appropriate in clinical contexts when dealing with illness, health promotion, exercise, diet, medications and many other health issues, but quick advice is not.

In those situations where advice is called for, I've found an effective way to offer it is through self-disclosure. If you have been in a similar situation, you can share what worked for you: "This might not work for you, but what I found helpful for me was to ...." The introductory phrase, "This might not work for you," softens the advice and makes the other person more likely to explore this option. When someone is facing a problem I have previously helped dozens of other people grapple with, I sometimes summarize three or four of the solutions my former clients arrived at for this situation, and then let the person consider if any of the alternative responses seems right for him or her. Now let's turn to some general recommendations for listening and helping.

GENERAL RECOMMENDATIONS FOR LISTENING AND HELPING

Develop a Wide Range of Helping Responses

One way to fulfill yourself as a helper is to increase your repertoire of helping skills. To do this, you will need to practice the different skills presented here and try using them in real helping situations. If you have moved to the stage of unconscious competence with a wide range of skills, you will avoid skill ruts and mechanical repetitions in your responses. Repeating "Sounds like you're feeling" begins to sound like you're feeling bored, and it will surely bore or annoy the person you are helping. By using a variety of response leads, a diverse vocabulary of feelings, and a wide range of skills, you will be a much more interesting and effective helping companion.

If you increase your skill repertoire, you will be able to generate many different helpful responses in any given situation. Remember, there is no single "correct" response; there are only effective and ineffective ones. As your skill repertoire increases, you will feel more confident; this in turn will enhance your creativity and instill more confidence in the people you care for. As these new skills become second nature to you, you will be able to, as Kennedy and Charles put it, "respond to the person instead of trying to make a good response."[23]

Use Different Skills in Different Phases of Helping

Many theorists divide helping into three general phases. These three phases are exploring, understanding, and acting.[24] The helper has different tasks in each of these three phases. In the exploring phase, the primary goal is to establish trust and rapport, communicate respect and empathy, and explore the problem. In this phase, sensitive listening is critical.

In the second phase, understanding, you can begin to facilitate a deeper exploration of the problem and start to help your client establish workable goals. Goals are, after all, the flipside of problems. For example, if a client is lonely, his or her goal might be to become better connected socially. In this phase, helper self-disclosure and additive empathy responses become more appropriate and useful because they foster the trust and insight necessary to examine inner barriers to change.

In the third phase, action, you can make sure your client's goals are clearly defined and support him or her in taking first steps toward the fulfillment of those goals. Here, advice and confrontation begin to play a larger role because the issue now is how the person can take his or her new awareness and act differently in the world.

In any given helping relationship, several different problems can be worked on simultaneously, and each can be in a different phase of the helping process. You might just be beginning to hear the outlines of one problem while you are well along in your progress on another.

Use the Least Amount of Authority and Control Necessary

In a nonauthoritarian helping relationship based on mutual participation, the kind we strive for in person-centered/patient-centered care, the helper is encouraging but not controlling, and exerts the least amount of authority and control necessary to achieve the desired results. Success or failure in this task is closely linked to the helper's communication skills. Take a second look at the list of microskills presented earlier in this chapter. Can you identify the quality or characteristic increasing as you move from the top of the list to the bottom? The quality is control or directiveness. Silence exerts almost no control or directiveness on the client, questions exert considerably more, confrontations exert yet more, and so forth.

Authoritarian helpers use more closed questions, give more advice, make more interpretations, allow for fewer silences, and generally dominate the helping encounter. The nondirective, flexible helper is highly active (a nondirective style must not be confused with passivity), but the content of the interview—and the solutions to problems—comes from the client. Advice, confrontations, interpretations, closed questions, and other more directive responses are not prohibited, and can often be used to good effect, but they should be used sparingly and with awareness of their intended and unintended outcomes.

In helping interactions, the goal is to keep the conversational ball in the client's court as much as possible. This has an empowering effect, giving the client time and psychological space to explore his or her feelings and ideas, and ourselves an opportunity to observe the other person, and to deepen our empathy. However, the barrage of questions in everyday conversation results in a ping pong dynamic: We ask a closed question, the other person answers with a single word, then the conversational ball is instantly back in our court. We then reply with another closed question, and the pattern continues.

Less directive interventions, like silence, minimal encouragers, paraphrases, reflections of feeling, and first-person responses, tend to keep the ball in the client's court. Using these microskills leads to more moments when you can respond, but the conversational rules don't demand you do so.

You should try to keep the ball in the client's court as much as possible. Making a checking-out response, such as "Is that it?," will often elicit an acknowledgment, but then the client can also go on to bring up something related or perhaps something different and significant. One way to describe this general interviewing style is you are helping people tell their stories.

Suspend Judgment

Our perceptions and our evaluations are often dangerously intertwined. To be an effective helper, we need to allow the client's statements to sink in without trying to make decisions (e.g., "Is this right or wrong, responsible or irresponsible?"). It is always tempting to overlay our values on the thoughts and actions of the people we help. But each of these judgments erodes the sense of we-ness we have with the other person. As much as you can, listen with an open mind and an open heart to the other's message, without making any decisions about it.

Listen for Themes

A technique I find helpful is to listen for themes. These themes can often help you organize and interrelate the different content shared with you. They might be things like "Nothing is going to work out," "Life is the pits," or "I'm someone who can't say no."

I note or "red flag" these themes and keep them in my mind as the conversation continues. I might explicitly describe or summarize the theme if it seems helpful, or I might instead simply add it to my perceptions of the client and our current interaction. Most helping conversations or dialogues, no matter how chaotic or disparate the content seems, are of a piece, and your challenge is to make sense of how it all fits together.

One organizing theme we should always pay attention to relates to important things being said about a client or family member's self—image, goals, disappointments, emotions, or other highly personal concerns. When this happens, your sole task is to concentrate on comprehending the individual's inner world.

An important goal for you as a helper is to facilitate the self-exploration of the person you are helping. Your clients routinely face the distress-disclosure dilemma, and your general task is to facilitate their self-disclosure while maintaining or enhancing their self-esteem. As we know from our earlier discussions of secrets and self-concealment in therapy (*see* Chapter 4), there are also exceptionally significant instances when clients are struggling with whether to conceal or disclose extremely important and treatment-relevant personal information.

In *Secrets and Lies in Psychotherapy*, Farber, Blanchard and Love offer suggestions for therapist responses in these moments, including: "Can you say more about that?"; "Please help me understand what you're trying to tell me."; "Is there something I can do to make this easier to talk about?"; or "It feels like you're really struggling to let me know what happened to you."[25] It is less important to hear the content of the secret than it is to acknowledge and empathize with the struggle to conceal it.

Meet the Request Being Made

As helpers, we should always try to empathize with the people we are caring for. However, it isn't always important for us to communicate this empathy to them. People seeking help make at least three different kinds of requests of their helpers: requests for action, requests for information, and requests for understanding and involvement.[26]

Requests for action include statements like "The light's in my eyes" or "My pain is acting up." Can I have the pain medication my doctor recommended?" Requests for information might include "Are you going to be working tomorrow?" or "Can this prescription be filled at the pharmacy?" Requests for understanding and involvement are communications wherein the client is asking for a relationship—not action or advice—and where the major message is an emotional one. Some examples would be, "I feel really helpless just watching her get worse and not being able to do anything about it," or "Being alone is what gets to me. No one seems to care. I feel pretty abandoned by all those people I thought were my friends." Identifying effective responses to these kinds of requests is a central goal of this chapter.

There can also be more than one request in a single statement: "I'm worried about the way things are heading (a request for understanding and involvement). Are the staff telling me everything about my illness (a request for information)?"

It is extremely important for us to know when each of these different kinds of requests is being made, and to respond accordingly. For example, Jenny, the patient we practiced responding to earlier in this chapter, was clearly making a request for understanding and involvement when she expressed such strong feelings. However, we could easily have seen only a request for action, and have left the room, or a request for information, and have left to find out more about her current medical condition and treatments. Neither of these responses addresses Jenny's request for understanding and involvement.

When a patient says, "The light is in my eyes," the appropriate response is to pull down the shade, not "You're really upset about the light in your eyes." It is an error to believe we should always or exclusively attend to deep existential and inner emotional concerns. In fact, clients' concerns about work or finances or physical pain are often most pressing. Problem solving, helping them take care of their daily concerns, or giving them a little information, would probably be the best way to help in these areas. On the other hand, because it is often much easier and more comfortable to deal with our patients' surface issues and obvious requests for action and information. This means we can easily miss their more subtle requests for understanding and involvement.

Frequently, however, clients and their families are unclear about what they want or need from us. They also often mix two different kinds of requests. If you hear more than one request in your client's communication, ideally you should try to address both requests.

However, demands on our time or limits to the situation often permit us to address only one.

Work Upstream When Possible

When we take action is also very important. There is a contemporary fable of a man walking beside a river who notices someone is drowning. He jumps in, pulls the person ashore, and revives him. Then, another drowning person calls for help. Again, the man successfully rescues him. As the man is about to walk away, a passerby shouts, "Hey, there's another person drowning out there! Where are you going?" The man replies, "I'm going upstream to see who's throwing all these people in!"

Much of our helping is downstream, rather than upstream, work. Patients and their families have already suffered a great deal before coming to us: their relationships are strained, psychological difficulties have taken a great toll, their bodies are ravaged, or death has occurred, and pain is deep. It is too late for prevention. You can't jump into a time machine, go back 30 years, and convince a patient to stop smoking. We have to work downstream most of the time, at the end of the line, even though it is often frustrating and exhausting to do so.

The mental health and health care fields are moving, albeit slowly, towards greater emphasis on prevention, wellness, and a more upstream approach. This makes sense because no disease has ever been conquered through downstream, curative interventions. Upstream approaches such as immunizations, pollution control, changes in health behaviors, and the acquisition of psychological skills, to name just a few, hold the ultimate answers to reducing and possibly eliminating the physical, psychological, and social problems that now plague us.[27]

As caregivers, it is helpful—both to us and to the people we assist—to look for any upstream interventions we can make. It is also less stressful to work upstream, where the problems begin and changes still can be made. For example, you might do community education work, make an early evening phone call to a family telling them what to expect during the night, or intervene with a timely end-of-life conversation.[28] These kinds of interventions can prevent some of the difficulties we repeatedly encounter downstream, and so reduce our stress.

Avoid Trivializing Distress

One empathic error we can make in helping is to under-respond to the distress someone is experiencing. For example, we can refuse to acknowledge suffering by blocking communication about it:

> I find myself trying to make everything all right! The patient is dying. She reveals her concern that her husband doesn't even care. Though I feel the same distancing of the spouse to his dying wife, I gloss it over. I refuse to let her talk about it. I make excuses for the husband. I cut off healing self-disclosure. The last 2 weeks of this patient's life were spent in uncontrollable pain.

Another way we can under-respond to suffering is to encourage people to be "super copers," or urge them to see their illness or grief as a challenge, not as a threat. This stance can lead people to conceal their suffering because they see it as a symptom of a failure to cope.

Richard Lazarus gave several reasons for this trivialization of distress in our society.[29; 30] First, in our culture, suffering is seen as a waste of time. Death is a problem, and grief is inconvenient. Second, the enormous popularity of the stress management principle of converting our threats into challenges has led to the misapplication of this simple wisdom to grief and grieving. For everyday stressors, neither clearly positive nor negative, this strategy can work, as research on stress hardiness has shown (see Chapter 3). However, the benefits of this attitudinal shift should not be romanticized as applicable to all stressors. Many tragic life events have little or no redeeming value.

When we encourage patients to "have a good attitude," there can be many unintended consequences for the management of suffering. Many cancer patients have shared with me they resent being told "Cancer is a challenge," or "Hope dispels fear," because they are left not knowing what to do with their negative feelings. One patient said to me, "I don't want to be a hero! I don't want to be challenged by this.

I just want to be healthy again." All these efforts to inject positivity usually have the well-meaning intention of trying to encourage hope and promote a more optimistic outlook. As a caregiver, you do have to be an ambassador of hope, someone who can help clients and family members overcome their pessimism, despair, demoralization, and helplessness; however, we must not offer false hope.

Finally, we trivialize distress in others because we often have an unconscious desire to avoid suffering. This is a very difficult motivation to identify in ourselves because we like to think of ourselves as being open to the suffering of others. Yet the natural human inclination to avoid distress can prompt us to focus only on the positive and to unconsciously discourage the disclosure of suffering by clients and family members.

Thus, our motivations for trivializing distress can range from the altruistic to the self-serving. Whatever the motivations for our responses, we are in effect saying to the victims of a tragedy they don't have a right to their painful feelings, and that their continued distress represents a failure of coping, or even spiritual failure. In these ways, our well-intentioned responses can have the effect of greater self-concealment and lowered self-esteem in our clients.

Some other psychonoxious forms this failure to empathize can take include clichés offering no real comfort. They can discourage further disclosure of one's distress: "They're better off now," "Be brave," "Time heals everything," or "Don't cry, you'll only make yourself worse." These platitudes are well intentioned, yet fail to offer the empathy and compassion the suffering person so deeply needs.

Don't Scratch Where It Doesn't Itch

The other error we can make is to overrespond to our clients' distress. With grief and life-threatening illnesses, this occurs when we assume everyone in this situation requires in-depth psychotherapy, and our role must be to probe their psyches for existential anguish. It is important to remember we most often work with normal people who are confronting abnormally stressful life events (something I frequently point out to my clients), and many of them do just fine without any additional psychosocial interventions. When we work tirelessly to uncover the hidden distress of our clients, we may indeed be scratching where it doesn't itch.

To avoid underresponding or overresponding to suffering, and to avoid other mistakes we can make as helpers, we need to listen more closely to the people we care for. They will tell us what is true for them—by their reactions, by the hopes and fears they express, and by the actions they take or don't take. If we pay close attention to these cues, we can respond to their painful feelings and encourage genuine hope in a way that respects the whole individual and his or her emotional world.

Grief and Grief Counseling: Models and Interventions[31]

Now let's examine in some detail how combined relational and technical expertise can be applied in grief counseling. My approach to grief counseling is shaped by my basic view of grief: Although grief is often intensely overwhelming, it is regarded as a natural condition—the human reaction to loss. However, grief is not a uniquely human experience. It is an ancient urge shared with other species, as Diane Ackerman reminds us when she describes elephants "visiting the remains of even long-dead relatives and gently turning over their bleached bones with trunk or foot... gorillas banging their chests with yowls of anguish during a wake for a fallen friend... sea lions wailing when their babies have been mutilated by killer whales... grief-stricken monkey mothers carrying dead infants around for days... geese singing both halves of a duet when their partners have died.[32]

In we humans, grief generally abates over time and often leads to psychological growth. Accordingly, the role of grief counseling is to accelerate or unblock this natural healing process—to get grief working—particularly if this process is moving slowly, or if the reaction to a loss is severe or protracted.[31] Given this central role of grief counseling, we need to examine the therapeutic style, conceptual models, and interventions most likely to achieve this healing outcome.

Despite the complex and idiosyncratic nature of grief and mourning, thanatologists have succeeded in identifying definite patterns and relations in their presentation to guide our interventions. Two of the most comprehensive and influential grief theories are Stroebe and Schut's[33; 34] dual-process model and the task-based model developed by Worden.[35] The dual-process model views bereavement in terms of two orientations: loss and restoration. Both orientations are present in the coping responses of each bereaved individual. In the loss orientation, the griever confronts loss—doing the *grief work* of yearning, going through memories, feeling the pain and finality of separation, crying over the loss, and exhibiting emotions ranging from despair to relief while coming to terms with the loss. As Stroebe and Schut say, "Healthy grief work…entails facing up to the reality of the loss."[36] In the restoration orientation, the grieving person focuses on adjusting to the secondary stressors that occur after the loss, and attempts to deal with all the changes the loss brings, finding distraction (and rest) from grief, and exploring new areas of growth.

As the grieving person struggles to come to terms with the loss, he or she oscillates between these two orientations. This oscillation serves as an adaptive regulatory function, optimized when movement between the two orientations is balanced and flexible.[37] When balanced oscillation breaks down and the griever becomes stuck in either the loss orientation (extreme rumination) or the restoration orientation (extreme denial and avoidance), complicated grief can develop. From the perspective of the dual-process model, counseling will be most effective if it helps the griever oscillate between loss-oriented and restoration-oriented efforts in a balanced and flexible fashion, without becoming stuck in either.

Worden's task-based model views mourning as entailing the completion of four tasks: (1) accepting the reality of the loss; (2) processing the pain of grief; (3) adjusting to a world without the deceased; and (4) finding a "way to remember the deceased while embarking on the rest of one's journey through life."[35] The third task of adjusting to a world without the deceased is similar to the restoration orientation of the dual-process model, with some qualifications.[36] The four tasks serve as markers for the natural healing process of grief and as keys to identifying when grief is not working. In the task-based model, complicated mourning reactions set in when one or more tasks are impeded, resulting in what Worden terms "abnormal grief reactions" (e.g., chronic, delayed, or exaggerated grief reactions). Successful grief counseling helps clients complete these tasks.

Both the dual-process and task-based models strongly support the roles of meaning making and meaning reconstruction in adapting to loss. Robert Neimeyer has led study of these phenomena and narrative clinical strategies targeting them.[38; 39] Major losses require grievers to re-evaluate and reconstruct their schemata of self, others, and the world as they search for the meaning of their loss, and the meaning of life without the deceased. Traumatic loss presents additional challenges to the bereaved, for it can shatter basic assumptions about life and require grievers to create a more viable assumptive world that is both credible and tolerable.[20] Efficacious grief counseling facilitates meaning making in clients.

Several integrated treatment models address the myriad clinical issues and challenges identified by the task, dual-process, reconstructive, and trauma models. The Complicated Grief Treatment (CGT) model created by Katherine Shear and colleagues[40] and the guide for treating traumatic bereavement by Laurie Pearlman and coauthors[20] systematically guide therapists and clients through a series of interventions and include engaging handouts for clients. Structured bereavement initiatives, such as the Family Bereavement Program developed by Irwin Sandler,[41] and Trauma-Focused Cognitive-Behavioral Therapy for traumatized children,[42] have proved efficient and successful. Cognitive Processing Therapy, Prolonged Exposure Therapy, Eye Movement Desensitization and Reprocessing (EMDR), and the Emotion-Focused therapy approach are also used in trauma treatment. Dignity Therapy, an individualized psychotherapy approach that focuses on patients' emotional needs in hospice and palliative care, provides guidelines and a program for compassionate care at the end of life.[43] Also helpful are the principles and practices of motivational interviewing (MI), an intervention model extending Rogers' person-centered approach that focuses on client ambivalence and resistance to behavior change. I find motivational interviewing skills useful when assisting clients to engage in exposure activities and move toward new goals.[44] I believe the relationship and communication skills discussed here are crucial to the success of these diverse programs and interventions.

In the rapid evolution of the bereavement field, research and clinical attention have turned to a wide range of clinically significant phenomena, including the adaptive value of continuing bonds with the deceased,[45] disenfranchised grief,[46] differing grief trajectories,[47] and prolonged, traumatic, or complicated grief.[48; 49] Therapeutic initiatives and the literature on grief have also focused on posttraumatic growth,[50] anticipatory mourning,[51] grief across the life span,[52] the role of rituals in grief and mourning,[53] and cultural factors.[54] Keeping abreast of these developments can sharpen your clinical skills and efficacy.

In this digital age, interventions for grief and trauma have become increasingly accessible online. Internet-based interventions are being tested, and large numbers of people are visiting mutual support sites.[55; 56; 57; 58] Some of these can be important resources in treatment if they are chosen with discrimination and due regard for their origin. Regardless, some familiarity with them is needed because many of your clients will be accessing these resources, and their online exchanges can be incorporated in your work together.

In contrast to the emergence, popularity, and availability of grief-counseling resources, some people have expressed a contrary view of grief counseling, claiming it is ineffective or possibly harmful to bereaved clients. Don't let these claims keep you from providing grief counseling to those who need and seek it. The claim of harmful effects has been shown to be invalid, and there is no other evidence of associated harmful effects.[59; 60] Grief counseling, like other therapeutic interventions, tends to be effective for those who seek it and need it.

But who should receive grief counseling? Gamino and colleagues offer probably the best answer when they suggest grief counseling is appropriate for all bereaved people who answer yes to the following two questions: "Are you having trouble dealing with the death?" and "Are you interested in seeing a grief counselor to help with that?"[61] Once a person has opted for counseling or some other form of bereavement support, he or she can work with their provider to assess the level of care desired and needed. Motivation is a reliable predictor of outcomes in all psychotherapy, and this is true in grief and trauma counseling as well.

A Person-Centered Approach
to Grief Counseling

A bereaved client who is motivated to directly address the nature of their bereavement and come to terms with it is highly likely to benefit from a generally person-centered counseling style for several reasons. This is because the needs of the bereaved person and the core conditions of the person-centered approach match up so well. First, bereaved persons need an empathic helper. Deep empathy is the hallmark of the person-centered approach. The empathically-attuned counselor successively forms more accurate constructions of the client's thoughts and feelings, assisting clients to develop a view of self more congruent with their actual lived experience.[62] Furthermore, they can accept and make sense of their loss and have the emotions of grief guide their adjustment to the loss. They will also be able to clarify, accept, and integrate their new sense of self, find new meanings in their painful events, and explore emerging directions for growth. Importantly, they will be able to establish continuing bonds with their lost loved ones, bonds that are not maintained through the pain of loss.

Second, people in the throes of grief need respect, to be accepted, and to accept themselves as they struggle with feelings of shame and guilt, worry and regret, and a widening gap between their inner experience and others' expectations. This acceptance is invaluable as grievers work to determine their inner timetable for grief and find their way through the pain of loss. To do this, they require a nonjudgmental listener, who is fully prepared to be present with the intense and often unsettling emotions and thoughts accompanying grief. Diana Fosha put it this way: "The emotional atmosphere should be one in which the patient feels safe and the therapist brave."[63] The griever's everyday support system can rapidly exhaust itself and is not often able to provide this kind of consistent "holding environment" for these strong reactions to loss.

Third, they need an authentic helper or companion as they grapple with existential issues touching core dimensions of the human condition. This is a great fit with the person-centered helper who strives to be genuine in the helping encounter.

Besides the distinctive, less content directive, person-centered way of working with bereaved people, other interventions can be particularly helpful. These include displaying a photo of the deceased during sessions, meeting with relatives and significant others, referring the client or family to local bereavement support groups, sharing readings on grief and loss, supporting the establishment of new goals that restore meaning to life, experiential focusing, and the empty-chair or imaginal dialogue technique. I also find the cognitive-behavioral *vertical arrow* technique helpful, because it gets at deeper meanings for the client. I ask, usually more than once, "If that were true, what would it mean?" and then continue responding in a more person-centered fashion.[64]

I believe that the core qualities and interventions of the person-centered approach are a necessary foundation for effectiveness in all interventions aimed at helping the bereaved. These qualities and interventions are key mechanisms of change as we assist clients to practice greater self-compassion, reduce counterfactual thinking, set new goals, or overcome patterns of experiential avoidance that can derail their healing. The case study of Bruce presented below highlights many of these qualities and interventions. Although the empty-chair work and other interventions I employ entail more counselor directiveness than is usual in the Person-Centered Approach (PCA), these interventions retain its quintessential inner-directed and client-centered qualities.

Counseling a Bereaved Father[31]

Bruce was a Caucasian Silicon Valley engineer I met with for 40 sessions over 2 years. Bruce's son, Adam, aged 7, had died suddenly from a cerebral hemorrhage. Bruce was in deep despair at the outset of counseling. A dedicated father, he was confronting the unimaginable: the loss of his beloved son. His grief and mourning were intense and prolonged and had a traumatic component, one typical for bereaved parents of young children. I also had several conjoint sessions with Bruce and his wife. They grieved differently; Bruce was actually the more intuitive griever, his wife more instrumental, but they worked together to give each other space to grieve while the other kept the home functioning as normally as possible for their surviving son.

As our initial sessions unfolded, Bruce often had extreme emotions of anguish and yearning. The intensity and frequency of the reactions gradually diminished during the course of therapy, but these "grief attacks," as we called them, were moments when Bruce confronted and lived through the trauma of the loss as he struggled to accept this reality, and to integrate the loss into his world and sense of self. In terms of grief's tasks, Bruce shared he only accepted the full reality of his loss when he visited the cemetery and saw Adam's tombstone for the first time.

Bruce consistently used evocative metaphors to describe his grief: as on a "long, painful road" with broken glass cutting his bare feet; his remaining family as "wobbly," like a "table with three legs" (himself, his wife, and their other son); the loss as an "earthquake," followed by aftershocks; himself as a "man with one arm." Bruce was able to reach deeper levels of feeling and meaning when I encouraged him to attend to the bodily felt sense he had for each of these images, and the richness and depth of the insights he achieved were remarkable.[65]

In general, my response style in the therapy was classically person-centered: few questions, almost no advice, and a majority of my responses focused on the feelings and meanings Bruce communicated. Throughout the session, a sense of loss stirring within me allowed my *pain compass*, as emotion-focused therapists refer to it, to guide my empathy and my responses to Bruce.[66]

Each week, Bruce brought a photo of Adam to our sessions, and he had extensive imaginal conversations with Adam in empty-chair work. In these conversations, Bruce often repeated: "I have not forgotten you, Adam. My love has not diminished." Extensively refined and researched within the ever-expanding person-centered tradition,[16] this experiential intervention is now used in grief counseling by therapists from many theoretical persuasions, including cognitive grief therapy (the "as if strategy"),[67] and cognitive-behavioral therapy for complicated grief.[40] The empty-chair dialogue facilitates integrating the loss, developing a healthy, continuing bond with the deceased, and adjusting to a life without the loved one.

I will never forget the day Bruce so eloquently and poignantly conveyed the suffering he confronted. He told me about the joy he felt when he tucked his sons into bed at night and told them stories. When he had a scary dream about his children, he would go into their bedroom to check on them, as many parents have done with their children, and be relieved to see them well and asleep. Now, he said, he doesn't waken from a nightmare; instead, he wakens to one, and his only solace is when Adam appears to him in a dream.

When Bruce asked me questions about grief and mourning, I answered to the best of my ability. An engineer, he wanted to know how things worked, and the task-based and dual-process models made sense to him. He would often point to what I had termed the zigzag nature of his grief journey, with profound moments of loss and yearning, followed by "vacations from grief" when he began to find pleasure again. He struggled with counterfactual thinking, as almost all bereaved parents do, obsessing about how he might have prevented Adam's death, even though he could not have realistically done so. Near the end of our work together, he described himself as coming back into his life, and now reflecting on what had happened while he had "been gone on a vacation in hell."

Bruce's grieving illustrates what the dual-process and task-based models emphasize: adaptation to loss involves more than the emotional aspects of grief work. There is also the work of adjustment and restoration—adjusting to a world without the loved one, setting new goals in life, approaching things previously avoided, and generally reinvesting in life. These restoration and adjustment processes of the task-based and dual-process models can include an element of avoidance or denial, of consciously or unconsciously diverting one's attention from the loss itself. The dual-process model says when grief is working, the griever flexibly oscillates in balanced fashion between loss and restoration orientations, and does not get stuck in extremes of either—neither excessive rumination nor rigid denial or repression.

When grief is working, adjustment and restoration-oriented coping are activated. Grief-related emotions are fully processed and worked through. Person-centered experiential theorists say "every feeling has a need, and every need has a direction for action."[16] This axiom is confirmed in bereaved clients who have sudden realizations, such as "I don't need to make the trip this year to the lake where we scattered our son's ashes," or "Now that Plan A is not going to happen, I need to make Plan B work for me." One day, after recounting cherished memories of his son, Bruce resolved to set up a scholarship in his son's name. This idea was a "direction for action" that emerged directly from Bruce's deep experience of loss. It is a good example of how clients can create meaning and establish healthy continuing bonds with their lost loved ones.

Insights into this pattern of deeply felt emotion leading to adaptive real-world actions can be found in the work of Pascual-Leone and Greenberg, who study "moment-by-moment steps in emotional processing" in therapy with clients in experiential therapy for depression and interpersonal problems. They identified patterns of productive emotional work, and showed how painful and unpleasant emotions can promote healing. They "propel the client on a healthy self-organizing trajectory that reaches its completion as a meaningful, emotionally differentiated, and integrative experience."[68] This therapeutic endpoint is perhaps similar to the adaptive grief outcome Zisook and Shear term "integrative" or "abiding" grief.[69] These detailed explorations of how feeling and meaning unfold in effective therapy help explain the paradoxical clinical reality that the pain of loss actually helps to process the loss: to change grief, you must experience grief.

To say it again, I believe the core person-centered counseling approach, with its emphasis on a deeply empathic and caring therapeutic relationship, fulfills fundamental criteria for effective grief counseling. The phenomenological and experiential focus of the person-centered approach, and the deeply empathic counseling relationship it promotes, match the needs of bereaved clients, and allow for flexible responses to their often idiosyncratic reactions. Empathic understanding, exploring, exposure, and most principally, experiencing, are at the heart of effective grief counseling and healthy grieving. These elements are brought to life in an authentic and caring helping relationship, with a counselor who believes in the client's healing capacities. They define the person-centered approach to grief counseling I strive for in my work with all my bereaved clients.

Losing one's child, and traversing the long journey to a life one can endure and even embrace, is probably the most difficult of all challenges. Bruce's courage on his journey inspired me as his companion on the journey. There were difficult moments for me. My son Evan was about the same age as Adam, and I had some dreams with Evan being threatened and not being able to rescue him. However, these instances of vicarious traumatization were far outweighed by my growth, as a therapist and as a father, in my work with Bruce. When counseling ended, Bruce reflected he had at last arrived at a different place, a place where he could hold Adam in his heart, not with the intense anguish of loss, but with cherished memories of the son he would always love dearly and never forget.

Conclusion

Good communication skills are the primary tools for exercising caring and compassion. We are naturally more helpful than unhelpful, but to express our helpful natures to the fullest, we need to continually learn new skills that support helping and delete others that detract from it.

Two caveats must be added to this discussion of skillful performance. First, no matter how skillful you are, any of your responses not grounded in a caring attitude and genuine concern for the person you are helping is likely to be unhelpful, despite how technically correct or dazzling it may be. Technique can never replace the genuine intention to help.

Second, no matter how skillful you become, you will continue to make errors. What helper has never asked too many questions, given too much advice, talked too much, feigned understanding, uttered a cliché, said the wrong thing, been impatient or defensive? If this person exists, I know I have never met him or her; it certainly isn't me. You might make fewer errors as you become more skilled, but you will always make them.

There is a saying an error doesn't become a mistake until you refuse to correct it. This might be the best piece of advice. The greatest mistake you can make as a helper is believing you don't make any mistakes. Your tribulations as a helper can be turned into personal and professional growth if you accept you do make mistakes and you are willing to listen to feedback and take the necessary self-corrective actions.

When our helping journey includes being a member of a helping team or leading a support group, opportunities for personal and professional growth and contributions, embarrassment too, are even greater. To be successful in these challenging contexts, we must learn yet other skills and add these to the caring connection and healing words that remain our core helping tools. We now turn to those challenges

PART THREE

Creating Caring Systems

7

We live by each other and for each other.
Alone we can do so little.
Together we can do so much.[1]

Helen Keller

If they don't have scars, they haven't worked
on a team.[2]

Balfour Mount

In medieval times, alchemy was a symbol
for transformation of what is most common
(lead) into what is most precious (gold). So,
too, do learning teams practice a special form
of alchemy, the transformation of potentially
divisive conflict and defensiveness into
learning.[3]

Peter Senge

The Caring Team

Working on a team can be both frustrating and fulfilling. As a team member, your success as a helper is interwoven with your teammates' success. If the team fails in its tasks, you will also fail. If the team doesn't safeguard and encourage you and your caring, your idealism and morale can be threatened, paving the way for disillusionment and burnout. But if your team invites you to grow and to learn, and supports you in doing what you care about, your team caregiving experiences can be among the most rewarding of all those on your helping journey.

This chapter concerns interprofessional caregiving teams—what they are and what makes them succeed or fail. We will see that many basic concepts explored earlier, such as mission and purpose, self-esteem regulation, resilience, approach and avoidance, self-concealment, and the principles of effective communication, are immediately applicable to the team context. The vignettes and examples I will use come mainly from the health care field, but the basic ideas developed here can be extended to all caring teams and organizations.

The Team Wave

Teamwork is now the number one trend in the global workplace trend, and this is perhaps most dramatically evident in health care.[4] Unfortunately, one reason for the intense focus on teamwork and teamwork training in health care is the recognition that teamwork failures contribute significantly to medical errors.[4] Another more positive impetus has been the emergence of the biopsychosocial model and person/patient-centered care, both calling for a team approach.

In tandem with the increasing recognition of the importance of teams and their failure in some instances to provide safe health care, has come an intense focus on training in teamwork and teaching inter-professional teamwork skills to students in the health professions.[5] In this process, research on teams has grown dramatically, identifying the many factors that support or undermine effective teamwork.[6] For example, in their review of surveys examining teamwork, Valentine and colleagues found that the most frequently assessed general dimensions of teamwork were communication, coordination, and respect. Scales they identified measured cross-functional cooperation, work group effectiveness, interdisciplinary collaboration, psychological safety, team learning, team process, team climate, and other constructs.[7]

Other studies have produced overlapping findings. Drawing upon prior theoretical and empirical work and expert input on the properties of teams that excel, Shoemaker and colleagues developed a conceptual framework of interprofessional team-based primary care. They identified 12 constructs as core characteristics of high-functioning teams. These features were viewed as "mediators"—the "dynamic or interactional properties that occur among members of the team and create an emergent property of *teamwork*."[8] The researchers then reviewed instruments used to measure teamwork and mapped the items in those scales to the mediator constructs in their model, then recorded the frequencies of the matches. The mediators they identified and assessed were "sense making," "continuous learning," "shared explicit goals and accountability," "evolving mental model of roles," "trust," "respectful interactions," "heedful interrelating," "commitment," "communication," "improvisation," "conflict resolution," and (shared) "leadership." Mediators most frequently represented in surveyed measures were communication, heedful interrelating, respectful interactions, and shared explicit goals, with each of the other mediators also significantly represented.

Shoemaker and colleagues' conceptual model and findings reinforce the central themes and points we will make here, namely, that high-functioning teams are characterized by effective communication, respectful and supportive relationships, a sense of collective purpose and commitment to worthy goals, shared leadership, an ability to address and resolve conflicts, flexibility in relation to roles, and a capacity to constantly learn as a team and improve the quality of care. High-functioning teams have greater team efficacy, promote resilience among team members, and are more able to provide person-centered care.

Team Mission and Goals

Why do we have teams? The answer is simple: because we need them. Caregiving teams are a response to complex human problems that demand the focused attention of experts from more than one discipline. No single health professional can address all the needs of a person who is terminally ill, or of a person coping with chronic illness or severe disability. The expertise of several disciplines is required to understand and care for people facing such difficult life circumstances. A caring team can meet this need by synergistically melding the expertise of multiple disciplines and achieving goals no single helper could accomplish alone. This reality is now widely recognized throughout health care.

Acting in concert, team members can convert a collective commitment to a worthy purpose into specific caring acts that fulfill this shared mission. One essential team task is to agree on the team's purpose or mission and on the best way of getting there. If you are currently a member of a caregiving team, how would you define the mission, the team's shared purpose or *why* of the work, and how would you define your role as a team member? Is your team's mission closely aligned with your own purpose in helping? What does the team allow you to achieve that you couldn't accomplish alone?

There is a big difference between the objectives and guidelines given to a team by the larger organization to which it belongs and the personal ownership that results from team members discussing and arriving at what they believe is the team's mission. Has your team owned its mission statement, or is the statement just a set of guidelines that has been handed down to you, which you couldn't accurately restate if you were asked to?

The team must also have a clear sense of the goals it is working toward, a vision of *what* it will actually do to fulfill its mission. This is the mission-to-vision process at the team level. In an ideal situation, there is a strong alignment between each team member's mission-to-vision process and the team's mission-to-vision process; ideally, these are aligned with mission-to-vision process of the larger organization the individuals and teams belong to. When such alignments exist within a caring organization, enlivening synergies and remarkable outcomes are possible. Prosocially motivated teams are most successful and cohesive when the actions of team members are aligned in pursuit of a common goal.[9]

Setting clear performance goals and priorities is something teams often bypass, but it is well worth taking the time to do so. This shared vision is like a compass that can keep the team moving on course toward its goals in difficult times. The commitment dimension in high-functioning teams reflects a sense of belonging to the team and dedication to group values and goals.[8]

Teams must also determine *how* they are going to work toward the goals that actualize their mission. The hows pertain to the ethics and principles of care that guide their helping efforts. When these ethics and principles conflict with ongoing practices, moral distress is possible, and effective team communication is needed to work through the issues raised.

The Interprofessional Team

In the health care field, the development of interprofessional or interdisciplinary teams has paralleled that of the biopsychosocial model, which says that *bio*logical, *psycho*logical, and *social* elements must all be considered when we attempt to understand and treat any health problem, and that the whole person in his or her social context is the appropriate focus of our interventions. Interdisciplinary clinical teams draw upon the expertise of specialists in each of these separate domains—biological/medical, psychological, and social—to diagnose and treat the whole person and the context of the illness because these are inseparable from the disease or problem the person seeking help brings to us, and so can include a wide range of providers.

Hospice care pioneered a comprehensive interdisciplinary team approach, extending the biopsychosocial model to include the spiritual needs of dying persons.[10; 11] Hospice teams typically include the patient's personal physician, the hospice physician or medical director, nurses, social workers, clergy or other counselors, home health aides, trained volunteers, and sometimes speech, physical, music and art therapists.

The interdisciplinary team represents one point or level in a developmental sequence of interprofessional team development. The sequence ranges from *unidisciplinary* (where there is no team at all) to *multidisciplinary* (where independent disciplines function largely unaffected by one another, but each adds their own contributions). Then there is the *interdisciplinary* context (where the interaction of the team is necessary to produce the final product, and decisions are made in collaboration, but team members do not expand their function beyond their role on the team). Finally, there is the *transdisciplinary* context (where team members train one another, and there is a phenomenon of "role release" wherein roles and responsibilities are shared in a more holistic process).[10; 12]

Working together in a truly interdisciplinary or transdisciplinary fashion is an ideal state most caregiving teams aspire to, but not all achieve. Batorowicz and Shepherd describe the transdisciplinary team as also being characterized by rich ongoing discussions among team members.[13] They developed the Team Decision Making Questionnaire (TDMQ) to measure the quality of transdisciplinary teamwork. TDMQ Questionnaire items ask whether team decision making processes help team members with decision making (e.g., "obtain support in clinical/technical decision making"), team support (e.g., "sharing success"), developing quality services (e.g., "ensure quality of services"), and learning (e.g., "becoming more competent"). Achieving transdisciplinary, or even true interdisciplinary team functioning, is challenging in the modern health care environment, where professional fragmentation, hierarchical authority, and traditions of individualism tend to dominate.[14]

Interdependent collaboration, the key to successful interdisciplinary and transdisciplinary teamwork, is often undermined by the failure of team members to understand the unique contributions and expertise of their colleagues from other disciplines. This lack of understanding and appreciation, or *interdisciplinary myopia*, can lead to a variety of communication problems and conflicts. One is a form of role competition commonly known as "turfdom":

> The major conflict in our hospice is a turf issue: Who is best able to deal with emotional/counseling issues with patients—the RN case manager or the MSW? The MSW wants nurses to deal only with physical problems and leave counseling to the MSW.

A related phenomenon is what I call the one-person interdisciplinary team—the caregiver who refuses to collaborate and attempts to do it all alone. This stance probably originates in feelings like these:

> I often feel no one cares as much as I do about the patients and their individual needs. Consequently, I feel ultimately responsible for the care the patients do or don't receive.

The resulting situation can look something like this:

> A nurse complains about carrying the whole load of a patient's and family's care. The other team members complain that the nurse refuses to call any of them into the care even when the care plan is developed to incorporate them. The nurse "controls" the case and is exhausted by it.

Situations like these pose tremendous challenges to teams. The nurse's teammates must find a way to communicate with her that recognizes her intention to give the best care possible, and at the same time communicates the need—for her and the patient and family—to share the responsibilities and resources for care.

Teamwork, Personal Vulnerability and Growth

Working collaboratively in a highly interdependent mode is intrinsically difficult, especially for the more autonomous individual. Every team and team member faces the challenges of blending cooperation and competition, working together and working separately. For the individual team member, meeting these challenges often entails a great deal of personal vulnerability.

When you are a member of a multidisciplinary, interdisciplinary, or transdisciplinary team, your work is constantly exposed to the critiques of others. You don't have the comfort of working in a uni-disciplinary context, where it is possible no one will see what you do, or how well you do it. The unavoidable close scrutiny of other team members forces you to look at your own behavior, and your ability to receive feedback, or give it. For example, I feel much more comfortable doing counseling in my private office, where no one can observe me, than I do intervening in a health care situation as a team member. In the team setting, if I fail to communicate effectively with a patient, especially when other team members are successful in doing so, all my credentials and degrees won't protect me from the judgments of my fellow team members. One social worker shared similar feelings:

> I am a social worker, and I am supposed to be the expert on our hospice team on psychosocial issues. However, during the course of everyday hospice practice, I see the nurse or volunteer providing this type of support as well or better than myself. Even though I am the one with the master's degree and experience, at times the work seems easier and more natural for others.

Being a team member means looking at yourself—at your needs for power and control, your difficulties with sharing or collaborating, and a host of other personal issues related to team functioning. This forced self-awareness can be painful, but it can also yield personal growth if you approach yourself and the members of your team with an attitude of openness, flexibility, compassion, and respect. Like in your personal relationships, working as part of a caring team will bring you face to face with your strengths and weaknesses. This usually leads to some combination of personal growth and personal distress. There is no pain-free way to be a team member, as suggested by Balfour Mount's comment about the scars that predictably come with working on a team.

However, sometimes our involvement as a team member woefully lacks the redeeming element of personal growth. If the team atmosphere is dominated by unresolved conflicts, put-downs, gossip, power plays, incivility, and other negative behaviors, the personal growth of team members, and the team's effectiveness in caregiving, will be severely limited.

Conflict in the Team

Interpersonal conflicts and other communication problems present the greatest challenges for most caregiving teams. Remember that the issue of communication problems with fellow team members is often the number one stressor reported by caregivers. These conflicts and communication problems can lead to the development of dysfunctional alliances or subsystems within the team. The structures of these team subsystems reflect the basic personal and interpersonal dynamics associated with the conflict or communication problem.

Kim and colleagues reviewed the literature on conflicts among health care professionals and summarized findings from articles on the individual, interpersonal, and organization sources of conflict.[15] Examples of individual factors included self-focus (e.g., "my own views are indisputable"), self-esteem (if jeopardized, conflict ensues), and conflict management style (varying degrees of skill). Interpersonal factors were reflected in communication breakdowns, incivility, and a lack of recognition, trust, and transparency. Organizational factors such as workflows and scope of practice issues were also identified as contributing to conflict in teams.

Donald Bailey, an interdisciplinary team theorist and researcher, outlines a number of possible dysfunctional team subsystems, each diverging from an ideal model of team functioning.[12] Bailey proposes that in the ideal model the leader acts as a member of the team, team members have comparable power and influence, and conflicts and other disagreements revolve around substantive issues, not personality conflicts. The dysfunctional subsystems Bailey identifies are illustrated in the following disclosures of team members:

Factions within the team

✧ Disagreements/conflicts are handled in twos or threes and avoided in a full-team discussion. Nursing area is the largest and tends to segment off at times.

✧ As our hospice grows, old-time staff members have difficulty accepting changes. They view change as preventing them from delivering "good care." Old-time staff view hospice as being too businesslike. They think there is too much concern over cost containment, and they feel this concern reduces quality of care.

Conflict between two team members

A personality conflict and power struggle between our medical director and executive director makes almost every discussion an issue of control.

A dominant leader

We have a dominant team leader who controls all meetings, but skirts direct discussion or solutions to problems.

A dominant team member

✧ A member of the psychosocial staff has comments on all patients and all aspects of their care. She interjects at all times during the meeting and at other times. She is the ultimate expert in everything and enjoys arguments.

✧ At the weekly team meeting, one nurse constantly runs on and on about peripheral details and many examples of patient/family behavior. Even though one of us may try to "rein her in," nothing changes from one week to another.

An isolated team member

A patient care nurse is consistently delinquent in turning in paperwork. Her body language in team conference reflects her feelings because she is always sitting alone at another table. How can we turn her around?

One person who is in conflict with the rest of the team

✧ The conflict is between the only male (a nurse) and three female nurses, one female MSW, and a female counselor. The male nurse functions as a one-man team, rarely seeks assistance from others or team, is not a collaborator, and if he's corrected or spoken to about a situation, he goes back to the others and confronts each person about "who told on him."

✧ One nurse on the team clearly shows very poor clinical judgment, and when she asks for advice she always responds with "Yes, but that won't work." No problem is ever solvable as far as she is concerned. The nursing supervisor refuses to intervene. Direct intervention by other nurses has not helped. Other nurses no longer trust her nursing judgments.

✧ There's a continuous conflict between the medical director and the hospice nurses. Whenever a nurse makes a suggestion, it is "cut-down" and "taken apart" by him. This causes the team to withdraw and become split and nonproductive.

Conflicts within the team sometimes stem from sharp differences of opinion about what to do in what are extraordinarily complex and difficult caregiving situations. There are no simple answers to the ethical, legal, and psychosocial problems modern caregiving teams often confront. Team members can have widely diverging views as to the best course of action to pursue, resulting in painful exchanges, and often moral distress. Here are some examples of caregiving situations that challenge the team in these ways:

✧ A 39-year-old patient with advanced cancer asks the RN about her prognosis. The RN states it is 3 to 4 weeks, which the MD has told the RN, and which the RN understands was communicated to the patient. The patient becomes upset. The husband is enraged. He directs criticism towards the RN and the hospice. The hospice coordinator and other staff are critical of the RN's blunt disclosure. A team conflict ensues.

✧ The team suspects that a patient and/or family members are abusing pain meds. The primary physician has pulled back from the situation. The patient needs more medication. The nurse has been hesitant to reveal the problem. The patient is in pain. The physician is unwilling to prescribe more or different medication. What should I do?

It is difficult to imagine any team could deal with these complex and trying situations without acquiring a few scars. Research shows that poor team communication is a root cause of moral distress, and it is easy to see why this is true.[16] However, if a team can deal openly with disagreements among its members, deeply reflect on what its mission is, and reach agreement on how its members are going to fulfill that mission, situations like these can lead to personal growth for team members and a strengthening of the team. Sometimes the team can even be surprised by how well it handled what seemed like an impossible situation. Moral courage and good communication skills can often transform moral distress into a moral victory for the team.

However, a less appealing alternative is too often the case. Ethical dilemmas that tear at the soul, unresolved conflicts among team members, rapid growth and organizational restructuring, the departure or serious illness of a team member—all these can disrupt and threaten the helping team and leave it uncertain as to whether it can cope with the new demands it faces.

Confronted by these threats, teams can opt to avoid difficult or uncomfortable feelings and engage in defensive maneuvers that could cripple the team's growth and well-being. Such defensive maneuvers often entail avoiding the pain of looking at core problems for the moment, but suffering the consequences of that avoidance later. Essentially, this is a group variation on the neurotic paradox. Here too, the short-term gains (anxiety reduction) of avoidance behavior outweigh the long-term pain associated with it, leading to what is ultimately self-defeating behavior.

UNHEALTHY AGREEMENT, TEAM SECRETS, AND DEFENSIVE ROUTINES

Many team and organizational experts emphasize that patterns of avoidance are among the most destructive and dysfunctional of all team dynamics. In *Groupthink*, Irving Janis documents how teams can make bad decisions even though some or all team members have serious misgivings about the wisdom of these decisions.[17] The team can ignore these misgivings and dissenting opinions as it works hard to be in a state of agreement, and then it takes the easy way out by accepting the first solution that arises. The guiding principle is that we are nice people, and nice people agree with one another. The problem is that important ideas and contributions can get lost along the way.

When unhealthy agreement emerges, a self-defeating pattern develops, and team members feel frustrated and powerless trying to deal with a specific problem. Worse still, they tend to blame one another for the problem. They also tend to discuss these issues in small subgroups of friends and trusted confidants, but don't directly communicate their ideas in team meetings. Additionally, in public situations they try to determine what the positions of other team members are without sharing their own. Ultimately, they often feel they should have said something, but they didn't do so. In this way, team secrets result in deleterious outcomes, much like individual helper secrets do. The pattern of collective avoidance and unhealthy agreement continues until the problem precipitates a major crisis. Even though all team members might be able to identify the problem or conflict, the entire group never discusses it openly. Because no one can talk about the problem, the team's decisions lack feedback and commitment from team members, and thus usually fail.

Low trust levels go hand in hand with this failure to deal openly with team conflicts. When team members don't trust one another's intentions, they feel threatened and perceive the risks of sharing information and addressing the conflict as outweighing the benefits. Ideally, team members should always feel safe enough to talk about not feeling safe. But the problem is that, once you begin talking about the "elephant in the room," it is hard to selectively deny the particular aspects you don't feel safe talking about, and it feels that even if a small piece of the truth is discussed, the rest inexorably follows, so denial is often carefully maintained.

In The Open Organization, Fritz Steele makes a strong case for openness:

> Unless there is the opportunity and ability to disclose information about what is actually happening in the system, including both behaviors and feelings, then it is very difficult for that

system's members to be masters of their own fate and for the system to be self-correcting. In this sense, the importance of disclosure is not only in doing the day-to-day work which requires information flow (that kind of disclosure happens fairly regularly), but also in examining how things are being done, so that maintenance can be done on the system to keep it healthy.[18]

Steele also notes that we often blame the sharing of information about a problem, as if it had created rather than simply signaled the problem. When information is not being shared openly, the team encounters more rumors and gossip, it doesn't learn and self-correct, and then there are the elephants in the room that can't be discussed. In other words, what the team doesn't know can hurt it.

In *The Fifth Discipline*, organizational expert Peter Senge describes the forces preventing productive dialogue in working teams.[3] Among the key culprits, Senge notes, are "defensive routines" he describes as "habitual ways of interacting that protect us and others from threat or embarrassment, but which also prevent us from learning." Examples of defensive routines include "smoothing over" differences or having big theoretical debates that go nowhere. "Yet," Senge adds, "the very defensive routines that thwart learning also hold great potential for fostering learning, if we can only learn to unlock the energy they contain."

Antidotes to Avoidance and Defensiveness

For Senge, the antidote to defensive patterns of behavior is a commitment to telling the truth about the team's current reality. This translates as a commitment to self-disclosure and to a quality of reflectiveness and openness that fosters a deeper understanding of what other team members are thinking and feeling. If these conditions are absent, although the individuals on the team may all be extremely intelligent, the team itself will have a subpar IQ.

But openness in the organization or team doesn't mean speaking out and airing every thought or feeling you have. It is a more demanding stance, a "reflective openness" as Senge describes it, one allowing us to challenge our own and others' thinking, to not be attached to the rightness of our views, and to share our feelings and ideas with a receptiveness to having them changed.

The successful management of conflict requires what Alfie Kohn calls a "cooperative framework for dealing with disagreement" so that competition and win/lose dynamics don't interfere with the healthy exchange of differing views by team members.[19] When a cooperative context exists, Kohn notes, conflicts can become opportunities for team learning." Senge also emphasizes that no team can avoid all conflicts and defensive maneuvers, but a healthy team is the one that learns from them.

As we have discussed, it is rare to enjoy significant and lasting personal growth without feeling any pain or suffering as an essential part of that growth. This idea applies to teams as well. Conflicts and defensive operations can make or break a team, but effective teams can recognize these phenomena, learn from them, and then continue to work toward the team members' shared goals. Teams often don't know or realize their full strength until they have been pushed to their limits.

INTERVENTIONS AND STRATEGIES FOR TEAM DEVELOPMENT

Outstanding teamwork is at the heart of successful outcomes in the health care and other team settings. As a valued member of a caregiving team you can make an important contribution to ensure a healthier and more productive unit. Here are some ideas that can help foster team collaboration, development, efficacy, and support.

See Conflict as Natural and Unavoidable

Openly dealing with conflicts and sharing potentially threatening information are tough assignments for any team. However, we can begin to develop a more workable approach to these tasks by first accepting that conflict is a natural, and often desirable, team event. When we see conflicts and disagreements as the inevitable concomitants of working so closely with others, we are more likely to approach these issues nondefensively, to feel less need to blame others, and to encourage a joint effort to solve the problem.

The examples of team conflicts presented earlier are good illustrations of the downstream consequences of not dealing effectively with conflict and disagreements over a long period of time. In the everyday work of the team, major problems like these often begin with a simple failure to communicate clearly about what team members expect of one another. These failures to communicate can result from role ambiguity, which exists when team members don't know what they should be doing, aren't clear about what other team members expect of them, or aren't clear about their own expectations of others. In a productive and healthy team, members have a clear understanding of what their own and others' job responsibilities are (i.e., there is a state of role clarity).

Role conflict is another source of these problems. Here there are inconsistencies in the expectations of team members. Team members can have expectations for themselves inconsistent with the expectations other team members have of them. Two or more team members can make conflicting demands of a colleague, or there can be role overload and there is simply not enough time for members to meet all the expectations of the other team members.

When not discussed and openly negotiated, role conflicts, role ambiguity, and differing views of what the team is trying to do can all lead to team strife and escalating patterns of conflict among members. Such conflicts eventually come to be seen as "personality clashes." When we consider how these different kinds of conflicts are mismanaged or not managed at all, a common theme emerges: The conflicts tend to become personalized, and team members make negative characterological attributions to each other.

This tendency to personalize conflicts is reinforced by our natural inclination to explain behavior by making attributions about the other person rather than the situation the person is in. This is another instance of the fundamental attribution error discussed in Chapter 5. Rather than seeing ourselves as struggling with a problem that is common to many teams, or viewing the problem as a consequence of team members not being clear about their goals and expectations, we tend to see ourselves as struggling against people who are "bad, stupid, or both." The result is that the ensuing patterns of behavior become self-reinforcing and tend to escalate over time.

The personalization of conflict also means that the potential recipients of feedback are less open to that feedback because it is likely to be delivered as an unwelcome message about some perceived flaw in themselves. We all want feedback, and yet we don't want it. We want to know how we are doing in the process of achieving our goals, but we don't want to know others don't like what we are doing, or want us to change how we are doing things.

It is instructive to think about similar situations in your personal life. What is your first reaction when someone tells you they don't like what you are doing, or asks you to change your behavior, and do something differently? For most people, there is a natural tendency to resist this kind of feedback and the corresponding behavior change. We respond in a way that will restore threatened freedom.[20] This is partly because we want to feel good about what we are doing, and accepting that we need to change our behavior implies we are wrong in some way.

This is the point when the request to change can be potentially threatening to our self-esteem and therefore potentially stressful. In our personal lives and on caregiving teams, we need to find ways to give and receive feedback and to change our behavior accordingly. The obstacle is that there usually isn't an easy and pain free (i.e., self-esteem maintaining or enhancing) way to ask someone else to change his or her behavior, particularly when the other person is not experiencing any difficult feelings associated with the behavior. In fact, it is usually the case that the other person is fairly attached to this particular behavior, and it is meeting his or her needs, thus making it even more likely he or she will resist changing. Thus, it is important to be nonjudgmental, to focus on specific, observable behaviors, and to follow up with supportive messages if you sense a negative response. As the recipient of feedback, we need to recognize that although how we are doing things might be excellent in many respects, we often need to do things differently to achieve optimal teamwork and team functioning.

Enhance Support, Collaboration, and Inspiration

Support and collaboration are pivotal to harmony, efficiency, and effectiveness in health care teams. Recognizing the value of these key attributes has galvanized the development of innovative team interventions. One such development is Schwartz Rounds, multidisciplinary meetings when caregivers discuss patient care with a focus on how that care is affecting them personally. This model, described by Lown as "an interdisciplinary approach to enhancing patient-centered communication, teamwork, and support," was developed by the Schwartz Center for Compassionate Healthcare and is now implemented in health care settings throughout the world.[21; 22] Each round includes a psychosocial facilitator and medical lead. After a panel of presenters speaks there is an open discussion. The rounds are unique in that they focus not on clinical problem solving, but on providing an opportunity for participants to tell their stories, often about particularly challenging family or patient situations, and to reflect on their reactions and connect with the purpose of their work. By offering support and inspiration to participants, Schwartz Rounds increase participants' awareness of, and appreciation for, the contributions of other disciplines, and thus reduce interdisciplinary myopia. Research shows that these rounds validate participants' feelings, provide more responsive and empathic care, and develop a greater connection to the purpose of the organization.[22]

Another example of a team development intervention is Enriching Moments, a practice that can be implemented in hospice interdisciplinary team (IDT) meetings.[23] Enriching Moments is described by Pangborn as a "collaborative narrative occasion" when team members have an opportunity to share "defining moments" and inspiring stories related to their care of patients and families. Enriching Moments, Schwartz Rounds, and other supportive and facilitative interventions can act as potent antidotes to caregiver stress because they enhance social support, normalize difficult caregiving encounters, and foster reconnection with a shared sense of purpose in the work. These team-enhancing interventions seem most likely to be effective if they are scheduled regularly.

Encourage Shared Leadership

Team development expert Irwin Rubin and his colleagues stress that leadership functions must be shared throughout the team to effectively achieve the team's goals.[24] Just as no single person can achieve the basic task or mission of the team, no single person can make the decisions, monitor and coordinate team progress, and lead the team in every situation. Instead, team members must assume shared leadership responsibilities. These leadership functions can be divided into two categories: those that focus on what (content/task) the group is doing, and those concerned with how (process) the group is working.

Task-oriented leadership functions include initiating problem solving or building work agendas, giving and seeking information and opinions, clarifying and elaborating on the inputs of group members, summarizing where the group is and where it needs to go, and checking to see if people are clear on the goals and decisions of the team.

Process-oriented leadership requires that everyone's contributions are considered, and that all group members are encouraged to participate with the common goal of harmonizing different points of view in order to find creative solutions to problems the group tackles. When these leadership functions are shared, an ethos of participation, empowerment, and a greater sense of commitment to the team's goals, can develop. When leadership is shared, team members are more likely to have *flow* experiences like those identified by Csikszentmihalyi.[25; 26] The sense of collective commitment and shared purpose created in this process provides a context for team members immersing themselves completely in their work and enjoying it for its own sake.

**Enhance Team Members' Self-Esteem
and Connection to the Team Mission**

Making team members feel good about themselves is another important leadership function that team members can share. Think back to our discussion of the central role self-esteem plays in buffering stress and guiding purpose-driven efforts. To a large extent, leadership involves just that: making people feel good about themselves and enhancing their self-esteem. The praise, awards, and recognition dispensed within the team are part of this core leadership function. Burnout is much less likely when team members feel they and their work are truly valued and valuable. This is particularly important in the helping professions, where self-doubt, helper secrets, and self-blame can lower a person's self-esteem. High self-esteem is an excellent buffer against stress, and inhibits burnout. We all need occasional affirmation of the good things we do and of our important contributions to the team effort.

How much do you feel your work is recognized and rewarded by your team? Although you can't change everyone else's behavior toward you directly, you can recognize and reward the work of your teammates. These positive actions will earn the goodwill of your colleagues, making them more likely to reciprocate in kind in the future, as Selye noted in his recipe for stress management (see Chapter 3). The moral is, if the world feels cold, light a small fire, and it will spread. An added benefit is that your caring expressions to your teammates will also benefit you by improving your own mood and self-esteem.

How can we increase affirming behaviors like these among teammates? Too often, months or even years go by without team members sitting down and sharing their appreciation of one another. Some people might say that to be genuine, positive feedback and expressing gratitude must be spontaneous, unplanned, and "from the heart," but some structured exercises can help build these "spontaneous and heartfelt" communications into our busy helping worlds. For example, I encourage teams to do a brief round of acknowledgments and thank-yous intermittently throughout the year. The feedback should be specific and as perceptive as possible, acknowledging things you have seen the other person do that have struck you as a positive contribution to the team effort or your own work. You might acknowledge a creative intervention, someone's sense of humor, or anything else about the person that inspires or supports you. Don't spend more than a minute or two on each person, but be sure everyone is included. You might think that doing this regularly would lead to all the positive comments being saved for "appreciations day" and that the number of spontaneous expressions of appreciation between these sessions would decrease. But the reverse is actually true: Acknowledging the efforts of others is a good habit that can be strengthened by occasionally making it the team's exclusive focus.

Build Caring Relationships

Your relationships with other team members will be most rewarding and productive if they are endowed with the same qualities of openness, trust, respect, and authenticity you are striving for in your helping relationships. When teammates are in the Helper's Pit, or in the midst of a personal crisis, it is natural to share our best helping selves with them.

An important kind of empathy to have for other team members, particularly members of other disciplines, is a clear understanding (intellectually and emotionally) of what it is like to do their job. The challenge here is to overcome interdisciplinary myopia. I've found that many, if not most, team members have surprisingly incomplete and often erroneous pictures of what the other team members do and how they feel about doing it. However you do it, a good team-building intervention is to have members provide a detailed picture of what they do and their inner experiences doing it. You could do this in group or one-on-one settings.

When there is empathy among team members, and an atmosphere of goodwill, there is greater openness, fewer negative interactions, and sustained personal growth of team members. Fear has exactly the opposite effect on these qualities of team life. If every team had a "fear detector" and used it, the possibilities for team development would be enormous. Of course, not all our fears need to be discussed in a group context, but when an atmosphere of fear replaces one of goodwill, the negative effects on the team are pervasive. Accordingly, the team should be aware this is occurring so it can address the problem creatively.

One anxiety-provoking behavior that can lower trust levels among team members significantly is spreading rumors and gossip. A rumor is a statement or opinion circulated among team members that has no known source. Rumors are hazardous to teams because innocent statements can change in context, meaning, and attribution as they are passed from person to person. In this fashion, an insignificant event could become an explosive "news" item with serious implications for particular team members.

Gossip—a rumor or rumors linked to a specific individual—is even more hazardous to the team. We all know this, but it is often difficult to politely resist participating in gossip. If all team members agree that gossip is unacceptable, and if each team member makes an effort to politely refuse to listen to gossip about teammates, the norm of no gossip will quickly develop.

An appropriate response to gossip is to say, in effect, that although you appreciate the other person just wants to keep you informed about what is happening, you don't think you need to know about this piece of information. Then shift the conversation to another topic.[27] Each person must find his or her own way to say no to gossip. A commitment to not say anything about anyone you would not say directly to him or her is best.

If you think it is impossible to avoid participating in gossip, given your network of friendships within the team, you might need to examine whether that network is healthy for you and the team. The dilemma with gossip is that people don't think they are doing anything wrong when they indulge in it, and therefore see no need to change their behavior. We often participate in gossip because we don't want to alienate the person who is sharing it with us, and consequently have him or her also talking about us behind our backs. But another part of us knows that a better response is to gently let the person know we are simply not interested.

Approach and Resolve Conflicts

People are particularly motivated to give feedback to someone when his or her behavior doesn't match their expectations. This simple fact is the basis for a model of conflict and conflict resolution that discourages the personalization of these kinds of problems within the team. This model defines conflicts simply as unmet expectations.[28]When we have a conflict with other people, they are either doing something we didn't expect them to do, or they are not doing something we did expect them to do. Virtually all conflicts will fall within this model.

Unmet expectations are a major source of team stress; they underlie many interpersonal communication problems team members typically cite as among the most stressful aspects of their work. When you are experiencing unmet expectations concerning another person's behavior, the first step toward conflict resolution is to let the other person know about these unmet expectations. Of course, these should be unmet expectations worthy of such attention, namely, conflicts that cause you stress, interfere with the optimal performance of your clinical duties, and so forth. There are more unmet expectations in our lives than we could—or should—ever address.

One striking phenomenon I've encountered is that when I ask people to think about the most troublesome unmet expectation they have regarding someone in their workplace, most of them admit they haven't told the other person about it. Their explanations include statements such as "She'll never change," "I've given him enough hints to sink a ship. If he wanted the feedback, he'd have figured it out by now," "She'd be devastated," or "I want to continue working here and don't want to make him my enemy."

Each of these reasons seems to have some validity. There are risks involved when you approach another person to ask for a change in his or her behavior. However, the consequences of the alternative course of action are more definite: If the other person is never directly told about your unmet expectation, there is no chance that his or her behavior will change, and the problem is likely to get worse.

A paradoxical finding is that, although most people say they would like feedback on their own behavior if someone has a problem with it, these same people insist the other person would not respond in a similarly positive and welcoming fashion. In these situations, we often believe the other person couldn't possibly have the same psychological maturity, win-win attitude, empathy, team spirit, or goodwill we see in ourselves, and so it is difficult to imagine the person will cooperate with our requests for a change in behavior.

There is self-deception operating here that also contributes to the perpetuation of conflicts within teams. Although few of us believe we are perfect, when we are experiencing problems on the team, too often our first thought when we arrive at work in the morning is something like this: "If only this other person or these people would get it together, things would be much better around here." If all 10 members of a 10-person team feel this way, the results are predictable. In contrast, if everyone approaches the team seeking ways that would help other members of the team, many conflicts would rapidly disappear.

Even if we recognize others might be amenable to changing their behavior, and that we might need to change our own too, dealing with these issues is usually uncomfortable for everyone. The good news is there can be many more positive outcomes than we actually believe are possible. These positive outcomes are even more likely if structures and norms exist that support the ongoing negotiation of roles and expectations in the team. Successful conflict resolution is more likely if there is a group norm that all team members should routinely discuss unmet expectations with other team members as part of continual team development.

Let's look at some skills that can make these exchanges of information safe enough for teams to embrace and practice openly. We will discover how you can ask others to change their behaviors in a way that doesn't lower their self-esteem and evoke angry and defensive responses.

A key first step is to see the problem as existing in the relationship, or in the fit, between you and the other person, rather than in you or the other person. This more systems-oriented perspective will help you avoid blaming yourself or the other person and distorting the reality of the situation. It is better to adopt the expectation that successful resolution of the conflict will involve change on both your parts.

During the first few seconds when you are presenting an unmet expectation to the other person, the outcome of the encounter is rapidly being decided. The encounter is likely to go in one of two possible directions: mutual discovery or combative defensiveness. Think about the encounters of this nature you have had in your personal and work lives. When the outcome was positive, you and the other person were probably able to listen to each other and understand the impact of the behavior in question without getting locked into a competitive, angry, and defensive state. You weren't thinking, "How can I protect myself?" or "What can I do to get my own way?"

How can we increase the likelihood of mutual exploration, empathy, and cooperation? One way to do this is to express our unmet expectations by using what are now widely known as "I-statements" or "I-messages." This is the same talk tool many self-help books recommend for parents, managers, and just about anyone who must solicit changes in the behavior of other people. When you present your conflict via an I-message, the key is to begin by stating it as a problem you have and not as a problem the other person has.

This way of stating things is effective for two reasons: First, it is in fact your problem: the other person might be perfectly happy with his or her behavior. Second, by stating it this way, you increase the likelihood that the other person will empathize with your position and not immediately adopt a defensive stance. It helps to maintain a belief that the other person is doing what they are because they believe it is the most effective thing to do. It might be something they learned in their first-rate educational program, and it might have been successful for him or her working in a different organization; it just isn't working in relation to you or in the current context.

The next parts of the message should include a description of the behavior that is troubling you, how it affects you (include your feelings), and why. Help the other person understand and empathize with your point of view. The emotional issues in the conflict must be approached and resolved before the content issues are handled. Understanding what the conflict looks like from the other side is essential.

The more strictly behavioral (as opposed to personal) your description of the troublesome behavior, the better. If your comments contain even an implicit evaluation of the general abilities or worth of the other person (e.g., "I guess you just don't care." Or, "You have an attitude problem.") the possibility of a defensive or hostile response is much greater.

Here are some examples of I-messages: "Jean, I'm having some difficulty because when I don't get the paperwork from you in time to do my own notes when they're due, I get lots of complaints from everyone else." Or "Ron, I'm struggling with something. When you don't let me know what happened on your shift, I'm left in the dark, and I'm afraid I could make a serious mistake as a result. What can we do about it?"

Although I might not be stating these messages exactly the way you would, it is the form that is important, not the content. Own the problem. Be specific when you discuss what it is about the other person's behavior that is causing problems for you. Describe how it is affecting you, and include your feelings. Then submit the problem for joint consideration, rather than making a unilateral demand for behavior change.

Think of your conflict resolution intervention as a *care-frontation* response (see Chapter 6). In other words, you are pointing to a discrepancy between something specific in the other person's behavior and your expectations of that person's behavior. There should be no aggressive element in your message. However, we often wait such a long time before bringing up a subject that by the time we do discuss it, our anger has built up and quickly surfaces if our comments meet with any resistance. This is why all members of the team should give one another feedback frequently as an essential part of team maintenance. When these communication channels break down, the team suffers, defensive routines strengthen, and the problems become increasingly more difficult to address in a productive manner.

Here are some additional principles that can make conflict resolution or role negotiation interactions more successful:

- Don't confront anyone in a group setting, and never encourage ganging up on one person so they will "get the point."
- Be supportive. Go one better than the Golden Rule and treat others better than you want them to treat you.
- Find ways to share information without lowering the other person's self-esteem. How would you like to hear the message you are about to convey?
- Imagine what the other person needs from you and offer it; the other person will be more likely to give you what you need.
- Negotiate frequently with all members on role expectations as part of the normal ongoing life of the team. This will prevent the

buildup of tensions that lead to crises and emotional eruptions that characterize dysfunctional teamwork.

- Ask what you can do to improve their success and satisfaction at work. The idea here is quid pro quo: something for something. If you want someone to change a behavior they believe in or are very attached to, you must be willing to change an equally important and central aspect of your own behavior. This quid pro quo element can elicit a sense of a shared mission and transform a potentially divisive exchange into a mutually-enhancing one.

- Be sure the other person wants to experiment with this new way of talking about working together before you initiate any conflict resolution sessions. Explain the model in some detail. You might even ask the other person to read this chapter before beginning.

Empower One Another

Empowerment has become somewhat of a cliché, but even so, it retains its relevance for all our clinical efforts. In essence, our human presence, support, and communication skills empower the people we care for: They gain a greater sense of control over the difficult situations they face, so they are able to live in more fulfilling ways.

This should also be our goal in relationships with our fellow caregivers. The helper's journey is not that of an isolated individual working wonders on a mountaintop. It is more like being part of a team of climbers who are working together interdependently to get to the top of the mountain. In the end, each member is able to achieve something he or she could not do alone.

High-performance teams are exciting to participate in because the group often generates solutions to problems all team members recognize as better than those any single member could have provided. A sense of collective efficacy develops, and team members empower one another by teaching skills and sharing their knowledge. Transdisciplinary team functioning gives the team added flexibility and confidence, and reduces interdisciplinary myopia and feelings of "This is my turf." The need for a transdisciplinary approach is particularly keen in the assessment of pain and spiritual distress in end-of-life care.

Establish a Staff Support Group

Creating a support group where problems, concerns, and feelings are communicated openly is an often used intervention for preventing burnout, reducing turnover, and improving team morale.[29] A support group is a place where you can talk with people who appreciate the difficulties and joys of your shared work and who understand your motivations for doing it. "The secrets of life," as Emerson noted, "are not shown except to sympathy and likeness."[30]

In staff support groups, as in personal support groups, members share a common concern (i.e., stress at work) and there is an emphasis upon peer help. Members meet to learn together and to support one another in their work as helpers. These groups provide a unique opportunity for interpersonal learning and for receiving assistance in coping with work stressors, dealing with issues of professional identity, and team building.

An important learning occurring among group members during these regular meetings is a shift from believing "I'm the only one having a difficult time with this" (i.e., the fallacy of uniqueness) to knowing "We're all in the same boat" and that everyone has a difficult time with these stressful situations. Sharing common concerns in an egalitarian atmosphere can lead to instant empathy and a sense of we-ness among group members; unrealistic self-expectations can be tempered and corrected. Difficult feelings and helper secrets can be shared and worked through. Once this occurs, the bias toward self-blame can be corrected, and one's energies can be directed toward developing better coping and problem-solving skills and strategies.

Many kinds of support and learning can occur in effective support groups. These include direct assistance, feedback, sharing and modeling problem-solving strategies, venting feelings, and giving wholehearted encouragement. Each of the six different forms of social support—listening, technical appreciation, technical challenge, emotional support, emotional challenge, and shared social reality—are typically exchanged among group members. These different support needs can also be met through unstructured interactions among team members.

In *Staff Support Groups in the Helping Professions*, Hartley and Kennard list keys to a successful staff support group: The request or proposal for the group should be based on realistic and agreed-upon expectations, and there must be transparency in establishing the group and agreement about the choice of a facilitator. The facilitator's style should match the group's needs and he or she must be careful not to let personal reactions get in the way. Finally, the group must ensure safety for its members, address important issues, stay on task, and self-evaluate.[31]

It is important to realize what these groups are not, as well as what they are. Most importantly, they are not psychotherapy sessions. In the support group, the focus is on problem solving, processing stressful events, and sharing good moments as well, with the goal of increasing team members' effectiveness and well-being and strengthening relationships on the team.

Although personal problems do arise and are appropriate topics in a professional support group because they affect our work with the team, serious personal problems should be taken to a counselor rather than to the group. Staff support groups should also not become a palliative treatment for organizational problems, such as a lack of space, work overload, or failures in leadership. Their use in this way will only further demoralize staff members.[31] Support groups can also fail for a variety of other reasons. Breaches of confidentiality, the presence of a dominant facilitator, and failure to establish and maintain trust and a caring atmosphere in the group are just a few of the many problems to avoid.

As Hartley and Kennard note, it is extremely important to have the support group study itself or evaluate how it is doing on an ongoing basis. A brief discussion at the end of each session to focus on the best and worst things about the session can be useful. You can periodically give group members a few minutes to answer these questions: "What is one thing you appreciate about our support group?" "How do you see your own participation in the group?" And, "How do you feel about the role you've played?"[32] The Kennard and Hartley text has chapters dealing with the many other challenges and potential benefits associated with staff support groups.[29]

Study Team Process

To be effective, a caring team, like a staff support group, needs to study itself and discuss how the team can work together more effectively and address any problems that may exist. This self-study requires precious time, time often not allocated for this endeavor, but needs to be. In their self-study, the team can look at its own process by asking about *how* they are talking and acting with one another, rather than only reviewing *what* they are talking about. Process questions the team can ask might include the following: How are decisions made? Are differing points of view encouraged or discouraged? Are there any "elephants in the room" everyone is aware of but no one addresses?

The content of the team's interactions is important, but if the team fails to look at how it is interacting, it will inevitably lose control of that process and of its helping outcomes. Team debriefing that offers constructive criticism and focuses on task-related (rather than person-oriented) factors, proves to be an incredibly efficacious team building intervention.[4] An atmosphere of respect, trust, and openness will encourage process awareness and self-study. It can also promote sensitivity to the changing needs of individual group members. A process orientation is proactive because it detects team problems in their earliest stages and leads to adjustments that ensure the continued productivity and well-being of the team and its members.[33] When something doesn't feel right, it is crucial someone says "Let's look at our process."

Questionnaires assessing different aspects of team functioning can also be useful for team self-study. One brief questionnaire I often use can serve as an example of what the team needs to look at. Respond to each of the following items as they apply to your team, using this Likert scale: (1) strongly disagree, (2) disagree, (3) neutral, (4) agree, and (5) strongly agree.

- There is a high degree of trust and openness in the group.
- The team is effective at achieving its tasks.
- I get all the information I need to do my work and make effective decisions.
- Good work is recognized and rewarded in this group.

- Assignments (who does what) are clearly defined.
- Differences and conflicts are recognized and worked through.[34]

Questionnaires like this can be an excellent starting point for team discussions. Responses from team members can be gathered anonymously, collated, and then reviewed by the entire team in a team-building session. Distressed teams suffering from severe communication breakdowns and organizational upheavals score poorly on all six dimensions of the questionnaire, but even high-performing teams sometimes indicate difficulties with trust and openness and addressing conflicts.

Does your team regularly evaluate its effectiveness? Many teams take a downstream, or reactive approach to the management of team problems and do something only after a problem develops. Fewer teams take an upstream, preventive stance. How does your team deal with its problems? Is its approach reactive or proactive?

It requires systematic and regular attention to team dynamics and process to identify some of the patterns that form the core of the team's process. Once these are identified, the team can choose behaviors to maintain or increase, or to decrease or eliminate. The proactive team also renews itself through regular team-building events. Diverse strategies teams use for self-renewal include having an outside facilitator work with the team, arranging retreats, holding brainstorming sessions, or organizing restorative group activities such as a happy hour, an informal social occasion, or a community activity day.

RESILIENT AND HEALTHY TEAMS AND ORGANIZATIONS

Caring teams and organizations need to effectively address a wide range of challenging issues, including intense cases, team conflicts, work overload, the absence of fairness and rewards, and other stressors we identified earlier. Despite these challenges, resilient and healthy teams and organizations find ways to resolve them and grow in the process.

Models of healthy work organizations now being developed can help diagnose these issues and identify efficacious team and organizational strategies to cope with them.[35; 36] However, positive psychologists are suggesting that an even higher order or optimal level of team functioning is possible. These theorists and researchers are advancing an expanded and inspiring vision and lexicon for healthy teams and organizations, introducing concepts such as *transformative cooperation*, the *broadening-and-building* effects of positive emotions, *team resilience* and *flourishing*.

As we explored in earlier chapters, positive psychologists and ancient philosophers have identified two basic kinds of well-being. The first is hedonic well-being, well-being consisting of global satisfaction with life and pleasant affect. The other is eudaimonic well-being, which incorporates dimensions such as meaning, growth, authenticity, and purpose in life beyond self-gratification. Barbara Fredrickson argues that human flourishing combines these states, encompassing "both feeling good and doing good."[37]

Fredrickson claims higher positivity ratios (ratio of positive emotions to negative emotions) in a team are associated with flourishing and other beneficial outcomes.[37] Her broaden-and-build theory posits that higher positivity ratios (within limits) promote a cognitive openness to new perspectives, more active discovery, stronger personal and social resources, the desire to create more goodness, and other positive characteristics supporting both hedonic and eudaimonic experiences in the team and organization.

Sekerka and Fredrickson apply these ideas, examining how positive emotional climates in a team or organization can lead to what they termed transformative cooperation.[38] They defined transformative cooperation as "a dynamic process that brings organizational members together to create innovation through social interaction, where positive change emerges through new organizational forms that provide benefits for all who participate."[38] When this kind of cooperation occurs, "individuals support others to discover positive meaning in their work, bringing forward what they value most," and "gratitude and enthusiasm emerge."[38] The team accomplishes its goals, and team members grow and learn through their work together.

Sekerka and Fredrickson gave an example of "Appreciative Inquiry" as a practice that can support transformative cooperation in an organization. In Appreciative Inquiry, team members reflect together on moments when the team or organization was at its best, and they share stories that capture these high points. Much like the mission moments presented in Chapter 1, these team or organizational mission moments reconnect team members with their larger shared purpose.

Working within the general framework of positive psychology, Luthans and Youssef developed a model of the "positive workplace" in which efficacy, hope, optimism, and resiliency are viewed as positive psychological resources or capacities that promote the accrual of "psychological capital."[39]

Alliger and colleagues studied resilient teams and "how they flourish under pressure."[40] They identified three key behavioral strategies that resilient teams employ in the face of challenging events and circumstances: minimizing, managing, and mending. Minimizing is a proactive strategy wherein the resilient team anticipates upcoming challenges, engages in "what if" discussions, detects warning signs, and prepares to meet any pending challenges. When challenging situations occur, the resilient team manages the challenges quickly and honestly, maintains basic processes when challenged, seeks out expertise and guidance from team members and others outside the team, and supports overly-stressed teammates. Resilient teams mend: They recover from the stressful demand and adapt to what might be a "new normal." They debrief, express appreciations, work through conflicts, and make adjustments to ensure they are prepared for similar events in the future. Gathering a team of resilient individuals does not necessarily create a resilient team, echoing our earlier point that some high-functioning team members can take a go-it-alone stance and not embrace the interdependent role that optimal teamwork requires.

Finally, in their model of a healthy organization, Schwartz and Hasson emphasize the central role of alignment. For them, alignment is "the lining up of different aspects of what is going on in an organization so they create a common thread."[41] One key alignment, they argue, occurs when employees are given the opportunity to perform at a high level in sync with the organization's goals or mission. This view echoes the one expressed here—that in a healthy caring team and organization, the mission-to-vision process of the individual helper and caring team and organization are synergistically aligned, each component enhancing the others.

Conclusion

We have seen how a high-functioning, caring team—like a high-performing or self-actualizing individual clinician—has a collective sense of efficacy and belief in making a valuable contribution to the world. High team efficacy and esteem are potent stress deterrents and support a team's continued success, resilience, and well-being. Openness, feedback, and addressing unmet expectations allow a high-functioning team to adapt and learn. In their most evolved forms, caring teams and organizations are distinguished by transdisciplinary, eudaimonic, and transformative processes that enhance both providers and outcomes of care. As Helen Keller reminded us, together we can do—and be—so much more.

The success of a healthy and high-performing individual, team, or organization ultimately depend on the health of the larger systems they exist within—the community, the nation, and the world. Can the concepts and perspectives we have explored throughout these pages also tell us something about caring, health and transformation in these larger systems? We will try to answer that question in the next chapter, as our exploration of the helper's journey leads us to this larger stage of empathy, compassion, and healing.

8

Love and compassion are necessities, not luxuries. Without them humanity cannot survive.

Dalai Lama

All of us, citizens of every nation, are now in the same family, are now in the same boat, walking the same tightrope, like it or not. The worst problems of the human predicament are common to all of us, from climate disruption, loss of biodiversity, and poisoning of the environment to pandemics, gross economic inequities, and the threat of nuclear war. Our tightrope is a line from humanity's past to its future.[1]

Paul Ehrlich and Robert Ornstein

Toward a Caring
Society and World

Within this book, we have traced your helping journey from your earliest sense of a mission to your current work on the front lines of caregiving. Our focus has shifted steadily outward, starting with your innermost experiences of helping and eventually moving to the interpersonal contexts of caregiving. At each step of this journey, we have addressed the different challenges you have faced: studying yourself, being open to others' and your own suffering, learning new communication skills, transforming stress, and being a member of a caring team. This final chapter will identify some of the caring challenges we face as a nation and global community. We will also explore how the ideas developed in the preceding pages can help us understand and confront these challenges head-on.

As you think about these collective challenges, imagine our entire nation and global community as a single caregiver entity. This collective caregiver faces many of the same psychological dilemmas felt by individual helpers and caring teams, such as balancing demands with resources, overcoming barriers to compassion, and evading the hazards of avoidance.

The challenges facing this caregiver are daunting, including pervasive poverty and homelessness, ongoing civil wars, gun violence, physical and sexual abuse, racism and discrimination of all kinds, disparities in health care, and the existential crisis of climate change. In our struggle to meet these challenges, and to have hope triumph over despair, one key will be strengthening the social connectedness scientific evidence tells us is essential for our individual and societal well-being.

Our aging Baby Boomer cohort is one of the major challenges facing our collective caregiver here in the United States. The needs of this huge generational group will severely tax our resources and compassion in all realms of care, including family caregiving, hospice and palliative care, and bereavement support. As Roth and colleagues note, increasing demands will be placed on family caregiving as the number of adults living at home with cognitive impairments and with physical disabilities will skyrocket in the coming decades.

Exacerbating the situation is the shrinking availability of potential caregivers. Roth and colleagues urge that caregivers must be integrated into the health care system more efficiently and more meaningfully, and that additional resources, including secondary caregivers, should be provided. The burgeoning requirements for accessible hospice and palliative care and bereavement support for survivors makes the provision of such additional resources imperative. The way in which we address these challenges will be a test of our collective compassion.

Commitment to the Common Good

To succeed on this collective helping journey, we must first dedicate ourselves as a social group to serving the public or common good by marrying individual and societal well-being.[3] Our commitment to the common good will find its fullest expression in a society and a world in which empathy and compassion are nurtured, valued, and expressed.

As argued in earlier chapters, our innate altruism and shared humanity can guide us into that desired future, as Jeremy Rifkin forcefully conveys in *The Empathic Civilization*: "A radical new view of human nature has been slowly emerging and gaining momentum, with revolutionary implications for the way we understand and organize our economic, social and environmental relations in the centuries to come. We have discovered *Homo empathicus*."[4]

By choosing to make caring a significant element of your life's work, you are already a force for this positive change. Each time you help someone or contribute to your caregiving team or organization, you advance the common good and reaffirm your commitment to it. And, as every professional or volunteer helper knows—and the research presented here confirms—doing good for others may be the best way to sustain a sense of meaning and purpose in life. In addition, this sense of purpose and meaning can be a powerful buffer against stress, provided you balance caring for others with caring for yourself.

The need to find meaning in our lives is perhaps the highest expression of the life process, and the direction it takes. All life forms move toward fulfillment and actualization of their potential. As we have seen, empathy, compassion, and helping are natural, healthy, and healing processes. They are expressions of the healthy human mind and heart and of the fundamental motivating forces of existence. This sense of purpose and meaning in life—this dedication to something beyond oneself—can engender a deep form of happiness and well-being that includes personal growth and expression of the best that resides within oneself.

Your Helping Journey

How has helping others made your life more meaningful? Picture yourself writing your autobiography. What is your life story, and what role does helping others play in that story? If you devoted a chapter to your helping journey, what would you title it, and what would the chapter be about? While writing on this subject, you would probably think of the people you have felt closest to and about those who have taught you the most about life, relationships, love, and courage. You would recall both painful and happy moments. How does helping others contribute to your sense of purpose and significance in life?

Take a few minutes and jot down the first ideas and memories that come to mind, and then save what you have written as a reminder of your commitment to caring and what it has meant to you. Be sure to store these reflections somewhere so you and those who follow you can enjoy and learn from them in the years ahead.

Now take a broader view of your helping journey, envisioning your caring efforts and their legacy beyond the current moment. See them rippling across generations: That daughter who sees you caring for her mother so lovingly, with such grace and skill, will become the next great nurse or physician; the children you help say good-bye to their beloved parent will remember that moment on their own death beds and bring their family together to say their own goodbyes; the client you help heal an early childhood trauma will not send that pain on to future generations; the grieving child you help will one day instill hope in children at a bereavement camp for kids. You are changing our culture. You are changing how we die and how we live. Your influence will go on and on, long after we leave this place we call home. It is your legacy.

The Growth of Compassion

There are many reasons to be hopeful about the future of compassion. One of my early publications was a survey of mental health training in a hospice community. In it, we contacted all 124 extant U.S. hospice programs.[5] Today, there are thousands of Medicare-certified programs in the United States. A majority of cancer centers report the presence of a palliative care program at some level of development.[6; 7] Hospice or palliative care teams serve millions of patients and their families annually worldwide. However, this population represents only a small percentage of the people who need such care.[8] Indeed, unmet need continues to persist in all arenas of care, most profoundly in low- and middle-income countries, where access to care is often nonexistent. Yet, on the bright side, efforts to expand the reach of compassionate end-of-life care throughout the world continue to increase in scope and number.

Other positive developments include, as documented here, the growing influence and presence of the person/patient-centered approach throughout health care. There has also been increased attention in the mental health field to the social and cultural factors contributing to psychological and physical well-being. In addition, research and theory in a variety of disciplines are significantly adding to our understanding of compassion, resilience, healing, and well-being. Bereavement theory, research, and practice continue to transform the ways we think about and treat grief and trauma. Finally, an emergent global mental health movement is seeking to address the woeful shortage of mental health specialists in low- and middle-income countries, where 75% of people struggling with mental health issues remain untreated.[9; 10] Though strained, our collective caregiver is showing signs of a deep-rooted resilience—a good sign for compassion's future.

Toward a Caring Society

Of course, the issues and dynamics of our individual, team, and organizational helping journeys are closely tied to those of our collective caregiver. Keeping balance in our lives and keeping your internal flame of caring burning brightly are difficult tasks, even in a highly supportive context. Doing so in a society that doesn't truly value the kind of work we do is doubly difficult. How can we as individuals and as a society begin to reverse some of the forces that oppose and threaten caring and helping? How can we achieve a balance between self-concern and collective concern?

The structural changes that will lead to a more caring, other-oriented society must ultimately include modifying the fundamentally egocentric patterns of socialization and cultural influences that shape our development. There are some obvious first steps we can take to work toward this goal: We can put greater emphasis on cooperation and prosocial behavior in our media, families, and schools. We know that exposure to prosocial television modeling of interpersonal skills, acceptance of diversity, cooperation, and discussion of feelings—as opposed to the more prevalent and often glamorized screening of violence—can enhance prosocial motivation and behavior in children.[11; 12] We can support childrearing that leads to secure attachments and parenting techniques—such as drawing your child's attention to others' feelings and explaining why people feel the way they do. These practices are associated with higher levels of prosocial behavior in children.[13] We can also implement school-based, social-emotional learning programs known to enhance students' social awareness and foster greater empathy, stress management, and positive social behavior.[14]

Healthy Caring Systems

If we are to meet the larger challenge of caring, we must work to realign our values and reward structures so that empathy and compassionate action are consistently rewarded and strengthened. We have reviewed efforts to accomplish this in our health care system (*see* Chapter 5). There, and in other settings, this will require creating healthy caring systems in which the empathy-compassion-helping-connection can flourish.

Two guiding principles for creating healthy caring systems emerge from our review. First, we must maximize the flow of health-related information. Second, in caring, as in politics and economics, we must resist the temptation to pursue short-term relief at the expense of achieving our long-term goals.

Systems theorists agree that a key feature in all healthy living systems (whether they be cells, individuals, caregiving teams, or nations) is a free flow of health-relevant information.[15; 16; 17] Without an extensive exchange of information, systems cannot maintain self-regulation and move toward their goals. Breakdowns in the exchange of critical health-related information disrupt healthy self-regulation. For example, when a team doesn't productively discuss a debilitating conflict, or an individual helper conceals troubling self-doubts, the health and efficacy of both are diminished. Unfortunately, these acts of avoidance often persist because they are immediately reinforced by reduced anxiety. These short-term gains from anxiety reduction outweigh the ensuing (and often unconsidered), long-term pain and losses. Both systems and individuals can behave in self-defeating ways when they fall prey to the dynamics of the neurotic paradox (*see* Chapter 3).

Even if we are highly motivated and free of any of these empathy-reducing influences, we can easily fail to accurately perceive the extent of others' suffering. Myriad psychological factors can lead us to avoid or misjudge the suffering of the people we care for. Even with the best intentions, we can trivialize their suffering or distance ourselves when their pain activates one of our own interpersonal allergies. We can also blame and stigmatize the victim, a practice common in our society's response to suffering. Such a failure to empathize derails the empathy-compassion-helping-connection.

One early study of the extent to which caregivers' accurately rate pain found that at the higher levels of sensed pain, there was a discrepancy between patients' ratings and those of caregivers (nurses and physicians).[18] Such an anomaly implies a lack of true empathy or deep understanding of the patient's experience of pain and has served as a strong argument for routinely using pain assessment tools to improve patient-caregiver communication. If we conducted a similar study on how well our assessment and treatment of suffering (understood as psychological distress) corresponded to the actual suffering of the people we care for, might we not come to a similar conclusion? The importance of continuing to develop and enhance our empathic skills and assessment tools cannot be overstated.

As we have seen, the phenomenon of self-concealment further complicates our efforts to respond accurately and sensitively to suffering. Many people who face personal distress hide it from everyone, even from available and caring helpers (*see* Chapter 4). Our co-workers feel burned out, but they are reluctant to share this fact. Terminally-ill patients are angry about dying but don't reveal their anger or pain because they feel they owe their helpers a peaceful death. Distraught teenagers secretly form suicide pacts or write lengthy suicide manifestos detailing pain they have never been able to communicate adequately. Bereaved family members and lovers/partners of people with stigmatized conditions have their grief disenfranchised by a society critical of nontraditional relationships and life-styles. Zerubavel and Wright here point to these clinical realities: "Avoidance, silence, secrecy, and shame are leading contributors to relapse, chronic dysfunction, and failure to recover from a variety of traumatic events and mental health difficulties."[19]

It is moot to determine which came first, the fear and shame that leads to self-concealment or a society that cannot compassionately face its own pain. Clearly, to open the lines of communication necessary for helping and healing, we need to cultivate respect, trust, and openness in all our relationships—at home, at work, at school, in the community, and at the local, national, and international levels. We also need to eliminate social stigmas related to health disorders, gender and sexual minority status, trauma and mental health struggles, culture, race, and help seeking.

Toward Global Compassion

Our compassion for the difficulties of people in the world is constrained both by how our media presents this suffering and by our limited emotional capacities. Major crises receive extensive media coverage, then quickly recede from the news—and our awareness—even though the victims continue to struggle. Also, constant exposure to the enormity of suffering in the world can overwhelm us if we open our hearts to it. We can agonize emotionally when confronting the pain of thousands of people dying of illnesses, or when pondering the severe long-term consequences of climate change for life on the planet.

This phenomenon, wherein our compassion decreases as the number of victims increases, is now studied as "compassion collapse."[20] Reviewing work in this area, Daryl Cameron offers two explanatory mechanisms. The first is that we have a limited capacity for compassion, one better suited for responding to individuals of whom we have a clear mental representation. A photo of a single starving child can elicit more compassion than reading about the starving thousands he represents.

A second explanation is that when confronted with multiple victims, such as those of an earthquake in China or a ferry disaster in the Mediterranean, we anticipate too great a cost (emotional or financial) for our compassion and helping. As a consequence, we then confront what is known as "anticipated exhaustion"; we down-regulate our compassion and helping, and often dehumanize the victims to avoid the cost.

Cameron suggests, however, that we can counteract this tendency by consciously choosing whether to limit or expand our compassion for mass suffering. He recommends compassion-focused meditation as a strategy to increase our awareness of these choice points and to help us upregulate, rather than downregulate, our compassion. We are also more likely to transcend perceived self-interest in these moments if we access an inner moral compass to guide our actions.

Pain, Power, and Empathy

In the ideal future, global society, responding with empathy and a firm caring ethic, will react swiftly and effectively to suffering around the world, unencumbered by political, economic, religious, and social barriers. However, for many of the major problems and kinds of suffering in the world, the people with the most pain have the least power to help themselves, and the people with the most power to help them have the least pain. Those in power might have altruistic intentions, but often lack the human encounters that could deepen their empathy and lead to compassionate action. For example, maybe no one in their family or circle of friends is unemployed, hungry, or mentally ill. Exposure to differences can expand we-ness and prosocial behaviors.

Consider again the example of the "altruistic" monkeys and rats, described in Chapter 1, who sacrificed their rewards to decrease the electric shock of their peers. Animals who had been shocked themselves or who had a special connection (e.g., who had been cagemates) with the other animal were the most likely to desist from shocking them.[21] We are like the monkeys and rats in these studies. We share an almost universal tendency to become aroused in the presence of a distressed member of our own species and to act in ways to reduce that distress. We are much more likely to use our power in the service of the other if we can understand the individual's pain and feel a sense of connection with him or her.

Unfortunately, for a variety of reasons, the distress of people who have little political and economic power usually doesn't reach the people who have the power to do something about it. Occasionally, someone acting from great personal pain and applying monumental efforts can exert enough influence to help others who share a similar plight. One person can make a difference. But the dominant power-pain relation too often prevails, and the resulting breakdown of the empathy-compassion-helping-connection leads to suffering that, however widespread, remains voiceless.

Kenneth Clark discusses how empathy balances egocentricity and power gratification with the concern for the needs of others:

> The inability of human beings with power to understand the legitimate needs and aspirations of other human beings—the inability of human beings to understand that their fellow human beings share their anxieties, their frailties, their posturing, their desire to make the most out of the limited interval of conscious and evaluative life—this lack of simple expanded empathy is…the basis of social tensions, conflicts, violence, terrorism, and war. The survival of the human species now appears to depend upon a universal increase in functional empathy. Trained human intelligence must now dedicate itself to the attainment of this goal.[22]

Skeptics might say that this vision is far-fetched and assumes a Pollyanna-like world. Our self-centeredness and greed, they would argue, and the self-interested intransigence of our institutions, will not permit such a future. However, I believe there is no other way to move toward a positive future for all of humanity, a future in which we actually address the difficult problems confronting us.

Psychologists Michael Lynn and Andrew Oldenquist reinforce the view that an increase in "functional empathy" holds the key to a healthier future.[23] They point out that many of the world's problems represent social dilemmas, each embodying a conflict between our short-term and long-term interests. The three defining features of social dilemmas are that (a) there is a common or public good to be attained through collective effort; (b) attaining this public good is costly to the individual, though not as costly as the failure to attain it; and (c) the actions of a single individual are not sufficient to determine success or failure in this task. They argue that the solutions to these kinds of dilemmas must ultimately come from three sources: altruistic motives linked to empathy, a stronger sense of community, and moral motives advocating cooperative, unselfish behavior.

Psychologist Albert Bandura articulates these themes in his epic work, *Moral Disengagement: How People Do Harm and Live with Themselves.* He writes, "The sense of common humanity is developed through shared relational experiences that link one's own well-being to the well-being of others. Commitment to humanitarian causes greater than oneself can further build commonalities. These interpersonal conditions are essential to the development of inclusive, socially just, and humane societies."[24]

In *The Philosophy of Civilization*, Albert Schweitzer warned that, if we lose our reverence for any part of life, we lose it for all of life.[25] On the national and international planes, we need to work toward an approach to conflict that is rooted in respect for ourselves, all others, and for life in all its myriad forms. As our work teaches us, nothing is more precious than life itself.

When we create a shared vision of caring and all parts of our social organism communicate openly, then our social system, and all the individuals and organizations that compose it, can function with a sense of purpose. This vision can help us self-regulate to achieve the twin goals of concern for self and concern for others.

To extend our empathy and caring beyond the people and suffering we intimately know requires a profound shift in consciousness, the kind Albert Einstein describes here:

> A human being is a part of the whole, called by us "Universe," a part limited in time and space. He experiences himself, his thoughts and feelings as something separated from the rest—a kind of optical delusion of his consciousness. This delusion is a kind of prison for us, restricting us to our personal desires and to affection for a few persons nearest to us. Our task must be to free ourselves from this prison by widening our circle of compassion to embrace all living creatures and the whole of nature in its beauty.[26]

The kind of expanded self-concept Einstein suggests is now studied as an all-inclusive identity wherein we construe ourselves and our identities in relation to the rest of existence.[27] In the realm of caregiving, this kind of expanded empathy begins with the acceptance of our own vulnerability and losses, and can grow to include compassion for the pain of all human beings.

There are no pain-free ways to do this. We must look into ourselves and beyond ourselves, and learn to trust our common humanity, as Einstein and Bandura urge. If we can do this, then our empathy will become a strong force in the world.

In *The Empathic Civilization*, Jeremy Rifkin asserts that global empathy is now possible, and is expanding in our highly interconnected and globalizing world. This transformation of our empathy into global compassion, guided by global ethics, is necessary to save ourselves and the Earth as we confront the catastrophic climate change threatening our planet and our very existence.[4]

Compassion and Conversations at the End of Life

End-of-life work has always captured my heart and imagination because it consistently brings me closer to the realities of death, grief, love, and meaning, thus deepening my existence and providing a perspective on life I could not have gained otherwise. At the heart of this work are end-of-life conversations—the exchanges between family members, their helpers, and all present as a loved one's life nears its end. The end-of-life conversations I have been part of have taught me more about empathy and compassion, their human significance and their fragility, than all my research ever could. As we near the end of our shared journey in these pages, I'd like to conclude with some thoughts about these conversations, and their role in the evolution of care and compassion at the end of life—indeed, in all of life.

In 1968, I was an undergraduate at the University of Chicago, working in medical records at the university hospital.[28] On my walks through the hospital, I often passed by Elisabeth Kübler-Ross's weekly seminars on death and dying. The seminars intrigued me—even then, they had a buzz about them—but little did I know how they, and the energetic Swiss doctor who led them, would eventually shape the field I was about to enter.

My view is that Kübler-Ross's most significant and enduring contribution lies not in her stage theory. Her stage model does capture many of the common thoughts and feelings of dying persons, but it has never been empirically supported. It fails to meet essential criteria for psychological stages, like irreversibility, an invariant sequence, and universality. It also fails to accommodate the uniqueness of each individual's dying or grief experience. Instead, her contribution lies in her call to action, her insistence that we listen to dying persons and stop avoiding the conversations essential for enhancing quality of life at its end. In her book *On Death and Dying*, she called for a tidal change in how we approach death and dying, saying, "It might be helpful if more people would talk about death and dying as an intrinsic part of life just as they do not hesitate to mention when someone is expecting a baby. If this were done, we would not have to ask ourselves if we ought to bring this topic up with a patient, or if we should wait for the last admission."[29]

A technique such as Lamaze for end of life has not yet been developed, but we have seen the continued growth of hospice and palliative care and with that, an increase in the kinds of conversations that hold the key to more humane care for dying patients and their families. This can include advance care-planning efforts, more frequent and efficacious treatment goal discussions, and a wide range of bereavement interventions, including the art therapy Kübler-Ross held dear.[28; 30]

The view that we can cope better or less well with death and dying is relatively new to our culture. This shift in perspective, combined with public and community awareness efforts that present a different image of dying, is an essential element in the evolution of end-of-life conversations. These conversations, whether short or long, between the patient, his or her loved ones, and professional and volunteer helpers, serve as turning points along the path to life's end. Sometimes awkward or grueling in their candor, these end-of-life conversations can heal and bring a sense of control. But too often, the words don't come easily, they come too late, or they pale in comparison with the painful emotions of the moment.

And it's no wonder. The patient can feel embarrassed, fearful, or overwhelmed. Physicians and other health providers tiptoe around these conversations or struggle to find a way to convey hope when it no longer means what we'd like it to mean. And loved ones try to "stay positive" or simply stay silent, having no idea what to say. The structure of the medical care system, in which coordination of these conversations is not a routine part of care, creates additional barriers to these discussions.[30]

As a culture, we are moving together toward two inevitable conclusions: One, there is no way to avoid the realities of death and dying, no matter how hard we try. And two, conversations can play a vital role in helping move us closer to whatever awaits us on the other side of our loss. They can be a pathway leading us to a better way of dying. Silence breeds separation, but as we talk through our fears of death, a sense of hope and connectedness may replace avoidance, fear, and denial.[31] The end of life, as Ira Byock and other leaders in palliative care tell us, need not only be all angst and agony. It can also be a time of personal growth.[32; 33; 34] In our final days of life, a window of opportunity can present itself, and these conversations can guide us to it.

In clinics, online sites, kitchen tables, church basements, public lectures, Death Cafes, and town hall meetings across the nation and the world, people are slowly learning to master a new vocabulary that will help them break the silence. We are collectively discovering that there are many steps in the process of dealing with death, from talking early about medical planning, to coping with the illness and its treatment; from grappling with the physical and spiritual dimensions of impending death, to mourning that death once it comes.

Along the journey, these positive steps can be thwarted in several ways. Yet even in the face of these obstacles, people can and do find ways to use conversation as a tool for coping and communicating their love and concern. In so doing, they navigate this labyrinth of loss with courage.

Americans are clear in surveys about what they want as they die: To maintain dignity. To be comfortable. To make peace with whatever higher power they choose. They also want to say goodbye to important people. What they may not know, though, is that the healing power of these challenging conversations is one of life's greatest gifts. A few words—perhaps those never uttered before—can lift the burden of a lifetime of disappointment, a shameful personal secret, or unexpressed love. In everyday words, such a conversation can sound like this: I forgive you. Please forgive me. Thank you. I love you. Good-bye.[35] A hospice worker shared one such moment:

> Searching for a relationship with God, yet cutting himself off
> from his children by not allowing them to visit, he revealed

he had never told his adult children that he loved them. Turning to me, he said, "You have to help me." I asked him to identify which child was easiest to talk with. Then having named one, I guided him to say, "I love you." He repeated it four times, once for each child. He told each one of his love the day before he died.

Each time I have facilitated or witnessed conversations like these, I feel more alive and aware of our shared humanity and the ties that bind us.

Conclusion

When we are able to confront and accept loss and the impermanence of life, our natural empathy can transform into a deep sense of compassion, binding us in a helping and healing way with the suffering of others. This transformation can serve as a compass to guide our helping journeys and awaken the spirit of caring that resides deep within us.

In my attempt to address the challenges before us, I may have painted too dire a picture of the state of caring in our world today. Perhaps I opened a Pandora's Box in which only the Furies may seem to have escaped, and haven't given Hope her proper due, although I have tried. We turn to an unlikely moment to discover hope and bolster our moral courage—a scene from the Holocaust.

The Holocaust taught us about both sides of being human—the very worst and the best. In sharp juxtaposition to the Nazis were the people who cared so much they risked their lives to help others. These people included members of the resistance and the rescuers of the Jews. My great uncle, a Yugoslavian partisan resistance fighter, was captured by the Nazis, incarcerated at Dachau, and freed on liberation day in April 1945. He showed me the camp serial number tattooed on his forearm. The numbers had faded; his memories had not.

In *The Courage to Care*, Carol Rittner and Sondra Myers recount the story of Hermann Graebe, a German engineer who saved the lives of more than 300 Jews in Europe by employing them in his construction company.[36] Graebe involuntarily witnessed a massacre in

Dubno. That critical event led to his involvement as a rescuer. Here, he describes this decisive moment:

> One of the most terrible things I remember seeing...was a father, perhaps in his fifties, with his boy, about as old as my son Friedel was at that time—maybe 10 years old—beside him. They were naked, completely naked, waiting for their turn to go into the pit. The boy was crying, and the father was stroking his head. The older man pointed to the sky and talked quietly to the young boy. They went on speaking like that for a while—I could not hear what they said because they were too far away from me—and then it was their turn. There were other members of the family there too—the man's wife and an older woman, a white-haired lady who was maybe the grandmother. She was holding and cradling a child, and singing to it softly. Then a soldier screamed for them to go down into the pit.... The boy cried and the father talked to him and stroked him. How do you explain that? And how do you see such a thing without being stirred into action against whatever or whoever caused it to happen?

Graebe's poignant words likely moved you to feel sadness, loss, or anger; those are your personal feelings, but they are also rooted in the connection among us all—in a human response—that holds the only hope for our collective future.

In the first chapter of this book, you reflected on your purpose in helping, on why you are doing what you are doing. Remember George Bernard Shaw's exuberant words, "This is the true joy in life, the being used for a purpose recognized by yourself as a mighty one"? Compassion is at the core of being human. It is the inner light, the "splendid torch" you have in your hands, and you can pass it on to future generations. With this torch, you bring light when it is dark, and warmth when it is cold. And when you reach the end of your journey, you will know that you have given to others the greatest gift you can give: your caring.

A Self-Diagnosis Instrument for Burnout

A SELF-DIAGNOSIS INSTRUMENT FOR BURNOUT

You can compute your burnout score by completing the following question-naire. How often do you have any of the following experiences? Please use the scale:

1	2	3	4	5	6	7
Never	Once in a great while	Rarely	Sometimes	Often	Usually	Always

_____ 1. Being tired.

_____ 2. Feeling depressed.

_____ 3. Having a good day.

_____ 4. Being physically exhausted.

_____ 5. Being emotionally exhausted.

_____ 6. Being happy.

_____ 7. Being "wiped out."

_____ 8. "Can't take anymore."

_____ 9. Being unhappy.

_____ 10. Feeling run-down.

_____ 11. Feeling trapped.

_____ 12. Feeling worthless.

_____ 13. Being weary.

_____ 14. Being troubled.

_____ 15. Feeling disillusioned and resentful.

_____ 16. Being weak and suscep-tible to illness.

_____ 17. Feeling hopeless.

_____ 18. Feeling rejected.

_____ 19. Feeling optimistic.

_____ 20. Feeling energetic.

_____ 21. Feeling anxious.

Computation of score:

Add the values you wrote next to the following items:
1, 2, 4, 5, 7, 8, 9, 10, 11, 12, 13, 14, 15, 16, 17, 18, 21 (A) _____.

Add the values you wrote next to the following items:
3, 6, 19, 20 (B) _____. Subtract B from 32 (C) _____.

Add A and C (D) _____.

Divide D by 21 _____. This is your burnout score—see page 59 for interpretation.

Note. Reprinted with the permission of The Free Press, a Division of Macmillan, Inc, from *Career Burnout: Causes and Cures* (p. 219) by Ayala Pines and Elliot Aronson. Copyright © by Ayala Pines and Elliot Aronson.

APPENDIX B

Self-Concealment Scale

SELF-CONCEALMENT SCALE

Please indicate the extent of your agreement with each of the following statements using the scale below:

1	2	3	4	5
Strongly Disagree	Disagree	Neutral	Agree	Strongly Agree

Circle one number for each item.

1 2 3 4 5 I have an important secret that I haven't shared with anyone.

1 2 3 4 5 If I shared all my secrets with my friends, they'd like me less.

1 2 3 4 5 There are lots of things about me that I keep to myself.

1 2 3 4 5 Some of my secrets have really tormented me.

1 2 3 4 5 When something bad happens to me, I tend to keep it to myself.

1 2 3 4 5 I'm often afraid I'll reveal something I don't want to.

1 2 3 4 5 Telling a secret often backfires and I wish I hadn't told it.

1 2 3 4 5 I have a secret that is so private I would lie if anybody asked me about it.

1 2 3 4 5 My secrets are too embarrassing to share with others.

1 2 3 4 5 I have negative thoughts about myself that I never share with anyone.

Larson, D. G., & Chastain, R. L. (1990). Self-concealment: Conceptualization, measurement, and health implications. *Journal of Social and Clinical Psychology, 9*(4), 439–455.

Notes

Chapter 1. The Helper in Us All

1. Shaw, G. B. (1963). *Complete plays with prefaces* (Vol. 3). New York, NY: Dodd, Mead. (Original work published 1903). (pp. 510–511)

2. Shaw, G. B. (1989). In E. Doan, C. (Ed.), *Speaker's sourcebook II*. Grand Rapids, MI: Zondervan. (p. 236)

3. Nightingale, F. (1979). *Cassandra: an essay*. Old Westbury, NY: Feminist Press.

4. Eley, D., Eley, R., Bertello, M., & Rogers-Clark, C. (2012). Why did I become a nurse? Personality traits and reasons for entering nursing. *Journal of Advanced Nursing, 68*(7), 1546–1555.

5. Rushton, J. P. (1980). *Altruism, socialization, and society*. New York, NY: Prentice Hall.

6. Davis, M. H. (1983). Measuring individual differences in empathy: Evidence for a multidimensional approach. *Journal of Personality and Social Psychology, 44*(1), 113–126.

7. Mehrabian, A., & Epstein, N. (1972). A measure of emotional empathy. *Journal of Personality, 40*(4), 525–543.

8. Jolliffe, D., & Farrington, D. P. (2006). Development and validation of the Basic Empathy Scale. *Journal of Adolescence, 29*(4), 589–611.

9. Hojat, M., Mangione, S., Nasca, T. J., Cohen, M. J. M., Gonnella, J. S., Erdmann, J. B.,…Magee, M. (2001). The Jefferson Scale of Physician Empathy: Development and preliminary psychometric data. *Educational and Psychological Measurement, 61*(2), 349–365.

10. Batson, C. D. (2017). The empathy-altruism hypothesis: What and so what? In E. M. Seppälä, E. Simon-Thomas, S. L. Brown, M. C. Worline, C. D. Cameron, &

Page numbers for quotations are provided following the reference. If more than one quotation for the same reference is cited, page numbers appear in order cited.

J.R. Doty (Eds.), *The Oxford handbook of compassion science.* (pp. 27–40). New York, NY: Oxford University Press.

11. Bucknall, V., Burwaiss, S., MacDonald, D., Charles, K., & Clement, R. (2015). Mirror mirror on the ward, who's the most narcissistic of them all? Pathologic personality traits in health care. *Canadian Medical Association Journal, 187*(18), 1359–1363.

12. Muris, P., Merckelbach, H., Otgaar, H., & Meijer, E. (2017). The malevolent side of human nature: A meta-analysis and critical review of the literature on the dark triad (narcissism, Machiavellianism, and psychopathy). *Perspectives on Psychological Science, 12*(2), 183–204.

13. United States Department of Labor (2016). *Volunteering in the United States, 2015.* Retrieved from https://www.bls.gov/news.release/volun.nr0.htm.

14. Naslund, J.A., Aschbrenner, K.A., Marsch, L.A., & Bartels, S.J. (2016). The future of mental health care: Peer-to-peer support and social media. *Epidemiology and Psychiatric Sciences, 25*(2), 113–122.

15. Post, S.G. (2005). Altruism, happiness, and health: It's good to be good. *International Journal of Behavioral Medicine, 12*(2), 66–77.

16. Pfaff, D.W., & Sherman, S. (2015). *The altruistic brain: How we are naturally good.* New York, NY: Oxford University Press.

17. Zahn-Waxler, C., & Radke-Yarrow, M. (1982). The development of altruism: Alternative research strategies. In N. Eisenberg (Ed.), *The development of prosocial behavior* (pp. 109–137). New York, NY: Academic. (p. 126)

18. Hallet, J.P. (1967). *Congo kitabu.* New York, NY: Fawcett World Library. (p. 381)

19. de Waal, F.B.M. (2008). Putting the altruism back into altruism: The evolution of empathy. *Annual Review of Psychology, 59,* 279–300.

20. Masserman, J.H., Wechkin, S., & Terris, W. (1964). "Altruistic" behavior in rhesus monkeys. *The American Journal of Psychiatry, 121*(6), 584–585.

21. Church, R.M. (1959). Emotional reactions of rats to the pain of others. *Journal of Comparative and Physiological Psychology, 52*(2), 132–134.

22. Ben-Ami Bartal, I., Rodgers, D.A., Bernardez Sarria, M.S., Decety, J., & Mason, P. (2014). Pro-social behavior in rats is modulated by social experience. *eLife, 3.*

23. Poulin, M.J. (2017). To help or not to help: Goal commitment and the goodness of compassion. In E.M. Seppälä, E. Simon-Thomas, S.L. Brown, M.C. Worline, C.D. Cameron, & J.R. Doty (Eds.), *The Oxford handbook of compassion science.* (pp. 353–367). New York, NY: Oxford University Press.

24. Hornstein, H.A. (1976). *Cruelty and kindness.* Englewood Cliffs, NJ: Prentice Hall.

25. Marsh, A. A. (2016). Neural, cognitive, and evolutionary foundations of human altruism. *WIREs Cognitive Science, 7*(1), 59–71.

26. Bonini, L. (2017). The extended mirror neuron network: Anatomy, origin, and functions. *The Neuroscientist, 23*(1), 56–67.

27. Zhang, J. W., Piff, P. K., Iyer, R., Koleva, S., & Keltner, D. (2014). An occasion for unselfing: Beautiful nature leads to prosociality. *Journal of Environmental Psychology, 37*, 61–72.

28. Hurlemann, R., & Marsh, N. (2017). Deciphering the modulatory role of oxytocin in human altruism. *Reviews in the Neurosciences, 28*(4), 335–342.

29. Israel, S., Weisel, O., Ebstein, R. P., & Bornstein, G. (2012). Oxytocin, but not vasopressin, increases both parochial and universal altruism. *Psychoneuroendocrinology, 37*(8), 1341–1344.

30. Poulin, M. J., & Holman, E. A. (2013). Helping hands, healthy body? Oxytocin receptor gene and prosocial behavior interact to buffer the association between stress and physical health. *Hormones and Behavior, 63*(3), 510–517.

31. Marsh, A. A., Kozak, M. N., & Ambady, N. (2007). Accurate identification of fear facial expressions predicts prosocial behavior. *Emotion, 7*(2), 239–251.

32. Hoffman, M. L. (2001). Toward a comprehensive empathy-based theory of prosocial moral development. In A. C. Bohart & D. J. Stipek (Eds.), *Constructive & destructive behavior: Implications for family, school, & society.* (pp. 61–86). Washington, DC: American Psychological Association.

33. Batson, C. D. (2011). *Altruism in humans.* New York, NY: Oxford University Press.

34. Coke, J. S., Batson, C. D., & McDavis, K. (1978). Empathic mediation of helping: A two-stage model. *Journal of Personality and Social Psychology, 36*(7), 752–766.

35. Riečanský, I., Paul, N., Kölble, S., Stieger, S., & Lamm, C. (2015). Beta oscillations reveal ethnicity ingroup bias in sensorimotor resonance to pain of others. *Social Cognitive and Affective Neuroscience, 10*(7), 893–901.

36. Hornstein, H. A., LaKind, E., Frankel, G., & Manne, S. (1975). Effects of knowledge about remote social events on prosocial behavior, social conception, and mood. *Journal of Personality and Social Psychology, 32*(6), 1038–1046.

37. Oliner, S. P., & Oliner, P. M. (1988). *The altruistic personality: Rescuers of Jews in Nazi Europe.* New York, NY: Free Press. (p. 249)

38. Maslow, A. H. (1971). *The farther reaches of human nature.* New York, NY: Viking.

39. Becker, E. (1973). *The denial of death.* New York: Free Press. (p. 82)

40. Kohlberg, L. (1981). *The philosophy of moral development: Moral stages and the idea of justice.* San Francisco, CA: Harper and Row.

41. Darley, J. M., & Batson, C. D. (1973). 'From Jerusalem to Jericho': A study of situational and dispositional variables in helping behavior. *Journal of Personality and Social Psychology, 27*(1), 100–108.

42. Tulsky, J. A., Fischer, G. S., Rose, M. R., & Arnold, R. M. (1998). Opening the black box: How do physicians communicate about advance directives? *Annals of Internal Medicine, 129,* 441–449.

43. Guéguen, N., & Lamy, L. (2013). Weather and helping: Additional evidence of the effect of the sunshine Samaritan. *The Journal of Social Psychology, 153*(2), 123–126.

44. Berkowitz, L., & Connor, W. H. (1966). Success, failure, and social responsibility. *Journal of Personality and Social Psychology, 4*(6), 664–669.

45. Isen, A. M., & Levin, P. F. (1972). Effect of feeling good on helping: Cookies and kindness. *Journal of Personality and Social Psychology, 21*(3), 384–388.

46. Isen, A. M., Clark, M., & Schwartz, M. F. (1976). Duration of the effect of good mood on helping: "Footprints on the sands of time". *Journal of Personality and Social Psychology, 34*(3), 385–393.

47. Piff, P. K., Dietze, P., Feinberg, M., Stancato, D. M., & Keltner, D. (2015). Awe, the small self, and prosocial behavior. *Journal of Personality and Social Psychology, 108*(6), 883–899.

48. Rosenhan, D. L., Salovey, P., & Hargis, K. (1981). The joys of helping: Focus of attention mediates the impact of positive affect on altruism. *Journal of Personality and Social Psychology, 40*(5), 899–905.

49. House, J. S., Landis, K. R., & Umberson, D. (2003). Social relationships and health. In P. Salovey & A. J. Rothman (Eds.), *Social psychology of health.* (pp. 218–226). New York, NY: Psychology Press.

50. Barth, J., Schneider, S., & Von Känel, R. (2010). Lack of social support in the etiology and the prognosis of coronary heart disease: A systematic review and meta-analysis. *Psychosomatic Medicine, 72*(3), 229–238.

51. House, J. S., Robbins, C., & Metzner, H. L. (1982). The association of social relationships and activities with mortality: Prospective evidence from the Tecumseh Community Health Study. *American Journal of Epidemiology, 116*(1), 123–140.

52. Dickerson, S. S., & Zoccola, P. M. (2009). Toward a biology of social support. In S. J. Lopez & C. R. Snyder (Eds.), *Oxford handbook of positive psychology* (2nd ed., pp. 519–526). New York, NY: Oxford University Press.

53. Cacioppo, J. T., Cacioppo, S., Capitanio, J. P., & Cole, S. W. (2015). The neuroendocrinology of social isolation. *Annual Review of Psychology, 66,* 733–767.

54. Friedman, M., & Rosenman, R. (1974). *Type A behavior and your heart.* New York, NY: Knopf.

55. Luks, A. (1988, October). Helper's high. *Psychology Today*.

56. Thoits, P. A., & Hewitt, L. N. (2001). Volunteer work and well-being. *Journal of Health and Social Behavior, 42*(2), 115–131.

57. Poulin, M. J., Brown, S. L., Dillard, A. J., & Smith, D. M. (2013). Giving to others and the association between stress and mortality. *American Journal of Public Health, 103*(9), 1649–1655. (p. 1652)

58. Schulz, R., & Beach, S. R. (1999). Caregiving as a risk factor for mortality: The Caregiver Health Effects Study. *JAMA: Journal of the American Medical Association, 282*(23), 2215–2219.

59. Pinquart, M., & Sörensen, S. (2003). Differences between caregivers and noncaregivers in psychological health and physical health: A meta-analysis. *Psychology and aging 18*(2), 250–267.

60. Roth, D. L., Fredman, L., & Haley, W. E. (2015). Informal caregiving and its impact on health: A reappraisal from population-based studies. *The Gerontologist, 55*(2), 309–319. (p. 311)

61. Schweitzer, A. (1963). *Memoirs of childhood and youth* (C. T. Campion, Trans.). New York, NY: Macmillan. (p. 311)

62. Riessman, F. (1965). The 'helper' therapy principle. *Social Work, 10*(2), 27–32.

63. Schwartz, C., Meisenhelder, J. B., Ma, Y., & Reed, G. (2003). Altruistic social interest behaviors are associated with better mental health. *Psychosomatic Medicine, 65*(5), 778–785.

64. Mongrain, M., Chin, J. M., & Shapira, L. B. (2011). Practicing compassion increases happiness and self-esteem. *Journal of Happiness Studies, 12*(6), 963–981.

65. Hutcherson, C. A., Seppala, E. M., & Gross, J. J. (2008). Loving-kindness meditation increases social connectedness. *Emotion, 8*(5), 720–724.

66. Allan, B. A., Duffy, R. D., & Collisson, B. (2018). Helping others increases meaningful work: Evidence from three experiments. *Journal of Counseling Psychology, 65*(2), 155–165.

67. Cohen, R., Bavishi, C., & Rozanski, A. (2016). Purpose in life and its relationship to all-cause mortality and cardiovascular events: A meta-analysis. *Psychosomatic Medicine, 78*(2), 122–133.

68. Steger, M. F., Frazier, P., Oishi, S., & Kaler, M. (2006). The meaning in life questionnaire: Assessing the presence of and search for meaning in life. *Journal of Counseling Psychology, 53*(1), 80–93.

69. Huta, V., & Waterman, A. S. (2014). Eudaimonia and its distinction from hedonia: Developing a classification and terminology for understanding conceptual and operational definitions. *Journal of Happiness Studies, 15*(6), 1425–1456.

70. Seligman, M. E. P. (2011). *Flourish: A visionary new understanding of happiness and well-being*. New York, NY: Free Press.

71. Fredrickson, B. L., Tugade, M. M., Waugh, C. E., & Larkin, G. R. (2003). What good are positive emotions in crises? A prospective study of resilience and emotions following the terrorist attacks on the United States on September 11th, 2001. *Journal of Personality and Social Psychology, 84*(2), 365–376.

72. McClelland, D. C., & Krishnit, C. (1988). The effect of motivational arousal through films on salivary immunoglobulin. *Psychology & Health, 2*(1), 31–52.

73. Ornstein, R., & Sobel, D. (1987). *The healing brain*. New York, NY: Simon and Schuster.

Chapter 2. The Challenge of Caring: Emotional Involvement in Helping

1. Maslach, C., & Leiter, M. P. (1997). *The truth about burnout: How organizations cause personal stress and what to do about it*. San Francisco: Jossey-Bass. (p. 34)

2. Pines, A., & Aronson, E. (1988). *Career burnout: Causes and cures*. New York, NY: Free Press.

3. Maslach, C. (1982). *Burnout: The cost of caring*. Englewood Cliffs, NJ: Prentice Hall.

4. Stotland, E., Mathews, K. E., Sherman, S. E., Hansson, R. O., & Richardson, B. Z. (1978). *Empathy, fantasy, and helping*. Newbury Park, CA: Sage Publications, Inc.

5. Richman, S. B., DeWall, C. N., & Wolff, M. N. (2015). Avoiding affection, avoiding altruism: Why is avoidant attachment related to less helping? *Personality and Individual Differences, 76*, 193–197.

6. Klimecki, O., & Singer, T. (2012). Empathic distress fatigue rather than compassion fatigue? Integrating findings from empathy research in psychology and social neuroscience. In B. Oakley, A. Knafo, G. Madhavan, & D. S. Wilson (Eds.), *Pathological altruism* (pp. 368–383). New York, NY: Oxford University Press.

7. Goetz, J. L., Keltner, D., & Simon-Thomas, E. (2010). Compassion: An evolutionary analysis and empirical review. *Psychological Bulletin, 136*(3), 351–374. (p. 351)

8. Batson, C. D., Fultz, J., & Schoenrade, P. A. (1994). Distress and empathy: Two qualitatively distinct vicarious emotions with different motivational consequences. In B. Puka & B. Puka (Eds.), *Reaching out: Caring, altruism, and prosocial behavior* (pp. 57–75). New York, NY: Garland Publishing.

9. Eisenberg, N., Fabes, R. A., Miller, P. A., Fultz, J., Shell, R., Mathy, R. M., & Reno, R. R. (1989). Relation of sympathy and personal distress to prosocial behavior: A multimethod study. *Journal of Personality and Social Psychology, 57*(1), 55–66.

10. Sinclair, S., Beamer, K., Hack, T. F., McClement, S., Raffin Bouchal, S., Chochinov, H. M., & Hagen, N. A. (2017). Sympathy, empathy, and compassion: A grounded theory study of palliative care patients' understandings, experiences, and preferences. *Palliative Medicine, 31*(5), 437–447.

11. Batson, C. D. (2011). *Altruism in humans.* New York, NY: Oxford University Press.

12. Eisenberg, N. (2000). Emotion, regulation, and moral development. *Annual Review of Psychology, 51,* 665–697.

13. Eisenberg, N., & Miller, P. A. (1987). The relation of empathy to prosocial and related behaviors. *Psychological Bulletin, 101*(1), 91–119.

14. Hoffman, M. L. (1982). Development of prosocial motivations: Empathy and guilt. In N. Eisenberg (Ed.), *The development of prosocial behavior* (pp. 281–313). New York, NY: Academic. (p. 294)

15. Back, A. L., Rushton, C. H., Kaszniak, A. W., & Halifax, J. S. (2015). "Why are we doing this?": Clinician helplessness in the face of suffering. *Journal of Palliative Medicine, 18*(1), 26–30. (pp. 27–28)

16. Harrison, R. L., & Westwood, M. J. (2009). Preventing vicarious traumatization of mental health therapists: Identifying protective practices. *Psychotherapy: Theory, Research, Practice, Training, 46*(2), 203–219. (p. 213)

17. Thirioux, B., Birault, F., & Jaafari, N. (2016). Empathy is a protective factor of burnout in physicians: New neuro-phenomenological hypotheses regarding empathy and sympathy in care relationship. *Frontiers in Psychology, 7,* 1–11.

18. Rifkin, J. (2009). *The empathic civilization: The race to global consciousness in a world in crisis.* New York, NY: Tarcher. (p. 41)

19. Klimecki, O. M., Leiberg, S., Ricard, M., & Singer, T. (2014). Differential pattern of functional brain plasticity after compassion and empathy training. *Social Cognitive and Affective Neuroscience, 9*(6), 873–879. (p. 877)

20. Singer, T., Seymour, B., O'Doherty, J., Kaube, H., Dolan, R. J., & Frith, C. D. (2004). Empathy for pain involves the affective but not sensory components of pain. *Science, 303*(5661), 1157–1162.

21. Kagan, N. (1984). Interpersonal process recall. In D. G. Larson (Ed.), *Teaching psychological skills: Models for giving psychology away* (pp. 229–244). Pacific Grove, CA: Brooks/Cole.

22. Wolf, A. W., Goldfried, M. R., & Muran, J. C. (2013). *Transforming negative reactions to clients: From frustration to compassion*. Washington, DC: American Psychological Association.

23. Bertman, S. L. (2015). *Facing death: Images, insights, and interventions: A handbook for educators, healthcare professionals, and counselors*. Washington, DC: Hemisphere. (p. 45)

24. Amenta, M. M. (1984). Death anxiety, purpose in life and duration of service in hospice volunteers. *Psychological Reports, 54*(3), 979–984.

25. Gama, G., Barbosa, F., & Vieira, M. (2014). Personal determinants of nurses' burnout in end of life care. *European Journal of Oncology Nursing, 18*(5), 527–533.

26. Combs, A. W., & Avila, D. L. (1985). *Helping relationships: Basic concepts for the helping professions* (3rd ed.). Boston: Allyn & Bacon. (p. 7)

27. Kennedy, E., & Charles, S. C. (1990). *On becoming a counselor: A basic guide for nonprofessional counselors*. New York, NY: Continuum. (p. 26)

28. Rogers, C. R. (1980). *A way of being*. Boston, MA: Houghton Mifflin.

29. Rogers, C. R. (1957). The necessary and sufficient conditions of therapeutic personality change. *Journal of Consulting Psychology, 21*, 95–103. (p. 99)

30. Lamm, C., Batson, C. D., & Decety, J. (2007). The neural substrate of human empathy: Effects of perspective-taking and cognitive appraisal. *Journal of Cognitive Neuroscience, 19*(1), 42–58.

31. Coke, J. S., Batson, C. D., & McDavis, K. (1978). Empathic mediation of helping: A two-stage model. *Journal of Personality and Social Psychology, 36*(7), 752–766.

32. Wills, T. A., & Sandy, J. M. (2001). Comparing favorably: A cognitive approach to coping through comparison with other persons. In C. R. Snyder (Ed.), *Coping with stress: Effective people and processes*. (pp. 154–177). New York, NY: Oxford University Press.

33. Schlosser, A. E., & Levy, E. (2016). Helping others or oneself: How direction of comparison affects prosocial behavior. *Journal of Consumer Psychology, 26*(4), 461–473.

34. Rosenhan, D. L., Salovey, P., & Hargis, K. (1981). The joys of helping: Focus of attention mediates the impact of positive affect on altruism. *Journal of Personality and Social Psychology, 40*(5), 899–905.

35. Grant, A. M. (2013). *Give and take: Why helping others drives our success*. New York, NY: Penguin. (p. 157)

36. Dill, J., Erickson, R. J., & Diefendorff, J. M. (2016). Motivation in caring labor: Implications for the well-being and employment outcomes of nurses. *Social Science & Medicine, 167*, 99–106.

37. Harris, M. B., Benson, S. M., & Hall, C. L. (1975). The effects of confession on altruism. *The Journal of Social Psychology, 96*(2), 187–192.

38. Worden, J. W. (2018, June 15).

39. Mruk, C. (2019). *Feeling good by doing good*. New York, NY: Oxford University Press. (pp. 30–31)

40. Clary, E. G., Snyder, M., Ridge, R. D., Copeland, J., Stukas, A. A., Haugen, J., & Miene, P. (1998). Understanding and assessing the motivations of volunteers: A functional approach. *Journal of Personality and Social Psychology, 74*(6), 1516–1530.

41. Ericson-Lidman, E., & Strandberg, G. (2007). Burnout: Co-workers' perceptions of signs preceding workmates' burnout. *Journal of Advanced Nursing, 60*(2), 199–208.

42. Kamal, A. H., Bull, J. H., Wolf, S. P., Swetz, K. M., Shanafelt, T. D., Ast, K.,... Abernethy, A. P. (2016). Prevalence and predictors of burnout among hospice and palliative care clinicians in the U.S. *Journal of Pain and Symptom Management, 51*(4), 690–696.

43. Melamed, S., Shirom, A., Toker, S., Berliner, S., & Shapira, I. (2006). Burnout and risk of cardiovascular disease: Evidence, possible causal paths, and promising research directions. *Psychological Bulletin, 132*(3), 327–353.

44. Figley, C. R. (Ed.) (2002). *Treating compassion fatigue*. New York: Brunner-Routledge. (p. 3)

45. Adams, R. E., Boscarino, J. A., & Figley, C. R. (2006). Compassion fatigue and psychological distress among social workers: A validation study. *American Journal of Orthopsychiatry, 76*(1), 103–108.

46. Klimecki, O., & Singer, T. (2012). Empathic distress fatigue rather than compassion fatigue? Integrating findings from empathy research in psychology and social neuroscience. In B. Oakley, A. Knafo, G. Madhavan, & D. S. Wilson (Eds.), *Pathological altruism*. (pp. 368–383). New York, NY: Oxford University Press.

47. Gentry, J. E., Baranowsky, A. B., & Dunning, K. (2002). The Accelerated Recovery Program (ARP) for compassion fatigue. In C. R. Figley (Ed.), *Treating compassion fatigue*. (pp. 123–137). New York, NY: Brunner-Routledge.

48. Adams, K. B., Matto, H. C., & Harrington, D. (2001). The Traumatic Stress Institute Belief Scale as a measure of vicarious trauma in a national sample of clinical social workers. *Families in Society, 82*(4), 363–371.

49. Larson, D. G., & Bush, N. J. (2006). Stress management for oncology nurses: Finding a healing balance. In R. M. Carroll-Johnson, L. M. Gorman, & N. J. Bush (Eds.), *Psychosocial nursing care along the cancer continuum* (2nd ed., pp. 587–601). Pittsburgh: Oncology Nursing Society.

50. Dudzinski, D. M. (2016). Navigating moral distress using the moral distress map. *Journal of Medical Ethics, 42*(5), 321–324.

51. Austin, C. L., Saylor, R., & Finley, P. J. (2017). Moral distress in physicians and nurses: Impact on professional quality of life and turnover. *Psychological Trauma: Theory, Research, Practice, and Policy, 9*(4), 399–406.

52. Fumis, R. R. L., Junqueira Amarante, G. A., de Fatima Nascimento, A., & Vieira Junior, J. M. (2017). Moral distress and its contribution to the development of burnout syndrome among critical care providers. *Annals of Intensive Care, 7*(1), 71.

53. Whitehead, P. B., Herbertson, R. K., Hamric, A. B., Epstein, E. G., & Fisher, J. M. (2015). Moral distress among healthcare professionals: Report of an institution-wide survey. *Journal of Nursing Scholarship, 47*(2), 117–125.

54. Corley, M. C., Elswick, R. K., Gorman, M., & Clor, T. (2001). Development and evaluation of a moral distress scale. *Journal of Advanced Nursing, 33*(2), 250–256.

55. Austin, W. (2017). What is the role of ethics consultation in the moral habitability of health care environments? *AMA Journal of Ethics, 19*(6), 595–600.

56. Lamiani, G., Borghi, L., & Argentero, P. (2017). When healthcare professionals cannot do the right thing: A systematic review of moral distress and its correlates. *Journal of Health Psychology, 22*(1), 51–67.

Chapter 3. Beyond Burnout: Finding Balance and Enhancing Resilience

1. Pines, A., & Aronson, E. (1988). *Career burnout: Causes and cures.* New York, NY: Free Press. (p. 11)

2. Hill, H. L. (1991). Point and counterpoint. *Journal of Psychosocial Oncology, 9*(2), 97–112. (pp. 107–108)

3. Connor, K. M., & Davidson, J. R. T. (2003). Development of a new resilience scale: The Connor-Davidson Resilience Scale (CD-RISC). *Depression and Anxiety, 18*(2), 76–82.

4. Lazarus, R. S. (1991). *Emotion and adaptation.* New York, NY: Oxford University Press.

5. Lazarus, R. S. (2012). Evolution of a model of stress, coping, and discrete emotions. In V. H. Rice (Ed.), *Handbook of stress, coping, and health: Implications for nursing research, theory, and practice.* (pp. 199–223). Thousand Oaks, CA: Sage Publications, Inc.

6. Hobfoll, S. E. (1988). *The ecology of stress.* Washington, DC: Hemisphere Publishing Corp. (p. 518)

7. Lazarus, R. S., & Folkman, S. (1984). *Stress, appraisal, and coping.* New York, NY: Springer. (p. 19)

8. Blackburn, E., & Epel, E. (2017). *The telomere effect: A revolutionary approach to living younger, healthier, longer.* New York, NY: Grand Central.

9. Claus, K. E., & Bailey, J. T. (Eds.). (1980). *Living with stress and promoting well-being: A handbook for nurses.* St. Louis, MO: C. V. Mosby.

10. Maddi, S. R. (2006). Hardiness: The courage to grow from stresses. *The Journal of Positive Psychology, 1*(3), 160–168.

11. Nakamura, J., & Csikszentmihalyi, M. (2002). The concept of flow. In C. R. Snyder & S. J. Lopez (Eds.), *Handbook of positive psychology* (pp. 89–105). New York, NY: Oxford University Press.

12. Crum, A. J., Akinola, M., Martin, A., & Fath, S. (2017). The role of stress mindset in shaping cognitive, emotional, and physiological responses to challenging and threatening stress. *Anxiety, Stress & Coping: An International Journal, 30*(4), 379–395.

13. Crum, A. J., Salovey, P., & Achor, S. (2013). Rethinking stress: The role of mindsets in determining the stress response. *Journal of Personality and Social Psychology, 104*(4), 716–733.

14. Lazarus, R. S. (1990). Stress, coping, and illness. In H. S. Friedman (Ed.), *Personality and disease.* (pp. 97–120). Oxford, England: John Wiley & Sons.

15. Smith, R. E., & Ascough, J. C. (2016). *Promoting emotional resilience: Cognitive-affective stress management training.* New York, NY: Guilford Press.

16. Smith, C. A., & Lazarus, R. S. (1990). Emotion and adaptation. In L. A. Pervin (Ed.), *Handbook of personality: Theory and research.* (pp. 609–637). New York, NY: Guilford Press.

17. McCarty, R. (2016). The fight-or-flight response: A cornerstone of stress research. In G. Fink (Ed.), *Stress: Concepts, cognition, emotion, and behavior.* (Vol. 1, pp. 33–37). San Diego, CA: Elsevier Academic Press.

18. Goleman, D. (1995). *Emotional intelligence.* New York, NY: Bantam.

19. Taylor, S. E. (2012). Tend and befriend theory. In P. A. M. Van Lange, A. W. Kruglanski, & E. T. Higgins (Eds.), *Handbook of theories of social psychology* (Vol. 1, pp. 32–49). Thousand Oaks, CA: Sage Publications Ltd.

20. Bandura, A. (1977). Self-efficacy: Toward a unifying theory of behavioral change. *Psychological Review, 84*, 191–215.

21. Cantor, R. C. (1978). *And a time to live: Toward emotional well-being during the crisis of cancer.* New York, NY: Harper & Row.

22. Perez, G.K., Haime, V., Jackson, V., Chittenden, E., Mehta, D.H., & Park, E.R. (2015). Promoting resiliency among palliative care clinicians: Stressors, coping strategies, and training needs. *Journal of Palliative Medicine, 18*(4), 332–337.

23. Tolin, D.F. (2016). *Doing CBT: A comprehensive guide to working with behaviors, thoughts, and emotions.* New York, NY: Guilford Press.

24. Craun, S.W., & Bourke, M.L. (2014). The use of humor to cope with secondary traumatic stress. *Journal of Child Sexual Abuse: Research, Treatment, & Program Innovations for Victims, Survivors, & Offenders, 23*(7), 840–852.

25. Maslach, C., & Leiter, M.P. (1997). *The truth about burnout: How organizations cause personal stress and what to do about it.* San Francisco, CA: Jossey-Bass.

26. Hlubocky, F.J., Back, A.L., & Shanafelt, T.D. (2016). Addressing burnout in oncology: Why cancer care clinicians are at risk, what individuals can do, and how organizations can respond. *Amercian Society of Clincial Oncology Educational Book, 35,* 271–279.

27. Vachon, M.L.S., Huggard, P.K., & Huggard, J.A. (2015). Reflections on occupational stress in palliative care nursing: Is it changing? In B. Ferrell, N. Coyle, & J. Paice (Eds.), *Oxford textbook of palliative nursing* (4th ed., pp. 969–986). New York, NY: Oxford University Press.

28. Maslach, C., & Jackson, S.E. (1982). Burnout in health professions: A social psychological analysis In G. Sanders & J. Suls (Eds.), *Social psychology of health and illness* (pp. 227–251). Hillsdale, NJ: Erlbaum.

29. Weisman, A.D. (1986). *The coping capacity: On the nature of being mortal.* New York, NY: Human Sciences

30. Moorey, S., Frampton, M., & Greer, S. (2003). The Cancer Coping Questionnaire: A self-rating scale for measuring the impact of adjuvant psychological therapy on coping behaviour. *Psycho-Oncology, 12*(4), 331–344.

31. Roth, S., & Cohen, L.J. (1986). Approach, avoidance, and coping with stress. *American Psychologist, 41*(7), 813–819.

32. Kashdan, T.B., Barrios, V., Forsyth, J.P., & Steger, M.F. (2006). Experiential avoidance as a generalized psychological vulnerability: Comparisons with coping and emotion regulation strategies. *Behaviour Research and Therapy, 44*(9), 1301–1320.

33. Bednar, R.L., Wells, M.G., & Peterson, S.R. (1989). *Self-esteem: Paradoxes and innovations in clinical theory and practice.* Washington, DC: American Psychological Association.

34. Senge, P.M. (2006). *The fifth discipline: The art and practice of the learning organization* (Revised ed.). New York, NY: Doubleday.

35. Solomon, R.L., & Wynne, L.C. (1953). Traumatic avoidance learning: Acquisition in normal dogs. *Psychological Monographs: General and Applied, 67*(4), 1–19.

36. Barlow, D.H. (2016). *The neurotic paradox: Progress in understanding and treating anxiety and related disorders* (Vol. 1). New York, NY: Routledge/Taylor & Francis Group.

37. Hayes, S.C., Wilson, K.G., Gifford, E.V., Follette, V.M., & Strosahl, K. (1996). Experiential avoidance and behavioral disorders: A functional dimensional approach to diagnosis and treatment. *Journal of Consulting and Clinical Psychology, 64*(6), 1152–1168.

38. Becker, E. (1973). *The denial of death*. New York, NY: Free Press. (p. 82)

39. Yalom, I.D. (1980). *Existential psychotherapy*. New York, NY: Basic. (pp. 147, 40)

40. Solomon, S., Greenberg, J., & Pyszczynski, T. (1991). Terror management theory of self-esteem. In C.R. Snyder & D.R. Forsyth (Eds.), *Handbook of social and clinical psychology: The health perspective*. (pp. 21–40). Elmsford, NY: Pergamon Press. (p. 23)

41. West, A.L. (2015). Associations among attachment style, burnout, and compassion fatigue in health and human service workers: A systematic review. *Journal of Human Behavior in the Social Environment, 25*(6), 571–590.

42. Shanafelt, T.D. (2009). Enhancing meaning in work: A prescription for preventing physician burnout and promoting patient-centered care. *JAMA: Journal of the American Medical Association, 302*(12), 1338–1340.

43. Cullen, A. (2016). Schwartz Rounds® Promoting compassionate care and healthy organisations. *Journal of Social Work Practice, 30*(2), 219–228.

44. Lindstrom, C.M., Cann, A., Calhoun, L.G., & Tedeschi, R.G. (2013). The relationship of core belief challenge, rumination, disclosure, and sociocultural elements to posttraumatic growth. *Psychological Trauma: Theory, Research, Practice, and Policy, 5*(1), 50–55.

45. Joseph, S., & Linley, P.A. (2005). Positive adjustment to threatening events: An organismic valuing theory of growth through adversity. *Review of General Psychology, 9*(3), 262–280.

46. Arnold, D., Calhoun, L.G., Tedeschi, R., & Cann, A. (2005). Vicarious posttraumatic growth in psychotherapy. *Journal of Humanistic Psychology, 45*(2), 239–263.

47. Kierkegaard, S. (1941). *The sickness unto death*. Princeton, NJ: Princeton University Press. (p. 29)

48. Rojas, J.I., Brand, M., Jeon-Slaughter, H., & Koos, E. (2014). Substance abuse patterns and psychiatric symptomology among health care professionals and

non–health care professionals evaluated in an outpatient program for impaired professionals. *Addictive Disorders & Their Treatment, 13*(2), 45–53.

49. Fox, R. W. (1985). *Reinhold Neibuhr: A biography.* New York, NY: Pantheon. (p. 290)

50. Stroebe, M., & Schut, H. (2010). The dual process model of coping with bereavement: A decade later. *OMEGA, 61*(4), 273–289.

51. Baughman, K. R., Ludwick, R., Fischbein, R., McCormick, K., Meeker, J., Hewit, M., . . . Kropp, D. (2017). Development of a scale to assess physician advance care planning self-efficacy. *American Journal of Hospice & Palliative Medicine, 34*(5), 435–441.

52. Weissman, D. E., Ambuel, B., Norton, A. J., Wang-Cheng, R., & Schiedermayer, D. (1998). A survey of competencies and concerns in end-of-life care for physician trainees. *Journal of Pain and Symptom Management, 15*(2), 82–90.

53. Antonovsky, A. (1998). The sense of coherence: An historical and future perspective. In H. I. McCubbin, E. A. Thompson, A. I. Thompson, & J. E. Fromer (Eds.), *Stress, coping, and health in families: Sense of coherence and resiliency.* (pp. 3–20). Thousand Oaks, CA: Sage Publications, Inc.

54. Shanafelt, T. D., Hasan, O., Dyrbye, L. N., Sinsky, C., Satele, D., Sloan, J., & West, C. P. (2015). Changes in burnout and satisfaction with work-life balance in physicians and the general US working population between 2011 and 2014. *Mayo Clinic Proceedings, 90*(12), 1600–1613.

55. Smeltzer, S. C., Cantrell, M. A., Sharts-Hopko, N. C., Heverly, M. A., Jenkinson, A., & Nthenge, S. (2016). Psychometric analysis of the Work/Life Balance Self-Assessment Scale. *Journal of Nursing Measurement, 24*(1), 5–14.

56. Barber, L. K., Grawitch, M. J., & Maloney, P. W. (2016). Work-life balance: Contemporary perspectives. In M. J. Grawitch & D. W. Ballard (Eds.), *The psychologically healthy workplace: Building a win-win environment for organizations and employees.* (pp. 111–133). Washington, DC: American Psychological Association.

57. D'Souza, F., Egan, S. J., & Rees, C. S. (2011). The relationship between perfectionism, stress and burnout in clinical psychologists. *Behaviour Change, 28*(1), 17–28.

58. Lo, A., & Abbott, M. J. (2013). Review of the theoretical, empirical, and clinical status of adaptive and maladaptive perfectionism. *Behaviour Change, 30*(2), 96–116.

59. O'Grady, H. (2005). *Woman's relationship with herself: Gender, Foucault and therapy.* New York, NY: Routledge.

60. Krestan, J.-A., & Bepko, C. (1990). Codependency: The social reconstruction of female experience. *Smith College Studies in Social Work, 60*(3), 216–232.

61. Jackson, S. W. (2001). The wounded healer. *Bulletin of the History of Medicine, 75*(1), 1–36.

62. Larson, D. G. (1987). Helper secrets: Internal stressors in nursing. *Journal of Psychosocial Nursing and Mental Health Services, 25*(4), 20–26.

63. Maslach, C. (1982). *Burnout: The cost of caring.* Englewood Cliffs, NJ: Prentice Hall.

64. Jordan, A. H. (2009). *Pluralistic ignorance in the perception of others' emotional lives.* (Doctoral dissertation). Available from ProQuest Dissertations and Theses database. (UMI No. 3364073).

65. Krycka, K. C., & Ikemi, A. (2016). Focusing-oriented–experiential psychotherapy: From research to practice. In D. J. Cain, K. Keenan, & S. Rubin (Eds.), *Humanistic psychotherapies: Handbook of research and practice, 2nd ed.* (pp. 251–282). Washington, DC: American Psychological Association.

66. Germer, C. K., & Neff, K. D. (2013). Self-compassion in clinical practice. *Journal of Clinical Psychology, 69*(8), 856–867. (p. 255)

67. Raes, F., Pommier, E., Neff, K. D., & Van Gucht, D. (2011). Construction and factorial validation of a short form of the Self-Compassion Scale. *Clinical Psychology & Psychotherapy, 18*(3), 250–255. (p. 255)

68. MacBeth, A., & Gumley, A. (2012). Exploring compassion: A meta-analysis of the association between self-compassion and psychopathology. *Clinical Psychology Review, 32*(6), 545–552.

69. Gilbert, P., & Procter, S. (2006). Compassionate mind training for people with high shame and self-criticism: Overview and pilot study of a group therapy approach. *Clinical Psychology & Psychotherapy, 13*(6), 353–379.

70. Rockliff, H., Gilbert, P., McEwan, K., Lightman, S., & Glover, D. (2008). A pilot exploration of heart rate variability and salivary cortisol responses to compassion-focused imagery. *Clinical Neuropsychiatry: Journal of Treatment Evaluation, 5*(3), 132–139.

71. Park, E. R., Traeger, L., Vranceanu, A.-M., Scult, M., Lerner, J. A., Benson, H., . . . Fricchione, G. L. (2013). The development of a patient-centered program based on the relaxation response: The Relaxation Response Resiliency Program (3RP). *Psychosomatics: Journal of Consultation and Liaison Psychiatry, 54*(2), 165–174.

72. Kabat-Zinn, J. (2003). Mindfulness-based interventions in context: Past, present, and future. *Clinical Psychology: Science and Practice, 10*(2), 144–156. (p. 145)

73. Garland, E. L., & Thomas, E. (2015). Neuroscience, resilience, and the embodiment of 'mental' disorder. In B. Probst (Ed.), *Critical thinking in clinical assess-

ment and diagnosis. (pp. 111–131). Cham, Switzerland: Springer International Publishing. (p. 124)

74. Shapiro, S. L., & Carlson, L. E. (2017). How is mindfulness helpful? Mechanisms of mindfulness. In S. L. Shapiro & L. E. Carlson (Eds.), *The art and science of mindfulness: Integrating mindfulness into psychology and the helping professions.* (pp. 99–112). Washington, DC: American Psychological Association.

75. Epel, E., Daubenmier, J., Moskowitz, J. T., Folkman, S., & Blackburn, E. (2009). Can meditation slow rate of cellular aging? Cognitive stress, mindfulness, and telomeres. In W. C. Bushell, E. L. Olivo, & N. D. Theise (Eds.), *Longevity, regeneration, and optimal health: Integrating Eastern and Western perspectives.* (pp. 34–53). Hoboken, NJ: Wiley-Blackwell.

76. Kangas, N. L., & Shapiro, S. L. (2011). Mindfulness-based training for health care professionals. In L. M. McCracken (Ed.), *Mindfulness and acceptance in behavioral medicine: Current theory and practice.* (pp. 303–340). Oakland, CA: Context Press/New Harbinger.

77. Chaukos, D., Chad-Friedman, E., Mehta, D. H., Byerly, L., Celik, A., McCoy, T. H., & Denninger, J. W. (2017). Risk and resilience factors associated with resident burnout. *Academic Psychiatry, 41*(2), 189–194.

78. Hogan, C. L., Mata, J., & Carstensen, L. L. (2013). Exercise holds immediate benefits for affect and cognition in younger and older adults. *Psychology and Aging, 28*(2), 587–594.

79. Toker, S., & Biron, M. (2012). Job burnout and depression: Unraveling their temporal relationship and considering the role of physical activity. *Journal of Applied Psychology, 97*(3), 699–710.

80. Schuch, F. B., Vancampfort, D., Rosenbaum, S., Richards, J., Ward, P. B., & Stubbs, B. (2016). Exercise improves physical and psychological quality of life in people with depression: A meta-analysis including the evaluation of control group response. *Psychiatry Research, 241*, 47–54.

81. Shirom, A. (2011). Vigor as a positive affect at work: Conceptualizing vigor, its relations with related constructs, and its antecedents and consequences. *Review of General Psychology, 15*(1), 50–64. (p. 50)

82. Puterman, E., Lin, J., Blackburn, E., O'Donovan, A., Adler, N., & Epel, E. (2010). The power of exercise: Buffering the effect of chronic stress on telomere length. *PLoS ONE, 5*(5).

83. Zahrt, O. H., & Crum, A. J. (2017). Perceived physical activity and mortality: Evidence from three nationally representative U.S. samples. *Health Psychology, 36*(11), 1017–1025.

84. Whitebird, R.R., Asche, S.E., Thompson, G.L., Rossom, R., & Heinrich, R. (2013). Stress, burnout, compassion fatigue, and mental health in hospice workers in Minnesota. *Journal of Palliative Medicine, 16*(12), 1534–1539.

85. Meldrum, H. (2010). Exemplary physicians' strategies to avoiding burnout. *The Health Care Manager, 29*(4), 324–331.

86. Dyrbye, L.N., Eacker, A., Durning, S.J., Brazeau, C., Moutier, C., Massie, F.S., . . . Shanafelt, T.D. (2015). The impact of stigma and personal experiences on the help-seeking behaviors of medical students with burnout. *Academic Medicine, 90*(7), 961–969.

87. Yasko, J.M. (1983). Variables which predict burnout experienced by oncology clinical nurse specialists. *Cancer Nursing, 6,* 109–116.

88. Vachon, M.L. (1987). *Occupational stress in the care of the critically ill, the dying, and the bereaved.* Bristol, PA: Hemisphere.

89. Sansó, N., Galiana, L., Oliver, A., Pascual, A., Sinclair, S., & Benito, E. (2015). Palliative care professionals' inner life: Exploring the relationships among awareness, self-care, and compassion satisfaction and fatigue, burnout, and coping with death. *Journal of Pain and Symptom Management, 50*(2), 200–207.

90. Stamm, B.H. (2002). Measuring compassion satisfaction as well as fatigue: Developmental history of the Compassion Satisfaction and Fatigue Test. In C.R. Figley (Ed.), *Treating compassion fatigue.* (pp. 107–119). New York, NY: Brunner-Routledge.

91. Slocum-Gori, S., Hemsworth, D., Chan, W.W.Y., Carson, A., & Kazanjian, A. (2013). Understanding compassion satisfaction, compassion fatigue and burnout: A survey of the hospice palliative care workforce. *Palliative Medicine, 27*(2), 172–178.

92. Roth, D.L., Fredman, L., & Haley, W.E. (2015). Informal caregiving and its impact on health: A reappraisal from population-based studies. *The Gerontologist, 55*(2), 309–319.

93. Selye, H. (1978, March). On the real benefits of eustress. *Psychology Today,* 70.

94. Janoff-Bulman, R. (1992). *Shattered assumptions: Towards a new psychology of trauma.* New York, NY: Free Press.

95. Haan, N. (1993). The assessment of coping, defense, and stress. In L. Goldberger & S. Breznitz (Eds.), *Handbook of stress: Theoretical and clinical aspects* (2nd ed., pp. 258–273). New York, NY: Free Press. (p. 259)

96. Gama, G., Barbosa, F., & Vieira, M. (2014). Personal determinants of nurses' burnout in end of life care. *European Journal of Oncology Nursing, 18*(5), 527–533.

97. Gazelle, G., Liebschutz, J. M., & Riess, H. (2015). Physician burnout: Coaching a way out. *Journal of General Internal Medicine, 30*(4), 508–513.

98. Pines, A., August, 2000). [Personal communication].

99. Smith, A. W., & Baum, A. (2003). The influence of psychological factors on restorative function in health and illness. In J. Suls & K. A. Wallston (Eds.), *Social psychological foundations of health and illness.* (pp. 432–457). Oxford, England: Blackwell Publishing.

Chapter 4: Secrets: Concealment and Confiding in Helping and Healing

1. Martin, G. (2009). *Gabriel Garcia Marquez.* New York, NY Alfred A. Knopf. (p. 198)

2. Bok, S. (1983). *Secrets: On the ethics of concealment and revelation.* New York: Vintage Books. (pp. 37, 41)

3. Jung, C. G. (1970). *The collected works of C. G. Jung.* Princeton, NJ: Princeton University Press. (p. 192)

4. Baldwin, J. (1993). *The fire next time* (First Vintage international edition ed.). New York, NY: Vintage Books. (p. 95)

5. Luft, J. (1969). *Of human interaction.* Palo Alto, CA: National Press Books.

6. Slepian, M. L., Chun, J. S., & Mason, M. F. (2017). The experience of secrecy. *Journal of Personality and Social Psychology, 113*(1), 1–33.

7. Larson, D. G. (1986). *Health and self-disclosure survey.* Santa Clara University. Santa Clara, CA.

8. Petronius. (1930). *Petronius* (M. Heseltine, Trans. T. E. Page, E. Capps, & W. H. D. Rouse Eds.). London, England: William Heinemann Ltd.

9. Wood, N., & Ward, S. (2010). Stigma, secrets, and the human condition: Seeking to remedy alienation in PostSecret's digitally mediated environment. *Symbolic Interaction, 33*(4), 578–602.

10. James, W. (1902). *The varieties of religious experience: A study in human nature.* New York: Random House. (pp. 453, 452)

11. Ellenberger, H. F. (1970). *The discovery of the unconscious: The history and evolution of dynamic psychiatry.* New York, NY: Basic Books.

12. Freud, S. (1963). *Therapy and technique.* New York, NY: Collier Books. (p. 84)

13. Fromm, E. (1955). *The sane society.* Oxford, England: Rinehart & Co.

14. Jourard, S. M. (1971). *The transparent self* (rev ed. ed.). New York, NY: Van Nostrand Reinhold.(pp. 32–33)

15. Pennebaker, J. W. (1990). *Opening up: The healing power of confiding in others.* New York, NY: William Morrow.

16. Pennebaker, J. W., & O'Heeron, R. C. (1984). Confiding in others and illness rate among spouses of suicide and accidental-death victims. *Journal of Abnormal Psychology, 93*(4), 473–476.

17. Pennebaker, J. W. (1985). Traumatic experience and psychosomatic disease: Exploring the roles of behavioural inhibition, obsession, and confiding. *Canadian Psychology/Psychologie Canadienne, 26*(2), 82–95. (p. 82)

18. Frattaroli, J. (2006). Experimental disclosure and its moderators: A meta-analysis. *Psychological Bulletin, 132*(6), 823–865.

19. Smyth, J. M., Pennebaker, J. W., & Arigo, D. (2012). What are the health effects of disclosure? In A. Baum, T. A. Revenson, & J. L. Singer (Eds.), *Handbook of health psychology* (2nd ed., pp. 175–191). New York, NY: Psychology Press.

20. Nils, F., & Rimé, B. (2012). Beyond the myth of venting: Social sharing modes determine the benefits of emotional disclosure. *European Journal of Social Psychology, 42*(6), 672–681.

21. Sheese, B. E., Brown, E. L., & Graziano, W. G. (2004). Emotional expression in cyberspace: Searching for moderators of the Pennebaker disclosure effect via e-mail. *Health Psychology, 23*(5), 457–464.

22. Ruwaard, J., & Lange, A. (2016). Online structured writing therapy for post-traumatic stress disorder and complicated grief. In N. Lindefors & G. Andersson (Eds.), *Guided Internet-based treatments in psychiatry* (pp. 121–141). Cham, Switzerland: Springer International Publishing.

23. Smart, L., & Wegner, D. M. (2000). The hidden costs of hidden stigma. In T. F. Heatherton, R. E. Kleck, M. R. Hebl, & J. G. Hull (Eds.), *The social psychology of stigma* (pp. 220–242). New York, NY: Guilford Press.

24. Wegner, D. M., Lane, J. D., & Pennebaker, J. W. (1995). From secrecy to psychopathology. In J. W. Pennebaker (Ed.), *Emotion, disclosure, & health* (pp. 25–46). Washington, DC: American Psychological Association. (p. 33)

25. Slepian, M. L., Masicampo, E. J., & Ambady, N. (2014). Relieving the burdens of secrecy: Revealing secrets influences judgments of hill slant and distance. *Social Psychological and Personality Science, 5*(3), 293–300.

26. Slepian, M. L., Camp, N. P., & Masicampo, E. J. (2015). Exploring the secrecy burden: Secrets, preoccupation, and perceptual judgments. *Journal of Experimental Psychology: General, 144*(2), e31–e42.

27. Farber, B. A., Blanchard, M., & Love, M. (2019). *Secrets and lies in psychotherapy.* Washington, DC: American Psychological Association.

28. Burgoon, M., Callister, M., & Hunsaker, F. G. (1994). Patients who deceive: An empirical investigation of patient-physician communication. *Journal of Language and Social Psychology, 13*(4), 443–468.

29. Heaven, C. M., & Maguire, P. (1997). Disclosure of concerns by hospice patients and their identification by nurses. *Palliative Medicine, 11*(4), 283–290.

30. Cagle, J., & Bunting, M. (2017). Patient reluctance to discuss pain: Understanding stoicism, stigma, and other contributing factors. *Journal of Social Work in End-of-Life & Palliative Care, 13*(1), 27–43.

31. Larson, D. G., & Chastain, R. L. (1990). Self-concealment: Conceptualization, measurement, and health implications. *Journal of Social and Clinical Psychology, 9*(4), 439–455.

32. Larson, D. G., Chastain, R. L., Hoyt, W. T., & Ayzenberg, R. (2015). Self-concealment: Integrative review and working model. *Journal of Social and Clinical Psychology, 34*(8), 705–729.

33. Winnicott, D. W. (1965). *The maturational processes and the facilitating environment: Studies in the theory of emotional development.* New York, NY: International Universities Press. (p. 186)

34. Ullrich, P. M., Lutgendorf, S. K., & Stapleton, J. T. (2002). Social constraints and depression in HIV infection: Effects of sexual orientation and area of residence. *Journal of Social and Clinical Psychology, 21*(1), 46–66.

35. Potoczniak, D. J., Aldea, M. A., & DeBlaere, C. (2007). Ego identity, social anxiety, social support, and self-concealment in lesbian, gay, and bisexual individuals. *Journal of Counseling Psychology, 54*(4), 447–457.

36. Dogan, U., & Colak, T. S. (2016). Self-concealment, social network sites usage, social appearance anxiety, loneliness of high school students: A model testing. *Journal of Education and Training Studies, 4*(6), 176–183.

37. Magsamen-Conrad, K., Billotte-Verhoff, C., & Greene, K. (2014). Technology addiction's contribution to mental wellbeing: The positive effect of online social capital. *Computers in Human Behavior, 40*, 23–30.

38. Wertheim, R., Hasson-Ohayon, I., Mashiach-Eizenberg, M., Pizem, N., Shacham-Shmueli, E., & Goldzweig, G. (2016). Self-concealment among couples who cope with chronic illness: development and preliminary validation of the Couples Illness Self-Concealment (CISC) questionnaire. *Supportive Care in Cancer, 24*(12), 4951–4959.

39. Wertheim, R., Hasson-Ohayon, I., Mashiach-Eizenberg, M., Pizem, N., Shacham-Shmueli, E., & Goldzweig, G. (2018). Hide and "sick": Self-concealment, shame and distress in the setting of psycho-oncology. *Palliative and Supportive Care, 16*(4), 461–469.

40. Hartman, J. D., Patock-Peckham, J. A., Corbin, W. R., Gates, J. R., Leeman, R. F., Luk, J. W., & King, K. M. (2015). Direct and indirect links between parenting styles, self-concealment (secrets), impaired control over drinking and alcohol-related outcomes. *Addictive Behaviors, 40*, 102–108.

41. Wheaton, M. G., Sternberg, L., McGFarlane, K., & Aditi, S. (2016). Self-concealment in obsessive-compulsive disorder: Associations with symptom dimensions, help seeking attitudes, and treatment expectancy. *Journal of Obsessive-Compulsive and Related Disorders, 11*, 43–48.

42. Aldao, A., Nolen-Hoeksema, S., & Schweizer, S. (2010). Emotion-regulation strategies across psychopathology: A meta-analytic review. *Clinical Psychology Review, 30*(2), 217–237.

43. Uysal, A., Lin, H. L., & Knee, C. R. (2010). The role of need satisfaction in self-concealment and well-being. *Personality and Social Psychology Bulletin, 36*(2), 187–199.

44. Uysal, A., & Lu, Q. (2011). Is self-concealment associated with acute and chronic pain? *Health Psychology, 30*(5), 606–614.

45. Gross, J. J., & Levenson, R. W. (1993). Emotional suppression: Physiology, self-report, and expressive behavior. *Journal of Personality and Social Psychology, 64*(6), 970–986.

46. Gross, J. J., & John, O. P. (2003). Individual differences in two emotion regulation processes: Implications for affect, relationships, and well-being. *Journal of Personality and Social Psychology, 85*(2), 348–362.

47. John, O. P., & Gross, J. J. (2004). Healthy and unhealthy emotion regulation: Personality processes, individual differences, and life span development. *Journal of Personality, 72*(6), 1301–1333.

48. Appleton, A. A., Buka, S. L., Loucks, E. B., Gilman, S. E., & Kubzansky, L. D. (2013). Divergent associations of adaptive and maladaptive emotion regulation strategies with inflammation. *Health Psychology, 32*(7), 748–756.

49. Rogers, C. R. (1961). *On becoming a person.* Boston, MA: Houghton Mifflin.

50. English, T., & John, O. P. (2013). Understanding the social effects of emotion regulation: The mediating role of authenticity for individual differences in suppression. *Emotion, 13*(2), 314–329.

51. Rodebaugh, T. L. (2009). Hiding the self and social anxiety: The core extrusion schema measure. *Cognitive Therapy and Research, 33*(1), 90–109.

52. Nathanson, D. L. (1992). *Shame and pride: Affect, sex, and the birth of the self.* New York, NY: W. W. Norton. (p. 321)

53. Tangney, J. P., Burggraf, S. A., & Wagner, P. E. (1995). Shame-proneness, guilt-proneness, and psychological symptoms. In J. P. Tangney & K. W. Fischer

(Eds.), *Self-conscious emotions: The psychology of shame, guilt, embarrassment, and pride* (pp. 343–367). New York, NY: Guilford Press.

54. Dickerson, S. S., Gable, S. L., Irwin, M. R., Aziz, N., & Kemeny, M. E. (2009). Social-evaluative threat and proinflammatory cytokine regulation: An experimental laboratory investigation. *Psychological Science, 20*(10), 1237–1244.

55. Dickerson, S. S., Gruenewald, T. L., & Kemeny, M. E. (2004). When the social self is threatened: Shame, physiology, and health. *Journal of Personality, 72*(6), 1191–1216.

56. Nam, S. K., Choi, S. I., Lee, J. H., Lee, M. K., Kim, A. R., & Lee, S. M. (2013). Psychological factors in college students' attitudes toward seeking professional psychological help: A meta-analysis. *Professional Psychology: Research and Practice, 44*(1), 37–45.

57. Boelen, P. A., & van den Bout, J. (2010). Anxious and depressive avoidance and symptoms of prolonged grief, depression, and post-traumatic stress disorder. *Psychologica Belgica, 50*(1–2), 49–67.

58. Stroebe, M., Boelen, P.A., van den Hout, M., Stroebe, W., Salemink, E., & van den Bout, J. (2007). Ruminative coping as avoidance: A reinterpretation of its function in adjustment to bereavement. *European Archives of Psychiatry and Clinical Neuroscience, 257*(8), 462–472.

59. Lichtenthal, W. G., Nilsson, M., Kissane, D. W., Breitbart, W., Kacel, E., Jones, E. C., & Prigerson, H. G. (2011). Underutilization of mental health services among bereaved caregivers with prolonged grief disorder. *Psychiatric Services, 62*(10), 1225–1229.

60. Doka, K. J. (2008). Disenfranchised grief in historical and cultural perspective. In M. S. Stroebe, R. O. Hansson, H. Schut, & W. Stroebe (Eds.), *Handbook of bereavement research and practice: Advances in theory and intervention.* (pp. 223–240). Washington, DC: American Psychological Association.

61. Larson, D. G. (1993). Self-concealment: Implications for stress and empathy in oncology care. *Journal of Psychosocial Oncology, 11*, 1–16.

62. Malladi, S., Macalinao, D. G., Jin, X., He, L., Basnet, H., Zou, Y., … Massague, J. (2016). Metastatic latency and immune evasion through autocrine inhibition of WNT. *Cell, 165*(1), 45–60.

63. Schachter, S. (1959). *The psychology of affiliation.* Palo Alto, CA: Stanford University Press.

64. MacReady, D. E., Cheung, R. M., Kelly, A. E., & Wang, L. (2011). Can public versus private disclosure cause greater psychological symptom reduction? *Journal of Social and Clinical Psychology, 30*(10), 1015–1042.

65. Stiles, W. B. (1987). 'I have to talk to somebody': A fever model of disclosure. In V. J. Derlega & J. H. Berg (Eds.), *Self-disclosure: Theory, research, and therapy.* (pp. 257–282). New York, NY: Plenum Press.

66. Rawlins, W. K. (1983). Openness as problematic in ongoing friendships: Two conversational dilemmas. *Communication Monographs, 50*(1), 1–13.

67. Lepore, S. J., & Revenson, T. A. (2007). Social constraints on disclosure and adjustment to cancer. *Social and Personality Psychology Compass, 1*(1), 313–333.

68. Lepore, S. J., Silver, R. C., Wortman, C. B., & Wayment, H. A. (1996). Social constraints, intrusive thoughts, and depressive symptoms among bereaved mothers. *Journal of Personality and Social Psychology, 70*(2), 271–282.

69. Littleton, H. L. (2010). The impact of social support and negative disclosure reactions on sexual assault victims: A cross-sectional and longitudinal investigation. *Journal of Trauma & Dissociation, 11*(2), 210–227.

70. Glover, D. A., Loeb, T. B., Carmona, J. V., Sciolla, A., Zhang, M., Myers, H. F., & Wyatt, G. E. (2010). Childhood sexual abuse severity and disclosure predict posttraumatic stress symptoms and biomarkers in ethnic minority women. *Journal of Trauma & Dissociation, 11*(2), 152–173.

71. Walsh, W. A., Banyard, V. L., Moynihan, M. M., Ward, S., & Cohn, E. S. (2010). Disclosure and service use on a college campus after an unwanted sexual experience. *Journal of Trauma & Dissociation, 11*(2), 134–151.

72. Coates, D., & Winston, T. (1987). The dilemma of distress disclosure. In V. J. Derlega & J. H. Berg (Eds.), *Self-disclosure: Theory, research, and therapy* (pp. 229–255). New York: Plenum.

73. Slepian, M. L., & Kirby, J. M. (2018). To whom do we confide our secrets. *Personality and Social Psychology Bulletin, 44*(7), 1008–1023.

74. Corson, K., & Colwell, M. J. (2013). Whispers in the ear: Preschool children's conceptualisation of secrets and confidants. *Early Child Development and Care, 183*(9), 1215–1228.

75. Miller, P., & Ingham, J. G. (1976). Friends, confidants, and symptoms. *Social Psychiatry, 11*, 51–68.

76. Ferrell, B., Otis-Green, S., Baird, R. P., & Garcia, A. (2014). Nurses' responses to requests for forgiveness at the end of life. *Journal of Pain and Symptom Management, 47*(3), 631–641.

77. Byock, I. (2004). *The four things that matter most: A book about living.* New York: NY: Free Press.

78. Panagopoulou, E., Mintziori, G., Montgomery, A., Kapoukranidou, D., & Benos, A. (2008). Concealment of information in clinical practice: Is lying less stressful than telling the truth? *Journal of Clinical Oncology, 26*(7), 1175–1177.

79. Altiere, K. (2010, June 25). [Release to use interview].

80. Wampold, B. E., Baldwin, S. A., Holtforth, M. G., & Imel, Z. E. (2017). What characterizes effective therapists? In L. G. Castonguay & C. E. Hill (Eds.), *How and why are some therapists better than others? Understanding therapist effects* (pp. 37–53). Washington, DC: American Psychological Association.

81. Larson, D. G. (1985). Helper secrets: Invisible stressors in hospice work. *American Journal of Hospice Care, 2* (35–40).

82. Larson, D. G. (1987). Helper secrets: Internal stressors in nursing. *Journal of Psychosocial Nursing and Mental Health Services, 25*(4), 20–26.

83. Maslow, A. H. (1971). *The farther reaches of human nature.* New York, NY: Viking. (p. 187)

84. Norton, R., Feldman, C., & Tafoya, D. (1974). Risk parameters across types of secrets. *Journal of Counseling Psychology, 21*(5), 450–454.

85. Farber, B. A., & Heifetz, L. J. (1981). The satisfactions and stresses of psychotherapeutic work: A factor analytic study. *Professional Psychology, 12*(5), 621–630.

86. The SUPPORT Principal Investigators. (1995). A controlled trial to improve care for seriously ill hospitalized patients: The study to understand prognoses and preferences for outcomes and risks of treatments (SUPPORT). *JAMA: Journal of the American Medical Association, 274*(20), 1591–1598.

87. Leape, L. L. (2002). Reporting of adverse events. *New England Journal of Medicine, 347*(20), 1633–1638.

88. Hannawa, A. F., Shigemoto, Y., & Little, T. D. (2016). Medical errors: Disclosure styles, interpersonal forgiveness, and outcomes. *Social Science & Medicine, 156,* 29–38.

89. Petronio, S. (2006). Impact of medical mistakes: Navigating work-family boundaries for physicians and their families. *Communication Monographs, 73*(4), 462–467.

90. Pope, K. S., Sonne, J. L., & Greene, B. (2006). *What therapists don't talk about and why: Understanding taboos that hurt us and our clients.* Washington, DC: American Psychological Association.

91. Farber, B. A., Berano, K. C., & Capobianco, J. A. (2004). Clients' perceptions of the process and consequences of self-disclosure in psychotherapy. *Journal of Counseling Psychology, 51*(3), 340–346.

92. Schindler, C., & Lapid, G. (1989). *The great turning: Personal peace, global victory.* Santa Fe, NM: Bear and Company. (pp. 91–92)

Chapter 5. The Person-Centered Helper and Helping Relationship

1. Perlman, H.H. (1979). *Relationship: The heart of helping people.* Chicago, IL: University of Chicago Press. (p. 19)

2. Nouwen, H.J. M. (1974). *Out of solitude: Three meditations on the Christian life.* Notre Dame, IN: Ave Maria Press. (p. 34)

3. Osler, W. (1904). The master word in medicine. *The Johns Hopkins Hospital Bulletin, XV*(154), 1–19. (p. 17)

4. Engel, G.L. (1977). The need for a new medical model: A challenge for biomedicine. *Science, 196,* 129–136.

5. Lown, B.A., Rosen, J., & Marttila, J. (2011). An agenda for improving compassionate care: A survey shows about half of patients say such care is missing. *Health Affairs, 30*(9), 1772–1778. (p. 152)

6. Laine, C., & Davidoff, F. (1996). Patient-centered medicine. A professional evolution. *JAMA: Journal of the American Medical Association, 275*(2), 152–156.

7. Fuertes, J.N., Mislowack, A., Bennett, J., Paul, L., Gilbert, T.C., Fontan, G., & Boylan, L.S. (2007). The physician-patient working alliance. *Patient Education and Counseling, 66*(1), 29–36.

8. Sakallaris, B.R., Miller, W.L., Saper, R., Kreitzer, M.J., & Jonas, W. (2016). Meeting the challenge of a more person-centered future for U.S. healthcare. *Global Advances in Health and Medicine, 5*(1), 51–60.

9. Taylor, L.E. V., Stotts, N.A., Humphreys, J., Treadwell, M.J., & Miaskowski, C. (2013). A biopsychosocial-spiritual model of chronic pain in adults with sickle cell disease. *Pain Management Nursing, 14*(4), 287–301.

10. Sulmasy, D.P. (2002). A biopsychosocial-spiritual model for the care of patients at the end of life. *The Gerontologist, 42* (Special Issue 3), 24–33.

11. Grassi, L., Riba, M., Bras, M., & Glare, P. (2016). Person-centered palliative care. In J.E. Mezzich, M. Botbol, G.N. Christodoulou, C.R. Cloninger, & I.M. Salloum (Eds.), *Person centered psychiatry* (pp. 487–500). Cham, Switzerland: Springer International Publishing.

12. Epstein, A.S., O'Reilly, E.M., Shuk, E., Breitbart, W., Shah, M.A., Ly, M.,...Volandes, A.E. (2017). Development of an advance care planning paradigm for advanced cancer: Person-centered oncologic care and choices (P-COCC). *Psycho-Oncology, 26*(6), 866–869.

13. Washburn, A.M., & Grossman, M. (2017). Being with a person in our care: Person-centered social work practice that is authentically person-centered. *Journal of Gerontological Social Work, 60*(5), 408–423.

14. Donadio, G. (2005). Improving healthcare delivery with the transformational whole person care model. *Holistic Nursing Practice, 19*(2), 74–77.

15. Jakovljević, M., & Abou-Saleh, M. T. (2016). Person-centered psychopharmacotherapy. In J. E. Mezzich, M. Botbol, G. N. Christodoulou, C. R. Cloninger, & I. M. Salloum (Eds.), *Person centered psychiatry.* (pp. 235–245). Cham, Switzerland: Springer International Publishing.

16. Sinclair, S., Russell, L. B., Hack, T. F., Kondejewski, J., & Sawatzky, R. (2017). Measuring compassion in healthcare: A comprehensive and critical review. *The Patient: Patient-Centered Outcomes Research, 10*(4), 389–405.

17. Kelley, J. M., Kraft-Todd, G., Schapira, L., Kossowsky, J., & Riess, H. (2014). The Influence of the patient-clinician relationship on healthcare outcomes: A systematic review and meta-analysis of randomized controlled trials. *PLoS ONE, 9*(4), e94207.

18. Rogers, C. R. (1957). The necessary and sufficient conditions of therapeutic personality change. *Journal of Consulting Psychology, 21*(2), 95–103.

19. Rogers, C. R. (1959). A theory of therapy, personality, and interpersonal relationships, as developed in the client-centered framework. In S. Koch (Ed.), *Psychology: A study of a science, Formulations of the person and the social context* (Vol. 3, pp. 184–256). New York: McGraw-Hill.

20. Rogers, C. R. (1961). *On becoming a person.* Boston, MA: Houghton Mifflin. (p. 61)

21. Murphy, D., & Joseph, S. (2016). Person-centered therapy: Past, present, and future orientations. In D. J. Cain, K. Keenan, & S. Rubin (Eds.), *Humanistic psychotherapies: Handbook of research and practice* (pp. 185–218). Washington, DC: American Psychological Association.

22. Holland, J. C., Breitbart, W. S., Butow, P. N., Jacobsen, P. B., Loscalzo, M. J., & McCorkle, R. (2015). *Psycho-oncology* (3rd ed.). New York, NY: Oxford University Press.

23. Wampold, B. E. (2010). The research evidence for common factors models: A historically situated perspective. In B. L. Duncan, S. D. Miller, B. E. Wampold, & M. A. Hubble (Eds.), *The heart and soul of change: Delivering what works in therapy* (2nd ed., pp. 49–81). Washington, DC: American Psychological Association.

24. Bohart, A. C., Elliott, R., Greenberg, L. S., & Watson, J. C. (2002). Empathy. In J. C. Norcross (Ed.), *Psychotherapy relationships that work: Therapist contributions and responsiveness to patients.* (pp. 89–108). New York, NY: Oxford University Press. (p. xii)

25. Hill, C. E., Spiegel, S. B., Hoffman, M. A., Kivlighan, D. M., Jr., & Gelso, C. J. (2017). Therapist expertise in psychotherapy revisited. *The Counseling Psychologist, 45*(1), 7–53.

26. Bohart, A. C., & Tallman, K. (1999). *How clients make therapy work: The process of active self-healing.* Washington, DC: American Psychological Association. (p. 228)

27. Larson, D. G. (2013). A person-centred approach to grief counselling. In M. Cooper, M. O'Hara, P. F. Schmid, & A. C. Bohart (Eds.), *The handbook of person-centred psychotherapy and counselling* (2nd ed., pp. 313–326). New York, NY: Palgrave-Macmillan.

28. Freeman, B. (2015). *Compassionate person-centered care for the dying: An evidence-based palliative care guide for nurses.* New York, NY: Springer.

29. Roter, D., & Fallowfield, L. (1998). Principles of training medical staff in psychosocial and communication skills. In J. C. Holland (Ed.), *Psycho-oncology* (pp. 1074–1082). New York: Oxford University Press.

30. Wampold, B. E., Mondin, G. W., Moody, M., Stich, F., Benson, K., & Ahn, H. N. (1997). A meta-analysis of outcome studies comparing bona fide psychotherapies: Empirically, "all must have prizes". *Psychological Bulletin, 122*(3), 203–215.

31. Norcross, J. C. (1995). Dispelling the Dodo bird verdict and the exclusivity myth in psychotherapy. *Psychotherapy: Theory, Research, Practice, Training, 32*(3), 500–504.

32. Kennedy, E., & Charles, S. C. (1990). *On becoming a counselor: A basic guide for nonprofessional counselors.* New York, NY: Continuum. (p. 18)

33. Geller, S. M., Greenberg, L. S., & Watson, J. C. (2010). Therapist and client perceptions of therapeutic presence: The development of a measure. *Psychotherapy Research, 20*(5), 599–610. (p. 599)

34. Colosimo, K. A., & Pos, A. E. (2015). A rational model of expressed therapeutic presence. *Journal of Psychotherapy Integration, 25*(2), 100–114.

35. Arndt, B. G., Beasley, J. W., Watkinson, M. D., Temte, J. L., Tuan, W. J., Sinsky, C. A., & Gilchrist, V. J. (2017). Tethered to the EHR: Primary care physician workload assessment using EHR event log data and time-motion observations. *Annals of Family Medicine, 15*(5), 419–426.

36. Kennell, J., Klaus, M., McGrath, S., Robertson, S., & Hinkley, C. (1991). Continuous emotional support during labor in a U.S. hospital. A randomized controlled trial. *JAMA: Journal of the American Medical Association, 265*(17), 2197–2201.

37. Steel, A., Frawley, J., Adams, J., & Diezel, H. (2015). Trained or professional doulas in the support and care of pregnant and birthing women: A critical integrative review. *Health & Social Care in the Community, 23*(3), 225–241.

38. Fersko-Weiss, H. (2017). *Caring for the dying: the doula approach to a meaningful death.* Newburyport, MA: Conari Press.

39. Pedersen, A., & Hack, T.F. (2010). Pilots of oncology health care: A concept analysis of the patient navigator role. *Oncology Nursing Forum, 37*(1), 55–60.

40. Finset, A. (2014). 50 years of research on the effect of physician communication behavior on health outcomes. *Patient Education and Counseling, 96*(1), 1–2.

41. Katz, R.L. (1963). *Empathy: Its nature and uses.* New York, NY: Free Press of Glencoe. (p. 156)

42. Wampold, B.E. (2001). *The great psychotherapy debate: Models, methods, and findings.* Mahwah, NJ: Lawrence Erlbaum Associates Publishers.

43. Rogers, C.R. (1975). Empathic: An unappreciated way of being. *The Counseling Psychologist, 5*(2), 2–10. (p. 4)

44. Fromm-Reichmann, F. (1959). *Psychoanalysis and psychotherapy. Selected papers of Frieda Fromm-Reichmann.* Chicago, IL: University of Chicago Press. (p. 65)

45. Hill, C.E. (2014). *Helping skills: Facilitating exploration, insight, and action* (4th ed.). Washington, DC: American Psychological Association.

46. Reik, T. (1972). *Listening with the third ear.* New York, NY: Arena.

47. Greenberg, L.S., & Safran, J.D. (1987). *Emotion in psychotherapy.* New York, NY: Guilford. (p. 193)

48. Buber, M. (1923). *I and thou* (2nd ed.). New York, NY: Charles Scribner's Sons.

49. Gendlin, E.T. (1974). Client-centered and experiential therapy. In D.A. Wexler & L.N. Rice (Eds.), *Innovations in client-centered therapy* (pp. 211–246). New York, NY: Wiley.

50. Cantor, R.C. (1978). *And a time to live: Toward emotional well-being during the crisis of cancer.* New York, NY: Harper & Row.

51. Teding van Berkhout, E., & Malouff, J.M. (2016). The efficacy of empathy training: A meta-analysis of randomized controlled trials. *Journal of Counseling Psychology, 63*(1), 32–41.

52. Yalom, I.D. (1980). *Existential psychotherapy.* New York, NY: Basic. (p. 57)

53. Szalita, A.B. (1976). Some thoughts on empathy. *Psychiatry, 39*(2), 142–152. (p. 151)

54. Rilke, R.M. (1934). *Letters to a young poet* (M.D. Herter, Trans.). New York, NY: W.W. Norton. (p. 72)

55. Jackson, S.W. (2001). The wounded healer. *Bulletin of the History of Medicine, 75*(1), 1–36.

56. Jung, C.G. (1963). *Memories, dreams, reflections.* New York, NY: Pantheon.

57. Zerubavel, N., & Wright, M.O.D. (2012). The dilemma of the wounded healer. *Psychotherapy, 49*(4), 482–491.

58. Kearney, M., & Weininger, R. (2011). Whole person self-care: Self-care from the inside out. In T. A. Hutchinson (Ed.), *Whole person care: A new paradigm for the 21st century.* (pp. 109–125). New York, NY: Springer Science + Business Media.

59. Fraiberg, S., Adelson, E., & Shapiro, V. (1975). Ghosts in the nursery: A psychoanalytic approach to the problems of impaired infant-mother relationships. *American Academy of Child Psychiatry, 14*, 387–421. (pp. 396–397)

60. Mruk, C. (2019). *Feeling good by doing good.* New York, NY: Oxford University Press.

61. Gross, J. J., & John, O. P. (2003). Individual differences in two emotion regulation processes: Implications for affect, relationships, and well-being. *Journal of Personality and Social Psychology, 85*(2), 348–362.

62. Lebowitz, M. S., & Dovidio, J. F. (2015). Implications of emotion regulation strategies for empathic concern, social attitudes, and helping behavior. *Emotion, 15*(2), 187–194.

63. Pletzer, J. L., Sanchez, X., & Scheibe, S. (2015). Practicing psychotherapists are more skilled at downregulating negative emotions than other professionals. *Psychotherapy, 52*(3), 346–350.

64. Hyman, R. B., & Woog, P. (1989). Flexibility, the dominant characteristic of effective helpers: A factor analytic study. *Measurement and Evaluation in Counseling and Development, 22*(3), 151–157. (p. 152)

65. Carrard, V., Schmid Mast, M., Jaunin-Stalder, N., Junod Perron, N., & Sommer, J. (2018). Patient-centeredness as physician behavioral adaptability to patient preferences. *Health Communication, 33*(5), 593–600.

66. Wampold, B. E., Baldwin, S. A., Holtforth, M. G., & Imel, Z. E. (2017). What characterizes effective therapists? In L. G. Castonguay & C. E. Hill (Eds.), *How and why are some therapists better than others?: Understanding therapist effects* (pp. 37–53). Washington, DC: American Psychological Association.

67. Brown, L. S. (2013). Compassion amidst oppression: Increasing cultural competence for managing difficult dialogues in psychotherapy. In A. W. Wolf, M. R. Goldfried, & J. C. Muran (Eds.), *Transforming negative reactions to clients: From frustration to compassion.* (pp. 139–158). Washington, DC: American Psychological Association. (p. 139)

68. Cardemil, E. V., & Battle, C. L. (2003). Guess who's coming to therapy? Getting comfortable with conversations about race and ethnicity in psychotherapy. *Professional Psychology: Research and Practice, 34*(3), 278–286.

69. Fuertes, J. N., Toporovsky, A., Reyes, M., & Osborne, J. B. (2017). The physician-patient working alliance: Theory, research, and future possibilities. *Patient Education and Counseling, 100*(4), 610–615.

70. Hatcher, R. L., & Gillaspy, J. A. (2006). Development and validation of a revised short version of the Working Alliance Inventory. *Psychotherapy Research, 16*(1), 12–25.

71. Doran, J. M. (2016). The working alliance: Where have we been, where are we going? *Psychotherapy Research, 26*(2), 146–163.

72. Flückiger, C., Del Re, A. C., Wampold, B. E., & Horvath, A. O. (2018). The alliance in adult psychotherapy: A meta-analytic synthesis. *Psychotherapy, 55*(4), 316–340.

73. Falkenström, F., Granström, F., & Holmqvist, R. (2014). Working alliance predicts psychotherapy outcome even while controlling for prior symptom improvement. *Psychotherapy Research, 24*(2), 146–159.

74. Kelly, A. E., & Yuan, K. (2009). Clients, secret keeping and the working alliance in adult outpatient therapy. *Psychotherapy: Theory, Research, Practice, Training, 46*(2), 193–202.

75. Bar-Sela, G., Yochpaz, S., Gruber, R., Lulav-Grinwald, D., Mitnik, I., & Koren, D. (2016). The association between the strength of the working alliance and sharing concerns by advanced cancer patients: A pilot study. *Supportive Care in Cancer, 24*(1), 319–325.

76. Calvo, V., Palmieri, A., Marinelli, S., Bianco, F., & Kleinbub, J. R. (2014). Reciprocal empathy and working alliance in terminal oncological illness: The crucial role of patients' attachment style. *Journal of Psychosocial Oncology, 32*(5), 517–534.

77. Safran, J. D., Muran, J. C., Samstag, L. W., & Stevens, C. (2001). Repairing alliance ruptures. *Psychotherapy: Theory, Research, Practice, Training, 38*(4), 406–412.

78. Szasz, T. S., & Hollender, M. H. (1987). A contribution to the philosophy of medicine: The basic models of the doctor-patient relationship. In J. D. Stoeckle & J. D. Stoeckle (Eds.), *Encounters between patients and doctors: An anthology* (pp. 165–177). Cambridge, MA: The MIT Press.

79. Schellinger, S. E., Anderson, E. W., Frazer, M. S., & Cain, C. L. (2018). Patient self-defined goals: Essentials of person-centered care for serious illness. *American Journal of Hospice & Palliative Medicine, 35*(1), 159–165.

80. Rogers, C. R. (1974). In retrospect: Forty-six years. *American Psychologist, 29*(2), 115–123. (p. 116)

81. Gendlin, E. T. (1981). *Focusing* (2nd ed.). New York, NY: Bantam.

82. Kahn, R. L., & Cannell, C. F. (1957). *The dynamics of interviewing.* New York, NY: Wiley.

83. Rogers, C. R. (1973). My philosophy of interpersonal relationships and how it grew. *Journal of Humanistic Psychology, 13*(2), 3–15.

84. Hibbard, J. H., Mahoney, E. R., Stockard, J., & Tusler, M. (2005). Development and testing of a short form of the Patient Activation Measure. *Health Services Research, 40*(6, part1), 1918–1930.

85. Green, C. A., Perrin, N. A., Polen, M. R., Leo, M. C., Hibbard, J. H., & Tusler, M. (2010). Development of the Patient Activation Measure for mental health. *Administration and Policy in Mental Health and Mental Health Services Research, 37*(4), 327–333.

86. Gomberg, E. L. (1989). On terms used and abused: The concept of 'codependency'. *Drugs & Society, 3*(3–4), 113–132.

87. Cowan, G., & Warren, L. W. (1994). Codependency and gender-stereotyped traits. *Sex Roles, 30*(9–10), 631–645.

88. Calderwood, K. A., & Rajesparam, A. (2014). A critique of the codependency concept considering the best interests of the child. *Families in Society, 95*(3), 171–178.

89. Lazarus, R. S. (1990). Stress, coping, and illness. In H. S. Friedman (Ed.), *Personality and disease.* (pp. 97–120). Oxford, England: John Wiley & Sons.

90. Huang, C. (2015). Relation between attributional style and subsequent depressive symptoms: A systematic review and meta-analysis of longitudinal studies. *Cognitive Therapy and Research, 39*(6), 721–735.

91. Watson, D. L. (2008). The fundamental attribution error. In L. T. Benjamin, Jr. & L. T. Benjamin, Jr. (Eds.), *Favorite activities for the teaching of psychology* (pp. 248–251). Washington, DC: American Psychological Association.

92. Rae-Grant, Q. (1972). The art of being a failure as a consultant. In J. Zusman & D. L. Davidson (Eds.), *Practical aspects of mental health consultation* (pp. 71–82). Springfield, IL: Charles C. Thomas.

Chapter 6. Healing Words: Compassion in Action

1. Rogers, C. R. (1980). *A way of being.* Boston, MA: Houghton Mifflin. (p. 8)

2. Nathanson, D. L. (1992). *Shame and pride: Affect, sex, and the birth of the self.* New York, NY: W. W. Norton. (p. 320)

3. Brandon, D. (1976). *Zen in the art of helping.* New York, NY: Merloyd Lawrence. (p. 49)

4. Martin, D. G. (1983). *Counseling and therapy skills.* Pacific Grove, CA: Brooks/Cole.

5. Daniels, T. G., Rigazio-DiGilio, S. A., & Ivey, A. E. (1997). Microcounseling: A training and supervision paradigm for the helping professions. In C. E. Watkins,

Jr (Ed.), *Handbook of psychotherapy supervision* (pp. 277–295). Hoboken, NJ: John Wiley & Sons, Inc.

6. Moawad, R. (1978). *Increasing human effectiveness program guide.* Tacoma, WA: Edge Learning Institute.

7. Ericsson, K. A., Nandagopal, K., & Roring, R. W. (2009). Toward a science of exceptional achievement: Attaining superior performance through deliberate practice. In W. C. Bushell, E. L. Olivo, & N. D. Theise (Eds.), *Longevity, regeneration, and optimal health: Integrating Eastern and Western perspectives.* (pp. 199–217). Hoboken, NJ: Wiley-Blackwell.

8. Ericsson, K. A. (2015). Acquisition and maintenance of medical expertise: A perspective from the expert-performance approach with deliberate practice. *Academic Medicine, 90*(11), 1471–1486.

9. Chow, D. L., Miller, S. D., Seidel, J. A., Kane, R. T., Thornton, J. A., & Andrews, W. P. (2015). The role of deliberate practice in the development of highly effective psychotherapists. *Psychotherapy, 52*(3), 337–345.

10. Riess, H., & Kraft-Todd, G. (2014). E.M.P.A.T.H.Y.: A tool to enhance nonverbal communication between clinicians and their patients. *Academic Medicine, 89*(8), 1108–1112.

11. Ambady, N., Laplante, D., Nguyen, T., Rosenthal, R., Chaumeton, N., & Levinson, W. (2002). Surgeons' tone of voice: A clue to malpractice history. *Surgery, 132*(1), 5–9.

12. Egan, G. (2006). *Essentials of skilled helping: Managing problems, developing opportunities.* Belmont, CA: Thomson Wadsworth.

13. Johnson, S. (2012, May/June). The power of emotion in therapy: How to harness this great motivator. *Psychotherapy Networker.*

14. *The human dimension in health care: A tribute to Carl Rogers.* (1981, February 21–23). Palo Alto, CA.

15. Hammond, D. C., Hepworth, D. H., & Smith, V. G. (2002). *Improving therapeutic communication.* San Francisco, CA: Jossey-Bass.

16. Elliott, R., Watson, J. C., Goldman, R. N., & Greenberg, L. S. (2004). *Learning emotion-focused therapy: The process-experiential approach to change.* Washington, DC: American Psychological Association. (pp. 132, 24)

17. Robinson, F. P. (1950). *Principles and procedures of student counseling.* New York, NY: Harper & Brothers.

18. The client-centered approach. Interview conducted by Carl Rogers at *The Evolution of Psychotherapy Conference*, Phoenix, AZ. www.evolutionofpsychotherapy. com, www.erickson-foundation.org. (1985). In M. H. E. Foundation (Producer).

19. Rilke, R. M. (1934). *Letters to a young poet* (M. D. Herter, Trans.). New York, NY: W. W. Norton. (p. 35)

20. Pearlman, L. A., Wortman, C. B., Feuer, C. A., Farber, C. H., & Rando, T. A. (2014). *Treating traumatic bereavement: A practitioner's guide*. New York, NY: Guilford Press.

21. Goodman, G., & Esterly, G. (1988). *The talk book: The ultimate science of communicating in close relationships*. New York, NY: Ballantine

22. Mencken, H. L. (1049). *A Mencken chrestomathy*. New York, NY: Knopf.

23. Kennedy, E., & Charles, S. C. (1990). *On becoming a counselor: A basic guide for nonprofessional counselors*. New York, NY: Continuum.

24. Hill, C. E. (2014). *Helping skills: Facilitating exploration, insight, and action* (4th ed.). Washington, DC: American Psychological Association.

25. Farber, B. A., Blanchard, M., & Love, M. (2019). *Secrets and lies in psychotherapy*. Washington, DC: American Psychological Association. (p. 245)

26. Gazda, G., Childers, W., & Walters, R. (1982). *Interpersonal communication: A handbook for health professionals*. Rockville, MD: Aspen.

27. Larson, D. G. (Ed.) (1984). *Teaching psychological skills: Models for giving psychology away*. Monterey, CA: Brooks/Cole.

28. Larson, D. G., & Tobin, D. R. (2000). End-of-life conversations: Evolving practice and theory. *JAMA: Journal of the American Medical Association, 284*(12), 1573–1578.

29. Lazarus, R. S. (1984). The trivialization of distress. In B. L. Hammonds & C. J. Scheirer (Eds.), *Psychology and health* (pp. 125–144). Washington, DC: American Psychological Association.

30. Larson, D. G., & Hoyt, W. T. (2007). The bright side of grief counseling: Deconstructing the new pessimism. In K. J. Doka (Ed.), *Living with grief: Before and after the death* (pp. 157–174). Washington, DC: Hospice Foundation of America.

31. Larson, D. G. (2013). A person-centred approach to grief counselling. In M. Cooper, M. O'Hara, P. F. Schmid, & A. C. Bohart (Eds.), *The handbook of person-centred psychotherapy and counselling* (2nd ed., pp. 313–326). New York, NY: Palgrave-Macmillan.

32. Ackerman, D. (2011, July 3). The lonely polar bear. *New York Times*.

33. Stroebe, M., & Schut, H. (1999). The dual process model of coping with bereavement: Rationale and description. *Death Studies, 23*, 197–224.

34. Stroebe, M., & Schut, H. (2010). The dual process model of coping with bereavement: A decade later. *OMEGA, 61*(4), 273–289.

35. Worden, J. W. (2018). *Grief counseling and grief therapy: A handbook for the mental health practitioner* (5th ed.). New York, NY: Springer. (p. 50)

36. Stroebe, M., Boelen, P. A., van den Hout, M., Stroebe, W., Salemink, E., & van den Bout, J. (2007). Ruminative coping as avoidance: A reinterpretation of its function in adjustment to bereavement. *European Archives of Psychiatry and Clinical Neuroscience, 257*(8), 462–472. (p. 470)

37. Hansson, R. O., & Stroebe, M. S. (2007). *Bereavement in late life: Coping, adaptation, and developmental influences.* Washington, DC: American Psychological Association.

38. Gillies, J., & Neimeyer, R. A. (2006). Loss, grief, and the search for significance: Toward a model of meaning reconstruction in bereavement. *Journal of Constructivist Psychology, 19*(1), 31–65.

39. Neimeyer, R. A., Burke, L. A., Mackay, M. M., & van Dyke Stringer, J. G. (2010). Grief therapy and the reconstruction of meaning: From principles to practice. *Journal of Contemporary Psychotherapy, 40*(2), 73–83.

40. Shear, M. K., & Gribbin Bloom, C. (2017). Complicated grief treatment: An evidence-based approach to grief therapy. *Journal of Rational-Emotive & Cognitive-Behavior Therapy, 35*(1), 6–25.

41. Sandler, I., Tein, J.-Y., Cham, H., Wolchik, S., & Ayers, T. (2016). Long-term effects of the Family Bereavement Program on spousally bereaved parents: Grief, mental health problems, alcohol problems, and coping efficacy. *Development and Psychopathology, 28*(3), 801–818.

42. Cohen, J. A., Mannarino, A. P., & Deblinger, E. (2018). Trauma-focused cognitive-behavioral therapy for traumatized children. In J. R. Weisz & A. E. Kazdin (Eds.), *Evidence-based psychotherapies for children and adolescents* (3rd ed., pp. 253–271). New York, NY: Guilford Press.

43. Chochinov, H. M., McClement, S. E., Hack, T. F., McKeen, N. A., Rach, A. M., Gagnon, P., ... Taylor-Brown, J. (2013). Health care provider communication: an empirical model of therapeutic effectiveness. *Cancer, 119*(9), 1706–1713.

44. Miller, W. R., & Rollnick, S. (2013). *Motivational interviewing: Helping people change* (3rd ed.). New York, NY: Guilford Press.

45. Klass, D., & Steffen, E. M. (2018). *Continuing bonds in bereavement: New directions for research and practice.* New York, NY: Routledge/Taylor & Francis Group. 46. Doka, K. J. (2008). Disenfranchised grief in historical and cultural perspective. In M. S. Stroebe, R. O. Hansson, H. Schut, & W. Stroebe (Eds.), *Handbook of bereavement research and practice: Advances in theory and intervention.* (pp. 223–240). Washington, DC: American Psychological Association.

47. Bonanno, G. A., & Kaltman, S. (2001). The varieties of grief experience. *Clinical Psychology Review, 21*(5), 705–734.

48. Prigerson, H.G., Horowitz, M.J., Jacobs, S.C., Parkes, C.M., Aslan, M., K., G.,...Maciejewski, P.K. (2009). Prolonged grief disorder: Psychometric validation of criteria proposed for DSM-V and ICD-11. *PLoS Medicine, 6*(8), 1–12.

49. Shear, M.K., & Mulhare, E. (2008). Complicated grief. *Psychiatric Annals, 38*(10), 662–670.

50. Tedeschi, R., Orejuela-Dávila, A.I., & Lewis, P. (2018). Posttraumatic growth and continuing bonds. In D. Klass & E.M. Steffen (Eds.), *Continuing bonds in bereavement: New directions for research and practice.* (pp. 31–42). New York, NY: Routledge/Taylor & Francis Group.

51. Rando, T.A. (Ed.) (2000). *Clinical dimensions of anticipatory mourning: Theory and practice in working with the dying, their loved ones, and their caregivers.* Champaign, IL: Research Press.

52. Walter, C.A., & McCoyd, J.L.M. (2009). *Grief and loss across the lifespan: A biopsychosocial perspective.* New York, NY: Springer Publishing Co.

53. Imber-Black, E. (2004). Rituals and the healing process. In F. Walsh & M. McGoldrick (Eds.), *Living beyond loss: Death in the family* (2nd ed., pp. 340–357). New York, NY: W.W. Norton & Co.

54. Rosenblatt, P.C. (2008). Grief across cultures: A review and research agenda. In M.S. Stroebe, R.O. Hansson, H. Schut, & W. Stroebe (Eds.), *Handbook of bereavement research and practice: Advances in theory and intervention* (pp. 207–222). Washington, DC: American Psychological Association.

55. Eisma, M.C., Boelen, P.A., van den Bout, J., Stroebe, W., Schut, H.A.W., Lancee, J., & Stroebe, M.S. (2015). Internet-based exposure and behavioral activation for complicated grief and rumination: A randomized controlled trial. *Behavior Therapy, 46*(6), 729–748.

56. Hartig, J., & Viola, J. (2016). Online grief support communities: Therapeutic benefits of membership. *Omega: Journal of Death and Dying, 73*(1), 29–41.

57. Litz, B.T., Schorr, Y., Delaney, E., Au, T., Papa, A., Fox, A.B.,...Prigerson, H.G. (2014). A randomized controlled trial of an Internet-based therapist-assisted indicated preventive intervention for prolonged grief disorder. *Behaviour Research and Therapy, 61*, 23–34.

58. Ruwaard, J., & Lange, A. (2016). Online structured writing therapy for post-traumatic stress disorder and complicated grief. In N. Lindefors & G. Andersson (Eds.), *Guided Internet-based treatments in psychiatry* (pp. 121–141). Cham, Switzerland: Springer International Publishing.

59. Stroebe, M., Hansson, R.O., Schut, H., & Stroebe, W. (2008). Bereavement research: 21st-century prospects. In M.S. Stroebe, R.O. Hansson, & W. Stroebe (Eds.), *Handbook of bereavement research and practice: Advances in theory and intervention* (pp. 577–603). Washington, DC: American Psychological Association. (p. 598)

60. Larson, D. G., & Hoyt, W. T. (2007). What has become of grief counseling? An evaluation of the empirical foundations of the new pessimism. *Professional Psychology: Research and Practice, 38*(4), 347–355.

61. Gamino, L. A., Sewell, K. W., Hogan, N. S., & Mason, S. L. (2009–2010). Who needs grief counseling? A report from the Scott & White grief study. *Omega, 60*(3), 199–223.

62. Rogers, C. R. (1961). *On becoming a person.* Boston, MA: Houghton Mifflin.

63. Fosha, D. (2000). *The transforming power of affect: A model for accelerated change.* New York, NY: Basic Books. (p. 213)

64. Tolin, D. F. (2016). *Doing CBT: A comprehensive guide to working with behaviors, thoughts, and emotions.* New York, NY: Guilford Press.

65. Gendlin, E. T. (1996). *Focusing-oriented psychotherapy: A manual of the experiential method.* New York, NY: Guilford Press.

66. Goldman, R. N., & Greenberg, L. S. (2015). *Case formulation in emotion-focused therapy: Co-creating clinical maps for change.* Washington, DC: American Psychological Association.

67. Malkinson, R. (2007). *Cognitive grief therapy: Constructing a rational meaning to life following loss.* New York: W. W. Norton & Co.

68. Pascual-Leone, A., & Greenberg, L. S. (2007). Emotional processing in experiential therapy: Why 'the only way out is through.' *Journal of Consulting and Clinical Psychology, 75*(6), 875–887. (p. 886)

69. Zisook, S., & Shear, K. (2009). Grief and bereavement: What psychiatrists need to know. *World Psychiatry, 8,* 67–74. (p. 68)

Chapter 7. The Caring Team

1. Lash, J. P. (1980). *Helen and teacher: The story of Helen Keller and Anne Sullivan Macy.* New York, NY: Delacorte Press. (p. 489)

2. Mount, B. M., & Voyer, J. (1980). Staff stress in hospice/palliative care. In I. Ajemian & B. M. Mount (Eds.), *The R. V. H. manual on palliative/hospice care.* New York: NY: Arno Press. (p. 466)

3. Senge, P. M. (2006). *The fifth discipline: The art and practice of the learning organization* (Revised ed.). New York: Doubleday. (p. 240)

4. Lacerenza, C. N., Marlow, S. L., Tannenbaum, S. I., & Salas, E. (2018). Team development interventions: Evidence-based approaches for improving teamwork. *American Psychologist, 73*(4), 517–531.

5. Fox, L., Onders, R., Hermansen-Kobulnicky, C. J., Nguyen, T.-N., Myran, L., Linn, B., & Hornecker, J. (2018). Teaching interprofessional teamwork skills to health professional students: A scoping review. *Journal of Interprofessional Care, 32*(2), 127–135.

6. Bell, S. T., Brown, S. G., Colaneri, A., & Outland, N. (2018). Team composition and the ABCs of teamwork. *American Psychologist, 73*(4), 349–362.

7. Valentine, M. A., Nembhard, I. M., & Edmondson, A. C. (2015). Measuring teamwork in health care settings: A review of survey instruments. *Medical Care, 53*(4), e16–e30.

8. Shoemaker, S. J., Parchman, M. L., Fuda, K. K., Schaefer, J., Levin, J., Hunt, M., & Ricciardi, R. (2016). A review of instruments to measure interprofessional team-based primary care. *Journal of Interprofessional Care, 30*(4), 423–432. (p. 424)

9. Bolino, M. C., & Grant, A. M. (2016). The bright side of being prosocial at work, and the dark side, too: A review and agenda for research on other-oriented motives, behavior, and impact in organizations. *The Academy of Management Annals, 10*(1), 599–670.

10. Connor, S. R., Egan, K., Kwilosz, D. M., Larson, D. G., & Reese, D. (2002). Interdisciplinary approaches to assisting with end-of-life care and decision making. *American Behavioral Scientist, 46*, 340–356.

11. Larson, D. G. (2005). Becky's legacy: More lessons. *Death Studies, 29*(8), 745–757.

12. Bailey, D. B. (1984). A triaxial model of the interdisciplinary team and group process. *Exceptional Children, 51*, 17–25.

13. Batorowicz, B., & Shepherd, T. A. (2008). Measuring the quality of transdisciplinary teams. *Journal of Interprofessional Care, 22*(6), 612–620.

14. Casimiro, L. M., Hall, P., Kuziemsky, C., O'Connor, M., & Varpio, L. (2015). Enhancing patient-engaged teamwork in healthcare: An observational case study. *Journal of Interprofessional Care, 29*(1), 55–61.

15. Kim, S., Bochatay, N., Relyea-Chew, A., Buttrick, E., Amdahl, C., Kim, L., ... Lee, Y. M. (2017). Individual, interpersonal, and organisational factors of healthcare conflict: A scoping review. *Journal of Interprofessional Care, 31*(3), 282–290.

16. Whitehead, P. B., Herbertson, R. K., Hamric, A. B., Epstein, E. G., & Fisher, J. M. (2015). Moral distress among healthcare professionals: Report of an institution-wide survey. *Journal of Nursing Scholarship, 47*(2), 117–125.

17. Janis, I. L. (2007). Groupthink. In R. P. Vecchio (Ed.), *Leadership: Understanding the dynamics of power and influence in organizations* (2nd ed., pp. 157–169). Notre Dame, IN: University of Notre Dame Press.

18. Steele, F. T. (1975). *The open organization: The impact of secrecy and disclosure on people and organizations.* Reading, MA: Addison-Wesley. (p. 6)

19. Kohn, A. (1986). *No contest: The case against competition.* Boston, MA: Houghton, Mifflin and Company. (p. 156)

20. Rosenberg, B. D., & Siegel, J. T. (2018). A 50-year review of psychological reactance theory: Do not read this article. *Motivation Science, 4*(4), 281–300.

21. Lown, B. A., & Manning, C. F. (2010). The Schwartz Center Rounds: Evaluation of an interdisciplinary approach to enhancing patient-centered communication, teamwork, and provider support. *Academic Medicine, 85*(6), 1073–1081.

22. Cullen, A. (2016). Schwartz Rounds® Promoting compassionate care and healthy organisations. *Journal of Social Work Practice, 30*(2), 219–228.

23. Pangborn, S. M. (2017). Reimagining interdisciplinary team communication in hospice care: Disrupting routinization with narrative inspiration. *Journal of Applied Communication Research, 45*(5), 455–473.

24. Rubin, I. M., Plovnick, M. S., & Fry, R. E. (1975). *Improving the coordination of care: A program for health team development.* Cambridge, MA: Ballinger.

25. Aubé, C., Rousseau, V., & Brunelle, E. (2018). Flow experience in teams: The role of shared leadership. *Journal of Occupational Health Psychology, 23*(2), 198–206.

26. Nakamura, J., & Csikszentmihalyi, M. (2002). The concept of flow. In C. R. Snyder & S. J. Lopez (Eds.), *Handbook of positive psychology* (pp. 89–105). New York, NY: Oxford University Press.

27. Gazda, G., Childers, W., & Walters, R. (1982). *Interpersonal communication: A handbook for health professionals.* Rockville, MD: Aspen.

28. Dyer, W. G. (1977). *Team building: Issues and alternatives.* Reading: MA: Addison-Wesley.

29. Hartley, P., & Kennard, D. (2009). *Staff support groups in the helping professions: Principles, practice and pitfalls.* New York, NY: Routledge/Taylor & Francis Group.

30. Emerson, R. W. (1921). *Essays and poems of Emerson.* New York, NY: Harcourt, Brace, and Company. (p. 367)

31. Kennard, D., & Hartley, P. (2009). Ten keys to a successful staff support group. In P. Hartley & D. Kennard (Eds.), *Staff support groups in the helping professions: Principles, practice and pitfalls.* (pp. 26–33). New York, NY: Routledge/Taylor & Francis Group.

32. Kirschenbaum, H., & Glaser, B. (1978). *Developing support groups.* La Jolla, CA: University Associates.

33. Pearson, P. H. (1983). The interdisciplinary team process, or the professionals' "Tower of Babel". *Developmental Medicine and Child Neurology, 25*(3), 390–395.

34. Ucko, T. J., & Kazemek, E. A. (1986). Creating effective work teams. *Healthcare Financial Management, 41*, 80–81.

35. Cartwright, S., Cooper, C. L., & Murphy, L. R. (1995). Diagnosing a healthy organization: A proactive approach to stress in the workplace. In L. R. Murphy,

J. J. Hurrell, Jr., S. L. Sauter, & G. P. Keita (Eds.), *Job stress interventions.* (pp. 217–233). Washington, DC: American Psychological Association.

36. Wilson, M. G., DeJoy, D. M., & McGrath, A. L. (2001). Making health care organizations healthy: Conceptual model and intervention process. In J. de Jonge, P. Vlerick, A. Büssing, & W. B. Schaufeli (Eds.), *Organizational psychology and health care at the start of a new millennium* (pp. 3–21). Munich, Germany: Rainer Hampp Verlag.

37. Fredrickson, B. L. (2013). Updated thinking on positivity ratios. *American Psychologist, 68*(9), 814–822. (p. 816)

38. Sekerka, L. E., & Fredrickson, B. L. (2010). Working positively toward transformative cooperation. In P. A. Linley, S. Harrington, & N. Garcea (Eds.), *Oxford handbook of positive psychology and work.* (pp. 81–94). New York, NY: Oxford University Press. (pp. 83, 85)

39. Luthans, F., & Youssef, C. M. (2009). Positive workplaces. In S. J. Lopez & C. R. Snyder (Eds.), *Oxford handbook of positive psychology* (2nd ed., pp. 579–588). New York, NY: Oxford University Press.

40. Alliger, G. M., Cerasoli, C. P., Tannenbaum, S. I., & Vessey, W. B. (2015). Team resilience: How teams flourish under pressure. *Organizational Dynamics, 44*(3), 176–184.

41. Schwarz, U. v. T., & Hasson, H. (2013). Alignment for achieving a healthy organization. In G. F. Bauer & G. J. Jenny (Eds.), *Salutogenic organizations and change: The concepts behind organizational health intervention research* (pp. 107–125). New York, NY: Springer Science + Business Media. (p. 107)

Chapter 8. Toward a Caring Society and World

1. Ehrlich, P. R., & Ornstein, R. E. (2010). *Humanity on a tightrope: Thoughts on empathy, family, and big changes for a viable future.* New York, NY: Rowman & Littlefield. (p. 3)

2. Roth, D. L., Fredman, L., & Haley, W. E. (2015). Informal caregiving and its impact on health: A reappraisal from population-based studies. *The Gerontologist, 55*(2), 309–319.

3. Ruger, J. P. (2015). Governing for the common good. *Health Care Analysis, 23*(4), 341–351.

4. Rifkin, J. (2009). *The empathic civilization: The race to global consciousness in a world in crisis.* New York, NY: Tarcher. (p. 43)

5. Garfield, C. A., Larson, D. G., & Schuldberg, D. (1982). Mental health training and the hospice community: A national survey. *Death Education, 6*, 189–204.

6. Hui, D., Elsayem, A., De La Cruz, M., & et al. (2010). Availability and integration of palliative care at U.S. cancer centers. *JAMA: Journal of the American Medical Association, 303*(11), 1054–1061.

7. *NHPCO Facts and Figures: Hospice Care in America.* (2018). Retrieved from https://www.nhpco.org/sites/default/files/public/Statistics_Research/2017_Facts_Figures.pdf

8. Connor, S. & Sepulveda, C. (Eds.). (2014) *Global Atlas of Palliative Care at the End-of-Life.* London UK, Geneva CH: Worldwide Palliative Care Alliance and World Health Organization. Retrieved from: http://www.who.int/cancer/publications/palliative-care-atlas/en/

9. Heisler, E. J. *The mental health workforce: A primer.* Retrieved from www.crs.gov

10. Patterson, J. E., & Edwards, T. M. (2018). An introduction to global mental health. *Families, Systems, & Health, 36*(2), 137–143.

11. Mares, M.-L., Palmer, E., & Sullivan, T. (2008). Prosocial effects of media exposure. In S. L. Calvert & B. J. Wilson (Eds.), *The handbook of children, media, and development.* (pp. 268–289). Malden: Blackwell Publishing.

12. Mares, M.-L., & Woodard, E. H. (2007). Positive effects of television on children's social interaction: A meta-analysis. In R. W. Preiss, B. M. Gayle, N. Burrell, M. Allen, & J. Bryant (Eds.), *Mass media effects research: Advances through meta-analysis.* (pp. 281–300). Mahwah, NJ: Lawrence Erlbaum Associates Publishers.

13. Eisenberg, N., Spinrad, T. L., & Morris, A. S. (2013). Prosocial development. In P. D. Zelazo (Ed.), *The Oxford handbook of developmental psychology, Vol. 2: Self and other* (pp. 300–325). New York, NY: Oxford University Press.

14. Malti, T., Chaparro, M. P., Zuffianò, A., & Colasante, T. (2016). School-based interventions to promote empathy-related responding in children and adolescents: A developmental analysis. *Journal of Clinical Child and Adolescent Psychology, 45*(6), 718–731.

15. Schwartz, G. E. (1984). Psychobiology of health: A new synthesis. In B. L. Hammonds & C. J. Scheirer (Eds.), *Psychology of health: The master lecture series* (Vol. 3, pp. 149–193). Washington, DC: American Psychological Association.

16. Andersen, S. C., & Loftager, J. (2014). Deliberative democratic governance. *Administrative Theory & Praxis, 36*(4), 510–529.

17. Sayin, H. U. (2016). A short introduction to system theory: Indispensable postulate systems and basic structures of the systems in quantum physics, biology and neuroscience. *NeuroQuantology, 14*(1), 126–142.

18. Grossman, S. A., Sheidler, V. R., Swedeen, K., Mucenski, J., & Piantadosi, S. (1991). Correlation of patient and caregiver ratings of cancer pain. *Journal of Pain and Symptom Management, 6*(2), 53–57.

19. Zerubavel, N., & Wright, M. O. D. (2012). The dilemma of the wounded healer. *Psychotherapy, 49*(4), 482–491. (p. 487)

20. Cameron, C. D. (2017). Compassion collapse: Why we are numb to numbers. In E. M. Seppälä, E. Simon-Thomas, S. L. Brown, M. C. Worline, C. D. Cameron, & J. R. Doty (Eds.), *The Oxford handbook of compassion science* (pp. 261–271). New York, NY: Oxford University Press.

21. Church, R. M. (1959). Emotional reactions of rats to the pain of others. *Journal of Comparative and Physiological Psychology, 52*(2), 132–134.

22. Clark, K. B. (1980). Empathy: A neglected topic in psychological research. *American Psychologist, 35*(2), 187–190. (p. 190)

23. Lynn, M., & Oldenquist, A. (1986). Egoistic and nonegoistic motives in social dilemmas. *American Psychologist, 41*(5), 529–534.

24. Bandura, A. (2016). *Moral disengagement: How people do harm and live with themselves.* New York, NY: Worth Publishers. (p. 446)

25. Schweitzer, A. (1959). *The philosophy of civilization* (C. T. Campion, Trans.). New York, NY: Macmillan.

26. Sullivan, W. (1972). The Einstein papers: A man of many parts. *New York Times.* (p. 1)

27. Leary, M. R., Tipsord, J. M., & Tate, E. B. (2008). Allo-inclusive identity: Incorporating the social and natural worlds into one's sense of self. In H. A. Wayment & J. J. Bauer (Eds.), *Transcending self-interest: Psychological explorations of the quiet ego.* (pp. 137–147). Washington, DC: American Psychological Association.

28. Larson, D. G. (2013). Taking stock: Past contributions and current thinking on death, dying, and grief. *Death Studies,* 1–4.

29. Kübler-Ross, E. (1969). *Valentine.* New York: Macmillan. (pp. 141–142)

30. Larson, D. G., & Tobin, D. R. (2000). End-of-life conversations: Evolving practice and theory. *JAMA: Journal of the American Medical Association, 284*(12), 1573–1578.

31. Larson, D. G. (2002, August). Tough talk: Finding the words for living with loss. *Santa Clara Magazine, 44,* 12–18.

32. Byock, I. (2012). *The best care possible: A physician's quest to transform care through the end of life.* New York, NY: Avery.

33. Gawande, A. (2014). *Being mortal: Medicine and what matters in the end.* New York, NY: Metropolitan Books/Henry Holt and Company.

34. Ostaseski, F. (2017). *The five invitations: Discovering what death can teach us about living fully.* New York, NY: Flatiron Books

35. This section draws upon "It's time to talk: The most important conversations often are the most difficult to have," an article by Dale Larson that was part of the 2001 national newspaper series, *Finding Our Way: Living With Dying in America.* Funnded by the Robert Wood Johnson Foundation, the series consisted of 15 articles by national experts on end-of-life issues and reached nearly seven million American readers.

36. Rittner, C., & Myers, S. (Eds.). (1986). *The courage to care: Rescuers of the Jews during the Holocaust.* New York, NY: New York University Press. (pp. 40–42)

Index

About the Author

Dale G. Larson (BA, University of Chicago; PhD, U. C. Berkeley) is Professor of Counseling Psychology at Santa Clara University, where he directs graduate studies in Health Psychology. A clinician and researcher, Dr. Larson is a Fulbright Scholar, a Fellow in three Divisions of the American Psychological Association, and a Member of the International Work Group on Death, Dying and Bereavement. A leader in end-of-life care and training, he codirected the pioneering Berkeley Hospice Training Project and was Senior Editor and a contributing author for *Finding Our Way: Living with Dying in America,* the national newspaper series that reached seven million Americans. His publications on end-of-life issues, professional stress, grief and grief counseling, and secrets and self-concealment are widely cited, both in the scientific literature and popular media. Dr. Larson has keynoted conferences throughout North America, as well as Europe and Australia. For his contributions, he has received the Death Educator Award from the Association for Death Education and Counseling and was honored as an Innovator of Hospice and Palliative Care by the National Hospice Foundation.